Everyday Crimes

Social Violence and Civil Rights in Early America

Kelly A. Ryan

NEW YORK UNIVERSITY PRESS
New York

NEW YORK UNIVERSITY PRESS
New York
www.nyupress.org

References to Internet websites (URLs) were accurate at the time of writing. Neither the author nor New York University Press is responsible for URLs that may have expired or changed since the manuscript was prepared.

Library of Congress Cataloging-in-Publication Data
Names: Ryan, Kelly A., author.
Title: Everyday crimes : social violence and civil rights in early America / Kelly A. Ryan.
Description: New York : New York University Press, [2019] | Includes bibliographical references and index.
Identifiers: LCCN 2018042916 | ISBN 9781479869619 (cl : alk. paper)
Subjects: LCSH: Violence—United States—History. | Violence—Social aspects—United States. | Civil rights—United States—History. | United States—History—Colonial period, ca. 1600–1775. | United States—Social conditions—To 1865.
Classification: LCC HN90.V5 R93 2019 | DDC 303.60973—dc23
LC record available at https://lccn.loc.gov/2018042916

New York University Press books are printed on acid-free paper, and their binding materials are chosen for strength and durability. We strive to use environmentally responsible suppliers and materials to the greatest extent possible in publishing our books.

Manufactured in the United States of America

10 9 8 7 6 5 4 3 2 1

Also available as an ebook

For Adam and our families, with love.

CONTENTS

Introduction

In 1741, a slave master in Roxbury, Massachusetts, believed one of his enslaved women had stolen money from him, but she "deny'd" any involvement. Unconvinced by her pleas of innocence, the master "gave her the Discipline; upon which she confess'd she had." Turning to physical coercion was natural to the slave master. Most early Americans believed that corporal punishment was an effective means of reforming petulant slaves. Indeed, the narrative of events justified violence because only when the master whipped the enslaved woman was she honest. In her confession, she admitted giving the money she had stolen to another slave named London. London denied taking the money, even after money was found on him. London's and the enslaved woman's masters "thought proper to whip him till they could bring him to it, but in vain, for he would own nothing of it."[1] London's refusal to admit fault made the beating harsher, and the masters tied him down and whipped him repeatedly until he could no longer walk. The article in the *Boston Post Boy* reported the incidents without questioning the ethics of the punishment or portraying the enslaved persons' versions of the events.

Legally and socially dependent peoples, such as London and the enslaved woman, are the central figures of this narrative.[2] Until the end of the eighteenth century, slaves, wives, and youthful servants all lived in a society that condoned their corporal punishment and hindered their access to justice and safety. *Everyday Crimes* is a study of their experiences in Massachusetts and New York, but the broader geographic areas of New England and the Northeast provide context and examples for the varied lives covered. A major cause of most early Americans' acceptance of using corporal punishment against individuals such as London was that they were legally and socially dependent peoples. Early Americans believed that youthful servants, slaves, and wives needed the oversight of guardians for their own well-being and the good of larger communities, and legal texts prescribed the status of youthful servants, slaves, and wives. The guardianship of children and young adults transferred to their masters upon becoming servants or apprentices, husbands had authority over their wives, and masters had extensive powers over slaves. With the emergence of gradual and immediate emancipation in New York and Massachusetts, free African Americans join our story. Emancipation initiated trends in violence against free African Americans aimed at limiting their mobility, economic prospects, and family life, and laws established their status as lesser than whites. Whites no longer had direct and legal guardianship over adult African Americans, but laws and social practices meant they were often in the households of whites.[3] With the exception of free African Americans, most of this narrative is dedicated to the dependent's resistance to violence perpetrated by legal guardians. This focus elucidates how rationalizations of violence against dependent peoples occurred and the ways resistance to violence reshaped ideas regarding the rights of dependents.

Local communities decided what cases were criminal. In Massachusetts and New York, early Americans largely accepted corporal punishment of legally dependent peoples so long as it was used as a reformative tool and not taken to extremes, and this was unlike other cases of violence against more legally empowered peoples. Corporal punishment against legally empowered persons was only acceptable in a context of court-ordered punishment for crimes.[4] In cases when legally empowered individuals brought suits about assaults or murders, governments and communities recognized their right to bear witness and tried cases based on evidence and merit. This was not uniformly the case with legal dependents. After the slave masters beat London, he was "unty'd and laid on the Grass, and being carry'd home dyed soon after." Rather than acknowledging that the slave masters caused the death, the community created alternatives to excuse the slave masters' roles in London's death. *Boston Evening Post* reported it was "generally tho't, that being very old, his laying with his fore Body upon cold Ground expos'd to the Dew and open Air in the evening was a means of hastening his Death." Limited medical knowledge allowed for these kinds of explanations, but the lack of concern expressed in the article over London's death suggests other intentions. Even more fantastically, the article said that some believed London "was sullen, and died, as it were out of Spite," thus blaming London for his own murder.[5] Armed with this rationale, whites constructed explanations for their violence and did not question the morality of violence nor did they consider slaves' perspectives. For many, physical punishment played a role in creating an orderly society by hindering bad behavior and punishing offenders.[6] Had London and the enslaved woman continued committing theft successfully, they could have weakened slavery and societal trust in the authority of masters by showing how the enslaved outsmarted the largely white population.

When assaults and murders went unpunished, it often meant no perpetrator could be found or that the community felt no public breach of the peace occurred. In the case of a slave such as London, it was clearly the latter. The slaveholders admitted they intended to beat London until he confessed, but in the absence of London's declaration of guilt, the only restraint on their conduct was their own exhaustion or their fears he would die. Certainly, no repercussions would be forthcoming, and the slave masters knew this.

Though cases such as London's show little would be done to protect slaves murdered by their masters, this was not the norm for other legally dependent peoples. Studying resistance to violence from multiple perspectives in early America shows the ways inequalities intersected and differed.[7] Murdered, maimed, or especially badly beaten wives and youthful servants had some redress, and their abusers could suffer criminal trials and penalties. Intersectional analysis uncovers why differing rationalizations of violence were accepted and reveals the flexibility of early Americans in adapting violence to the social order. The righteousness of servitude and marriage became questionable if abuse became extreme and repeated, and if the victim acted in good faith. This was not always the case with slavery. Rather than inhibiting violence against African Americans, whites' fears of retaliatory violence issued by slaves was used to rationalize extensive violence against slaves. Assuring that African Americans were orderly was a priority, and many early Americans characterized the government's and masters' disabling or murderous violent acts against them as protection for whites. Yet not all African Americans were the same—black women, men, and children each had distinctive circumstances that were "not the sum" of adding race to ideas about childhood, gender, or poverty.[8] African American children in the early republic, for example, received assistance from whites more often than African American adults in cases of cruelty, but children's status as servants or slaves was often the most legally settled and accepted.

Legally dependent people had to find a means of protesting abuse in a society that accorded them with lesser status than those who were empowered to abuse them. As London's situation makes clear, their very survival demanded it. Slaves, wives, and youthful servants did not have the same legal rights as husbands and masters, making their legal and extralegal protests difficult to locate in historical records. However, the resistance of legally dependent people shows the boundaries of masters' and husbands' authority, as well as the extent to which whites would be allowed to harass African Americans in the era of emancipation. From the colonial era, slaves, servants, and wives established four main methods of seeking help and asserting their right to safety. First, they sought allies who could assist them in finding safe spaces or intervene on their behalf. These allies would be essential in their second tactic: reporting violence to legal authorities. Justices of the peace (JPs), judges, and juries offered more favorable outcomes when the abused had witnesses who could attest to the violence they experienced. Access to JPs was uneven for wives, youthful servants, and slaves. In New York, slaves did not have the right to testify against whites, and children and young adults in the United States would lose some of their authority in legal matters by the nineteenth century as legal theories, in addition to judges and juries, questioned their competence. Third, when allies could not be located or legal options did not appear fruitful, wives, servants, and slaves ran from their abusive situations. Moments of societal dislocation, such as the Revolutionary War and the War of 1812, were particularly opportune times to seek self-emancipation. Finally, many individuals chose to use violence to combat their subordinate status or abusive situation. Arson, assaults, riots, murders, and planned uprisings were among the many tactics used by legal dependents to resist violence. The question of whether nonviolent or violent tactics could best alter civil and structural liabilities has been an issue for activists since the colonial era.

Resistance revealed the human and civil rights issues of legal and social dependency and, most important, the rights of individuals to live without violent molestation. Modern interpretations of human rights hold that certain basic rights exist for all persons. Human rights are not granted by an authority, and they include rights to safety, protection from compulsory labor, and freedom from torture. This study reveals how individuals asserted their belief in the human rights to safety and freedom from coercive labor, and concomitantly, how this resistance affected the ideas of the legally empowered. In their resistance, wives, slaves, and youthful servants showed a keen understanding that the assaults they experienced were neither just nor reformative—they were dangerous and wrong.[9] Without legally and socially dependent peoples protesting the violence used against them, the emergence of human rights and humanitarian discourses aimed at ameliorating their abuse and suffering is impossible to imagine.[10] Human rights advocacy and humanitarianism are often situated as movements that begin with antislavery activism in the nineteenth century.[11] Wife, servant, and slave resistance to violence shows efforts by the legally dispossessed to shed light on cruelty prior to the full awakening of humanitarianism in western society. African Americans, wives, and youthful servants lived in a world in which the perspectives of masters, husbands, and more broadly whites were predominant. In bearing their scars and telling their stories, dependent persons put their narratives about abuse on the map to be discovered. They forced would-be allies to visualize their pain and suffering.

Though legal activism for civil rights is most often associated with the twentieth- and twenty-first-century battles to end racial segregation and expand marriage rights, dependents targeted and identified legal advocacy to advance their freedoms and safety from the colonial era.[12] In protesting violence, legally subject peoples challenged communities and the criminal justice system to deal with their complaints, thus creating an argument about their rights to testify and bear witness against their masters, husbands, and aggressive whites. Cases of abuse forced communities to mediate different perspectives and learn about the effects of violence on dependents' daily lives. Although each petition to a JP or government authority might not have resulted in a win, the government did have to make decisions with the input of community members on how to handle violence. Legal cases established and maintained community standards about abuse and had the power to chip away at the immunity of whites, masters, and husbands to abuse African Americans, youthful servants, and wives.

Locating and developing allies in the quest for safety was essential, and such partnerships are a common trend in civil rights activism in

United States history.[13] The first allies for legally dependent people were each other—and their planned resistance and building of support networks were crucial. Encouraging individuals outside of one's social group to act was onerous and often took repeated attempts. Until the beginning of the nineteenth century, the belief that corporal punishment promoted order was deeply entrenched in the North, and slaves, wives, and servants could not ask for protection unless they had proven themselves to be worthy of interdiction. Similar psychological motivations exist today in individuals' decisions to assist others. Often, people do not want to help those who they perceive as to blame for their situation.[14] The relationships created out of these moments required diplomatic feats of legally dependent peoples, who had to balance their own claims for safety with the presumed authority of those who assaulted them. Even with those limitations, the relationships that were developed with household members, bystanders, and neighbors created knowledge about the realities of violence that moved people to act. Allies helped alter violent situations, but they also cooperated to end some of the legal and social impairments of dependent peoples. In early America, lawyers and other compassionate community members cooperated to overturn slavery, limit the use of corporal punishment, and curtail the legal powers masters and husbands held.

One of the major factors in the success of protests against violence was the ability of dependent peoples to connect their plight with other social movements and trends. From the Enlightenment, philosophers criticized corporal punishment, and new theories of childhood development would gain steam during the eighteenth century to include larger criticisms about the use of force. By the nineteenth century, northeasterners were revising their legal codes to reduce public and capital punishments, and this altered the landscape of violence, reducing the visibility of it in public spaces.[15]

Studying resistance reveals the social economy of violence built and maintained in Massachusetts and New York. "Social economy of violence" is a term used to describe the social, cultural, and governmental systems that permitted certain people and institutions to commit acts of violence against peoples, as when the slave masters murdered London without interdiction or when states and colonies executed criminals. An often-unspoken agreement existed among individuals to accept violent acts as appropriate or necessary in certain cases. Those who witnessed the violence against London chose not to intervene by either reporting it to authorities or directly assisting him. Social economies of violence are not static, and individuals and their communities built environments in which violence was ignored or unpunished. Governments created and sustained the social economy of violence by producing and enforcing laws that characterized violence against dependents as part of a process of organizing social relations. In some cases, governments passed laws to protect individuals from abuse and murder but failed to enforce them. In addition, governments punished certain groups more harshly than others, thereby naturalizing and maintaining knowledge that youthful servants, wives, and slaves were more appropriate to discipline and punish than others. The culture of early America was hostile to the independence of people of color, women, and minors, and this, too, supported the social economy of violence.[16] Their status as subject peoples was clear, and this allowed for some violence to occur without reprisal.

Resistance to violence could have the unintended effect of supporting the social economy of violence. The social economy of violence had a circular logic to it, and depictions and acts of cruelty—even those protesting its dehumanizing qualities—normalized the use of it.[17] When slaves, wives, and youthful servants engaged in violent acts or verbal threats, they perpetuated pre-existing ideas about dependents that exaggerated their passionate natures, as well as their moral and intellectual deficiencies to make rational decisions.[18] Acts of violence by dependent peoples threatened society, and the government's role was to construct an infrastructure of laws and policing that supported safety. Laws and the criminal justice system stipulated harsher punishments for wives, slaves, and servants for their violence against masters and husbands, and in the early republic, the criminal justice system was eager to discipline and punish free African Americans. The power of violent resistance was that it impacted more than its direct victims, striking fear in those with authority. News and gossip about poisonings, arson, assaults, and riots could be as powerful as witnessing the actual events, leading individuals to wonder if violent retribution was a possibility in their own homes and communities. Such thinking was particularly concerning during times of dislocation and war, when the loyalty of dependent peoples was needed but unreliable. Laws enacted in reaction to slave insurrections are an example of the ways legislatures emboldened the power of masters in the wake of resistance. The narratives of violence created by the abused to resist violence could also end up supporting the social economy of violence. Tales of violence added to the already existing reservoir of information that situated wives, slaves, and youthful servants as proper vessels upon which to inflict violence.

The people who fought against assaults and murders of dependent peoples in early America most often protested for and about particular individuals, and this is where civil rights activism in early America differed from that of other nineteenth- and twentieth-century civil-rights movements. Defiance often started with the actual cries or pleas for help by the abused, who would later find allies, take their cases through courts, or flee. Cases of individual suffering moved people to intervene and could bring about significant changes in the rights of individuals. Modern studies of the effects of individualized narratives of violence and suffering show that people are more moved to act when narratives aim to inform the public about an individual over a group or class of people. Individual stories draw people in and exploit the sympathies of readers and bystanders.[19] People also feel more compelled to take action on behalf of individuals, as they can better relate to them, rather than social groups. Some allies would partner with the abused to fight for their broader civil rights by serving as witnesses, acting as legal counsel, or finding ways to share the story of their suffering in print. Medical doctors and lawyers, in particular, were often connected with larger movements to end cruelty in the Atlantic World.[20] Others did not seek to expand the rights of youth, wives, and African Americans. They simply wanted to protect the peace in their communities or prevent disorders from occurring in the future. For this group, punishing abusers was a way to secure the authority of masters and husbands and even governments. Though the motivations of those engaged in aid and resistance varied, the actions taken by those who protested violence were most often singular. These were not the mass and popular civil rights movements associated with later eras. Even the antislavery associations and the movement against corporal and capital punishments in the antebellum era would not constitute the kinds of mobilization realized in the twentieth century.

Because of the individualized nature of much of the contestation of violence in early America, it most often makes sense to study it through the eyes of local communities. Though transatlantic and world histories offer us much in the way of understanding larger trends, the fight for freedom from violence was one that was directed from the bottom up. Indeed, unless initiated by slaves, wives, or youthful servants, it was rare that any action was taken on their behalf until the early nineteenth century. Individuals suffering in bondage, in cruel marriages, and in a racially hostile society were not always connected to broader movements to foment social change. They reached out to the individuals nearest to them for empathy and assistance, making their plights best known in the local community. Many struggles for safety were also ultimately about freedom from abusers and abuse, and the ability to secure that freedom depended on several factors, including population size and geographic isolation. Targeting options to attain freedom meant taking in the context of the local community and fashioning an individualized plan. Local communities had their own social economies of violence and differential pathways to freedom and safety, though some similarities exist across early America.

Situating this study in local contexts—primarily those of Massachusetts and New York—allows for analysis of the ways emancipation, access to divorce, and changing conceptions of youth and childhood affected the ways people resisted and tolerated violence. Though legal impairments decreased, wives, youthful servants, and African Americans still struggled to find safety and combatted societal beliefs promoting their need for oversight and dependence. New York and Massachusetts did not simply replicate each other in these major transformations. Massachusetts (and New England) would more quickly offer options of divorce and separation to abused wives, while New York would be among the last of the states to allow full access to divorce. New York would also be among the last of the northern states to begin a gradual emancipation of slaves, and only offered it in 1799 to the children born of slaves after that date when they reached the age of 25 (for women) and 28 (for men). The policies of the state related to their conservative reactions to the threat of violence from dependent peoples, the imperial crisis, and war. Massachusetts acted much more swiftly, and in 1783 became one of the first states to adopt emancipation. In other ways, New York outstripped Massachusetts in responding to the rights of the abused— New York developed and maintained processes for abused white servants that resulted in white servants and apprentices attaining freedom at greater rates in the colonial era. Before New York was taken over by the English in 1664, it was a Dutch colony, called New Netherland, and the colony was more attuned to the rights of children and servants. Both Massachusetts and New Netherland would be organized by those interested in trade and development, and early modern trends in thoughts about gender, race, and generation meant similarities existed between some locations in New York and New England. Letter writing, reading, the economy, and travel meant the wider world intersected with local households, neighborhoods, towns, colonies, and later, states.

The freedoms of legally subordinate peoples often varied more between urban and rural areas in the same state or colony than from colony to colony. Urban locales such as New York City and Boston play large roles in this study because resistance is most visible in areas where bystanders could readily intervene. As two of the largest cities in North America, New York and Boston were havens for runaways seeking anonymity, and individuals had easier access to courtrooms. Regions such as Essex, Plymouth, Middlesex, and Worcester Counties in Massachusetts have rural areas and large and small towns, making different forms of resistance necessary. Finding allies was critical to any intervention, which was often extralegal. Contrasting records from these locales provided an understanding of differing relationships to violence and demonstrations against it. Upstate New York and Maine (part of Massachusetts Bay colony) provided the starkest contrast with these regions, with smaller populations and much greater isolation. Patterns there mimicked those of rural Massachusetts.

Though many acts of resistance were singular, resistance to violence grew during the early republic as wives, African Americans, and youthful servants repeatedly pressed for safety. Recurring activism created a trend as more people turned to JPs and other persons with access to governmental or legal authority to prevent or punish abuse. Taken together, individual protests against abuse altered the way cruelty was handled by communities. JPs, judges, and juries created and maintained practices that offered slaves, wives, and free African Americans greater access to freedoms and security than they had in earlier eras, which advanced their human and civil rights. Other escalations in resistance related to moments of opportunity. Wives, servants, and slaves ran away in greater numbers during wartime, and elopement and runaway advertisements expanded knowledge about their flight. The threats they posed to security and production created a groundswell of concern often related to the larger welfare of the United States. Knowing how dependent peoples secured and maintained rights to habeas corpus, to bear witness, and to serve as plaintiffs, among other rights, is key to understanding the growth of civil rights activism in the United States.

Protests against violence in early America are important to understand because they shed light on how individuals perceived themselves, their rights, and community institutions. Wives, servants, and African Americans saw themselves as legitimately aggrieved, revealing their recognition that human and civil rights existed. Some forms of their resistance showed they believed local communities had a role in discerning what was acceptable. When they challenged abuse through legal means—in serving as plaintiffs in civil or criminal suits, petitioning the government, or writing and describing their abuse to others—they protested for their safety and inclusion in their communities and governmental processes.[21] Studies of violence show that societies and individuals with lesser access to and faith in criminal justice systems sometimes turn to violence as a means of solving disputes.[22] Wives, youthful servants, and slaves had reason to believe communities would not assist them, perhaps leading them to seek extralegal solutions to abuse when prudent. Sometimes extralegal actions solved immediate problems—as when individuals wanted to defend themselves during an assault. The ways the abused created support systems and protested to enhance their safety show reactions to the changing governmental and community norms about violence and their legal subordination.

This resistance was not wholly successful, and human rights and civil rights were not fully realized. Indeed, as I conducted research, analyzed data, and wrote up my findings, the United States grappled with public cases of violence against women and African Americans that resulted in the Black Lives Matter and #metoo movements. Historical analysis shows that the advancement of rights does not simply occur over time. Though some laws declared abuse wrongful in early America, communities often ignored violence against dependent peoples, choosing to view their abuse as proper and lawful even though it was harmful and dangerous. It was during the colonial era that much of the social economy of violence was built, and it did not evaporate during the eras of the American Revolution or early republic. In fact, by the eighteenth century, the power of masters and husbands grew. The successes in resistance lie in the creation of new partnerships and protections for dependent peoples. The social economy of violence proved flexible and persistent even as some individuals and communities showed an awakening to the problem of cruelty in society.

Though this narrative tells many stories, it does not tell all the stories; difficult choices were made about whom to discuss, which modes of violence to consider, and when topics entered this narrative. Analysis of children's abuse by their parents is not a major theme, though constructions of childhood, youth, and guardianship are central to this narrative. Violence occurring in master-servant relationships in which victims were children or young adults is covered instead because it allows for discussion of legal dependency based on age and provides a meaningful counterpoint to slavery. Servitude and marriage were both contractual in nature, and certain rights and expectations were part of those agreements. Exploring the contours of these relationships allows for meaningful approaches to the ways that poverty, race, and gender influenced experiences and access to resistance. Analysis of the violence against free African Americans in the colonial and revolutionary eras is not discussed thoroughly in the first section of this narrative, though free African Americans were important members of communities and suffered from targeted attacks on their independence. Enslaved wives are not a focus in the first section either. Interventions were rare and communities did not prioritize the safety and welfare of enslaved women.[23] Free African Americans are included in part two of this narrative, to follow the history of African Americans as they experienced freedom in greater numbers. Some forms of violence are not considered here. The violence studied in this text is physical, not verbal in nature, with murder and assaults being the most commonly addressed. Early Americans understood that slander, gossip, and scolding were problematic for communities, and they targeted legally dependent peoples often in their prosecutions. Much literature exists on that topic and it informs this work, but space did not allow for a lengthy discussion of it as human rights to safety and freedom from torture are more pertinent.

The deep research for this work covers a large period—from the colonial era through the early republic—and decisions about where to investigate were calculated. The voices of women, youth, and African Americans are particularly difficult to locate in sources, but through careful examination of legal records, print literature, diaries, and letters a base of primary sources revealed how and when individuals sought help. The evidence presented here is not randomly chosen or anecdotal; the trends in the ways communities handled violence against legally dependent people are clear. Legal records were particularly helpful in sorting through violence and resistance because the government was a popular space to settle disputes, and some extralegal resistance resulted in punishments. Finding the race of litigants was particularly difficult in the early national era. A comparison of plaintiffs' names, occupations, and addresses with city directories and censuses helps identify litigants. Of course, not all violence was recorded and neither did legally dependent people always seek help from authority figures. Discovering numerical trends in violence against dependents is not possible or meaningful given these limitations in the early period. The many volumes of legal records examined in this study were meticulously recorded to discover changes in resistance, however. Resistance often resulted in the creation of laws and other processes codified by governments, so records of governmental activity were additional sites of discovery. Access to education and publishing meant published and private writing most often recorded the thoughts and perspectives of those empowered to abuse others, but reading these sources for signs of violence and dissent proved valuable, particularly after the eighteenth century. Some print literature created by and about dependent peoples has revealing insights into motivations and survival methods. Religious documents—ministers' sermons and some church records—provided indications of the ideologies of violence and the ways communities set standards about violence outside of the government. However, most religious communities (other than the Society of Friends, also called the Quakers) were not great sites of mediation and were more important in public discussions about violence. Words were not always followed up by action. Like today, many people wrote against the use of violence while they simultaneously ignored the use of it in their communities.

Part I explores the status of wives, youthful servants, and slaves during the colonial era in separate chapters, ensuring readers have a grounding of their status and experiences. Resistance to abuse in the colonial era most often focused on finding safety and freedom from abuse, but some activism pointed out the harmful nature of legal dependence and coercive labor arrangements. By the eighteenth century, courts reduced their punishment of abusers, as patriarchal mandates empowering husbands and masters gained greater force. Wives, slaves, and youthful servants established means to survive and protest violence, but their agency in doing so fluctuated over time. Slaves suffered from the most extensive abuse, but wives and servants were not meaningfully protected by existing codes either, particularly as local courts became less active in penalizing their abuse. Intervention by allies was the key to finding safety and security in the colonial era.

Part II explores the way the imperial crisis and Revolutionary War impeded and enhanced previous opportunities to resist violence and abuse. Conservative ideologies and reactions to the crisis and war shored up some powers over wives and servants, but African Americans found pathways toward freedom and away from violence, as Massachusetts and other New England states ended slavery. From masters' and husbands' perspectives, the loyalty of dependents took on increased importance, but new opportunities to resist proved both tempting and risky to wives, servants, and slaves. Running away and privately negotiating out of abusive situations were valuable options, because local courts and governments restricted adjudications and courts temporarily shut down in some regions. The imperial crisis marked a turning point in the arbitrations of servant abuse. Servants and apprentices decreasingly made use of civil suits as their power as plaintiffs and witnesses in the legal system declined. For slaves, government petitions and legal suits were among the more successful means of exposing their perspectives in Massachusetts, but like youthful servants, they also turned to military service to express their antipathy toward masters.

Part III illustrates how the surging protests of African Americans, wives, and servants in the early republic forced society to confront abuse and consider their human and civil rights, with each chapter focused on a decade of events and resistance. The early republic was marked by both opportunities and setbacks, as local communities sought to restore or replace older orders. African Americans gained gradual emancipation in New York, but the northeast also adopted new measures aimed at reducing African Americans' newfound independence. For wives and African Americans, legal strategies and ally-building were of primary importance in resistance during this era, as judges and juries proved accessible and optimal in redressing grievances. They secured their legal rights to access the courts, but justice was not equal, and they remained impaired in critical ways. Youthful servants saw a continuing decline in their ability to leverage legal suits and used private mediations through neighbors and family to support themselves, as their roles as servants and apprentices went through a major transformation. They also turned to violence. Records from the early republic are better preserved than those from earlier periods, and this allows for greater recognition of the ways urban versus rural contexts determined some of the resistance and assistance legally dependent peoples received. For those in rural areas, allies were essential to the fight, but they were difficult to locate, and in urban areas, associations and access to the government altered legal contestations of violence. The final chapter shows the impact that resistance had on the civil and human rights of African Americans, wives, and young adults, and some of the problems they would face in the antebellum era as violence grew.

It's no secret that the United States has a problem with violence, and it's imperative we understand how our history plays a role in this. Echoes of the social and cultural institutions that rationalized violence in early America are visible today. As scholars of colonization and empire-building have shown, violence secures territories and maintains rule, and interpersonal conflict is also about power. Violence was critical to the founding of the colonies, to asserting independence, and to securing the republic.[24] Our agency in creating or resisting cultures that condone violence is writ large in this narrative. The desire for security and safety goaded early Americans to use violence to assert authority, but they would act to delimit violence for stability when the case was made in a way that connected the goals of the powerful with those of dependents. Within this narrative, you will see moments of hope and clarity, as well as horrifying violence and powerlessness. Researching and writing about violence reveals the dark side of our institutions and human nature, but if we shy away from learning about violence, we miss an opportunity to evaluate how our social and cultural institutions support it. Making the violence they suffered visible to the public was the priority of dependent peoples. In the past, socially and legally empowered people often chose to look away from the pain and suffering of others. They made laws that made it seem like protections existed but did not enforce them. Uncovering the truths about how violence operates in society shows us how we arrived at this moment and, perhaps, what we can do to choose a better path forward.

PART I

The Colonial Era

Chapter 1

Young Servants and Apprentices

In 1718, Benjamin Franklin had reached the age of twelve in Boston, Massachusetts, a time when parents and their children customarily began making decisions about what trade their children would pursue. Parents of some financial means, such as Franklin's father, secured their children's contracts for servitude or apprenticeship to ensure the children developed the skills and education to become productive members of society. Franklin rejected his father's vision of his becoming a clergyman, and he refused to join the family business as a soap and candle maker. Franklin was fortunate to have options. The best apprenticeships for boys involved serving for skilled artisans and usually required a fee on the part of parents; it was not regularly available to girls, the poor, and servants of color, who commonly received lesser training. Poor children, who often included Indians and African Americans, were bound to servitude or apprenticeship by Overseers of the Poor and they had little input on where they were sent. Though differences in the quality of experiences existed, the terms "servant" and "apprentice" were often used interchangeably because servitude in the early modern era simply meant a contract to work for the head of the household for wages, training, and room and board. Parents and Overseers expected masters to fulfill the basic needs of children, demanding they receive proper clothing, food, and lodging, and contracts stipulated a "decent and Christian education" in addition to any trade skills learned as part of their broader training.[1] Benjamin Franklin and his father decided to apprentice him to Benjamin's brother, James, to learn the skills of printing. Parents often chose to send their children to family members, as it was a way of ensuring their good training and treatment. Franklin quickly took to printing; he had increased access to books and he spent time outside of his apprenticeship learning to write and read more deeply.

Franklin was as assertive and resolute in his relationship with his new master as he was with his father in choosing his trade, and the re-

lationship between James and Benjamin Franklin soon soured. Franklin secretly delivered several short written pieces for publication in
his brother's newspaper "suspecting" that his brother "would object
to printing any Thing of mine in his Paper if he knew it to be mine."
Once they were published, Benjamin Franklin's esteem among friends
rose while the conflict with his brother intensified. James Franklin beat
Benjamin repeatedly, citing his hubris and dilatoriness. "Tho' a Brother,"
Benjamin explained, James "considered himself as my Master, & me as
his Apprentice; and accordingly expected the same Services from me as
he would from another." James Franklin likely believed that giving his
brother special treatment would not benefit Benjamin's development or
training. Throughout the seventeenth and eighteenth centuries, masters
had a responsibility to educate and promote order among their charges.
Allowing an unruly servant to do as he or she pleased had negative effects on the broader community, which expected masters to control their
servants. Benjamin admitted that he had become somewhat vain, but he
also believed James "demean'd me too much in some he requir'd of me."[2]

James Franklin's power to discipline Benjamin derived from early
Americans' belief in the needfulness of authority figures over children
and youth and obedience as a trait among them. A master's judicious use
of discipline along with kindness supposedly created peace and tranquil-
ity within the household and community.[3] Masters had clear rights to
use physical force, but they needed to temper this with the situational
needs of individuals and the right of servants to live free from extreme
bodily harm. Benjamin Wadsworth, a clergyman and educator in Cambridge, Massachusetts, suggested that "If [a servant is] so foolhardy, high
and stout as not to be mended by words; then correction should be us'd
for his reformation." Wadsworth proposed that limits existed on the use
of corporal punishment, and the laws and practices of communities
agreed. "Yet you should not correct them (as we said before of Children)
in rage and passion; nor upon uncertainties, unless you are sure of their
faults; nor should your corrections be cruel and unmerciful; if milder
ones will do, more severe ones should ever be avoided."[4] Masters had to
check their violence and aggression to maintain their authority among
servants and ensure that they raised their youth properly. In addition to
concerns about the futility of extreme violence as a means of correction,
communities worried about the physical well-being of servants. They

wanted young servants and apprentices well cared for and not perma-nently injured by their masters.

Benjamin Franklin was like many young men and women in New England when he rejected being beaten by his master. He claimed James "was passionate & had often beaten me, which I took extreamly amiss." Benjamin Franklin cited James's "passion," portraying him as unjust and challenging his authority in the workshop. The relationship between the brothers continued to deteriorate.[5] White servants and apprentices, like Franklin, were among the first of the dependent classes in early Amer-ica to receive the right to legally redress their grievances about physical abuse, though Franklin did not take this route. When masters failed to fulfill their part of the contract, servants could petition the court. In the seventeenth century, courts responded favorably to the pleas that made their way through the formal court system by investigating many cases and freeing some servants from abusive masters. Young servants who did not have access to the courts or did not believe courts would effectively prevent their abuse opted to contest and prevent abuse by alternative means, including running away, fighting back, and hiding from abusive masters. The court did not approve of such behaviors. Al-though young servants had various options to redress abuse, not all ser-vants found justice; courts and communities sometimes ignored claims of abuse or returned servants to abusive masters. Girls and servants of color were particularly susceptible to abusive situations. When ne-glected, abused servants suffered in dangerous situations with their best hope being to find a person (usually a parent) willing to help them.

By the time James Franklin began beating Benjamin, colonists in Massachusetts and New York were changing in terms of how they per-ceived and handled servant abuse. Young servants clearly had different conceptions than their masters of what constituted abuse. They had to assiduously assert their innocence and seek out intervention because communities were not equally disposed toward accepting servants' claims that masters wrongfully assaulted them. During the eighteenth century, judges and juries decreasingly issued fines to masters who abused their servants. The decriminalization of abuse occurred over the long term and did not mean that servants could no longer access justice. What it did mean was that as communities' craving for watchful mas-ters magnified, they would intervene only in cases of severe abuse. The physical scars of violence became more important as communities lost trust in the testimony of young servants and apprentices. Even as the eighteenth century saw a decline in legal interventions, advice literature increasingly contested the use of violence in proper child rearing, and colonists began viewing adolescence and youth as stages of life requiring affection to build character.[6] Children and youth protested abusive masters, and like Benjamin Franklin, they spoke up against violence or ran away, as many still had considerable agency in their lives. Youth created awareness about the dangers of abuse in servitude through their protests but did so among a culture attuned to maintaining obedience and discipline.

Processes of Contestation

Benjamin Franklin was not the first apprentice or servant to resent his treatment or suffer abuse at the hands of his master. Throughout the colonial era, youthful servants and apprentices assertively staked out their right to serve and learn a trade free from abuse in a society that accepted corporal punishment of servants within vaguely specified limits. Servants had their own conceptions of what constituted abuse, and in at least forty-four instances, servants and apprentices reported abuse to legal authorities.[7] Massachusetts and New Netherland had developed and maintained processes whereby servants could redress their grievances regarding excessively cruel treatment, but these varied by region and over time. Both regions prosecuted and imposed criminal penalties on some masters who abused their servants, but New York offered abused servants freedom and fined masters for abuse more often than did Massachusetts. Extralegal protests by servants are difficult to locate in this period because of the paucity of records, but servants assiduously searched for allies, fought back, and ran from violence too. Parents proved the most reliable allies because nonfamilial bystanders often did not intervene in ways that helped servants. While protections existed for servants, their fight against abuse was critical to ensuring their safety because standards could not be set without drawing public attention to it.

Communities would not accept the murder of young white servants, but the investigations occurring after the death of white servants and apprentices show the weaknesses in community interventions to protect servants. In 1652/3, Massachusetts Court of Assistants, the colony's highest court, prosecuted John Betts for beating his white servant Robert Knight to death "w'th a great plough staff . . . [and a] Goad upon y'e Backe, both which we find to be unlawfull weapons to strike w'th." It was not the plough staff, however, that led to Betts's indictment and conviction; it was the extreme cruelty with which he wielded the staff causing his servant's death. Betts broke Knight's back with his fierce blows, in addition to the suffering he inflicted with his fists and a stick. After the assault, Betts "neglected him and cruelly used him in sickness" by not giving him proper medical attention for the wounds. One witness who saw Knight prior to his death described him as "much maciated & decayed, strength [in] y'e inferious Limbs much decayed & somewha't paralitick." Neither did Betts allow Knight to rest, and the work of animal husbandry proved much too difficult to complete while suffering from a broken back. Witnesses for Betts testified that Knight was an insolent servant who stole and did not fulfill his work duties, but regardless, the court deemed the violence that Betts inflicted on Knight as criminal. As punishment, Betts was paraded to the gallows and stood with a rope around his neck for onlookers to taunt and harass him; he also suffered a severe whipping and paid a fine and the costs of the trial. In addition, the court required him to make a twenty-pound bond to ensure his good behavior in the future.[8] Importantly, courts waited until Knight's death to criminalize Betts's behavior and little appears to have been done to ameliorate the dangers Knight faced. Colony-wide governments occasionally found fault with the practices of local communities, but they only did so in cases of murder. Such interventions were too late.[9]

Murder cases reveal the importance of community allies and bystanders who helped servants secure safety prior to escalation of abuse. In the 1600s, white servants routinely turned to legal authorities and neighbors when they experienced cruel treatment, as well as lack of food, clothing, shelter, and training in their professions. New England, New Netherland, and later New York stipulated that servants had a process to redress their grievances. When masters "Tyrannically and Cruelly abuse their Servants," servants could make an actionable complaint to court officials. According to laws in New York, upon a servant's first complaint, the court warned the master against such treatment, but if the abuse continued, Overseers or constables would "protect and Sustain such Servants in their Houses till due Order be taken for their Relief" at the next sitting of the court. In Massachusetts, legal protections also extended beyond the courts, and servants fleeing from "the Tyranny and Cruelty of his or her Master" could arrive at any free man's household and expect protection until the "Magistrate or Constable" settled the affair. In cases of more egregious violence, the courts put other measures in place. In colonial New Netherland and New England, laws stipulated freeing maimed servants.[10]

Servants confronted a variety of difficulties when protesting abuse, including societal beliefs about the authority of parents and guardians to physically discipline unruly children and young adults. Early Americans viewed children as being at a developmental stage that required oversight, and English and Dutch societies accepted physical punishment so long as it was not excessively used.[11] The Dutch Reformed Church, like Puritans and Pilgrims, had a more moderate stance than the Catholic Church toward the development of children, believing that proper religious and educational guidance had positive results.[12] In cases of stubborn children, early modern parents generally agreed that physical discipline played a role in shaping them; in such cases, ministers and writers warned against exacting punishment during throes of anger and to always explain the reasons for physical punishment. It's clear that physical discipline was acceptable, but both the English and Dutch had measures and writing that suggested abuse could harm the development of children.

The ambiguity in the laws regarding "Immoderate correction" and "cruelty" required that protesting servants establish two points: their behavior had not warranted the punishment and the assault was unreasonably severe. Servants and apprentices petitioned for relief, claiming masters meted out abuse without any "just Reasonable Cause" or "just Occasion" for doing so. Courts used servants' testimonies and their witnesses to establish the veracity of complaints, and court officials also saw for themselves the wounds suffered by apprentices and servants. To make the best cases possible, servants understood that it was important to report abuse quickly. Bruises, cuts, and welts helped make cases, as well as any testimony they could find about their good behavior. Masters tried to persuade the court that their servants' bad behavior demanded assaults. When Jan Everzen Bout found himself on trial for abusing a servant in New Amsterdam, he claimed his servant "is a stiffnecked thing and will not listen to what is said to her."[13] The two holes he bored through the child's head indicated that more than the servant's impudence caused the violence.

Servants believed the use of whips or rods was illegitimate in discipline, but the wielding of implements was hardly the only determining factor in deciding an abuse case. In 1710, a servant in Boston complained against his master for "Striking him with unlawful Instruments" and "grievously bruising and wounding" him. The court, however, returned him to his master, whom the court forced to make a bond to "not Abuse him by cruel and unmerciful Punishment." The bond required a master and two other persons (serving as "sureties" for the bond) to agree that if the master abused the servant again within a stipulated time period the master and sureties would all lose the money bonded. While the potential loss of funds was significant, it did not constitute a punishment for the act committed and was only a preventative measure against future abuse. Another servant complained of the same master again in 1714, maintaining he received a "cruel Whipping," but again courts returned the servant to his master, posed no fine, and told the master to avoid "Cruelty." In addition to these cases, in 1639, a servant boy sought help by showing his battered body to several persons who looked specifically to see the marks of the whip, "but no blood" was found on the body. The witnesses did not report the abuse to JPs, but admonished the master that he had given the boy "sufficient correction for that time." They also sought to ensure the child had proper sustenance. The child eventually died and only after that did the court say the use of rods was unlawful, which suggests the mixed messages in communities.[14] Community members did not object to the use of whips and rods, and the courts deemed them unlawful only when they resulted in death or maiming.[15] Northern masters rationalized the use of tools as a suitable means to punish servants so long as the tools were means to reform behavior and did not leave lasting marks.

Communities accepted young white servants' ability to redress their grievances in court, and officials heard and processed their petitions even if they did not always agree with servants. Between 1630 and 1685 in Plymouth, at least six servants brought forth charges of abuse, and the courts removed three of these servants from their masters, admonished one master for the abuse, reproved one servant for being disorderly, and, in the final case, dropped the charges because the servant died.[16] In Massachusetts Court of Assistants, an additional eight servants pushed for relief, but only one servant received freedom. Similar contestations and outcomes of abuse appear in Essex County, Massachusetts, where, between 1640 and 1682, fifteen servants protested, with the court deciding nine in favor of servants. In only one of these cases did the court place the abused servant in another household. In more remote Maine, no records of servants' complaints exist prior to 1700, though suspicious murders of servants had occurred both there and in Plymouth.[17] The landscape of Maine likely made self-emancipation through running away more attractive than turning to legal authorities.

Servants actively protested abuse in Dutch New Netherland as much as they did in Massachusetts. However, New Netherland offered white servants more room to get out of their servitude contracts when they protested abuse. Servants, the sheriff, or the schout (a public prosecutor) bought fifteen cases to the courts in New Netherland and New York between 1652 and 1674, and the most successful cases were those in which servants used the proper channels to contest abuse. The council presiding over court cases sided with servants and issued fines or took other action to protect servants in all but one of the cases with known outcomes. Councils in New Amsterdam, Fort Orange, and Beverwyck often suggested servants return to their masters, but they also offered ways out of servitude by ordering servants to return to their masters or pay for their room and board or other costs claimed by their masters. New masters who took on abused servants and apprentices likely bore these costs. The flexibility of the Dutch courts in offering white servants a way out of abuse through paying these costs provided a practical measure to ensure they were protected. One reason for the high level of negotiated exits was that in five of these cases, masters reported the servants to the court for refusing to work or for running away. The council discovered wrongdoing in the process of exploring these cases and changed the trajectory of the trial, showing a commitment to securing the safety of young servants.[18] Yet the council also protected the masters' financial interests and authority by granting them remuneration for the costs associated with maintaining servants.

By reporting abuse, servants influenced the creation of standards for safety in the community even if community members disagreed about what constituted acceptable violence. Servants' reports of abuse could result in fines against their masters, suggesting the criminality of their acts. Severity of abuse was important in the issuance of fines, but no government followed the practice of fining only those masters who had egregiously abused and maimed their servants in the early period. At least seven masters paid fines during the seventeenth century in Massachusetts and Plymouth, and in New York, at least six masters received fines. The fines issued in Massachusetts were generally below five pounds, while those in New Netherland were usually between ten and thirty guilders, which is roughly equivalent; however, in one case, the court deemed the abuse so extreme that the council issued a fine of 100 guilders.[19] The use of fines, even when only rarely issued, signaled the importance of servants' and apprentices' safety within the community and the criminality of wrongful abuse. The courts' decisions to release servants was not necessarily a punishment for an assault because new masters often bought out the remainder of servants' previous contracts.[20] In paying a fine for their abuse of servants and apprentices, masters had to accept the consequences of their wrongdoing. Massachusetts Bay and Plymouth were less punitive toward masters in cases of abuse, but servants were still essential in establishing a standard to restrain excessive violence. When Massachusetts courts found masters guilty of abusing their servants, they most commonly held masters to a bond to "keep the peace" toward their servants and apprentices. In cases where masters signed bonds, the servants' safety remained imperiled because the onus was on servants to report future mistreatment. Nevertheless, the reporting and processing of incidents resulted in restraints on masters' powers that were not imaginable without servant protests.

Although some differences existed, both English and Dutch communities created a structure that supported judicious violence against servants by denying young apprentices and servants the same range of liberties as adult free persons. Moreover, the government's willingness to serve as disciplinarians for servants and youth likely bolstered masters' conceptions of their own authority to assault their servants. All servants and apprentices experienced limited freedoms, and differential laws and punishments existed for them as opposed to the general public. Legislators in Massachusetts and New York stipulated that "if any Children or Servants become Rude, Stubborne or unruly refusing to hearken to the voice of their Parents or Master the Constable or Overseers . . . have the power . . . to Inflict Such Corporall punishment as the merit of the fact of in their Judgment shall deserve, not exceeding ten Stripes." These laws did not serve as mere warnings. In the 1650s, the court ordered Allexander Maxell of Maine to be whipped thirty stripes on his "bare skine" for "grosse offence in his exorbitant & abusive carages towards his Maister Mr. George Leader & his Mistresse." The court further threatened to sell him to "Virginia, Barbadoes, or any of the of the English Plantations" if he did not behave. In the seventeenth century, masters found threats to sell white servants to the South or to the West Indies useful in pacifying intractable servants. In addition to the aforementioned tactics, most northern colonies also had laws empowering JPs, magistrates, or Overseers of the Poor to imprison "Rogues, Vagbonds, Common Beggars, and other Lewd Idle, and Disorderly Persons . . . stubborn servants, or children," for disorderly conduct.[21] From the government's perspective, taking an active role in the maintenance of discipline ensured public safety, and the government used the means at its disposal to uphold the authority of masters and punish servants.

Cities and towns admonished tavern keepers not to provide alcohol to servants to limit servants' disorderly and drunken behavior, as well as their mobility. As with other regulations regarding servants' behavior, colonists actively prosecuted these laws. Several crimes resulted in differential punishments with servants receiving corporal punishment rather than fines due to their financial dependence on masters. For example, the courts convicted John Barton, a servant in Maine, of swearing and drunkenness. For punishment, he had to pay a fine of three pounds or receive "20 lashes on the barre skinne."[22] Barton's position as a servant compromised his ability to pay the fine, and he likely suffered the whipping. Some masters preferred to pay these fines on their servants' behalf instead of seeing their servants whipped, but other masters sanctioned whippings to send a message about behavior.

The power masters accrued from these laws and practices meant that some servants had difficulty accessing government authorities to resist abuse. Servants and apprentices needed to secure time away from work to register a complaint, and masters who engaged in physically abusive behavior were likely to closely monitor the movement of servants. More-over, abusive masters did not respect the rights of their servants to com-plain about their ill treatment to others. In 1654, the court fined Thomas Huckens four shillings for forcing his servant to return home from his way to Plymouth, where he was heading to complain of abuse.[23] While bystanders could help in abusive situations, servants needed to live in proximity to community members for the court system to be an effective remedy for abuse. This was possible in some of the tightly constructed towns, but it was difficult in rural areas and new towns where JPs lived significant distances from servants in need of assistance. In addition, court officials may never have entered some petitions into court records because the officials did not believe the complaints merited responses. The relationship between court officials and certain masters may have meant officials did not want to record petitions, and their own preju-dices regarding the behavior of servants and apprentices were additional impetuses to dismiss complaints.[24]

For some servants, self-emancipation provided an option outside of legal interventions, but it proved difficult and came with risks and pen-alties. Numerous servants protested abuse by absconding, as suggested by the hundreds of runaway advertisements published in colonial news-papers. The law penalized servants for running away, so servants had to weigh the risks and rewards of fleeing an abusive environment even as legislation claimed they had a right to seek out a haven from abuse. Leg-islation against the harboring of servants existed throughout the North, but some individuals would intervene to help. In Massachusetts, Mary Adams successfully defended herself against charges of "withholding" a servant from her master when the servant revealed she ran away be-cause of "ill treatment and hard usage." Showing concern for the servant, Adams was essential to providing a haven while the community resolved the abuse. Although the court relieved Adams of charges, it forced the servant to return to her master.[25]

Servants avoided interactions with cruel masters and engaged in work slowdowns, which was a less risky method of avoiding abuse. Not all tasks required constant oversight by masters, and young apprentices and servants sought to prolong those moments when chores took them away from their masters. Other servants struck back by poorly complet-ing or not doing the work assigned to them. One servant admitted lying to his master about completing a chore because he and his fellow servant would "plot by all meanes they could to get away and be freed from their master." By combining forces, they hoped to find a way to avoid abuse.[26] Taking time away from work might anger a master further, but some servants found it an expedient measure to obtain space to rest.

Because communities and courts did not always take a strong stance against abuse, alternative means of prevention were necessary. Some servants fell victim to violence no matter how much they protested. After the death of John Walker, a fourteen-year-old white servant to Robert Lathem in Marshfield, Massachusetts, a jury examined the body and determined Lathem killed him. Walker's body was black and blue, his extremities frostbitten, and strange holes and scars riddled his body. Lathem's indictment noted his "felonious cruelty," and the court found him guilty of manslaughter and denying Walker appropriate food, clothing, and housing. Three men testified to Lathem's cruelty, including two who heard Lathem describe the whipping he gave to Walker the day he died. The court sentenced Lathem to be burned in the hand and have all his property taken away.[27] By attempting to uncover the causes of the servant's death, the Marshfield community followed the law in regard only to the murder of servants. The three men who testified to the Walker whipping did not intervene prior to Walker's death and their inaction speaks to the difference between rhetoric and practices in Puritan New England.

Cases of murder and maiming of white servants reminded locals they needed to protect servants who protested abuse prior to the escalation of conflict, and parents were important in safeguarding servants because they stepped in when they saw their children ill-used or not receiving the training or education they desired. Some parents even struck back at abusive masters. In 1751, Samuel Nobel of Philadelphia "had bo't a servant girl . . . and for some misdemeanor of her's, had given her proper Correction." Chagrined at the assault, the girl's mother attacked Nobel and his family "in a very gross manner" and demanded money. She even persuaded her friends to try and extort money from Nobel for his misdeeds. Other parents used the courts. In 1731, Samuel Magoo reported to New York City officials that "Thomas Hall hath several times very Immoderately Corrected his son Alexander Magoo." After hearing testimony and "seeing the Marks upon the head arm and body of the said

Alexander Magoo," the court freed the younger Magoo.[28] Parents tried to keep their children near them so that they could witness their growth and training, and they protested when masters tried to move their children to different locations. They could buy back the time or sue masters in court for failing to fulfil their expectations.[29] Parents were often the best allies youthful servants and apprentices had, and they went to great lengths to make sure their children were safe.

Only by informing parents, neighbors, and legal authorities could servants establish the limits of abuse and challenge the larger authority of masters to discipline them. As the deaths of several white servants showed, some masters still abused their power. Advice literature, laws, and the adjudication of abuse in courts revealed that excessive corporal punishment was illegal when it occurred outside the confines of an intention to correct poor behavior and when it resulted in a lifelong injury. Servants used this understanding to prove they had been good servants and not deserving of extreme violence. While New York was more generous in its protection of servants and apprentices, Massachusetts was less willing to provide a fuller relief for servants, though it did take its role in safeguarding youth seriously by hearing and processing complaints. From servants' perspectives, not enough was actively done outside of servants' and their parents' activism to protect them, and they believed whips and rods were illegal tools in a masters' arsenal. Bystander intervention was not a common enough practice to protect servants, though servants clearly sought help from community members. Courts responded to existing complaints, and a larger groundswell against violence was needed to prevent excessive abuse and death.

Eighteenth-Century Cracks in the System

By the 1720s, when Benjamin Franklin was determining how to handle his abusive apprenticeship to his brother, servants' ability to redress violence had not necessarily increased. Franklin may not have been aware of the changes, but courts altered the way they criminalized abusers, and society was in the process of reconceptualizing the nature of young adulthood and best practices in their development. Benjamin Franklin had much to consider as he tried to negotiate the situation, and his familial relationship with James dictated his method of resistance. He first challenged his brother's authority to beat him and then sought the help of his father rather than protesting through the court system. Amid the tension between Benjamin and James, the Franklin family was under pressure because officials in Boston arrested James Franklin for printing a libel. Benjamin did not want to make it worse for his brother, who he ultimately felt was not an "illnatur'd man."[30] Boston officials warned James he could not publish a paper under his own name again, so he turned to Benjamin to take the lead in the shop and publish under Benjamin's name thereafter. Benjamin sought more autonomy in his training and feared returning to a state of dependence after James returned home. Many young men and women chafed at their subordination as they reached young adulthood and youth protested abuse according to their unique situations.

During the eighteenth century, adult supervision of children and young adults took on new importance as perceptions of young adults' maturity and right to independence shifted, and these transformations affected the way society dealt with abuse. Young adults found that legal provisions chipped away at their autonomy by extending the age of independence to the age of twenty-one and increasing the authority of parents and masters.[31] Making labor contracts, serving as witnesses, and engaging in the body politic required reason and independence, traits not commonly associated with young adults, who were at an age when great temptation and willfulness clouded their minds. Courts continued to safeguard some white servants and apprentices who made complaints about abuse by freeing them, particularly in New York. However, new difficulties emerged for servants to legally establish masters' assaults as cruelty, and courts decreasingly issued penalties to abusive masters beyond loss of servants' labor. Slavery and pauper apprenticeship simultaneously grew in economic and social importance during the eighteenth century, and this too would influence experiences of servitude. Servants of color found it more difficult to prosecute their cases of abuse than whites, and they were more likely to suffer from unfair contracts and assaults. Young women were underrepresented in abuse cases as well, though they found ways to resist abuse. Running away, engaging in retributive violence, and creating networks of communication about abusive masters were means for all servants and apprentices to achieve safety and autonomy outside of the legal systems.

Servants continued protesting abuse and undoubtedly preferred freedom from abusive masters, as this was the best method to ensure their safety. In the eighteenth century, Massachusetts and New York continued to diverge in their responses to the issue of abuse. New York City was more generous in granting freedom to servants and apprentices who proved their masters assaulted them. Between 1695 and 1770, New York City freed all twenty-eight servants protesting abuse from their masters, and servants had the same level of success in the twenty-six complaints they made regarding lack of provisions and absentee masters between 1730 and 1770.[32] In contrast, in Suffolk County, Massachusetts, the government granted freedom in three out of the thirteen cases, and courts required masters to post bond in three other cases.[33] Courts were likely to free a servant who made a second complaint, but masters made that difficult by restricting their servants' mobility after being brought to court. While courts in Massachusetts were less likely to free servants in cases of cruelty, they did uphold their laws ensuring that servants did not return to their masters until the conclusion of the case. When William More deserted his abusive master in Maine, the court permitted him to stay with his parents until the case concluded.[34] Allowing servants to live apart from their masters during investigations afforded servants with some protection from immediate reprisal and indicated the government's concern about servants' safety.

Courts decreasingly made use of fines when masters assaulted their white servants, and only in rare cases of abuse nearly resulting in death would governments and juries act to punish and criminalize assaults. In 1756, a New York City court indicted Rice and Dorothy Williams for assaulting their white servant. The case showed the Williamses repeatedly engaged in abusive behavior toward Mary Mozhor and the violence was so extreme that her "life was greatly despaired of." New York City indicted and prosecuted the Williamses for "beating and bruising [Mozhor] . . . in a Most Cruel and Barbarous Manner at Sundry times."[35] Because Mozhor's abuse nearly resulted in her death, the court also registered it as a case of assault rather than a petition to be released from contract, but this had become extremely rare after the 1700s, and this is the only case resulting in a fine in New York City. Massachusetts acted just as rarely in criminalizing assaults.[36] Without assigning penalties to masters beyond the loss of labor or bonds to keep the peace, the trials became principally civil suits about a breach of contract. Private adjudication became preferable in Massachusetts with the Overseers of the Poor and other officials increasingly avoiding taking cases through the court system. It is important to recall that during the eighteenth century, petitioners maintained the same processes as they had when courts used fines against abusers, but newer interpretations of petitioners' cases resulted in declining use of indictments and fines, and Overseers privately negotiated with masters.

Behind the declining use of penalties for abuse were changes that emphasized the importance of caring for youth and preparing them for autonomy. Ironically, much of this literature eschewed corporal punishment as a means of preparing youth for the world. Among the signs of shifting ideas was a new emphasis on the role of affectionate families over authoritarian and abusive patriarchs. The desire for independent, logical, and civic-minded citizens who could act responsibly in a republican form of government required that children be trained toward proper decision-making. Philosophers and moralists encouraged minimal use of corporal punishment to attain these goals, and colonists read texts by writers such as John Locke and Francis Hutcheson in addition to sentimental literature and newspapers popularizing their ideas. John Locke believed parents must train children to accept physical and emotional hardship through physical and emotional denial, but he advocated a system of rewards and punishments for children's behavior that was based on a parent's denial and bestowing of affection. Francis Huthcheson theorized that children had an innate moral sense of justice and compassion, and he believed parents should appeal to these traits within children to guide them.[37] Adapting this literature to servants, John Barnard, a former mayor of London, suggested in the 1740s that disciplining servants required both severity and understanding, and he worried that servants would disobey both kind and violent masters alike. He warned masters not to overwork or overburden their servants, but he also suggested leniency would do a master no good. Barnard surmised, "the capricious tyrant is better obeyed than the man of gentleness and forbearance who refines too much on the dictates of his own compassion, and suffers himself to be persuaded out of his will." Although he claimed that being strict was important, Barnard also believed severity undermined a master's authority. Establishing

a middle ground between fear and respect for their master was paramount, as mistreatment of servants created even worse behavior. "If
thunder itself was to be continual," Barnard argued, "it would excite no
more terror than the noise of the mill, and we should sleep in tranquil-
ity when it roared the loudest. . . . If ever then you give way to the trans-
ports of anger let it be extremely rare; and, never, but upon the highest
provocation."[38] The increased availability and circulation of these ideas
emphasized educational development over corporal punishment when
guiding children's moral compass. The message underlying these texts
was that youth would resist abuse and even be encouraged in their defiance if they suffered violence without just cause.

Although advice literature deemed unwarranted abuse unjust, society
remained wary of the temptations of young adults and worried about
their penchant for disobedience. Barnard advised servants on how to
best conduct themselves and wrote they must "be guarded against all
the snares to which youth is obnoxious." Admonishing servants not to
lie, gossip, be vulgar, or befriend loose women, Barnard's suggestions
centered on warning servants against the bad behavior to which he assumed youth were attracted. He also tried to lead them toward a righteous path by urging apprentices to be industrious, deport themselves
with manners, and dress appropriately. Barnard's views about servants as
a potentially disorderly group were not isolated. Ministers, laymen, and
employers offered a bevy of advice such as Barnard's in newspapers, sermons, and their day-to-day lives, underscoring the general suspicion of
adults regarding their servants' and children's behavior.[39] The authors of
such literature assumed their audience consisted mostly of young males,
although girls and young women were a vital component of household
labor and made up large numbers of servants. Literature advising young
women to be obedient, humble, and diligent more than made up for this
omission by instructing them on the ruinous effects of poor choices.
Growing populations of youth in the colonies, England, and the Netherlands meant these common themes about young adults circulated in
Europeans' transatlantic literature.

Early Americans had viewed children and young adults with suspicion in the seventeenth century, and negative perceptions of their
competency further compounded judgments about their truthfulness
and their right to appear in court. Over the course of the eighteenth

century, courts decreased the use of, and trust in, children's testimony, which affected their willingness to criminalize masters' actions.[40] Children's and young adults' bodies and words played a central role in the evidentiary base upon which judges and juries made decisions about abuse. As young adults' words lost impact, their bodies took on new importance. Scars, bruises, and other visible marks of violence became essential for masters to be found criminally culpable. Bystanders proved far more likely to intervene in extreme cases of violence as well. The effects of these newer understandings of young adults were particularly pronounced in New York, where courts had more often criminalized assaults in the previous century. These changes culminated in the practices of criminalizing only life-threatening abuse or that which maimed servants and apprentices. The freeing of servants in New York, however, remained a vital means of securing their safety, even if courts did not find masters criminally culpable for their abuse.

Some counseled servants to temporarily accept even unjust punishment for their betterment although processes existed for their contestation. It was a contradictory message that suggested the skepticism surrounding community support of abused youth and early American views about enduring pain.[41] Writing in the eighteenth century, Reverend Wadsworth surmised, "if their Masters thro' mistake or passion, sometimes chasten them wrongfully; they should yet strive to bear it as patiently as they can." Josiah Quinby had similar advice for those who bore discipline, and his recommendations came from real-world experiences of having served a prison sentence for debt in New York. Quinby recounted that rather than seeing his punishment as unwarranted, he opened himself up to it and used it to better himself. "I have no more Resentments lodged on me on that Account," Quinby related, "than a Child or a Servant that well knows he justly deserves for his Misdeeds, many heavy Stripes, and instead of his receiving them all, he received a few, and they but light." Both writers characterized withstanding punishment as a virtue and said that it was important not to feel "overwhelmed in Vexation and Bitterness of Mind" and become "entrapped in the Plague and Torment of Discontent."[42] Advice literature directed those suffering abuse to bear it with humility and an eye toward reformation even when they received such abuse unfairly. In advocating that servants tolerate illegitimate discipline, the writers supported the authority of masters and promoted tolerance of abuse beyond what the law allowed.

From servants' perspectives, such writing was anathema. The singling out of their behavior for correction by the government and masters, as well as the assumed righteousness of masters, were twin poles that undermined servants' sense of justice and the full realization of their rights compared with their masters. Elizabeth Ashbridge, a white servant who arrived in New York in 1732, recalled that her master asked the town whipper to come to his home to punish her for spreading a false rumor. Ashbridge was shocked to find that when the whipper arrived, no man intervened to decide whether the punishment was fair. No hearing bore out the truth of her master's claims, and she said the town whipper "never asked me Whether I had told such thing but ordered me to strip." She begged her master to reconsider and deliver the punishment himself, if he must, because she was horrified by the shame of having to be both whipped and undressed before a man she hardly knew. Her master sent the whipper away, perhaps mollified by Ashbridge's pleading, but she believed his conscience may have gotten the better of him because she claimed that she was the honest party in their disagreement.[43] Though Ashbridge escaped the lash, she did not have access to legal intervention; she had to rely on her own pleading and her master's reconsideration of the punishment. Ashbridge eventually purchased her way out of her servitude and secured her independence for herself.

New opportunities offered young adults more autonomy and they showed a willful disregard of authority figures even as contemporary ideas and practices stressed the need for young adults' further development. Economic transformations of the eighteenth century made it more difficult for young adults to attain the financial independence required to establish their own households. Many youth moved to cities or the frontier in search of opportunities, breaking free of the bonds of families and communities of origin. Religious diversity opened new avenues for expressing independence as young men and women asserted beliefs and practices different from their parents. Youth culture was another means for young persons to turn away from the power of adults, and youth identified with one another as a group and took part in common activities that authorities viewed with suspicion.[44] Colonists' engagement in war was perhaps the greatest threat to youthful dependence as new prospects existed to break free of unhappy circumstances.

During the French and Indian War, running away was a primary means for abused servants to protect themselves. Richard Iverson of West New Jersey reported that his seventeen-year-old servant girl had left with the army and should have returned, but she kept her freedom and traveled in the colonies since that time.[45] The colonies needed manpower, and it was during this moment that Massachusetts lawmakers reiterated their commitment to fining masters in cases of abuse.[46] Massachusetts enacted a law in 1758 that masters who harmed indigent servants and apprentices—those whom the Overseer of the Poor bound—would receive fines up to five pounds, and the court would free apprentices if it deemed it necessary. The court did not actively engage in the prosecution of masters, however. Passed amidst war, the legislation may have aimed to stem the tide of runaways who were taking advantage of the conflict to escape from masters. New York and other northern colonies simultaneously passed laws to protect masters in times of war, demanding that individuals under the age of twenty-one, as well as servants or apprentices, get handwritten permission from parents, guardians, or masters to serve in the military. Dislocations from war, nevertheless, provided ample opportunity for young men and women to leave their stations and take up work elsewhere, and servants did not wait for consent.

Extralegal resistance by servants and apprentices included engaging in violence against their masters, with a few even attempting to murder their masters. Laws protected the power of masters in such cases, and penalties for acting out resulted in whippings or added time for disobedience.[47] Women servants more often initiated murderous violence against their masters and mistresses than against others outside of their families. Historian Randolf Roth attributes women's violent acts to the "deadly hatred" that could develop between masters and servants who worked closely together.[48] Their violence may also suggest a sense that the courts would fail them. Arson provided another common means of revenge and resistance, and in 1757 in Watertown, Massachusetts, one white servant was jailed for "setting Fire to his Master's House, with intent to destroy it." Assaults and arson gave servants a way to disrupt abuse and assert independence, but the courts held servants accountable. The court sentenced Isaac Parker to receive twenty-one stripes for "evill Entreating his Master," and that was not the end to his punishment. If he did not repay his master for the forty-five-shilling fee the court issued to him—a large sum for a servant—he was to serve an additional twelve months.[49] Although these penalties existed, some white servants deemed retributive violence a better method of disrupting unfavorable conditions than utilizing the court system.

The actions by servants contesting abuse became part of the narrative on why physical correction was an important component of masters' powers. Colonists accepted that unruly servants and children needed correction, and when servants moved beyond acceptable standards of behavior during moments of protest or defense, people drew on that very behavior to justify corporal punishment. Servants who challenged the contours of their relationships through violence ultimately did not always serve to contest the larger societal structure that supported their abuse. Indeed, it undermined their claims to rationality and independence. For example, early Americans so associated arson with the servant class that when a fire erupted in Boston in 1760, "a Report spread thro' this Town abot the late Fire was owing to the Carelessness of the Maid Servant living with Mrs. Mary Jackson and Son."[50] Although the rumor proved false, Bostonians immediately connected the fire with servants, and this was commonplace. However, finding ways outside of the courts to fight abuse proved especially important for the servants for whom the legal system was anything but just.

Indian and African American servants' complaints for abuse and lack of training, education, or sustenance had even less success than their white counterparts' in courts. White apprentices' and servants' petitions in Massachusetts Bay and Plymouth were effective 34 to 50 percent of the time prior to 1750, while Indians' and African Americans' were effective at rates of 9 and 2 percent respectively.[51] Indians' petitions to the General Court in Massachusetts show a familiarity with processes the court used in cases of abuse, and Indian complainants also sought JPs to interdict wrongdoing. In 1733, Susanna Manchester, an American Indian, petitioned the court in Bristol, Massachusetts, on behalf of her grandson James, whom she believed William Hicks had illegally bound as a servant and abused. James Manchester's parents had died, and his grandmother suspected Hicks intended to sell him to another

master even though she contested the legitimacy of the original contract. Indentures of Indians required the consent of JPs as well as their
legal guardian, and James's contract was made "Without her Consent or
knowledge."[52] The court practiced due diligence in calling upon Hicks to
appear in court with James Manchester, but ultimately the court decided
against her petition, as it did in so many other cases involving servants
of color. Manchester appealed the court's decision, but Hicks never appeared to defend himself. The deputy sheriff tried on multiple occasions
to deliver the summons to Hicks, but he was never at the house, and
the sheriff left the summons without personally serving it. The court set
aside Susanna Manchester's petition due to Hicks's absence. Her case
reveals the ways that Indians actively used the court system to negotiate
a settlement. By first calling upon justices and then appealing the court's
decision, she used all the means at her disposal to get a favorable settlement to the case.

Evidence suggests that courts were particularly disinclined to view
abuse of Indians as problematic because of their familiarity with and
preference for the accused whites involved. In New York City, white petitions proved overwhelmingly successful, but no Indian petitions exist
in the official records of the General Sessions. Indians' use of the courts
in Massachusetts suggests that perhaps New York City may not have
made official notes when Indians petitioned regarding maltreatment or
dubious contracts. Plymouth General Sessions investigated a case of an
Indian servant who reported a sexual assault by her master; however,
the records suggest that the court did not fully indict or prosecute the
master. In fact, Peter Hunt, the accused, went on to serve as a juror and
deputy of the court in several instances after this event, indicating that
community members likely trusted him more than the servant who
made a complaint.[53] It clearly was difficult for Indian servants and their
guardians to find justice, even as they tried to use the judicial system to
petition against wrongdoing.

By the eighteenth century, courts were disposed to viewing Indians
and African Americans as having less of a right to their autonomy than
whites. During the seventeenth century, a desire for Indian servants and
slaves contributed to warfare with Indians, and the resulting trade in
Indian servants would be one of the precursors to racially based slavery.[54] In the eighteenth century, Indians living near white settlements

suffered from white encroachments on their land and increased indebtedness to whites. Merchants extended credit eagerly to Indians to force a "debtor-creditor" relationship on Indians unfamiliar with English laws. In return for credit and goods, indentured servitude rose to pay off debts as Indians were left with few alternatives.[55] Massachusetts's legislators attempted to reduce the number of Indians indentured by having two JPs oversee Indian financial agreements, including servitude contracts of adult men. The legislation intending to ameliorate Indians' indebtedness, however, did not adequately protect Indians. Gideon Hawley, a missionary to the Mashpee Indians, recalled that in the 1760s, Indian children "were sold or bound as security for the payment of their fathers debt as Soon as they were seven or eight years old ... at the desire of their creditors." The system had become exploitative and he remembered, "These Indians and their Children were transferred from one to another master like Slaves."[56] Population statistics underestimate the number of indentured Indians in New England and New York because colonists rarely identified Indians living with whites as Indians. Historian David Silverman estimates that in Rhode Island in 1774, 38 percent of Indian boys under the age of sixteen were servants, and 39 percent of Indian men over the age of sixteen; 32 percent of Indian girls under the age of sixteen were servants, and 36 percent of Indian women over the age of sixteen.[57] New England clearly created bondage practices to make use of Indian labor, and evidence exists that southern New York residents had similar aims.[58]

Even in the seventeenth century, communities did not respect Indian and African American servants' contracts as much as whites' and could force them into bondage. Threats to send white servants to the South or the West Indies proved a useful tool in maintaining discipline, but officials in Massachusetts and New York readily delivered on such threats for servants of color, in addition to trading them into slavery. The courts treated other Indians more mercifully. When Joseph Peter stole some animal hides, he was "released from bodily punishment" because he expressed regret, but the court still forced him into service for two years for his crime and for debts. While this was a harsh punishment, Peter was at least able to stay near his community and regain his freedom after service.[59] The courts implemented more legal processes during the eighteenth century to ensure that whites oversaw people of color. Boston, for example, required Indian and African American parents to bind their children as servants to whites by the age of four, and if the parents did not create the contracts, the court empowered Overseers or selectmen to do so.[60] Race and ethnicity affected the courts' handling of cases of abuse and servitude.

Indian and African American servants undoubtedly received harsher treatment than other servants, and communities condoned this disparity, particularly by the eighteenth century with the growth of African slavery and Indian servitude. In 1758, Aaron Forman Jr. of Westchester, New York, reported that his "Indian Servant Wench" had taken advantage of the dislocations caused by war to seek her freedom. Kate, his servant, was about "15 years of Age . . . and . . . Had an Iron Collar about her Neck."[61] The runaway advertisement provides a rare example of a servant description including an iron collar, a device more common among African American slaves in the North. Forman's neighbors would have been familiar with Kate's situation because she was a mobile servant, and Forman gave her a pass to look for a master. The use of the collar seems not to have disturbed community standards regarding Indian servants because the advertisement gave no explanation for it. Other evidence illustrates how communities accepted greater severity in the treatment of slaves and other servants of color. In 1731, Grace Pearson, a white woman, petitioned JPs on behalf of her daughter, whose master, she complained, treated her daughter cruelly. Asking that the court release her daughter from her indenture, Pearson described her daughter's servitude "as near Slavery," a plea that acknowledged different standards of treatment for white versus black servants.[62]

Young white women appear infrequently in the official records of the courts, but it is also likely that they more often took other opportunities to contest abuse. Between 1740 and 1770, six white female servants and apprentices in New York City used the courts to argue that their masters had cruelly beaten them, that they had absentee masters, or that their masters had not provided sufficient clothing or food. The women petitioners composed 13 percent of all servant petitions for relief during this time span, and their cases were successful with the court discharging them from their labor contracts.[63] In Suffolk County, Massachusetts, young women represented five of the eleven cruelty cases between 1702 and 1732, and in all of the cases the court returned them to their masters, as it did in males' cases during the same period.[64] Though young women represented a sizable number of registered complaints, it is certain that more young women and girls experienced abuse and deprivation than those who opted to use the local courts. Apprenticeship and servitude contracts were far less likely to be made for girls than for boys; impoverished girls bound out by contract composed between 19 and 39 percent of indentures in southern New England and New York, though it is clear girls served in households as domestics in higher numbers.[65] Overseers arranged servitude for impoverished girls, and abused girls would have needed to return to an Overseer or find an adult nearby who would assist them. Without contracts, girls and young women likely contested treatment more often through their parents and relatives. It is unknown how many young women might have used informal networks or privately sought help to resist abuse. Girls serving in households did not hold the esteemed occupations of males, however, which lessened their weight and authority in communicating distress. Although poor girls and young women would have been in a particularly disempowered situation, they did use speech outside of the courtroom to protest the abuse they suffered.

Acceptance of sexual violence against girls and young women affected their conceptions of whether they had the ability to contest abuse, particularly for young women of color. Some masters assumed they had a right to sexually touch and copulate with their female servants, and though some wives tried to limit that behavior, they were not always present. Neither was it always in wives' interests to prevent such abuse. Servants often waited until they suffered ramifications from sexual coercion—such as pregnancy and scars of violence—to protest abuse. They often reported these incidents to JPs, but they were recorded as fornication and bastardy suits rather than cases of "ravishment" or assault. Rape trials in early America reveal that only white young girls and married women had hope of successfully pursuing their cases, and servants of color had little success. JPs rarely left records denoting sexual assaults against any servants, suggesting both that young women did not see them as the best avenue to seek justice and that JPs did not pursue these cases.[66]

In addition, the broader cultural acceptance of violence against women may have deterred some girls from protesting abuse. In one particularly noteworthy incident, servant women admonished the community for allowing the mistreatment of women servants, which gives us a glimpse into the daily treatment of domestic help. In 1733, several women created an advertisement in the *New-York Weekly Journal* to protest the abuse they received in their domestic employment. They noted that "many Women in this Town . . . intend to go to Service," but they had certain "Terms" that households must agree to if they were to take up employment. "We think it reasonable we should not be beat by our Mistresses Husband, they being too strong, and perhaps may do tender Women Mischief." They intended to serve only those "Ladies" who "will engage for their Husbands."[67] The women acknowledged that their mistresses had a right to discipline them, but the women banded together to demand more humane standards. Setting terms of acceptable treatment prior to entering a household was important. Parents and Overseers avoided putting their children in households known for violence, just like adult women servants.

Examining young women's servitude shows how impoverished and immigrant children may have been underserved in contesting abuse because their families may have been distant or less empowered to help them negotiate out of abusive situations. Finding empathetic persons to help act on their behalf was a problem, as the numbers of poor and bound servants rose. Between 1733 and 1751, Boston made indentures for 247 children, who would serve until the age of eighteen for girls and twenty-one for boys. New York was similarly concerned about the poor being raised properly, and from 1665, it expressed the desire that the poor be brought up "in some honest and Lawfull Calling."[68] Immigration to the colonies increased for adult and child servants in the eighteenth century. Boston and New York City engaged in the immigrant labor trade, as runaway advertisements for Irish, Welsh, and Dutch servants in the North indicate, though the practice of holding immigrants as servants was more common southward.[69] The servant population posed challenges, but one writer from New Jersey felt positive about the ability of society to prevent and manage cases of servant abuse. "We have an excellent Law that is well guarded in Favour of such as may fall into severe Hands." Though the law clearly stated that servants had ways to contest abuse, the advantages society saw from Overseers binding out the poor to masters may have limited interventions. The same writer believed the benefits accrued from even abusive masters were "greatly in . . . [the] Favour" of those who bonded themselves to servitude because they did not miss the chance at learning an occupation and "Improvement."[70] The fear that the poor would be left without a calling or instruction could affect the dispositions of bystanders, Overseers, JPs, and juries from interfering. The rising numbers of poor children and young adults entering servitude may have also been a factor in the declining penalization of masters in the eighteenth century.

Servants' resistance to violence shows both the changing and continuous contours of ideas about children and servitude during the seventeenth and eighteenth centuries. Region, race, sex, and poverty affected the ability of servants to attain justice and secure safety. Servants of color became increasingly susceptible to violence as the growth of slavery and ideas about race converged to disempower them; later chapters further explore slavery. Some servants found solutions to their abuse through the courts, while others enlisted the help of neighbors and family members or turned to running away or retaliating with violence. The declining use of fines against masters who abused their servants, regardless of race or gender, shows society placing a higher value on empowering adults when it came to supervising children and young adults. Young adult apprentices and servants now held a legal standing more akin to children, and this decreased their successes in the courtroom. Their beaten and battered bodies became critical to the evidentiary base courts used to discern what constituted cruelty, and the difficulty of establishing cruelty heightened the stakes for abused servants and apprentices in need of safety.

Benjamin Franklin's story of abuse ended with his flight from Boston. When he decided to leave James Franklin's service, Benjamin noted that "the Blows his Passion too often urg'd him to bestow upon me" were of primary importance in his decision. Franklin's father and James refused to end his contract, and they forbade other Boston printers to accept him as an apprentice. Though the Franklin family tried to prevent his departure, in 1723, Benjamin Franklin set sail for New York and then Philadelphia, where he continued work as a printer. Franklin found the independence and security he desired in Philadelphia and would play a major role in the United States seeking and declaring independence from Britain.

Chapter 2

White Wives

In 1671, Katherine Naylor asked the governor and magistrates of Massachusetts Bay to support her in "freeing her from such an Intolerable bondage & oppression." Like servants, white wives made contracts with their husbands that were legally dissolvable only through official channels. She was married to Edward Naylor, whose abuse put her "in danger of her life." Katherine Naylor implored that she needed "releife agt cruelty and oppression and many abuses so frequently & indeede daily receives from her husband." In addition to the abuse, she and her witnesses testified that her husband had had an affair that resulted in the birth of a child.[1] Establishing that Edward Naylor had committed adultery was crucial because Massachusetts allowed a divorce only in the case of adultery. Wives who claimed cruelty as the sole cause for their petitions were only allowed separations, regardless of their desire for a more permanent division. For abused African American wives, as will be shown in the next chapter, it was even more difficult to attain assistance. The enslaved faced major impediments in turning to institutions and bystanders for safety.

Naylor's case is exceptional for the willingness of community members to bear witness against her husband. Innkeepers and the servants who lived in the Naylor household had sufficient evidence to convince the court that Edward Naylor and Mary Read had committed adultery, and witnesses told of the couple moving from bed to bed. It was Edward Naylor's notorious sexual transgressions, including getting Mary Read pregnant, that truly upset community standards.

When Katherine Naylor referred to her marriage as a form of bondage, she was not using hyperbole. White wives needed to find ways to secure their freedom from abuse and manage familial conflict. Naylor's experiences demonstrate the considerable effort abused women went through to attain freedom from abuse. Abused wives took action in an era in which "moderate correction" was as acceptable to mete out to wives as to young servants. Patriarchs held sway over their dependents, and only rarely would courts penalize them for their transgressions—and, just as with abuse of servants, the judiciary in the eighteenth century less actively indicted men for abuse of wives than it had in the seventeenth. During the eighteenth century, no new statutes defined spousal assault as illegal, and the courts tended to treat wife abuse as a noncriminal act. The power of husbands grew in ways similar to that of masters, and courts processed indictments against men only in cases of life-threatening abuse, murder, or maiming. Witnesses and bystanders, moreover, proved no more willing to step forward than they had in the previous century.

White wives worked with the limited options they had available to them to advance conversations about their rights and secure their safety. They told neighbors about their abuse and turned to them for protection, and in some cases, abused wives found solace, assistance, and even intervention. Court processes forcing husbands to make a bond promising not to abuse them proved useful in some instances, but only rarely would their cases go to trial.[2] As with servants, local courts and communities accepted moderate abuse of wives and would not act unless they viewed the abused as an innocent party who did not need discipline. Women also used expanding print literature to articulate their perspectives and alter perceptions of spousal assault. The legal and cultural challenges against abuse stimulated conversations about women's larger rights and demanded that society give more weight to women's voices. Patriarchal ideals, however, proved more resilient than concerns for wives' safety.

Creating a Baseline for Change

When Katherine Naylor petitioned for a divorce, fewer witnesses spoke about the violence within the household than had testified to the adultery, but the entire family suffered under Edward Naylor's drunken episodes. Waking the family and servants up in the middle of the night, Edward Naylor demanded obedience to his will and would not tolerate crying as he exposed his family to the outdoors in cold weather without sufficient clothing. He threw household objects at the children, kicked them, and threw one down the stairs. Edward Naylor and Mary Read targeted Katherine Naylor in a plot to poison her, according to several witnesses who reported overhearing Read boasting of the plan.[3] Naylor had hope for success in her petition because of the seventeenth-century legal climate in Massachusetts and New York.[4] Massachusetts Bay and Plymouth legislated against spousal assault as they had against servant abuse, and New Netherland inherited laws and practices from the Dutch that penalized wife abuse. Massachusetts Bay and Plymouth courts punished some husbands for abuse, and several colonies established legal separations for women seeking an end to abusive marriages.

As with servants, communities drew a line in the sand regarding wife murder. Egregious cases of violence resulting in maiming and those nearly resulting in death also had penalties regardless of the perpetrator's relationship to the victim, and some courts and communities found husbands' flagrant disregard for their wives especially heinous. Plymouth ordered Richard Marshall to sit in the stocks and endure public shaming for "kiking [his wife] of from a stoole into the fier," which went beyond moderate correction because his actions could have maimed or killed her.[5] The Massachusetts Court of Assistants indicted and punished two other men for murdering their wives, and one received the death sentence. Reverend Cotton Mather held that murder of a spouse was a grave sin. At the execution of Hugh Stone for stabbing his wife to death, Mather condemned Stone for murdering "*Her* whom you should have Loved above all the world; *Her* whom you should have Cherished with all the Kindness and Goodness of an Holy conversation." Mather may have been particularly aghast at rumors that Stone's wife was pregnant with a child at the time of her death, and he declared Stone's execution as "just."[6]

Condemnations and prosecutions for murder and maiming established an extreme standard for abuse, and white women had to speak against violence if they wanted those protections to extend to lesser forms of abuse. English common law and Roman-Dutch law established that women could bring complaints to court officials about abusive and intimidating husbands, but the Dutch also imposed penalties even when abuse was not life-threatening. As with servants, English common law did not explicitly state that correction of a wife was illegal.[7] Instead, English common law established that abused and threatened spouses should report ill treatment to JPs, who in turn would hold abusers to bonds to keep the peace. When a husband faced bonds for peace, he and his guarantors promised to pay if he abused his wife again before the next sitting of the court. It was up to wives to report any wrongdoing in the interim. England's courts rarely issued penalties for abusive behavior unless the violence involved maiming or death.[8] In contrast, in the Netherlands, criminal penalties were inscribed into the law. Hugo Grotius, a Dutch jurist, explained that "if either spouse behaves badly to the other, the local law imposes a fine, and sometimes a severer penalty appropriate to the circumstances." He did assert, however, that "a wife owes obedience to her husband." Cases of spousal assault in the Netherlands resulted in reprimands, fines, and imprisonment, but the court system also used bonds for peace and commitment as a means of stemming abusive situations.[9] These practices did not necessarily transfer to the colonies, and the Dutch accepted husbands' rights to discipline their wives within customary bounds.[10]

Massachusetts made new laws more clearly prohibiting spousal abuse. White women, by bringing forward suits, were partly responsible for these alterations from English practice. In 1641, Massachusetts Bay's Body of Liberties stipulated that husbands were not empowered to physically correct their wives unless they were defending themselves. Instead, magistrates ordered husbands to hand over unruly wives for correction. Plymouth, Rhode Island, and New Hampshire had similar statutes. Although New England law proscribed correction, courts at first attached no criminal penalties to the laws, giving local judges considerable leeway to fix punishments as they saw fit. By 1649, Massachusetts Bay altered its laws and stipulated criminal penalties for spousal assault: "No man shall strike his Wife, nor any Woman her Husband, on penalty of such fine not exceeding ten pounds for one offence, or such Corporal punishment as the County Court shall determine."[11] The strengthening of this law suggests the emergence of greater concerns about wife abuse and the government's intention to extend protections for women. Notably, Massachusetts Court of Assistants and the General Sessions in Essex County both heard at least two cases of wife abuse prior to 1649. Although the details are not available, in one case the abuse proved sufficiently severe that the Court of Assistants granted a separation based on cruelty.[12] The formal establishment of penalties was likely motivated by the court's hearing and handling of such cases, as well as the religious disposition of colonists. By bringing forward complaints of abuse, wives were making a difference.

Abused wives employed legal interventions in Massachusetts, with at least thirty abused white wives seeking legal mediation for marital conflict in Essex County, Massachusetts, Plymouth Bay Colony, and Maine during the seventeenth century. Their activism resulted in establishment of penalties for some men's abuse, though New Englanders remained far more likely to punish only perpetrators of extreme violence. Fifteen women in Essex County, Massachusetts, protested abuse between 1636 and 1683, and the Essex General Sessions stands out for establishing penalties for wife abuse at a greater rate than other county-wide governments. Essex County penalized men in nine of the fifteen wife abuse cases that entered the court. Standards for punishment were not always related to severity of abuse: Essex fined William Smith for pushing his wife in a common area. The public nature of Smith's display of anger likely offended authorities, who accepted that men should face consequences when they behaved outside the dictates of using corporal punishment as a means of correction.[13] Although the number of penalized cases suggests a high rate of criminal convictions, the record books do not offer a complete picture of wife abuse, and rates of spousal assault were likely much higher.

Many complaints by women likely never made it to the county court or its record books. No record in this study revealed complaints by women of color about their husbands prior to the American Revolution. However, this does not mean that Native American and African American women did not pursue solutions to wife abuse. It is likely that Native American and African American women viewed the courts with skepticism and believed them to be arms of the white men who ran them rather than as arbiters that would act to protect their safety. Native Americans often avoided use of colonial courts for issues within their nations, pursuing justice instead within their own community. Moreover, Native American marital practices allowed women self-divorce. In cases of enslaved African American women, their first step would be to look toward their masters for intervention, and masters had some self-interest in seeing their slaves well treated. The practice of not legally codifying enslaved African Americans' marital vows also gave African American women the ability to take leave of their husbands without requiring petitions or the support of others.[14] Free African American and Native American women had access to the legal system, but JPs may not have officially recorded their complaints. Race and ethnicity clearly played a role in the way women contested abuse.

Puritans and Pilgrims did not practice racial or sexual egalitarianism, and this influenced their construction of new legal codes and practices related to spousal abuse even as they believed in women's spiritual equality.[15] Patriarchal values held that women should be subservient to their husbands, and the doctrine of coverture removed women's independent legal and economic status upon marriage. According to the law, women could not make their own contracts, sue or be sued, or make use of familial assets without the permission of their husbands. However, companionable marriages played a crucial role in the reproduction of society and its orderly governance, and Puritan and Pilgrim ministers spoke out against spousal abuse and noted that households troubled by disputes undermined patriarchal governance and marriage. Maintaining a healthy family—and thereby a healthy society— became more difficult in a marriage wracked with fighting. Benjamin Wadsworth held that unhappy marriages created a "vile example before Inferiors." Children and servants, according to Wadsworth, needed examples of orderly and responsible adults. Ministers and communities in Massachusetts felt motivated to speak and legislate against spousal assaults because of the friction such violence caused and the ways it affected patriarchal norms. Wadsworth encouraged the husband to be "kind, loving, tender in his words & carriage" and preached that a man who acted differently would "shame his profession of Christianity, he breaks Divine Law." He spoke against husbands "beating or striking of her (as some vile wretches do) or in [using] any unkind carriage, ill language, hard words, morose, peevish, surly behaviour." Other ministers agreed and decried corporal punishment of wives. A woman was to be "a help to the man" and should not be "sharply driven, but sweetly drawn. Compassion may bond her, but Compulsion will break her."[16] For these ministers, the kind treatment of women secured the authority of men and the marriage contract. Men held the power within marriages, but they should not abuse this power because it upset the marital covenant. Quarrelling households also spilled into the streets as rumors and gossip spread from house to house, undermining the connections between neighbors and disrupting communities. By shaming spousal assault, ministers' sermons created momentum to further establish standards against wife abuse. Such talk encouraged women's use of legal outlets where courts worked for them.

The way local communities handled cases of abuse affected the way women contested abuse. The fifteen reported cases of abused white wives in Plymouth and Massachusetts Bay are in stark contrast with the colony of New Haven, which did not indict men on charges of spousal assault before 1665, when it merged with Connecticut colony. Only two cases appear between 1665 and 1700 in New Haven, and the gravity of the cases in New Haven reveals the court's reluctance to penalize abuse. Of the two men who faced charges in New Haven, one caused his wife's miscarriage.[17] It seems that women in Connecticut knew little would be done to protect them and did not choose the courts as the best site to contest abuse.

Abused women in New Netherland turned to families and bystanders instead of using the courts, which is surprising given that their legal and social heritage gave them more opportunities for independence. The Netherlands experienced major economic, political, and religious transformations during the sixteenth and seventeenth centuries, an era known as the "Golden Age" of Dutch history. Roman-Dutch law accorded women more control over financial arrangements than did the English, allowing them greater involvement in the expanding economy and judicial system.[18] Women had the right to retain the property they brought to marriage, and women actively defended and sued others in court over property, as they took part in independent as well as familial businesses. The changes that brought about the "Golden Age," with its expansion of the arts and urban centers, also affected Dutch understandings of women's roles. Women's independence was not heralded, but the circulation of competing ideas in print about women's roles created conversations about their nature, as Calvinists spread beliefs about women's spiritual equality. The legal pluralism of the Dutch gave abused women greater opportunities to obtain safety and rein in their husbands' behaviors through courts, churches, guilds, and neighborhood associations. The urbanity of places like Holland also made access to justice easier. Most often, women in Holland used lower courts that confined men, but they also exploited neighborhood and church interventions that did not imprison men and so offered wives greater economic security because they retained access to their husbands' financial support.[19]

White women in New Netherland more often mediated household conflict through extra-institutional means. Governmental and community handling of abuse in New Netherland underserved women, and Dutch wives lost some powers to contest wife abuse as they settled in the colony. New Netherland lacked the institutions of its home country, leaving women with fewer options to pursue justice, and they turned to their friends and neighbors as a greater support system than legal outlets. Abused wives in New Netherland found that court officials did not follow the Dutch practice of meting out punishment to abusive husbands. Women needed to see effective monitoring and sentencing of abusers if they were to trust formal mediation. Courts, however, held men to bonds for good behavior even though community members knew that wife abuse should result in fines, with several persons insisting that the court hold some men accountable for the damage caused to the community. In 1656, Johannes de Deckere, who served as a lawyer for the Dutch West India Company, petitioned the court at Fort Orange "that the defendant be fined fl. 100 for having last week scandalously beaten and wounded his wife and thrown firebrands at her, so that the sparks or embers flew through the partition door into the plantiff's residence." De Deckere's complaint likely reflected his concerns about the safety of the community and his own household given that his house could have burned. Jacob Hap, the defendant, acknowledged the abuse and that "he beat his wife and drew blood." In contradiction with Dutch law and practices, the court did not impose a penalty, ruling that "the defendant is not punishable for it as it happened between man and wife."[20] The court's dismissal of the petition shows the way New Netherland placed a protective barrier around men who abused their wives. The courts did not break this pattern even in cases when men appeared multiple times for abuse. Patriarchy proved a strong cultural undercurrent that flowed into the colony even though married women's economic power was greater than in New England.[21] The newer courts chose to preserve men's power to corporally punish their wives, prioritizing women's obedience to their husbands over their safety.

The actions of the courts in New Netherland show the community would countenance abusive husbands, and this was an additional stimulus for white women to seek extra-institutional means of combating abuse. In the 1660s, Beletje Lodowycx fled the home of her husband, Arent Jurriaansen Lantsmen, because of his routine assaults on her. She sought the help of her family rather than the courts, but her family turned to the legal system. The courts denied the community's and her parents' repeated requests to restrain and punish Lantsmen, and instead it favored admonishments rather than penalties. By 1665, Beletje Lodowyckx's father, Lodowyck Pos, noted that Lantsmen "has now been full three different times before the Court regarding the improper treatment of his daughter . . . and he each time promised amendment, but never performed his promise." Community members also complained about Lantsmen, but the court averred that "on the proposition of some of his friends we yet abstain from any extreme measures," and it worked to try and reconcile the couple. As in New England, men successfully petitioned to reduce their friends punishments, revealing a larger sense of men's right to assault their wives under certain conditions. The court ordered her parents to release her, claiming the "parents are the chief and principle cause" of the couple's dispute.[22] As time would tell, it was not her parents' fault that the couple was at odds, and Lantsmen continued to abuse his wife.

The Dutch policy of avoiding penalization of wife abuse persisted under English rule as the Dutch and English "settled" upon new legal practices.[23] In 1667, after the English took over the colony, Pos asked the court to allow his daughter to take refuge at his house, again complaining that his son-in-law "has severely beaten his, the petitioner's daughter . . . contrary to his previous promise in contempt of the Court's order." The sheriff also entered a petition regarding the abuse. The court forced Lantsmen to make a bond for his good behavior and allowed Lodowycx to remain with her parents. Lantsmen again promised reformation, and after a time his wife agreed to return, but neighbors continued to request intervention. In 1669 and 1671, they complained to the court, but the court resisted laying out a penalty for his multiple and proven episodes of abuse. The court asserted "he deserves to be severely punished as an example to others," but it again pardoned him, hoping it would be the last time. The court "strictly warn[ed] him, to let his wife be unmolested and that he, on the first complaint of his unbecoming conduct made to the Court, shall forthwith be banished beyond the jurisdiction of this City as an example to others, without the hope of any further favor."

The court's admonishment proved an empty promise, and Lantsmen appeared in court yet again in 1673 but did not face banishment.[24]

The legal activism of abused white wives and the courts in Massachusetts contrasts with New Netherland, and this divergence relates to community involvement and trends in punishing "moral" offenses, such as swearing oaths, fornication, adultery, excessive drinking, and working on the Sabbath, among other concerns. Both communities saw it as part of their duty to interfere and report wrongdoing to court officials to protect themselves and ensure the success of their new settlements. Massachusetts Bay and Plymouth, however, were more vigorous in prosecutions of sexual offenses. Their willingness to punish men for some sexual offenses was part of a larger readiness to moderate patriarchal privileges that damaged the community's well-being.[25] They viewed wife abuse the same way—as a threat to communities and the women involved—and therefore worthy of intervention. The court did not fully penalize men's abuse or punish them to the extent of women who committed adultery or abused their husbands, but it did deem some intervention necessary. These prosecutions likely gave women faith in the court system to work on their behalf. Massachusetts also had greater regulation over sites of community gathering outside of religious worship such as taverns, which limited spaces in which governmental and church discipline could be questioned.[26] These controls on social spaces reinforced community norms. The outing of familial matters was routine, and for abused wives this proved a formula that made them comfortable seeking help through public venues.

Though Massachusetts and New York differed in specific details, courts in both places most often resorted to holding men to bonds for their good behavior over prosecutions and penalties. As in the case of servants, this limited the courts' effectiveness in establishing standards against abuse and protecting white women. The Massachusetts Court of Assistants most often returned indictments for spousal assault to the lower county courts as petty crimes and did not issue penalties. In these cases, the court's behavior was in contrast with its involvement in cases of servant abuse, in which it issued fines.[27] Colonial records of men's bonds to keep the peace are often difficult to locate and in most cases no records remain. In York County, where some records of bonds do exist, of the eleven extant complaints from before 1711 against men for wife abuse, the court admonished one husband, dismissed one, held five to bonds, and whipped or fined four. The court issued whippings only in cases of life-threatening abuse, and it turned to bonds with regularity, thus minimizing the criminality of spousal assault. In York, the severity of abuse cases resulting in bonds ranged from moderate to more extreme and dangerous. Complaints varied from "sleighting & abuseing" to "Actions as tend to her great injury, if not the apparent Hazard of her life." Strikingly, in two of the cases, men simultaneously faced additional charges along with assaulting their wives, and the court penalized the men for the other petty offense, but only held them to bonds for wife abuse. The court held Francis Morgan to a bond for his assault on his wife, but it fined him "for swearing severall oaths 10s." Thomas Crawley, who faced charges of "being drunke & for beateing and abuseing his wife," was to sit in the public stocks for four hours for being drunk and "to bee bound to the peace in a bond of Tenn pounds or to be Corporally punished" for his crimes against his wife. Similar events occurred elsewhere.[28] Courts showed little motivation to uphold marital abuse as a criminal offense, and Massachusetts and New Netherland preferred maintaining marital unions and upholding patriarchal rule unless they discovered a particularly dangerous situation.[29] In this regard, the two colonies had more similarities than differences.

Although Massachusetts's communities prosecuted some abusive husbands, the court was ineffective in following up on sentencing in routine white wife abuse cases, and this affected the safety of white women and how they viewed the legal system. Courts commonly revoked punishments in wife abuse cases, which was different from their handling of masters who faced punishments for abusing servants. Plymouth issued sentences of whipping to wife abusers, but the court vacated these sentences when men petitioned not to face such punishments. After the court convicted Charles Thurston of abusing his wife, the "yeong men of Ply" asked the court to release him, and the court did remit his sentence and held him to a bond instead. The petition showed men's chafing at the doling out of public punishments for wife abuse. Public punishments in colonial America signified to the community the wrongfulness of criminal acts, and holding Thurston to a bond revealed a lack of intent to reform wife abuse in the community. Plymouth was not the only colony to apply lesser sentences. In York, the court convicted Ephraim Joy of

"Cursing Swearing and abusing of his wife both in words and blows" and ordered him to be whipped ten stripes or pay a sixty-shilling fine. Joy's conviction was especially serious. Neighbors testified that Joy said that he would kill his wife by stabbing her and that they witnessed him kicking his wife and beating her with a stick. She admitted fearing she would be crippled for life.[30] It was common to allow fines in place of whippings in many petty crimes, but this level of abuse was extreme. Abusive husbands showed themselves empowered to beat their wives despite laws suggesting otherwise. Women had to face this fact as they decided where to turn.

White women in the colonies would contest abuse, but they often demurred when it came to seeing their husbands punished, and this proved another obstacle when sentencing husbands and setting standards against abuse. Marriage imposed restrictions on white women that were different from those on servants and apprentices, which is why wives could both protest abuse and desire commutations of sentences. In Plymouth, John Dunham's wife contacted JPs about the abuse she suffered, noting that he beat her and threatened to kill them both. Although she took the case to court, she prevented the court's proposed punishment of whipping through a petition asking for a remission of his punishment.[31] Women like Dunham had many motivations for asking for a reduction in their husbands' sentences. They likely hoped the public humiliation of appearing in court would stem the abusive behavior but feared that further punishment by the courts would incur retributive violence. Concerns for their family's financial welfare contributed to women's requests for a reduction in sentences too. In New Amsterdam when the court jailed Abraham Pieters Corby for stealing, Elsje Gerrits asked that the court allow him to return home to "work for her." The court professed it heard reports that "he beat her and her child," and Gerrits admitted it was true "but that it happened to the child unexpectedly." She likely believed her child was not in danger, and the court returned Corby to the family even though he might engage in further violence.[32] For some white women, the very real pecuniary costs of pressing charges against an abuser proved more important in the short term than their safety.

Since courts proved all too willing to accept community members' and white women's petitions that abusive husbands be returned to their spouses, bystander intervention played an important role in establishing standards against abuse. Community members' testimony about the discord caused by abuse made a difference in the type of punishments meted out for abuse and in providing safety for abused families. On one occasion, Essex County rejected a white wife's appeal for a reduced sentence for her husband, and neighborly intervention and testimony was key in its decision. In 1681, Elizabeth Ela ran to neighbors for safety, expressing that she feared for her life. Her neighbors initially hoped to resolve the situation by returning her to her husband and serving as mediators, but when they arrived at Daniel Ela's home, he refused to let his wife back in the house, and he came at her with a stick. At this point, the neighbors called a local JP to intervene because Daniel Ela was recalcitrant. When Elizabeth Ela ran for safety, Daniel Ela perceived it as a slandering of his name and as a betrayal of their covenant and his authority. He told their neighbors that "if he ever had her come home without a humble acknowledgement, he hoped his hands might rot off or his legs never carry his body more." One neighbor testified to Daniel's sense of righteousness in assaulting his wife: "Ela said his wife was his servant and his slave and he would have her whipped but that it would be a disgrace to him, for he would never have a quiet hour until he did." Resenting his wife's sense that she suffered wrongful abuse, Daniel Ela hoped his wife would reform and succumb to his will. His wish was affirmed in 1682 when Elizabeth returned to court asking that it stop the prosecution against her husband. She claimed her original complaint was "in A passhon" and that "I am twoe apte to speake more then I doe allow my self." The court did not accept Elizabeth Ela's demurring petition. It pushed through the prosecution of her husband and issued him a fine of forty shillings after it was found he had held up a knife and threatened to kill her.[33] In this case, the involvement of neighbors meant that the court did not need to rely on Elizabeth's testimony.

The courts fully penalized and had different forms of punishment for white wives who abused their husbands; this was parallel to their policies in regard to servants, who were more severely punished for disobedience and assaults than their masters. Courts more easily established the wife's guilt for causing violence than her husband, illuminating the key distinction in abuse cases: men used violence to "correct" wayward wives and the community often found this acceptable. Wives were certainly in a position to offer correction, but their form of violence was categorized as unnecessary and unlawful to maintain distinctions in the marital hierarchy. In Plymouth, two white women accused of abusing their husbands received physical punishment without the option to make bonds, an option that would have been available to their husbands. In York and Essex Counties, similar criminal penalties existed.[34] The doctrine of coverture left the maintenance of property to husbands, and if courts demanded wives make bonds for peace they would therefore be effectively imposed on the victim, the husband. These concerns were not animating factors in sentencing, however. Courts often made bonds for peace for women and slaves who engaged in violence and slanderous acts toward people who were not their masters or husbands. Punishing abusive women boosted men's sense that they had power over their wives, who were to obey, not command, their husbands. The greater punishments doled out to women are incomparable with those for men, who were usually held to bond and often found their fines remitted. The public nature of these punishments, in addition their severity, served to remind the community about women's place in marriage and the importance of adhering to those prescriptions.

In one case, a court directed a husband to corporally punish his wife, which further supported men's sense they had a right to abuse their wives. Joane Miller, from Taunton, was to be "Punished at home" after being charged with "beating and reviling her husband, and egging her children to healp her, biding them knock him on the head, and wishing his victuals might choake him." Joane Miller's actions turned the household order upside down, and this unique punishment empowered her husband to beat her in contradiction to the statute ordering men to bring their wives to the government for correction. Through punishing his wife, Obadiah Miller restored his patriarchal prerogative and set his household in order.[35]

White women had to find ways to get community members to help them in an environment that prioritized their obedience and their husbands' rights. When an opportunity to speak emerged, wives needed to begin the process of converting individuals to their perspective and showing their scars of violence. When Richard Pray was on trial for assaulting his wife, Jabish Hackett admitted that he heard rumors that Richard Pray hit and cursed his wife and had heard him curse her before in his presence. Hackett waited to intervene until Mrs. Pray used his visit to their household to get him to intercede on her behalf. She "stripped up the sleeve of her shift and said 'Here are ye marks of ye blowes' that her husband had given her, which were two great places black and blue." Mrs. Pray was not the only wife to use such tactics. When Samuel Harris faced indictment for assaulting his neighbor's wife, testimony emerged that he had routinely beaten his own wife, but she never sought an injunction against him. Prior to the trial, a neighbor named Woodbury asked Mary Harris, wife of Samuel, if her husband beat her. She "answered yes and pulled up her sleeve and showed her arm which was black and blue, saying that her husband did it with a great stick that he had used when he was lame. She also said that her back was a great deal worse."[36] Mary Harris's willingness to show her bruises illustrates her readiness to share the trials of her marriage, but she may have been unwilling to do it without the invitation of neighboring Woodbury, given the socialization of women in their use of speech.[37] The importance of bystander intervention cannot be understated, as wives needed the assistance of neighbors to attain a safe haven and often to gain the courage to press a suit in an atmosphere that accepted women's subordination to their husbands. Samuel Harris and Richard Pray were certainly not going to stop the abuse on their own.

White women had to maintain their level of activism once initial conversations with bystanders occurred, and some even tried threatening neighbors to get help. When Elisabeth Ela appeared at her neighbor's doorstep crying, she told him "if you will not entertaine mee & lett mee abide in yor house I will lie in the street and snow & if I perish, my blood be on yor head." Other neighbors took action on their own accord after learning of abuse. When Samuel Harris came looking for his wife later at Woodbury's house, Mary Woodbury confronted him about the beatings, saying his wife had little reason to stay home given the way he treated her. Mrs. Woodbury's words did not move Mr. Harris, and he replied, "Well, what if I doe, If I doe she shall haue more of it." Faced with neighborly concern, Harris remained obstinate and promised greater violence, but his wife now had a person to whom she could turn in moments of violence and who would serve as a witness to the aftermath of his assaults. Jabish Hackett also decided to intervene after Mrs. Pray revealed her wounds. Hackett told Richard Pray it was a sin to curse and hit his wife, but Mr. Pray initially denied it. Again, Mrs. Pray had to stand up and assert her right to safety, and she pressed him in the presence of Hackett. Mr. Pray threw a dish at her for it and told Hackett he "would beat her twenty times a day before she would be his master." Mrs. Pray seized the opportunities she had to make use of bystanders and bring her husband to the bar, but he maintained his right to abuse her. After several witnesses stepped forward, the court fined him for cursing, beating her, and contempt. Prior to appearing in court, he stated "he did not care for the court and if the court hanged him for it he would do it."[38]

White women wanting to find freedom from abusive marriages took advantage of the options available in New Netherland and Massachusetts. Viewing marriage as a civil institution, both New Netherland and New England believed the marriage contract could be broken, though they reserved full divorces for adultery and made separations available to those suffering from desertion or cruelty.[39] Separations did not allow abused wives to remarry but did allow wives to live apart from their husbands, which gave them some measure of safety. As with servants, legally freeing wives from an abusive situation provided the best measure of protection. Between 1624 and 1674, the Dutch and English in New York granted at least eight divorces, three separations, and one annulment; in no case did the court grant divorce for cruelty alone. The separations, however, were all influenced by reported accounts of the husband's cruelty. As New Netherland transitioned to English rule, the governors continued to allow divorces and separations until 1681 despite English legal prohibitions on them.[40] In Massachusetts Bay, the court issued at least forty divorces and annulments, and among these, two individuals cited cruelty alongside other causes, including affinity (marrying a relative), adultery, bigamy, desertion, or incest. Plymouth granted at least six divorces, but none of these were for cruelty.[41] Connecticut, in contrast, did not allow separations for cruelty, though the court did grant thirty-seven divorces between 1639 and 1710, with four cases citing cruelty or abuse among other legal complaints.[42] In separations, the courts often made arrangements for husbands to provide for their wives so that women were not left without support, but payment was not guaranteed.

In cases when white men and women petitioned for divorces and separations, courts in New Netherland, New York, and New England generally tried to keep couples together and bring about peace in the home. Attaining a separation required considerable effort on the part of abused white women and their allies. After Nicholas Velthuyzen hit his wife with a pair of tongs, his wife fled their home, and Velthuyzen turned to the court in New Amsterdam to request a separation. The court asked them to live together again, but both refused, which eventually resulted in their official separation. Perhaps the most glaring case of a government trying to maintain an abusive marriage was that of Beletje Lodowycx and Arent Jurriaansen Lantsmen, mentioned earlier for their longstanding issues of abuse in New Netherland. After Lodowycx, her parents, and their neighbors complained, in 1667, the court began negotiating a separation settlement, but Lantsmen rejected it and asked that his wife be returned to him. She did return, but she ultimately ended up fleeing his abuse again. In 1673, he asked the court to order his wife to live with him again. Rather than enforce a separation, the court admonished Lantsmen to "conduct himself in future and henceforward so civilly, peaceably and friendly towards his wife, that by his good behaviour his wife may be induced to dwell again with him as she ought."[43] Having laws that made separation possible did not mean courts willingly offered it as a solution, and even when the courts did so, the husband could rebuff those attempts. Governments worked to reconcile marriages broken by abuse and used separations only as a last resort.

Although the courts may not have always acted in the best interests of women and men, the white wives who did challenge their husbands' abuse during the seventeenth century held governments to their stated laws. Bonds for peace did not effectively penalize white men for abuse, but the white women who told JPs and other court officials about their treatment brought to light the experiences of women in violent marriages. Had white women not reported their husbands or explained their experiences to bystanders, the community would not have had the opportunity to consider where it should draw the line between correction and abuse. The seventeenth century stands out as one of great possibility, a time in which some New England and New Netherland communities began the work of reconsidering wife abuse. However, as settlement increased and institutions grew, responses to spousal assault stagnated, and men's power within marriage continued to allow for moderate violence against their wives.

Stagnation and Resistance

By the turn of the century, it had been almost sixty years since Massachusetts Bay passed legislation breaking with English practices, officially codifying correction as wrongful, and nearly thirty years had passed since Katherine Naylor sued her abusive and adulterous husband for divorce. During the eighteenth century, governments in New York and Massachusetts decreased their assistance to abused white wives. Bonds for peace remained the most common way courts handled white wife abuse, but they also lessened the number of indictments and penalties for men accused of abuse. Evidence shows that, as with the earlier era, bystanders did not take enough action to prevent serious injuries and death, though courts did willingly and fully prosecute men for spousal murder, intent to kill, and maiming. In New York, divorce and separations became less accessible in the eighteenth century, though it would remain an option in much of New England for those who had the means. In this way, the courts' and communities' handling of white wife abuse in the eighteenth century mirrored that of servant abuse: white wives did not experience better conditions over time and the shoring up of husbands' powers hindered progress. Society and law continued to view moderate violent correction as the prerogative of husbands, and women like Katherine Naylor would have to assertively stake out their right to safety to achieve peace.

The eighteenth century afforded new opportunities for white women to protest abuse, but their activism would not see dramatic results before the American Revolution.[44] Print culture expanded, with newspapers, tracts, and broadsides proliferating in New England and New York.[45] Male and female authors discussed women's roles, and wife abuse was central to the arguments writers made to increase women's status. Wife abuse epitomized the legal and social liabilities that married women faced, and their scars and bruises became metaphors for the overall hardships women endured. The eighteenth century also saw a rise in the ideals of sentimentalism and companionate marriage, which reinforced the need for happy marriages and gave writers additional opportunities to expound upon the problems caused by wife abuse. Companionate marriage ideals emphasized that individuals should choose partners based on compatibility, and it was presumed these matches would re-

duce conflict. Community members and the court system did not increase their levels of intervention on the basis of these new cultural
trends. Rather, the expanding print culture and new ideals became tools
in women's arsenal for depicting abuse as wrongful. It would not be until
later decades that such positions affected community standards regarding spousal assault.

Massachusetts and New York retained its prosecutions of cases of
murder, manslaughter, and intent to murder, but in prosecuting only the
most egregious cases of abuse, women were underserved. Statistically,
wives were in more danger than were husbands. Historian Randolf Roth
has estimated that before 1800 in New England and the Chesapeake,
women were the victims in 80 percent of the marital homicide cases,
with 47 marital homicide cases occurring in New England.[46] In 1741,
the Supreme Court of Judicature heard a case against Richard Thomson,
who stood accused of boring out the eyes of his wife and blinding her.
The court ordered Thomson to be whipped while blindfolded as he hung
in the gallows, in addition to a twelve-month sentence of imprisonment.
Thomson's stiff penalty was not the norm, but his assault, described as
"barbarous & inhuman," exceeded the boundaries of correction and
maimed his wife. Part of the reason for the thorough punishment was
that Thomson had planned his assault; it was not a momentary lapse of
conscience. He used "a . . . Sharp Stick . . . he had prepared for that Purpose," along with his thumb to injure her eye.[47] The court could not deny
Thomson's premeditation. In addition to this case, Massachusetts prosecuted two men for murdering their wives between 1740 and 1789, and
the court found both not guilty. By contrast, in the seventeenth century,
the court found guilty both men who were tried for spousal murder,
but the sample size is too small and incomparable to draw more than
cursory conclusions.[48]

White women continued reporting abuse through the courts, but
rates of prosecution for wife abuse in the lower courts of Massachusetts
declined, and New York continued its pattern of not establishing penalties for men. Eighteenth-century husbands rarely found themselves
on trial for complaints made by their white wives, although they would
have if they had assaulted another woman or man. The small number of
eighteenth-century prosecutions is in contrast with the rising population in Massachusetts, which should have increased the number of abuse

cases, not lessened them. Over the eighteenth century, Massachusetts's population doubled roughly every forty years, with an estimated population of a more than 235,000 people in 1760, while New York reached 113,000 in the same year.[49] Records show that between 1740 and 1763 in Massachusetts, Suffolk and Middlesex Counties fully prosecuted and penalized only one man each and Plymouth and Worcester Counties did not prosecute any men, though they received complaints of abuse.[50] In contrast, during the seventeenth century, Plymouth established punishments for at least three men and two couples, though the courts often set aside punishments of men. The decreasing use of fines and prosecutions during the eighteenth century falls in line with the handling of servant abuse in Massachusetts.

Women used bonds as a tool to restrain abusive husbands in New York and New England, but bonds were difficult for some women to obtain and not the best solution for abuse. Women in populous areas and dense towns sought bonds for peace more frequently than those in more rural and geographically spread-out settlements. JPs' willingness to bring men to court also affected women seeking bonds. Between 1710 and 1790 in New Haven, a county with historically low levels of penalization for wife abuse, Cornelia Hughes Dayton found only nine cases of women suing the peace against their husbands.[51] In addition to problems of access to JPs, financial issues factored into women's decisions, because JPs charged for their processing of recognizances and bonds and often required abusive husbands to pay the court fees in these complaints. For some families, court fees stretched budgets beyond their means, and women had to weigh which financial and physical concerns they could withstand.[52] Records do not indicate women of color took up use of bonds in the eighteenth century either. As pauper apprenticeship and servitude hardened, options of legal redress did not appear more attractive to African American or Native American women.

Bonds provided a measure of security for white women, particularly when men were jailed for failing to make bonds, but restraining harmful men required persistent action on the part of women. In New York City, Mary William asked the court to bind her husband to the peace and the court agreed, but Frederick William was unable to find guarantors for his good behavior. Neighbors might not have believed Frederick would reform, which assisted Mary in attaining safety. The JP jailed him, which was a common practice throughout the colonies for individuals unable to make bonds. Confinement did not alter his behavior. In February 1739/40, Mary William returned to court and asked that he continue to be held to the peace because she still feared for her safety. The General Sessions ordered him to "Remain Committed until he find Sufficient Sureties to keep the peace," and it did not release him until May 1740, which gave Mary William the assurance of safety for several months. In May, Mary William could have objected to his release, but she did not.[53] Living without a partner likely strained her family's financial well-being, and she needed the wages Frederick William could bring to the household. Perhaps she also hoped that the months in confinement had reformed her husband, and if not, he at least knew that she could take action again if his behavior warranted it.

Bonds for peace were not equivalent to prosecutions, and in many ways, bonds were a failure of the entire community to take wife abuse seriously. Justices of the peace, aldermen, and attorneys general did not push indictments forward in cases that remained as bonds, which was an indication of the community's lack of interest in pursuing cases involving wife abuse. When the court released Jopthah Smith from his bond, the judges noted "no prosecution against him appearing the Defen't was discharged." The legal system required more threatening abuse or further complaints by his wife to take action, but as the history of the General Sessions showed, it would do little besides hold men to bonds. The courts exhibited a reluctance to bring men to the bar for abusing their wives except in very extreme cases.[54] While the bonds provided some measure of safety, they could not fully protect women against husbands who continued their abusive behavior. In the eighteenth century, in particular, having men go through a public trial for wife or servant abuse was uncommon, and this sent a clear message about the community's high tolerance for such violence.

Separation continued to be an option for many white women in New England suffering abuse, though white wives in urban areas were more likely to take advantage of it. Connecticut, however, was not one of the colonies offering separation, which left some women with more limited options. In Massachusetts between 1696 and 1786, forty-one white women sued for separation or divorce, noting they suffered cruelty, among other causes, in their marriages. Women who sued on the basis of cruelty were much more likely to come from Boston and other large towns. Large towns offered the most support for women seeking other types of legal intervention too, because women could find more witnesses in areas with close proximity to neighbors. Women suing on the sole grounds of cruelty did not fare as well in court as others. Twelve of the women were successfully separated, while the courts returned six cases for lacking evidence and did not move five cases forward. The courts granted divorces to eleven of the nineteen women who noted their husbands had committed adultery and practiced cruelty.[55]

Divorce was not accessible for those living in New York in the eighteenth century, since they were no longer under Dutch law, and abused white wives created extralegal settlements to achieve safety. Some white women continued to petition for the right to separate despite the government's unwillingness to publicly sanction it. In 1715, Elizabeth Sydenham asked the Supreme Court of Judicature for a separation and maintenance from her husband, George Sydenham. The couple's problems dated to at least 1710, when she complained her husband sold some of her property without her knowledge or consent. Elizabeth Sydenham claimed George had refused her clothing and provisions. By 1715, the issues had worsened. Sydenham claimed her husband "Threatens her with binding Imprecations . . . if She your [petitioner] dose make any complaint thereof he will certainly breake all her Bones and cut her Tounge out of her head." She alleged threats and poor treatment were a regular part of her life. George Sydenham refused to live with her, though he would not "Suffer her to any abiding place in Quietness" either. The records do not reveal that the court made her separation official, but it is clear that Elizabeth and George Sydenham lived apart the rest of their lives. Their unofficial separation could have left Elizabeth Syndenham in a precarious position both economically and physically; however, she was able to leave a will and dispense with items of value upon her death owing to the wealth she had obtained from a previous marriage.[56]

For those who successfully separated, either officially or unofficially, living without an abusive spouse did not always mean a return to safety. In 1744, John Courset and "his Negro" Peter assaulted Courset's wife, who had been living apart from him in a boardinghouse. The two men sneaked into her lodging and locked the door of her room so others would not be able to enter. They "Spread hot Tarr & peat in another Room." Before departing, the two men stole several small items and "did greatly terrifie & threaten the s'd Sarah" by their actions. Given the ease with which Mrs. Courset located witnesses, the court found both men guilty and fined them twenty shillings for the offense.[57] Yet Courset's inability to fully free herself from the marriage compromised her independence from her husband. Separations did not allow for remarriage, and Courset remained without the financial contributions or physical protection she required. Even in public lodgings, her husband was capable of entering and attacking her. Had Sarah Courset remarried, her former husband's crime of breaking into a household would have taken on greater significance for the courts who respected men's right to their own property and households, as well as their right to make suits on behalf of their dependents. Courset's new husband could have pressed the court to be more responsive.

Communities connected men's authority within marriage to their right to moderately "correct" their wives, which explains some of the courts' avoidance in making indictments when white women brought forward complaints of abuse. Discussions of the marital hierarchy often turned to the issue of wife abuse because the matters were connected. Some people arduously defended the existing gender hierarchy, arguing that it protected women from behaving in ways that would cause their husbands to act violently. One writer claimed that the happiness of marriage demanded men "relax Nothing from the Severity of those antient Laws by which Woman is for every [sic] placed in a State of Subjection." When women were freed from subjection, the author contended, husbands ended up in the untenable position of wives acting as "mistresses" in making demands and dissembling to fulfill their whims. In such a marital state, the writer believed, "The Good-natur'd as well as the Severe Husbands have equally Reason to think with Regret on the Comforts of a single Life." A demanding wife "stirs up certain Desires of Revenge by which [the severe husband] is dishon'rd." Though the writer maintained that wife abuse would taint the severe husband, positioning abuse as a natural response to wives that "will acknowledge no Law but their own" suggested that severe husbands would be granted great leniency if they had disorderly wives.[58] By this logic, patriarchy protected wives because it taught them to deny their desires to behave badly out of fear of reprisal from their husbands. Writing like this shows the other side to the sermons and tracts promoting marital harmony through companionability. It emphasized the role of wifely subordination and reveals how many early Americans denounced men's violence as shameful but ultimately did not find it criminal.

Companionate marriage ideals grew in importance over the eighteenth century, and ironically, these ideals often supported the decriminalization of wife abuse. Early Americans expected conflict to occur within marriages, and they reasoned that choosing a suitable marital partner was among the best means through which conflict could be reduced.[59] Writers urged better marital choices rather than intervention to stymie abuse even though they held abuse as regretful and dishonorable. Ministers, playwrights, novelists, and other writers regularly opined on the importance of developing friendships prior to courting to avoid passionate disagreements and to attain greater happiness in marriage. Marriage required a "similarity of disposition, and a perfect and mutual affection. If it is otherwise, marriage, instead of being a blessing, becomes a real curse." Writers posited dire predictions of "Poverty, Contempt, and Inquietude" as the result of arranged or hasty marriages. They viewed verbal and physical assaults as the outcome of wrong matches, not as larger systemic or behavioral problems.[60] Bad marriages became the fault of the individuals who chose bad partners, and this left little room for government or community interference and penalization in case of abuse.

While the above examples demonstrate that print culture could reinforce societal norms, the press also offered a space for women and men to challenge patriarchal views about their rights and place in society. Perhaps the largest change in the eighteenth century was the emergence of a print culture that included the discussion of white women's roles. Wife abuse served as a critical metaphor for those urging an expansion of white women's rights because men's violence served as an example of their unsuitability for the extensive privileges granted to them. Those who supported limited roles for white women often suggested that they lacked the intellectual and emotional capacity to move beyond the "private Life." In response to one such editorial, a writer positing the value of women's intellect questioned why more men did not do more to develop reason and virtue among their wives. The writer opined husbands bred "fear hatred and contempt. . . . You must know there are bad Husbands who destroy the Happiness of the Matrimonial State, as well as bad Wives." The writer claimed some men were "hurried by their Brutal Passions, their sensual Appetites . . . and follow the low life." The point was clear: abusive, unfaithful, and unreasonable men existed, and a bad woman could not be the exemplar of all women just as a bad man was not of all men. The implication was that communities could not ignore wife abuse just because of some women's disorderly behavior. The argument hinged, in part, on the belief that a wife who lived in fear of her husband was wrongfully treated. Promulgating this position in the press served to remind readers that physical correction was abuse. It was an important step in changing community standards.

Publications also stressed the idea that abusive men endangered women. Writings that prioritized the impact of wife abuse over the need to uphold men's authority proved necessary to foment change in communities. By renegotiating the cultural meaning of wife abuse against white women, writers' focus on women's perspectives implicitly questioned whether corporal punishment was a worthy tool in the reformation of wives or an abuse of power. As in the case above, some writers did this by highlighting the fear experienced by abused wives, which showed the personal effects of abuse. Others focused on how the law left women in untenable circumstances. One writer drew attention to Dutch laws that instituted guardianship over husbands who were abusive or who mismanaged family finances. Asking why English laws were not as generous with women, the writer concluded "Had *English* Law makers done the like it had saved many Families from Ruin."[61] Showing the harmful effects of abusive men and pointing out existing alternative practices to assist families cleverly countermanded ideologies and laws upholding patriarchal customs. Writing and conversations like this began the process of changing conversations about wife abuse, but altering community standards of acceptable violence against wives would take more frank and public conversations about the toll on women.

White women turned to more than print and the judiciary to seek safety and justice. Running away was another option for married white women, just as it was for servants, but women faced difficulties in attaining financial stability and establishing a new life while concealing their identities. Laws regarding runaway slaves limited this outlet for enslaved African American women abused by their spouses. Abused white wives and their neighbors reported violence to churches, but churches proved slower to react and less effective in defending women. Husbands had to be willing to let the church adjudicate the matter because ministers and committees could only withhold communion or church membership to offending men. Churches did, however, offer a place for women and congregants to report abuse, and they provided solace for abused wives and pressured abusive men to reform. They also served as a space to reflect on the suffering of abused wives.

Institutions may have failed to protect women, but some bystanders intervened to protect abused white women. Bystander intervention remained essential in the eighteenth century, as concerned neighbors provided safe havens for white women and acted as witnesses in petitions to court officials. Urban areas such as Boston and New York City offered dwellings that were shared spaces with little privacy. Enslaved African American women did not find succor in highly populous spaces, however, as masters' rights to oversee their households—which included slave marriages—were prioritized over abused African American women's safety. In rural regions and less populous new towns, the close-knit and planned communities were disappearing. New patterns of settlement did not favor oversight and interventions in familial matters, and this presented new challenges for white women facing abuse. Still, neighbors relied on one another for basic goods, and the interconnected economies of colonial North America presented all women in less populous regions occasions to share their suffering. Women's roles in bartering, selling, and purchasing household goods connected them with neighbors and communities and revealed to the public their beaten and battered bodies.

According to a 1735 newspaper article, several women in Chester County, Pennsylvania, took justice into their own hands and "apprehended" a white man who was "being unreasonably abusive to his Wife upon some trifling Occasion." The women had him "duck'd 3 Times in a neighboring Pond" and sheared his beard and hair "to the great Diversion of the Spectators."[62] While the article does not mention men's participation in the event, it is likely both sexes attended, and the jovial nature of the article suggested that the crowd approved of at least some of the activities. The man's assault against his wife occurred in public, and the article deemed it as "unreasonable." Given the trends in court-adjudicated abuse cases, it is likely the husband repeatedly and severely beat his wife for no community-sanctioned cause and that his wife had a good reputation. The article does not provide information about whether the abused white wife called attention to her suffering, but the public nature of his punishment suggests she previously notified neighbors or other family members about the abuse, possibly in the same way as women in the seventeenth century—by showing her scars. The abusive husband's punishment became the community's way of asserting that it would not condone such beatings, even if courts would not act. Their vigilante justice proved an important counterweight to the declining judicial activism by creating consequences for assaults, and early American communities had histories and cultures that supported their use of violence to set standards.[63]

Occasionally, white men stepped in amidst extremely abusive situations to protect and defend white women, and sometimes they even punished the abusers. In Connecticut, six men on a nearby boat saw Jeremiah Quimley quarrelling with his wife. When Quimley fired a weapon into his wife's back, the men came ashore and assisted his wife. They also decided to punish him by tying him to a tree for three hours and issuing "3 or 400 Lashes with a Whip prepared for that Purpose." Quimley promised reformation, and they "left him to consider the Justice of their administration."[64] The men's insistence on punishing Quimley in addition to protecting his wife reveals their sense that this violence was outside the bounds of acceptable corporal punishment. The musket fire endangered his wife's life, and that Quimley shot her in the back made his actions particularly dishonorable. The case is unusual for the men's intervention and extralegal punishment of Quimley, though courts would have agreed that Quimley's assault constituted unreasonable abuse. Not all women were so lucky to find witnesses to their attack, and without intervention and established penalties for wife abuse, many women lived in fear of untimely death.

White men also took up for abused wives in serving as witnesses in legal matters. In 1759, eleven men stepped forward in Dutchess County,

New York, to support the white wife of Isaak Wixum after she fled their home for safety. Because the law did not allow women to take leave of their husbands, men in the community took action to legally certify that she had no option but to flee. Writing directly to a local official, they asserted "We believe that Shee haith Sufered that Abuse and that . . . She tels the truth Concerning Him." The men supported her independence by establishing that she did not leave her husband out of malice but rather because of abuse. We do not know whether Wixum's wife sought the men out or they heard or saw her suffering first-hand, but they clearly believed the abuse was wrongful. Dutchess County was just below the median size for counties in New York, with a population of approximately 8,000. She likely bore the bruises and scars of his violence and revealed them as had other women. The men's certificate indicated that they had no doubts about the character of Wixum's wife, claiming "Shee haith bin a Peceble Harmless woman."[65] While these men may have accepted physical punishment of wives, this statement relayed their feeling that she was not deserving of the abuse she received. The men provided crucial evidence of abuse, which allowed Wixum's wife to support her case for safety and avoid officials who would want to see her returned to her husband.

The petition stands out for its all-male composition and interventionist strategy, which suggests white women's declining influence in legal matters even though women were more often involved in assisting abused wives. The men who reported Isaak Wixum's abusive behavior likely saw their defense of Wixum's wife as an extension of their own patriarchal duty to protect and defend women. These men broadened the scope of their authority to include a woman outside their own households whom they deemed worthy of assistance. (Ironically, their patriarchal motives gave Mrs. Wixum freedom from patriarchal oversight.) The men who signed this petition decided against having female signatories, including their own wives, who would have been familiar with the situation. The men likely reasoned that having all male signatories gave the petition more weight. The independence of women in New York became more circumscribed over time as English laws and custom overtook Dutch practices and initial settlement designs.[66] Yet abused wives often sought and benefited from the intercession of other women when seeking bonds for peace against abusive husbands. Abused wives listed their female neighbors as witnesses, and court officials accepted their testimony. Friendships and neighborliness strengthened women's connections, and they served as confidants and opened their homes as safe havens for one another.

Communities far too often looked the other way in cases of known abuse. In Stafford, Connecticut, Mr. Dyer murdered his wife, and the community had known about the abusive situation prior the fatal events. Neighbors described Mr. Dyer, a selectman in the town, as "somewhat violent in his Temper," though they felt he largely kept his anger "under a tolerable Restraint." Judging his temper as a work in progress, the community left Mrs. Dyer to suffer without intervention. The night of the murder, Mr. Dyer had threatened his wife's life with a quip that her "Dream [of being 'in Paradise'] shall be verified before morning." He issued this threat in the presence of neighbors who were at his house questioning him about stealing his neighbor's hay. Mrs. Dyer sided with the neighborhood in presuming his guilt. In addition to threating her life, Mr. Dyer "show'd a gloomy Displeasure, and utter'd some unkind Reflection upon [his wife's] Barrenness." Making little of the threats or his mood, neighbors left the couple alone, but did so with the knowledge that he had been abusive in the past and that his temper was riled. The next day, the neighbors found both of them dead, with Mrs. Dyer "murdered in a most cruel and shocking Manner. She seem'd to have been beat to Death with a Maul, supposed to have been made for that Purpose the evening before." The fashioning of the maul indicated Mr. Dyer's attack on his wife was premeditated. He had beaten her skull and neck "almost to a jelly" and had thrown her about the room. He continued to beat her even after she lay dead.[67] Neighbors expressed shock and horror after he had escalated beyond repair. Women such as Mrs. Dyer needed a way out of abusive situations before their murder.

To begin making the kinds of injunctions against wife abuse that would prevent death, communities needed to institute new standards of behavior, but the first half of the eighteenth century did not provide a new paradigm. Had Catherine Naylor lived to see the eve of the American Revolution, she would have recognized that the processes open to her in the seventeenth century were virtually the same as those in the latter half of the eighteenth century, though declining prosecutions were a new reality for white women in Massachusetts. In her case, a jury found Edward Naylor guilty of "Inhuman Carriag & several cruelties in abusing his wife and children" and of fornicating with Mary Read. The couple lived apart after that time, but Katherine Naylor was not free from his abuse. The court banished Edward Naylor for his crimes, and when he returned to Boston he sought her out and abused her. The court demanded he swear to keep the peace toward her and leave the town again.[68] While courts in the seventeenth century would find men guilty of crimes such as wife abuse, adultery, and fornication, in the eighteenth century, indictments against these acts decreased, suggesting that patriarchy grew stronger over the eighteenth century and men's rights expanded.[69] The cultural trend that measured a white woman's worth by her obedience to her husband continued to inhibit thinking about more extensive measures that would prevent and punish abuse. Had communities signified that abuse broke the marriage contract, they would have granted full divorces to women abused by their husbands and enabled women inside and outside the courtroom greater power to contest abuse and leverage the law on their behalf. It also would have dealt a severe blow to men's authority within the home. As northeasterners entered the American Revolution, patriarchal authority remained strong, and this included the right to abuse one's wife.

What had changed since Catherine Naylor suffered assaults from her husband were the more frequent and public pronouncements by women that wife abuse was wrongful, and more work like this needed to be accomplished. The emerging print culture offered women a new medium to posit that their safety, rather than men's authority, was what was at stake in issues of spousal assault. Naylor might have expressed surprise to see white wives compared with servants in print literature, and yet, in many ways, the experiences of white wives paralleled those of servants. Both suffered from legal impairments and cultural stereotypes that justified abuse. Servants and white wives did differ when it came to attaining freedom from abuse. In much of New England, legal separations were available to wives, but such freedom was not as readily available to servants. In New York, on the other hand, women had to make private arrangements or flee to safety, but servants gained freedom quite regularly. Bystander intervention proved critical to securing peace and legal remedies for both servants and white wives suffering from abuse, and community members played vital roles in the seventeenth and eighteenth centuries in helping them achieve a measure of safety. However, this intervention was all too rare, and for African American wives, the difficulties of finding allies was even tougher. Abused wives had to persist in their efforts to set new standards and create lasting change that offered them safe and financially sound options.

Chapter 3

Slaves

In 1755, Mark, Phillis, and Phoebe, who were enslaved to John Codman in Charlestown, Massachusetts, conspired to murder Codman in the hope of freeing themselves from his abuse. Mark told Phillis that some neighboring slaves killed their master and "were never found out, but had got good masters, & so might we." After much planning, Mark purchased the poison, and Phillis and Phoebe distributed the fatal dose. The timing of the poisoning may have related to Codman's recent abuse of Tom, another slave in the Codman household. The day before the murder, Phoebe entered the workshop where Mark and Tom worked to dress a wound in Tom's eye. In secrecy, Phoebe mocked Codman and impersonated him to alleviate the strains the group were under, given this most recent blow to the group's safety. Tom stated "he hop'd he [Codman] wou'd never get up again [from sleep] for his Eye's sake." The servants and slaves in Codman's household had no love for Codman, but whites in the area around Boston and Charlestown saw Codman's murder as a threat to their authority and responded fiercely. Phillis, Phoebe, and Mark were tried for murder. The court found them guilty and hanged Mark and set Phillis on fire. The court then sent Phoebe to the West Indies, where she would presumably die from disease, overwork, or mistreatment. After the executions, Mark's body was taken to Charleston, where it hung in a gibbet until the War for Independence from Britain.[1]

The violent reaction of whites to Codman's murder is an indication of the importance of slavery to the social and economic relations in the North, though smaller numbers of slaves existed there than in the West Indies or South. By the eve of the American Revolution, African Americans made up at least 2 percent of Massachusetts's total population, but coastal regions contained larger populations of up to 5 percent. The Dutch West India Company originally owned the slaves in New Netherland, until demand for slaves grew and individuals began purchasing Africans while the company leased out and sold others. By the 1760s, the enslaved in New York accounted for 6 percent of the population, and New York City had the highest number of African Americans in an urban center in British North America, nearing 15 percent of the population.[2] With commonly just a few enslaved individuals per household in the North, African Americans worked as domestic servants in wealthy and middling families, freeing up the familial labor of the household and serving as key indicators of their owners' social status. Shopkeepers and artisans employed slaves in skilled trades and as common day laborers, with some hired out to line the pockets of their masters. Although skilled trades drew more money, African Americans also worked in agricultural production and animal husbandry.[3] The smaller slave holdings and differing work patterns in the North did not reduce the physical discipline inflicted by masters, though the death rates and working conditions of slaves in the West Indies were far worse. Death rates among slaves declined by the mid-eighteenth century in the North, as slaves' economic value increased, but the brutality of slavery did not erode, as evidenced by Codman's cruel mistreatment of Tom. Domestic servants and other household workers remained continually under the supervision of whites, who used violence as a method of motivation and discipline.[4]

Violence was central to the racial controls of the colonial era. As with wives and servants, the laws of slavery in British North America imbued slaveholders and the government with power over slaves, and this included the right to physically assault slaves in the name of promoting order. Although there were laws against slaveholders maiming or murdering their slaves, communities did little to protect slaves or punish offenders, and this differed from the experiences of abused servants and white wives. Even in cases of murderous violence, communities rarely moved beyond initial investigations. Of the thirteen known cases of suspicious slave deaths by masters prior to the American Revolution in the North, merely three resulted in convictions, and a solitary case resulted in the punishment being exacted on the perpetrator. More deaths of slaves at the hands of their masters might have occurred.[5] The population of African Americans in the North did not threaten to overwhelm whites, as it did in the South, but fears of conspiracy existed and whites believed excessive force was an accepted tool to curtail slaves' aspirations—much more so than was the case with white servants and married women.

The murderous reactions of Mark, Phillis, and Phoebe to their abuse are part of the larger story of northern slavery, in which a limited range of possibilities existed for the enslaved to resist their masters.[6] African Americans suffered tremendous violence and hardship under the slave regimes of the North, and their peaceful and violent resistance to abuse added their own perspectives to local slaveholding narratives portraying northern slavery as humane. Indeed, like servants and wives, African Americans revealed their suffering in their interpersonal relationships with one another, as did Phoebe, Tom, and Mark when they took pleasure in mocking Codman. To escape violence, they also notified concerned whites, ran away, and made use of the legal system. African Americans had their own conceptions regarding violence and their rights.[7] From the colonial era, enslaved African Americans asserted that maiming, excessive whipping, and life-threatening violence were unjust, as were routinized violence without a precipitating cause and beatings resulting from honest mistakes or from masters' misdirected rage. Slaves' sense of their right to safety was similar to that of wives and servants, but they had fewer legal protections. Slaves were part of the community, and they conceived of themselves as legitimate plaintiffs and actors when masters threatened their lives. The protections the law and communities offered to African Americans were not commensurate with their needs during the colonial era, and most slaves were left to their own devices in their individual attempts to ward off violent masters.

Supporting Murderous Violence

Slavery relied on psychological and physical violence to maintain order, and runaway advertisements with descriptions of slaves' scars and missing fingers reveal the commonplaceness of severe assaults and maiming.[8] The fact that Mark, Phillis, and Phoebe struggled to find meaningful ways to defend themselves shows that colonists quickly adapted to slavery and supporting a racially based regime. All that remains of the violence from the seventeenth century are colonial legal codes, rare notes regarding the murders of the enslaved, and the planned and executed violence by African Americans. The vacancies in the records are telling silences about the wider acceptance of violence against African American slaves than against white wives and servants. The voices and protests of African Americans in these sources are difficult to locate but their corpses told stories that whites chose to ignore. African Americans tried appealing to the religious sense of whites and sought out allies in the white community, but bystanders did not do enough. The government constructed laws that seemingly gave slaves some protections but rarely allowed them the range of benefits the laws stipulated, unlike cases of wives or servants. In cases when slaves were murdered, white communities constructed fictive explanations for slave deaths and indemnified masters from having to suffer punishments. Although whites had legal and social power, they maintained that strict discipline of slaves was necessary to safeguard communities from African Americans' acts of violence or uprisings against slavery. Understanding the lack of empathy slaves faced is a vital first step in comprehending African Americans' unique struggles for safety during the seventeenth and eighteenth centuries as they encountered harsher violence than wives and servants, with fewer prospects for outside intervention.

Communities rarely successfully prosecuted and punished slave masters for murdering their slaves, which sent a message about how African Americans could be treated. Prior to the American Revolution, Maine, Rhode Island, Massachusetts, New Netherland, New York, and Pennsylvania indicted six masters for killing their slaves.[9] In addition to these cases, Massachusetts investigated two cases of murder by slave traders of Africans at sea and in Africa.[10] The rare trials for the murder of slaves by masters made it seem that communities invested in promoting the rights of all, yet courts fell short of punishing criminals. Courts found the offending slaveholders guilty in three of the eight cases above, and evidence suggests that the court followed through on punishment in only one case. In 1697, Nathaniel Cane paid five pounds when he killed his slave Rachel while disciplining her. Not punishing those persons found guilty of murder was an extreme abrogation of community norms even though juries often reduced charges to "intent" to murder in other cases.[11] Wives and servants received greater justice in murder cases. Though it was common to pardon individuals in capital cases, the rare prosecutions of masters coupled with pardons are telling. Peter Kalm, who recorded his perceptions of Pennsylvania's slaveholding population, observed that "a man who kills his Negro must suffer death for it: there is not however an example here of a white man's having been executed on this account." In cases of slave murder, the law acted as a cover in which northerners affected an interest in the physical well-being of their slaves through mock adherence to laws protecting the life of slaves. In practice, Kalm noted, "lenity" in the cases of slave murder occurred so "that the Negroes might not have the satisfaction of seeing a master executed for killing his slave; for this would lead them to all sorts of dangerous designs against their masters, and to value themselves too much."[12] Kalm's narrative is telling because contemporaries believed empowering slaves to redress their cruelty might lead to severe restrictions on masters' rights and a slave rebellion. Holding slave masters accountable would suggest that the government and community saw value in African Americans' lives beyond their significance to whites and that willful murder was dishonorable regardless of the victim.

One of the earliest reports of a slave death at the hands of his master in the North revealed the ways slaves fought back against routine violence. Rather than submitting to correction as young boys and slaves were expected to do, Lewis Barbese, a slave to Gysbert Opdyck, tried running and taking a defensive stance, but when those options failed, he fought back. In 1639, Opdyck, a fiscal at a New Netherland trading outpost, admitted to beating Barbese for bringing him a platter that was dirty. When Barbese "attacked" Opdyck in self-defense, Opdyck pushed Barbese and the "boy fell on his left side," at which point he tried kicking Opdyck away. Barbese ran to the door to escape Opdyck's blows, but Opdyck claimed that upon exiting, Barbese fell on the knife, which "bent like hoop," causing Barbese to die of "a wound in his body near the left arm." The court exonerated Opdyck, declaring the death an accident. In finding Opdyck not guilty, the court accepted that the knife that killed Barbese was upright, and only when Barbese fell on this strangely positioned knife did it enter his body. The facts provided by Opdyck imply Barbese dropped it or left it in the position that would ultimately kill him.[13] By allowing Opdyck to go unpunished, the court showed an early commitment to slaveholding and tolerating the murder of slaves when "correction" went too far. Barbese's behavior was interpreted as disobedient because he resisted the assault, and the court felt justified in finding Opdyck not guilty of the crime. They favored a view that faulty or disobedient slaves warranted punishment, even when it went very wrong.

The Dutch were establishing communities and quickly growing dependent on slave labor, which made Barbese's and other African American slaves' resistance threatening. From 1626, the first enslaved Africans arrived in New Netherland, and the Dutch West India Company used them to build the colony's basic infrastructure and defenses, including having them fight in wars against Native Americans. Their labor and residences, though degraded by Europeans, had allowed for the emergence of trading centers and the expansion of New Amsterdam. Although New Netherland would not establish a slave code, they "equated blackness with slavery," criminalized sex with African Americans, and punished criminals by having them work "with the Negroes in chains."[14] By the 1660s, when the English took over New York, African Americans composed 700 of the nearly 5000 inhabitants, and whites feared that empowering their resistance to abuse or officially chastising their masters for brutality would challenge slavery. By deeming slave deaths accidental, the government supported the development of the colony even though it was clear those slaves were victims of murder.

Slave resistance could prove deadly, and from early on in colonial development, masters and communities feared slaves turning against them. In 1664, Lysbeth Anthonijsen, an African American slave or servant to Martin Creiger, confessed to burning down Creiger's tavern. She put his life, home, and business in danger, and this was not the first time she had disobeyed or shown ill will toward her masters. In 1661, she stole from her previous masters, and the court chose to believe that a fellow enslaved woman induced her to behave poorly. This was an acknowledgement by whites that they knew African Americans conspired against them. The court ordered Anthonijsen's mother to beat her for stealing and reported that her mother and another woman had "whipped her daughter with rods in presence of the W: Magistrates."[15] Three years later when Creiger's house burnt, Anthonijsen was a natural suspect, as she had run away and was suspected of committing theft again. When interrogated, Anthonijsen admitted she had set the fire but only after "her mistress beat her unjustly" for the thievery. The court was not bothered by the beating, as Anthonijsen confessed to stealing and other crimes under further interrogation. The officials showed a willingness to accept physical abuse against poorly behaved slaves and might have used force to elicit her confessions. The court sentenced her to death by being "chained to the stake, strangled, and then burnt" but later remitted the death penalty. The court nevertheless insisted Anthonijsen be "conveyed to the place of execution . . . , that all the preparations for strangling and burning her be made, and then that she be pardoned and returned to her master."[16] Her master had the power to sell her abroad to make up for his loss, and the community would also be rid of her. Anthonisjen's case is a reminder that African Americans chafed at their servitude and had relationships with one another that were useful in resisting enslavement. They took wampum or other goods they deemed due to them, struck back in violence, or simply ran away to be free. This message was not lost on the early Dutch inhabitants of New Amsterdam. The two beatings Anthonijsen received, as well as the mock death penalty, showed their interest in maintaining order through force.

A remarkable uniformity exists in Massachusetts's and New York's laws regarding the treatment of slaves, and the laws mirrored much of the imprecise terminology used for wives and servants, with allowances made for "correction." In 1641, Massachusetts established the legal basis for slaveholding and the treatment of slaves, determining that slaves "shall have all the liberties and Christian usages which the law of god established in Israel concerning such persons doeth morally require." Vague in its conception, the law gave masters the right to discipline slaves while intending to limit excessive cruelty and murder, but it did not clarify the meaning of "Christian usages." The law stated that servants had the right to flee from cruel masters and that the community would grant slaves freedom in cases of maiming. New Netherland did not establish a slave code, but New York's slave law of 1665 mimicked that of New England. In fact, several New Englanders were influential in its construction, though it did not require "Christian usages."[17] Like Massachusetts's, New York's law had an ambiguous definition of cruelty, and to safeguard servants, the law stipulated JPs should hold masters to bonds to prevent further abuse.

Legal codes regarding the treatment of slaves eventually allowed for all but the willful murder of slaves, which may have already been in practice given Opdyck's exoneration from the murder of Barbese. In 1694, New Hampshire passed a law that came to represent white New

Englanders' broader legal understanding, though New Hampshire was the only New England colony to explicitly define it as such. It declared "That if any Person or Persons whatever within this Province shall willfully kill his Indian or Negro Servant or Servants, he shall be Punished with Death."[18] Other colonies avoided defining what constituted murder in cases of slaves, but New York's law stated it "may be lawful for any Master or Mistress of slaves to punish their slaves for their Crimes and offences att Discretion, not extending to life or Member."[19] With the passage of these laws, slaves' rights to protection became a chimera. Only willful murder and maiming (not as part of correction or discipline) were considered offenses, and all-white juries and governmental officials determined intent. England asked for further legal protection, but New York and New Hampshire reiterated their earlier stances, and other New England colonies did not respond with alterations to their original codes that specifically stipulated slaves could seek out JPs for redress.[20] The legal codes suggest that the North was united in its view that disciplining slaves required legal leniency and little culpability for slave masters who took their punishments too far.

In fact, communities might have believed that the death of slaves did not require investigation. Although records of investigations for abuse are missing, archeological studies of the African Burial Ground in New York City reveal cases of extreme cruelty and the lack of care given to African Americans' physical welfare. Of the 419 African Americans interred at the site, forty-one suffered from fractures, with an average of between 2.8 and 3.4 fractures per person. Four individuals had ten to thirty-two fractures, and for those with many factures, the authors of the study argue that "it is unlikely that they were the result of accidental injury." Alarmingly, a large percentage of total fractures found were located on the cranium (23.5% for men and 11.1% for women), suggesting the dangers posed to African Americans.[21]

Homicide cases that did not result in indictments reveal the ways northerners' legal practices were intended to indemnify them from the ignominy of slavery and its attendant violence. As with Barbese, white communities created fictive causes of slaves' deaths, and this was not seen as often in cases of servants and wives. In 1735, New York investigated the death of a slave after he was "corrected . . . with a Horse-Whip." Witnesses of the physical assault and several doctors testified at the coroner's inquest, and their remarks must have highlighted the needfulness of the whipping or their sense that the strokes did not cause the death. The jury determined "the Correction given by the Master was not the Cause of his Death, but that it was a Visitation of God," meaning the slave died of natural causes.[22] In the 1720s, Gilbert Livingston of New York severely punished a slave for running away, and the slave died ten days later. Livingston's mother, Aida, claimed the slave "died out of doggedness" rather than assault.[23] The fact that rumors circulated that masters caused these deaths shows some community discomfort with the willful or "accidental" murder of slaves, but the limited number of prosecutions and punishments of masters for murder and maiming suggests that a broader consensus in the North existed about slave masters' rights, just as it did in the South. In both regions, masters' rights to property superseded slaves' rights to life, and the deaths of slaves from "discipline" were not perceived as murder under the law.

Slaves tried to use religious figures to gain greater rights and freedom and to be part of the community; however, advocates of African American conversion used baptism and Christianization to maintain the racial hierarchy. In the late seventeenth century, a group of African Americans in Boston asked Cotton Mather to instruct them in Christianity, and Reverends Samuel Willard and Mather would repeatedly remind masters of their duty to Christianize slaves. By 1700, 1,000 slaves inhabited Massachusetts. They accounted for less than 1 percent of the total population, but their status and race loomed large in society, and baptism would not mean freedom. Cotton Mather, whom historians regard as fundamental to early New England critiques of slavery, largely dismissed slaves' present and temporal circumstances and instead focused on their spiritual welfare and afterlife. Mather believed that Christianizing slaves would make them more dutiful servants and would teach them "To be Patient in the Low and hard Condition." Others in Puritan New England followed his practice of connecting Christianization with obedience.[24] Religious conversion was less stressed in New Netherland, and access to baptisms declined after 1655. Writing in 1664, Reverend Henricus Selyns, a Dutch minister, informed the Dutch Protestant clergy that he did not baptize enslaved Africans owing to their "worldly and perverse aims" in using baptism as a means to "deliver their children from bodily slavery."[25] Selyns's writing shows African Americans pushed for conversion to better their circumstances, but ministers did not advocate for their freedom, even as their religious work made them familiar with the experiences of slaves. The efforts to Christianize slaves were more commonplace than broader humanitarian programs to ensure African Americans' worldly welfare.[26]

Ministers showed a willingness to acknowledge abuse but rarely strongly condemned it because of their acceptance of slavery. Cotton Mather, a slaveholder, acknowledged the need to physically discipline slaves and believed it could be a tool in their Christianization. He suggested that one method of inculcating slaves with a sense of their need for Christianity was to tell them "that all the *Stripes*, and all the *Wants*, and all the sad things they ever suffered in this World, are nothing, to the *many Sorrows*, which they shall suffer among the Damned, in the *Dungeon of Hell*" should they not accept Christianity.[27] Rather than arguing for slaves' rights to humane treatment, Mather recommended using slaves' memories of abuse as a tool to acquaint them with the miseries of the afterlife. In his later writings, Mather considered slaves' treatment but perhaps only did so to ensure that whites were aware of the spiritual danger they put themselves in when they mistreated slaves. In 1723, in the wake of an arson attempt by a slave, Mather proposed that the "Condition of such Slaves is worthy to be considered," and "whether our Conduct with relation to our African Slaves, be not one thing for which our God may have Controversy with us." Mather asked colonists to consider if "they always treated [slaves] according to the Rules of Humanity?" Though Mather did not directly point to the violence masters used against slaves, he opened the door to further examinations by considering their treatment more broadly. Mather's ultimate goal remained the Christianization of slaves, even after the arson attempt, and he reminded masters that spiritual life was primary to human existence. While Mather began questioning the humanity of slave masters, he encouraged slaves' submission to the authority of whites and maintained slavery in his own household when it proved financially and personally beneficial.[28] He is an example of a man who sought to improve the condition of slaves by acknowledging their poor treatment, but he did not overtly protest the abuse of slaves.

A more pointed rebuke of the abuse of slaves came from Reverend Samuel Willard, of Boston's Old South Church, who advocated corporal punishment only for reformation and spoke against murdering and maiming the enslaved. Willard accepted that masters had the "right of Command," but argued against "unjust threatenings, which carry in them the indication of fury and unbridled passions." As with writings against the abuse of servants and wives, Willard believed that cruelty tended "more to harden Persons in their wickedness, than to restrain or reform them, which is the next end of all Family Discipline." Willard was more progressive in that he saw fault with masters who engaged in corporal punishment while angered. Few individuals argued against using any corporal punishment, and he accepted it as a tool for creating an orderly society, writing it was a "good Means to prevent Disobedience, or humble them when in a Fault." Like other enlightenment writers, he advocated using moral and religious means of persuading and educating children, wives, and servants, and hoped masters and husbands would walk a fine line between abuse and discipline. Willard did not tolerate murder and stated unambiguously that "no Master as such, hath an Arbitrary Power over his servant as to Life and Death." He believed that it was the role of governments to intervene and prosecute cases of murder.[29] Northerners' lackluster history of prosecuting and investigating such cases made his sermon an important reminder to governments about the needfulness of their interventions in cases of abuse and murder.

The legal system was not as great a site of contestation for African Americans as it was for white wives and servants experiencing brutal treatment in New Netherland, New York, or Massachusetts in the seventeenth century. No government lived up to its promise of serving as a site of adjudication for slaves. Massachusetts Bay, Plymouth, and Dutch law allowed slaves access to the courts, and records show they made use of it, but African Americans' legal achievements were in cases over wages and property and in suits for freedom unrelated to cruelty.[30] Negative changes would occur in slaves' access to courts after the English took control of New York. Thereafter, New York did not accept slaves as legal plaintiffs or witnesses against whites, and slaves did not have jury trials unless the accused slave's master demanded it. Thus, New York's codes that professed servants' ability to redress abuse by making complaints to JPs must be met with some skepticism in regard to African Americans. Courts remained accessible to slaves in Massachusetts, but records of their interventions for abuse have not been found for the seventeenth century. Suits for freedom, wages, and property likely took priority in African American communities, as these issues provided greater assurances of familial and individual welfare. Successful suits could result in access to separate living spaces or freedom, which was the best way to avoid abuse in the cases of servants and wives too.

Given the legal and social barriers to freedom, African Americans used a variety of extralegal measures to avoid abuse. Daily struggles with temperamental masters required managing difficult personalities, and as with wives and servants, African Americans used their speech and actions to mollify abusers. To appease their masters' tempers, slaves appeared obedient or complimented masters. Running away, feigning illness, and avoiding interactions with abusive masters were other strategies slaves employed to remain safe. Seaports provided the best refuge for self-emancipated slaves, as crews often included African Americans and Indians; however, boarding vessels and finding freedom was a challenge in a world that increasingly associated Africans with enslavement. Self-emancipated African Americans could turn to other small communities of whites along the eastern seaboard or further into the frontier where they were unknown, but slavery continued to grow and to penetrate these communities, limiting slaves' ability to be perceived independently of slavery. Other options included turning to Indian nations, but they were not known to countenance runaway slaves in the North. Finding a safe cover and transportation to areas where they were unknown were vital concerns of the self-emancipated. By the end of the seventeenth century, Connecticut passed a law requiring passes when abroad. Massachusetts tried to forbid ships from leaving ports with African Americans.[31] For many slaves, proactively managing abusive situations and masters proved a more promising means of dealing with cruelty. Bystanders played vital roles in the lives of runaways. They gave them safe havens, sustenance, and cover from the outdoors.

Northern commitment to slaveholding grew during the eighteenth century, which made access to justice difficult for African Americans, as whites did not consider seriously prosecuting masters for murders, let alone abuse. New Englanders and New Yorkers invested heavily in the Atlantic slave trade and economy, and they bought and sold Africans to themselves and other colonists at great profits. By the 1760s, the Massachusetts census listed 2,818 men and 2,048 women of African descent, making up 5.2 percent of Boston's population. The vast majority of these African Americans were enslaved, and the statistics likely underestimate the numbers of African Americans in the colony. New York experienced similar growth, with African Americans reaching a height of 20 percent of New York County's population in 1746. In addition to purchasing Africans, northerners invested in the broader slave trade and economy, from the transportation of captured Africans to the production of rum, ships, and other goods that were essential to the Atlantic World. Jobs in the maintenance of these industries, such as coopers, tradesmen, and sailors, were important in maintaining the early American economy, particularly in port cities. White colonists had familial connections in the West Indies, too, which strengthened their bonds to slave regimes.[32] The growth of slavery and its profits meant that considerable changes needed to occur to induce whites to see the inhumanity of the system and their own culpability in its perpetuation.

Northern governments sustained slavery and the racial divide by normalizing the physical punishment of slaves in their criminal codes, creating a pattern that supported the social economy of violence against African Americans. Colonial governments sanctioned harsher penalties for slaves than for other members of society for the same criminal acts, and it created legal codes specific to slaves that resulted in corporal punishment in the name of promoting order. Local courts were more likely to convict, whip, and condemn to death (or sell southward) African Americans and Indians than whites.[33] Whipping was a common punishment for all those found guilty of crimes on the order of theft or fornication or other misdemeanors, but individuals able to pay fines avoided public whippings. In some cases, masters petitioned the courts to lessen the physical or capital punishment of their slaves, and they often met with success. Crimes stipulating whippings for slaves but not for non-slaves supported a culture of violence against African Americans. For example, in cases when enslaved African Americans bought goods directly from shippers, destroyed lamps, cursed, or got drunk, the law ordered that slaves be whipped while other offenders only paid a fine or were deposed in the stocks for several hours. The desire to maintain racial order also meant the government created laws for African Americans that did not apply to whites. Slaves were to be whipped for having weapons or meeting in groups of three or more, and in 1738 and 1751, Boston issued orders that slaves out after 9 p.m. without permission from their masters would be sent to the House of Correction "to receive the Discipline of the House." In areas without a House of Correction, slaves were to be "openly whipp'd by the Constable, not exceeding Ten Stripes." Physical punishment of slaves was part of the government's mandate in New York, which determined that "it shall and may be Lawfull hereafter for every City Town and Mannor within this Colony to have and appoint a Common whipper for their Slaves . . . to be paid him by the Master of Mistress of Slaves."[34] The routine use of public and physical punishments against African Americans, who faced a higher conviction rate, reinforced the acceptance of more brutal treatment of slaves and the social economy of violence.

Slaves used violence and destructive acts to fight for their safety and freedom from the seventeenth century, and one of the primary reasons for these laws and the acceptance of violence against African Americans was fear of slave violence. In 1681, Massachusetts executed two slaves for committing arson, a crime that would come to be associated with African Americans and servants. Jack, one of the executed slaves, lived with a master who "always beates him sometimes with 100 blows so that he hath told his master he would sometime or other hang himself." Fearing for his own life and feeling the abuse unbearable, Jack ran away rather than commit suicide, but authorities captured him and sentenced him to jail. After he escaped, the Court of Assistants found Jack guilty of arson, though he claimed the fire was an accidental result of his search for food as he struggled to avoid recapture in Northampton. The court's verdict was likely influenced by Jack's previous resistance to enslavement; he had run away and little consideration was given for his suffering of extreme whippings. Enslaved women also engaged in arson. Maria, a slave in Roxbury who was found guilty of arson, had the assistance of two men when she set fire to two homes, including her master's house. Massachusetts's fear of slave resistance was clear in the sentencing of both—Jack was to be hanged and his body burnt, and Maria was to be burned alive.[35] Though whites may have hoped this harsh punishment would inhibit African Americans' violent resistance, in 1690, a slave from New Jersey traveled through Massachusetts seeking enslaved allies to foment an insurrection in which *"the English should be cut off, and the negroes should be free."*[36] African Americans' collusion in acts of violence reminded residents that slaves had dreams of safety, independence and, in some cases, revenge.

Uprisings against slavery did not have to occur nearby to reinforce whites' sense of danger and desire for discipline; they interpreted news about slave conspiracies committed outside of their colonies as relevant to their own lives. In 1737, the *New-York Weekly Journal* ran a series on a planned slave conspiracy in Antigua and noted that the major leaders in this revolt were "very kindly used"—meaning they believed the masters treated their slaves well. The leaders of the conspiracy reportedly could not "justly complain of the Hardships of Slavery . . . ; their Manner of Living much more plentiful than that of our common Whites." Rather than examining brutality within slave regimes, writers turned to lack of discipline as a cause for rebellions. Reports on Antigua noted that one slave "perverted" his ease of living and used it in "propagating his vile purposes."[37] Slave insurrections reinforced whites' sense that order necessitated retributive violence and limiting slaves' freedom, yet slaves pushed forward and resisted.

By the eighteenth century, Massachusetts and New York had found their way toward excusing murderous violence against slaves. They never truly lived up to their laws regarding murder or cruelty, let alone allowing African Americans to seek reprieve from extreme abuse through the legal system. Whites justified their violence when it went too far by focusing on the victims' behavior rather than the perpetrators', which was also a common practice in cases regarding servants and wives. With slaves, the excusal of violence went further. Because whites were largely inured to the rights of slaves to live without molestation, they did not perceive the assaults on African Americans by their masters as a crime. African Americans tried resisting, but they found few allies in their quest for justice. Managing the abuse of masters, running away, and seeking solace in a fellowship of African Americans were vital means of dealing with the hardships of cruelty in the seventeenth century. Enslaved African Americans would continue trying to build relationships with whites to better ensure their safety, but the process was painfully slow and resulted in few successes.

Protesting Violence in the Eighteenth Century

In an era that allowed the enslaved few opportunities to resist, they acted where they could, and this included planning and executing violence, as did Mark, Phillis, and Phoebe. Slaves rarely engaged in that level of violent activity and instead tried to manage the effects of abuse and resist it. The planned murder was not Mark's, Phillis's, and Phoebe's first attempt to get clear of Codman. "Finding his rigid discipline unendurable," they set fire to his workshop about six years prior to the poisoning in the hope that he would sell them to better masters. Mark, Phillis, and Phoebe sought to spend time away from Codman to avoid abuse, too.[38] Running away and pursuing justice in the legal system were other options, but these actions were limited by the geographical, legal, and social situation of slaves. Slaves nevertheless spoke back against violence in pressing freedom suits and seeking help from neighbors. The growth of slavery and the challenges slaves faced in securing allies stymied resistance to violence in the eighteenth century, as white northerners became more, not less, committed to the institution over time. Whites neglected to consider the perspectives of northern slaves or the quality of their lives and instead sided with white masters in cases of conflict. Even so, resistance to violence opened a dialogue about slavery and forced white colonists to consider the realities of slavery from the perspectives of African Americans.[39]

Slave uprisings against enslavement were often stimulated by the violence experienced by slaves. During the course of the 1700s, major fires and plans for conspiracies to attain freedom were uncovered in New York City (1712 and 1741), Boston (1723 and 1741), Schenectady (1761), and several smaller episodes through the century.[40] In the New York plot of 1712, Governor Robert Hunter admitted some slaves' motivations stemmed from the "hard usage they apprehended to have received from their masters." Hunter stated he "can find no other cause" for their actions, though his writing ultimately questioned the legitimacy of the slaves' complaints.[41] In the New York conspiracy of 1741, some of the same causal factors reappeared. Several slaves who acknowledged being party to the plot described receiving whippings prior to the event. John Stevens reportedly whipped his slave Sam a few days before the planned arson attack, and other slaves told of being scolded by their masters or struck by the town watchmen. African Americans tried to draw attention to abuse even as they underwent interrogations for rebellions. Although these facts were in plain view in the interrogations, whites negated the treatment of the enslaved as causal factors for resistance.[42] Whites had constructed a society in which violence was wedded to controlling slaves, and they could not fathom that what they deemed "correction" caused insurrections.

Just as white wives and servants were punished for their resistance, slaves received like treatment. Many whites had no interest in improving the living conditions of slaves, and sought only their obedience, blinding themselves to other options in responding to slave insurrections. In reaction to New York City's slave rebellion in 1712, the legislature encouraged slave masters to take more initiative in overseeing their slaves and elaborated slave codes to ensure proper discipline and controls existed. The legislature also executed seventeen persons. The slave conspiracy of 1741 further supported many whites' belief that slaves needed to be better managed and controlled. Daniel Horsmanden's published narrative about the conspiracy and trial repeatedly pointed to the relative freedom of New York City's slaves and their want of discipline. He urged "for everyone that has negroes, to keep a very watchful eye over them, and not to indulge them with too great liberties" because his experience taught him that those slaves "who had the kindest masters, who fared best, and had the most liberty" were the most likely to rebel.[43] In the wake of suspected rebellions and arson, Massachusetts also passed more and stricter laws that limited African Americans' mobility and stipulated whippings as punishments.[44] Most whites saw slaves' use of violence as illegitimate, and they reviled slaves who participated in conspiracies as "monsters in nature" or "detestable wretches" even though evidence indicated slaves suffered wrongful treatment and violence.[45]

Slaves also engaged in direct physical altercations with masters to assert their right to fair treatment and in self-defense. During the 1760s, Jeffrey Brace, a slave in Connecticut, pushed a child in his master's family down the stairs. He explained he "designedly pushed his boy" because he "began whipping me & chirping to me, as would a driver to his horse" while he was hauling items. Brace suggests he turned to physical force to establish boundaries between himself and the child. Whether he tried to reason with the child prior to the attack is unknown. The father of the boy he pushed down the stairs, a man named Gibbs, "took a peculiar delight" in whipping Brace and gave him "about four whippings per day." The child had quickly learned that one of the ways masters asserted their identity was through their use of force.[46] During his nearly ten years of enslavement with several masters, Brace expected ill treatment, though he condemned it as unchristian and inhumane. The high stakes involved in physical conflict made resistance such as Brace's rare. Gibbs did not take him to JPs for his actions; instead the next day, Gibbs whipped him "fifty lashes with a horse-whip."[47] Though he faced extreme repercussions, Brace refused to tolerate unwarranted violence and he turned the household hierarchy on its head.

Self-emancipation was a common way to resist violence and find safety, as well as to propagate knowledge about slave abuse. As northern populations and cities grew, fleeing from abusive masters proved somewhat easier, though still a very difficult proposition in a society that connected race and slavery. African American men runaways outnumbered women runaways, and many slave men and women struggled with the choice between running and staying with their children. Arthur, a slave to Richard Godfrey in Taunton, Massachusetts, ran away because he "was so unhappy as often to incur the Displeasure of my Mistress," Theodona Godfrey. He reported he was "treated very kindly by my master," but he could not count on Richard Godfrey to serve as a bulwark against his wife's violence. While Arthur did not describe how Theodona Godfrey manifested her displeasure, Arthur noted it was her treatment of him that "caused me then to run away." By running away, Arthur saved himself from further violent retribution—at least for a time—and also protested it. Arthur's flight became a topic of discussion in the Godfrey household and though there may have been chagrin at his insolence, his message was clear: he would not suffer violence in their household. Arthur also shared his narrative of mistreatment with those who sheltered him. Running away took courage and connections, and Arthur had both. He also ran away from his final master, Thomas Clark, who was determined to sell him for his disobedience, too. Arthur's sense of independence would consistently undermine his masters until Massachusetts's highest court ordered he be put to death for raping a woman in Massachusetts.[48]

Self-emancipated African Americans concerned whites because they lost an investment, and whites feared that African Americans used independence to undermine slaveholders. Whites' feelings of discomfort at the specter of independent African Americans gave lie to their feelings of being dutiful and kind masters. In 1706, when a group of runaways coalesced in Kings County, New York, Governor Edward Hyde reported he had complaints they "assembled themselves in a riotous manner." Specific details about their behavior are lost, but the governor feared the group "may prove of ill consequence." Neighboring whites might have feared the destruction of their homes and property or perhaps that the African Americans would draw their own servants and slaves away from them. The governor ordered JPs to seize runaways or those "assembled in such a manner" whom they suspected of "ill practices or designs." The governor gave JPs the authority to "fire on them, kill or destroy them, if they cannot otherwise be taken." Once in the "safe custody" of whites, the governor desired "that their crimes and actions may be inquired into."[49] The order suggests the governor did not have specific criminal activity to ascribe to the group, outside of running away, and desired charges brought against the African Americans for behavior that he could not delineate. African Americans' independence portended ill news to colonists who viewed them as properly placed under the supervision of whites.

African American women took part in all the resistance efforts noted above, but they also used their voices and their maternal relationships with children to influence the household. In 1717, Cadwallader Colden, who would later serve as governor of New York, complained about a "Negro Woman" whose "Alusive Tongue [and] her sullenness" had beleaguered him. He did not have complaints about her work; he claimed she was a "good House Negro and understands the work of the Kitchen perfectly & washes well." She rebuked Colden by using her speech and body language, likely talking back to him and undermining his sense of authority. The enslaved woman had several children, and Colden felt her influence over them would contaminate the household. He decided upon selling her far away from them—to the West Indies—to prevent her influence, explaining "I know if she should stay in this country she would spoil them."[50] Mothering in a way that valued the contributions of their children and themselves, enslaved women's connections to their families threatened some slaveholders because children learned to speak and think against slavery and deride masters. The enslaved woman's relationships with her children cowed Colden, who valued the labor and obedience of her children but knew he could not compete with her. She suffered greatly for her displays of resistance.

Like white women servants, African American women who served in the homes of whites had greater interaction and intimacy with their masters and families and they suffered different types of violence. The findings of the African Burial Ground show that women's bodies had fewer fractures, but they were also differently located. Women had more fractures on their upper and lower limbs than men, suggesting both the type of labor they engaged in and that they may have experienced violence from their masters in different parts of their bodies. In addition to routine assaults, enslaved women more commonly faced sexual abuse as their reproductivity and labor were claimed by their masters. Studies of slavery show that "the obligation to provide sex might be seen as a central characteristic of enslavement."[51] Although coercive sex and concubinage were not as visible as they would be in some southern cities during the antebellum era, the patterns of sexual abuse seen elsewhere necessarily occurred in the North. Studies of sexual exploitation show that men often chose young, lighter-skinned women who worked in domestic service, though all enslaved women faced the possible threat of sexual coercion. Enslaved women throughout the North lived in close proximity to masters and other men, often within the same households.[52] Outside intervention would not be forthcoming for those facing threats of sexual coercion, and women had to turn to their own communities and families for support. The children born of coercive sexual relations did not lead to inquiries regarding illicit sexual relations. Indeed, New York and New England practiced the same laws as other colonies and understood that children derived their slave status from the mother, which gave masters license to rape and enslave their offspring. No legal records show slaves successfully using the legal system to combat sexual abuse in the colonial era or any interventions provided by northerners in such cases.[53]

In other ways, masters used violence against enslaved women in the same way as against enslaved men. Colden believed physical abuse could remedy the situation with the enslaved woman he decided to send to the West Indies, but he claimed "the Custome of the Country . . . will not allow us to use our Negroes as you doe in Barbados." While Colden claimed he did not beat her, he may have lied to get a higher price for the woman because he would not want others to think she was irredeemable. New Yorkers and New Englanders made claims about their slaveholding practices that did not jibe with the reality of slaves' lives. He proved a believer in the use of violence to reprove slaves in his decision to sell her abroad. He argued "she'l make as good a slave as any in the Island after a little of your Discipline or without it once she sees that she cannot avoid it."[54] While Colden claimed he could not beat her, he was not above removing her from her family for the rest of her life and sending her to others who would assault her.

African Americans' best chance of stopping violence was to seek out individuals who would intervene for them, legally or interpersonally, but it proved difficult to locate persons willing to do so. Jeffrey Brace, the man who pushed a white boy down the stairs, had several cruel masters in Connecticut. John Burwell and his wife were among Brace's first masters in British North America, and they fed him poorly, did not properly clothe him, and beat him ruthlessly with their chairs, fists and feet, horsewhips, and distaff. On one occasion, because he had not fully understood his master's commands, they beat him until he passed out and awoke in a pool of blood. Burwell scarred and bruised Brace and then did not properly attend to Brace's wounds. Nearby whites did not assist Brace, even though he bore physical scars, until Samuel Eals, a neighbor, found Brace nearly frostbitten and with a severe cut on his foot from chopping wood. Eals intervened and told Burwell "that such abuse was inhuman and unchristian." The two men "quarreled for some time." Eals took Brace into his home, gave him a pair of shoes as well as a coat, and provided him with "the first bed I had slept upon after I was taken into bondage."[55] For two weeks Brace stayed with Eals to recover, but Burwell quickly sold Brace to another master. Eals was not an antislavery activist, and he did not work to free Brace, but he did believe some standards should exist about the treatment of slaves that protected their lives and limbs.

Slaves targeted allies who knew about their suffering because bystanders like Eals were the best chance that slaves had in the face of judicial inactivism. For those two short weeks, Eals protected Brace by keeping him in his home, a comfort that the criminal justice system did not provide, despite the laws. Evidence shows other whites would also occasionally step in for abused slaves. In Rhode Island, Reverend James MacSparran "exposed" his slave Hannibal "to the whip," and Hannibal ran to Christopher Phillips, one of his neighbors. Hannibal left to prevent further abuse and to protest MacSparran's repeatedly cruel behavior. Eleven days earlier, MacSparran had tied, stripped, and whipped Hannibal "till he begged." Neighbors were likely aware of the abuse because of Hannibal's scars and MacSparran had an iron collar fitted to Hannibal. It was only when Hannibal sought out safety, however, that whites offered it. Phillips returned Hannibal to MacSparran and wrote a note asking MacSparran to "Spare him." Unlike Eals, Phillips did not provide a safe place for Hannibal by protecting him in his home, but his note did confront the severity of MacSparran's punishments. MacSparran heeded Phillips's wishes after attaining a promise from Hannibal not to disobey or run away again.[56] The notoriety of MacSparran's abuse tells us much about what the community would willfully ignore and the level of violence needed to make individuals intervene. Slaves had to suffer repeated abuse and then seek out help from men and women willing to take up their cause, as did wives and servants. The process of obtaining protection or assistance was slow and put the onus on slaves to seek out assistance from their communities.

The ongoing project of constructing and maintaining whiteness undermined African Americans' ability to find allies and whites willing to prosecute slave murders, let alone intervene in cases of abuse.[57] In 1751, a grand jury in Connecticut investigated Nicholas Lechmere for the willful murder of his nine-year-old slave, Zeno, after he beat her with a horsewhip. After three days of suffering, Zeno died, and neighbors reported their suspicions that Lechmere was at fault. Historian Allegra di Bonaventura argues that community members were aware that Lechmere was a brutal master, but that they chose not to report it prior to the death because they "were perhaps intimidated by his high rank and connections." Ultimately, the grand jury did not indict him. As is still the case today, individuals were less prone to assist persons they perceived as unlike them, and racial thought continued developing and differentiating whites from African Americans as it had since the introduction of slavery and African Americans into the colony.[58] Community members' identification with Lechmere as a leader in the community were among the influences that sanctioned his assaults on Zeno. Legal processes that held masters accountable for their brutality would undermine the racial hierarchy and property rights of slave masters. Though individuals might not have been conscious of these motives, it affected their thinking about indicting masters in cases of slave murder. Other motivations to brush aside slaves' deaths existed, including the growing number of slaves and investments into the slave trade, all of which denied African Americans the right to humane treatment and explicitly delineated whites as superior to African Americans. As communities continued to embrace such a racial hierarchy, and their ideas about race matured, the deaths of slaves went largely unpunished and unprosecuted.

Slaves used the judicial system to protest, but New York and New England differed in their willingness to allow African Americans access to it. Massachusetts had no law forbidding slaves from testifying in court or bringing suits against whites, and slaves harnessed the judicial system at least six times between 1700 and 1760 to petition for their freedom.[59] Some individuals in New England believed slaves' status made them ineligible to serve as plaintiffs or witnesses, though governments would uphold the right of slaves in the legal system.[60] New England tried slaves for crimes in the same courts as whites rather than setting up differential processes, which further supported slaves' rights and access to the justice system. However, they were not treated as equals within it. In contrast, New York did not create opportunities for slaves within the judicial system to make suits or testify. In 1702, alongside the laws that set up a common whipper for slaves as a public office, New York established that slaves could not testify against anyone other than a fellow slave. "No slave shall be allowed good evidence in any matter, Cause or thing whatsoever, excepting in Cases of Plotting or Confederacy amongst themselves, either to run away, kill or destroy their Master or Mistress, or burning of houses . . . and that against one another."[61] This act, which continued through the American Revolution, considerably weakened slaves' access to justice. To redress wrongful enslavement, slaves in New York petitioned governmental officials, usually the attorney general, who would ask courts of admiralty to intervene.[62] New York also made a separate process for slaves in capital cases, as did Pennsylvania, though their masters could request a jury trial. For African American slaves in New York, the judiciary was not a place open to their perspectives and testimony.

In New England, evidence indicates that some slaves in the eighteenth century tried to use authorities to effect changes in their masters' behavior. Venture Smith, a slave in Connecticut, complained to a
JP after his master's excessive violence threatened his life. Thomas Stanton, Smith's master, struck him over the head with a club, which "very
badly wounded my head," Smith stated, and he was left with a scar for
many years. Smith resisted Stanton's second attempt to crush his skull,
and "snatched the club out of his hands and dragged him out of the
door." Stanton called for his brother Robert to assist him, while Smith
took the club and "carried it to a neighboring Justice of the Peace, and
complained of my master."[63] Smith's decision to take his complaint to
a JP suggests his understanding of his own right to life and laws forbidding murder. Several prominent jurists, in addition to the legal statutes, argued that slaves held the right to life and to seek redress for cruel
punishments through JPs. Justice Tapping Reeve asserted that prior to
emancipation statutes, New Englanders recognized that a "master was
liable to be sued by the slave, in an action for beating or wounding, or
for immoderate chastisement, as he would be, if he had thus treated an
apprentice." Reeve wrote in the 1800s, and like other New Englanders, he
believed slavery in New England "was very far from being the absolute,
rigid kind"; he was part of a cultural milieu that promulgated a myth
about the ease of enslavement in New England.[64] Smith's actions suggest
that slaves in New England understood their right to testify against their
masters and hold abusive persons accountable through bonds for peace.
Samuel Eals, who confronted John Burwell about his mistreatment of
Jeffrey Brace, "threatened to complain of him to the authority," implying
broader community protection could be put into place for slaves whose
masters subjected them to extreme abuse and provided poor living conditions.[65] Eals never took the case to JPs, and Smith's record of this event
is singular; the ability of other slaves to make use of this process and access JPs remains unclear despite the promises of jurists and lawmakers.

JPs would do little besides reprove the offending master. In Smith's
case, the JP did not offer protection, nor did he punish his master, and
he did not hold his master to a bond to act as a deterrent for further
abuse. This was a different process for slaves than for servants and wives,
who had bonds for peace processed by JPs on their behalf. After hearing Smith's complaint, the JP "advised me to return to my master, and

live contented with him till he abused me again, and then complain." Although the JP sent Smith back to his master, the JP inquired into the matter, which suggests he believed Smith had a right to seek intervention. Indeed, when Thomas and Robert Stanton appeared at the JP's office to collect Smith, Smith remembered that the "Justice improved this convenient opportunity to caution my master."[66] Even with the discussion, it was an unsatisfactory resolution to Stanton's aggression. Smith's assertive actions of self-defense, when he took up the tools intended to crush him and pushed his master, may have accounted for the JP's lack of action. The legal and social context of the era, in which slaves were routinely beaten without intervention, further prevented the legal system from taking real action against masters. JPs could suffer community derision for punishing masters, which would ultimately negatively affect community trust in JPs' decisions. Nevertheless, the case offers insights into how communities conceived of the rights of the enslaved and slave masters, with slaves allowed to approach JPs about their abuse, and JPs hearing them out and occasionally speaking to masters about slaves' right to life and freedom from excessive violence. For this process to work, however, JPs needed to be located nearby and slaves had to assert themselves in demanding their assistance.

At least one case of abuse made its way through the legal system, but it was so extreme that it compares with only the most egregious cases of violence against white wives and servants. In 1717, John Pettell, a rigger in Boston, cut off "his Negro Man's Ears." Little is known about Cogno, the maimed slave, but his injuries would have been difficult for the community to ignore. It is unclear how the case found its way to the court—whether through Cogno or through bystanders who witnessed his injuries—but the grand jury did not fail to make an indictment. The case against Pettell stands out for the rarity of the prosecution, especially given society's failure to indict masters for manslaughter or to punish those that they did find guilty. Pettell pleaded guilty to the charges, and the court demanded he pay five pounds and court costs.[67] According to Massachusetts law, maimed servants should be freed, but no indication from this case suggests Cogno found his way to freedom. Colonies proved unwilling to part masters from their slaves even in acts of egregious violence. Pettell's confession was critical to the issuance of a fine, given the reluctance of courts to punish slave masters. By the eighteenth century, court prosecutions of and punishments for abusive husbands and masters of servants and apprentices also required brutality to make it through the court system. The difference in regard to cases of cruelty against slaves was the lack of seventeenth-century prosecutions of slave masters.

African Americans did successfully persuade some whites to partner with them against enslavement when they sued their masters for freedom. African Americans needed white men to serve as their lawyers, but even with white representation they did not often receive justice. Most slaves in the colonial era sued for their freedom based on their status of having been born of free parents, since wrongful imprisonment was a criminal act. Juries in Massachusetts most often sided with African Americans in freedom suits, which acknowledged the mistreatment of the illegally enslaved, particularly when they awarded damages from former masters. After finding for their freedom, JPs, grand juries, or attorneys general could have referred cases in which assaults against slaves occurred while they were wrongly enslaved to the General Sessions, but they chose not to take this action. The legal system only helped African Americans find their freedom; the courts did not pursue the criminal acts by masters who abused their slaves or wrongfully enslaved them.

Slaves revealed their independence and cracked away at the veneer of the humanity of New Englanders' slave system in their freedom suits.[68] The legal format freedom suits took was as trespass suits. Writs of trespass were originally marshalled in England to sue for justice in cases of kidnappings and assaults, including the forceful taking of land, property, or violence against another person. By the eighteenth century, persons suing for breach of legal contracts, debt, and property disputes used writs of trespass, but these suits continued to adhere to legal formats that commonly used the terms "force and arms" and "assaults" to describe wrongdoing. Lawyers and judges understood this verbiage to be fictive and not actually suggestive that physical assaults occurred. In cases of African American freedom suits, however, slaves and their lawyers challenged the boundaries of this customary language and gave substance to legal format. In freedom suits, lawyers declared that masters used "force and arms" and wrongfully imprisoned and assaulted their slaves. For example, in 1769, James, a slave, accused his master, Richard Lechmere, of having "with Force & Arms assaulted the said James and him took & imprisoned & restrained him of his Liberty and held him in Servitude from the same eleventh Day of April until . . . the Second day of May AD 1769."[69] Lechmere was the brother of Nicholas Lechmere, the slave master in Connecticut who was suspected of murdering Zeno, a slave girl. Jurors and spectators may have speculated and made connections between the Lechmere brothers' treatment of their slaves. By bringing forth freedom suits, communities were forced to see that slaves had limited mobility, suffered wrongful assaults, and were denied basic freedoms, even though the major focus of freedom suits was to parse out the legal status of the plaintiff as either a slave or free person.

The cases turned slavery on its head, with slaves and their lawyers directing how the court would parse the language and terms of slavery. In 1701, when a JP summoned John Saffin to answer to a freedom suit brought by his slave Adam Saffin, John Saffin called it a "Negromatick Summons." While the court considered the case, Adam Saffin reputedly "went about the Town swaggering at his pleasure in defiance of me his Master." John's chafing at the summons shows how such cases inversed the dynamics of slavery, placing masters in the uncomfortable position of defending themselves against slaves' charges. In another case, in 1763, Prince sued for his freedom, and his putative owner, David Bull, confronted the charges that he "took imprisoned detained and restrained of his Liberty for the Space of Time set forth in the Plt's [plaintiff's] Declaration." Bull's defense did not deny that he restrained and imprisoned Prince, only that he did so illegally. Believing his ownership and the custom of slaveholding would mute Prince's suit, Bull's lawyers declared Prince "Ought not to . . . maintain his Action . . . against him because he says that the Plt. [Plaintiff] . . . was a Negroe & Slave and Servant . . . after the Manner and Way in which Negroes in the American Government and Colonies . . . are Servants and Slaves."[70] Freedom suits posed a linguistic challenge to defenders of slavery by requiring that they acknowledge the similarities between imprisonment and slavery. Bull never denied his treatment of Prince; he argued only that Prince's status and race meant he could legally do so. While freedom suits about wrongful contracts suggested that it was acceptable to hold certain persons as slaves, they also challenged slavery by showing the harm done to enslaved persons.

Freedom suits often led to discussions about the use of violence against slaves, though masters were quick to excuse their behavior and blame violence on the disorderly conduct of slaves. Since violence was so often swept aside, such discussions were important moments in considering rationalizations of violence. Adam Saffin's freedom suit led to his masters' frequent explanations of Adam's misbehavior. John Saffin contracted with Thomas Shepard to lease out Adam Saffin's labor. Both John and Thomas denied abusing Adam, though they claimed the right to do so and substantiated existing societal views that slaves deserved correction. Few masters admitted their abuse of slaves. Thomas plainly admitted "I could beat him and lay him at my foot," but he claims to have chosen to not assault Adam in the hopes that his kindness would lead to Adam's reformation. Like Colden, Thomas claimed to be a more humane master and feared for his own family's welfare and productivity if Adam stayed in his family. He wondered whether a man "*that doth not value his own life, can command anothers,*" and viewed correcting Adam as a misstep because correction would not positively affect his behavior. In fact, he feared further bad behavior from Adam. Thomas's decision not to correct Adam also stemmed from the concern that "he should do him or his Children some mischief," showing the very real fear some whites had of slaves living within their households. Ultimately, Thomas returned Adam to John because he felt he had run out of options.[71] Thomas's admission that Adam may not have valued his own life is a telling sign that slaveholders saw the terrible effect slavery had on men and women in bondage.

In 1703, Adam won the case and gained his freedom, and along the way, he also incited discussion about the nature of slavery and the abuse of slaves. Among the assaults uncovered in this case that may have influenced the community was an instance in which the night watch, a force of constables who patrolled the streets to ensure the safety of citizens and maintain order, picked up Adam at the urging of John, who wanted him back to work. The watch admitted using a stick to strike a pipe out of Adam's mouth and to shoving him. Still unsatisfied, the captain hit Adam on the shoulders with the stick. Adam defended himself against their actions by breaking the stick used to beat him and throwing a shovel at the arm of the captain. It ultimately took six or seven men to restrain Adam; this was a fight reminiscent of Venture Smith's bold defense.[72] The freedom suit laid bare the true experience of slaves who were legally subject to such beatings. The case would not focus on this violence, but Adam's experiences aired publicly in the courtroom and in writings about the case.[73]

Samuel Sewall, a justice on the Superior Court of Judicature, reconsidered slavery in the wake of Adam's suit and he propounded against slavery publicly. Though Sewall shared Cotton Mather's focus on the afterlife and the effects of slavery on whites, Sewall sided with Adam in his suit for freedom, and published a tract condemning slavery as religiously unjustifiable. Unable to envision a future for the colony in which African Americans and whites labored and lived together, Sewall saw African Americans' presence as a detriment to whites. He nevertheless issued an indictment against the violence of slavery, asserting that murder of slaves was wrong. Biblical masters had "no more Authority to *Sell* him, than to *Slay* him," Sewall opined, using African Americans' basic right to life as a tool to argue against slavery.[74] New Englanders often stated that their laws did not allow for the murder of slaves, but their actions did not support this, so Sewall's intervention was important.

African Americans continued turning to religious authorities and using conversion as means of joining communities and expressing their shared humanity, but successes were limited in getting full religious condemnations of slavery. African Americans' most profound influence emerged in the writings and actions of several Quakers, who took the first organized efforts to end slavery in the eighteenth century. African Americans relayed their experiences to those who would listen, but often whites' antislavery writings emphasized the slave trade and the assaults and murders of slaves elsewhere.[75] From the 1730s to the 1760s, Benjamin Lay continuously criticized Pennsylvania Friends (Quakers) for their ties to slavery and the slave trade. Focusing his writing on the cruelty of places such as Barbados, Lay described practices where men whipped their slaves excessively to "keep them in awe." Among Lay's confidants in Barbados was a slave whose master would "whippe whippe poor Negro evee Munne Morning for notin tall," and the slave killed himself rather than continue to suffer the abuse. Antislavery writing that chastised the practices of masters in the West Indies reinforced the idea that slavery as practiced there was isolated in its horrors. African American suffering at home influenced Lay's eventual push to end Quaker slaveholding, but Quakers would disown Lay for his criticism of slavery and the racial hierarchy. Among other notorious activities of Lay, he put himself in danger by placing his own foot in the snow to shed light on the suffering of slaves in Pennsylvania. Lay was not alone in being reprimanded for speaking against slavery.[76] William Burling of Long Island published several tracts advocating abolition and Quakers tried to quash his critiques too. In the 1740s, Anthony Benezet, a Quaker leader in the antislavery movement, published his assault on slavery and laid out that the slave trade would not exist if not for purchasers, and he detailed the suffering of Africans abroad and on voyages to the Americas. Benezet chastised slaveholders, yet most antislavery arguments transferred concerns about the brutal treatment of slaves onto the slave trade rather than on treatment at home.

Although no antislavery organization emerged in the North until the American Revolution, the attention slaves received from antislavery writers opened the door to broader considerations of slavery and its inhumanity, which resulted in some action in several northern communities.[77] In revealing the physical distress of African Americans, antislavery writers called on whites to assess their complicity in the institution. Quakers were far ahead of other white northerners. During the 1720s, Friends in Chester County, Pennsylvania, proposed a ban on their members purchasing imported slaves, and in the 1750s, Philadelphia's Quakers forbade their membership's involvement in the slave trade. New England's Friends followed suit several years later.[78] The Quakers made greater strides to eradicate slavery than other groups, but even their efforts failed to seriously consider the welfare of African Americans in the northern colonies.

Because enslaved African Americans faced far greater obstacles in seeking community interventions from religious figures, the courts, and bystanders, a few turned to extreme measures, including suicide, to free themselves from abuse. In 1758, one slave reportedly "threw himself into the Mill Pond and was drowned" after his master threatened to assault him. The slave clearly told others about the pending physical assault, but no one intervened for him. *Boston Evening Post* editorialized that he took his own life because he was "not relishing a little necessary Correction which was administered to him for his Misconduct."[79] By highlighting that the correction was "necessary," the writer reinforced the idea that slaves required correction and, in doing so, slave masters were ensuring the safety of the community. White thoughts about slavery and African Americans hindered empathetic reactions and limited bystander interventions. The slave committed suicide to avoid harsh punishment and slavery, but white northerners did not reflect on this form of slave resistance.[80]

Communities deemed excesses in violence unfortunate, but these deaths did not lead to alterations in the treatment of African Americans, nor to the establishment of protections for them. The colonial era saw the growth of slavery in the North and its embedding in the legal system. Overall, perpetrators' rights were the primary concern in cases of slave abuse and murder. Jurors and justices proved unlikely to interrogate masters vigorously on behalf of slaves or to interview African Americans' friends and family for evidence or patterns in their masters' abuse. To effectively prosecute and investigate a murder, the community had to understand the rights of the victim and respect the testimony of African Americans who may have witnessed an event. Similarly, understanding the cruelty of slavery at home required acknowledgement of slaves' perspectives on violence. The lawyers who represented slaves in their freedom suits, like those who wrote against slavery abroad, provided some impetus for change by targeting the institution itself as immoral and publicizing certain slaves' perspectives.

Although the violence against slaves was more extreme and murder was tolerated, similarities exist in the overall patterns of resistance among the wives, servants, and slaves. Slavery left African Americans with limited options, so to protect themselves, they had to fight back physically, find allies, run away, and seek out freedom in the courts. The few bystanders who witnessed and interceded in violent acts laid groundwork for setting community-wide standards against violence and the basic rights of individuals held in bondage. Religious figures did step forward and speak against misdeeds, as did a few bystanders who intervened to protect individuals. The resistance against violence by African Americans, wives, and white servants did not result in community partnerships aimed at preventing it, and most whites gave only lip service to the laws designed, but not enforced, to ensure African Americans' safety.

Violence was implanted in the daily practices of slavery and structured race relations in the North. After the executions of Mark and Phillis, *Boston Evening Post* reported that they "died very penitent" after confessing their guilt, but their remorse for the repeated acts of violence against Codman remain in question. White northerners often ignored the violent acts in their communities, and situating Mark and Phillis as sorrowful fit into their desire to contain and dismiss it. Northeasterners created justice systems that did little to hinder slave masters' murderous violence and maintained a culture that tolerated abuse in the name of preventing slaves from mounting a rebellion or engaging in other acts of aggression. No law could curtail the aspirations of slaves, and Mark, Phoebe, and Phillis ultimately tried to flee from the violence of slavery through their murderous acts. The societal response to their acts tell us much about the limitations placed on slaves and their struggles to attain liberty from abuse. African American efforts to achieve safety continued into the revolutionary era as they worked to situate their welfare as a primary concern for society. Many whites failed to envision African Americans' safety and ambitions as central to promotion of good order, and the Revolution would test the prudence of ignoring their perspectives.

PART II

The Imperial Crisis and War

Chapter 4

Suspicious Servants and Slaves

In March 1770, British soldiers and a group of Bostonians engaged in a conflict that would result in the death of five men, including an escaped slave, Crispus Attucks. For some, the Boston Massacre was a momentous occasion that highlighted how the unruly behavior of a few—among whom were notably servants, wageworkers, and African Americans—could lead to danger. Reports after the event described it as emerging from "a quarrel . . . between some of the soldiers of the XXIXth, and the rope maker's journeymen and apprentices, which was carried to that length as to become dangerous to the lives of each party." Edward Garrick, a wigmaker's apprentice, ignited an argument with one of the soldiers, and an increasingly hostile crowd appeared around the soldier. Attucks took a leadership role in the dispute as people began throwing rocks and other objects at the sentries, and he was the first to die. John Adams, who defended the British soldiers in court, reminded the jury and its spectators about the disorderly conduct in Boston's streets since the Stamp Act. Questioning the general character of the crowd that day, he ascribed the events to "a motley rabble of saucy boys, negroes and molattoes, Irish teagues and outlandish jacktars," arguing they were "shouting and hazing and threatening life . . . whistling, scream[ing], and rendering an Indian yell . . . throwing every species of rubbish they could pick up in the street."[1] Adams convinced the jury that six of the eight soldiers were not guilty, which is significant because some colonists disagreed with the British policies they believed caused disorder. Colonists had also come to see that riots were ultimately a threat to their property rights, peace, and the social order of society.

Regardless of the position of colonists in this case, during the ten years before the declaration of independence, the public saw their streets turn into battlegrounds.[2] The threatening specter of racial and youthful rebellion were motivators for both change and stasis during the imperial crisis. Just a few months before the Boston Massacre, New York saw similar tumult with troops in the Battle for Golden Hill. Even colleges became havens of disruption as youthful students from at least five northern schools between 1760 and 1776 resisted what they saw as the determination of their lives by others.[3] Identifying with many of the themes of the imperial crisis, youthful white servants, apprentices, and slaves looked for ways to claim their own liberties. Their resistance challenged their masters' powers and required local communities to learn about their perspectives to create stability. Servants found their resistance to abuse was best mediated outside of the government during the imperial crisis, and they ran away or sought out allies who would privately negotiate exits from abusive situations. This was the beginning of an overall decline in governmental resolutions of abusive relationships between servants and masters. On the other hand, slaves renewed suits for freedom and petitioned the government to redress their grievances. Some whites participated in conversations about cruelty and abuse as part of their overall considerations about the political and social implications of the imperial crisis, yet these conversations were usually a means of forwarding their own political agendas. Nevertheless, a clear trend existed in the more frequent considerations of slavery from multiple perspectives.

Prior to declaring independence, governments and local communities did little to improve the safety of African Americans and white servants. The changes that occurred during the imperial crisis harkened back to the experiences of the two previous centuries in Massachusetts and New York. Society maintained its belief that physical discipline was a useful tool of masters, though they would make different allowances for masters of African American slaves than of youthful white servants and apprentices. Courts and communities indemnified slave masters in cases of slave murder, maiming, and abuse, and in the case of white servants, courts decreasingly made criminal charges against abusive masters as children's and young adult's testimony was increasingly doubted. Yet society remained willing to assist young white servants and apprentices when masters disobeyed certain rules of conduct. Bystanders stepped in to assist young whites in far more meaningful ways than they did for African Americans.

Suspicious White Servants

Young white servants and apprentices continued pressing suits forward to attain safety, but beginning in 1774, New York City's century-plus history of freeing all young white servants complaining of abuse or ill treatment ended. By the mid-eighteenth century, Massachusetts's and New York's policies merged as both lessened the criminal consequences of abuse, except in extreme cases. Ideas about white servants and masters had changed and this, alongside the chaos of the imperial crisis, fundamentally altered the ways the courts handled assaults. The adjustments in New York's legal system resulted from multiple interacting factors, and fundamental to understanding these changes are the colony's protests leading up to the movement for independence. Servants' and young persons' activism in resisting the British and other authority figures decreased the willingness of officials to free servants as readily as they had in the past. The stress was immense on court officials and the populace to maintain peace and order during the overall social upheaval associated with the crisis. Communities tried chipping away at young adults' autonomy as the imperial crisis worsened, but they faced resistance from youth along the way. Mediations of servant abuse would become more private affairs, taken on by Overseers and parents, with servants instigating arbitration.

While the court system in New York City provided a particularly valuable space for white servants to contest abuse in the colonial era, those same courts were abandoning servants and were no longer disposed to freeing them. They would maintain that stance through the 1780s. The trend toward privileging masters' testimony was paramount to this change. Between 1774 and 1776, seven servants complained of cruelty, but the court released only two of the petitioners from their masters, and the court returned four petitioners to their masters after it determined they had not proven the alleged abuse. Other servant protests show similar trends toward deciding in favor of masters. The court heard fourteen white servants' and apprentices' petitions alleging lack of training, clothing, or other provisions, and it returned two to their masters. Most telling was that the two cases in which the court returned the servants to their masters were also the only two cases in which the masters appeared in court to rebut their servants' testimonies. The court discharged servants for their masters' failure to fulfill their duties only when the masters had absconded, failed to show up in court, or willingly gave up their servants.[4] In Massachusetts, though they had stipulated it was illegal to assault servants in the 1750s, the General Sessions was not active in hearing cases of abuse, with cities and towns charging the Overseers of the Poor with administering to pauper servants and helping to redress grievances. In these cases, news of assaults experienced by children and youth never reached the courtroom, which lessened public discussions about servant abuse.

In the cruelty cases that New York City rejected, the court no longer automatically accepted white servant testimony over masters. Individuals testifying to the poor behavior of servants and their need for correction won the day in servants' unsuccessful cases, and this connected to the view that recalcitrant servants needed discipline. New York City, like Massachusetts, turned to an understanding of cruelty in which the scars of abuse had to be visible and substantiated to overcome prejudices that favored masters' testimonies. The amorphous categories of "cruelty" and "immoderate correction" had always been a problem outside of New York City, with servants, masters, and court officials disagreeing on the extent of correction allowed. Now New York became more critical of what constituted abuse. In 1775, Sarah Cotterill, a white apprentice to Elizabeth Williams, complained to the court "that she is very ill used." Williams had recently married William Williams, and the marriage changed Cotterill's circumstances, as he became a source of cruelty and put Sarah "in great Danger of her life." The court determined Cotterill's "Complaint is just" and released her from her contract, as it did for Nicholas Crocheron after he petitioned the court with similar causes. In Crocheron's case, the court found the master "doth immoderately beat and correct the said Apprentice."[5] Establishing severity of treatment required some signs of abuse because of competing testimony from masters. In one case, the court noted "immoderate correction not proved," implying that while the servant authenticated the use of corporal punishment, he had not adequately proven the level of cruelty.[6] Judges altered standards of what constituted cruelty in ways that reinforced the power of masters. As courts continued to downgrade young adults' testimony in relation to their superiors', the marks and scars of violence now became the sine qua non in attaining freedom, and only those who could show extensive damage received freedom.

Servants and apprentices had always been suspect to a certain degree, but before the American Revolution, this had not prevented courts from siding with them; it had only reduced criminal penalties. Understanding that New York City made the transition to more private mediations of abuse during the midst of its highly contentious and violent revolutionary experience explains some of the courts' hesitancy in empowering servants to resist their masters' abuse. During times of political instability, colonial British North American courts in the South were also less likely to side with servants and apprentices in cases of abuse.[7] New York was particularly divisive and disorderly in the time leading up to independence, and individuals used violence to assert their point of view and presented narratives of cruelty to secure their innocence.[8] Factions in support of the Crown vied against radical Patriots, and officers of the court found themselves under attack on numerous occasions, as renters' strikes broke out throughout the colony of New York and in parts of New England. In addition, the elite in New York felt the precariousness of their positions when the populace responded to British legislation and the government by protesting and publishing condemnations of their policies.

Resistance to British rule included destruction of property and disorder in the streets in Massachusetts and New York. The violence was ascribed to "the mob"—a group that became associated in the minds of many with the poor, young, and African Americans. After the much-hated stamped paper arrived from England in 1765, protestors in New York City paraded through town, threatened soldiers at Fort George, and destroyed property. Invading the home of Major Thomas James, the commander of Fort George, citizens demolished the family's goods and destroyed the governor's carriage, as well as street lamps and bawdy houses. Numbering into the thousands, the individuals who protested the Stamp Act created and burned effigies, signaling threats to leaders in the government in New York and elsewhere. Boston had a similarly hostile response to the Stamp Act. Resistance to the British continued thereafter, with several riots instigated by disagreements between soldiers and citizens, leading to assaults and causing unrest in the streets and theaters. In 1770, an infamous "battle" erupted over British soldiers' destruction of the liberty pole in New York City just weeks before the Boston Massacre. Aldermen had tried to prevent violence on Golden Hill by persuading soldiers and citizens to disarm, and the mayor attempted to draw the soldiers off the streets and to Fort George. "Citizens requested him not to quit the Fields," but at the end of the day, one writer noted "there has been Blood spilt on both sides."[9] Unrest became a constant struggle as colonial subjects responded to new British legislation, and riots required the deft handling of radicals to disassociate the rebellion from disorder.

Conservative cries for more restraint became commonplace, and they directed some of these concerns at the lower orders, including servants, youth, and African Americans. Public disturbances in the streets caused alarm, and courts in New York City turned to siding with the masters of apprentices and servants while the city faced the threat of commotions similar to those of 1765 and 1766. Massachusetts maintained its stance of supporting masters during the same time period. By 1773, colonial tensions had radicalized New York City and Boston with the Tea Act and the Intolerable Acts threatening to bring them into chaos again. When news of the Tea Act reached New York, William Smith, a member of the Governor's Council, reflected, "I suppose we shall repeat all the Confusions of 1765 & 1766." As cities like Boston began organizing against the Act, he surmised similar sentiment existed in New York: "The Flame ready to burst out here & rage all along the Continent."[10] The fear of continued unrest led to calls for more quietude and reasoned consideration, a boon to those seeking to restore authority. One writer in Massachusetts reflected that the colony required "A general *Reformation of Manners,*" which "cannot be accomplished without universal *Family Government*—of which every sober person sees the Degeneracy." His complaints included the breach of the Sabbath and that the "Servants and Children, and even Masters themselves are waking and sauntering in Streets and Fields. Young People act uncontroul'd—their tender Minds early receive the Impressions of Iniquity and leap boundless in Sin." In response to these disturbances, communities called for orderly family government, which coincided with the trends of prolonging the oversight of youths.[11]

Artisans and other skilled craftsmen, who were often labeled "mechanics," served as a lightning rod to which radicals were drawn. Their rise to power was synchronous with the period in which courts increasingly rejected apprentices' and servants' petitions. Making themselves a forceful coalition during the 1770s, mechanics loudly voiced their desire for a pact against the importation of British goods, while conservatives desired a more measured approach that was less threatening to the local economy and political structure.[12] Mechanics in New York City and Boston, who made and sold goods, repeatedly challenged merchants and others who desired alternative protests that protected their trade interests. In resistance to moderates, craftsmen in New York City created a coalition to protest the Tea and Intolerable Acts. Dubbing their gathering place "Mechanics Hall," their plan to siphon off leadership from other radical and moderate groups was clear. They tried to direct policies and programs through the imperial crisis by placing important stakeholders on committees and by courting public opinion.[13] Local governments that addressed factions understood the mechanics' involvement in the resistance movement, and those who sought to shape the course of the revolution tried partnering with them.

Land riots in New York and New Hampshire broke out simultaneously with the imperial crisis, as farmers rose against landowners whose policies eliminated the option of owning the land. Adding to the overall atmosphere of instability, the land riots partly influenced local courts' change in position regarding white servants and apprentices because government officials faced attacks for their role in protecting property. The riots broke out as landowners forced tenants off their lands, and tenants responded by destroying property and threatening those who replaced them as renters. The landowners, including the Livingston family, were among the wealthier and more politically active families in the colony and often had homes in New York City, which rioters occasionally threatened. New York speculators had investments in the land grants and they were connected to the judiciary and government, who called in British soldiers to protect their property claims in the Hudson Valley. By 1772, the conflict between the tenants and landowners in New Hampshire and New York reached a new height, and vigilantes attacked several of New York's JPs as punishment for supporting landowners in their execution of summons and for jailing those who broke the law. John Munro, a JP in Albany, wrote to the governor after rioters destroyed his potash works in retribution for jailing a protester. "The Mob has broke loose," he informed the Council, and the rioters continued to threaten and raid his property through 1773. Munro asked, "What can a Justice do when the whole Country combinds against him?" The Governor's Council read Munro's plea aloud, and it was clear that respect for law and order had dissipated.[14] In 1773, threats against JPs became more severe, as rioters extralegally tried two JPs for "accepting their Offices." The rioters woke up the men in the middle of the night, forced them to dress, assaulted them, and removed them by gunpoint to the place of their "trial." In a petition for use of armed forces against the rioters, several New Yorkers claimed the "Chiefs of the Mob" sentenced the JPs to have their houses and property destroyed unless they "renounce their Commissions and engage that they would no longer execute the Duties of their Stations." The rioters did not exclude the sheriff and constables from attacks, and the news of the assaults on JPs and other government officials spread quickly throughout the colony.[15]

Court officials' authority was simultaneously eroding and becoming politicized, prompting their protection of masters' rights over servants'. Property holders throughout the colonies repeatedly called on both the judiciary and the larger government to protect their rights and individual safety, but many persons viewed governmental actions as disloyal when they supported law and order in the face of protests, which some connected to the British.[16] After the Intolerable Acts in Massachusetts, Patriots attacked court officials and supposed Loyalists in Berkshire, Middlesex, Bristol, Suffolk, Plymouth, Cambridge, and Worcester. Aldermen and JPs had the responsibility of stymying violence where it affected daily life—including the right to property and to live free from assaults—but these roles became more difficult and mired in competing loyalties. Local government and court officials' favor with the populace swung like a pendulum. Communities asked them to intervene in cases of violence, but editorials and crowds proved quick to criticize when the actions of the government opposed their agendas.

In one particularly well-known case, a "mob" undermined the government's ability to prosecute an individual. At fault in this circumstance was a servant who seemingly betrayed his master. In 1770, Alexander McDougall, a merchant and radical, was arrested for writing a libelous piece criticizing New York's decision to pay for the British soldiers stationed there. The case was much discussed because McDougall was an emerging leader among the resistance in New York City. The grand jury found an indictment against McDougall, and "a mob was in readiness to escort and attend the culprit from the prison to the City Hall . . . consisting of about two or three Hundred of the rabble of the town." No prosecutor was willing to take the case under these circumstances, and the court eventually dropped the charges.[17] The radicals supporting McDougall expressed concerns about the white apprentices and journeymen—trained workers, employed by mechanics, who had never achieved the status of masters—who turned against their masters and reported the printing of the libel to court officials. Their testimony was a detriment to the larger political cause and a reminder of the needfulness of young men's oversight. The first person to supply evidence against James Parker, the printer of the libel, was one of his former journeyman named Cummins, "a young Strippling" who had been "discharged for bad Behaviour." Characterizing Cummins as a disobedient servant made his testimony immediately suspicious. Without Cummins's testimony, the cases against McDougall and Parker would have been compromised, and this created more ire among Patriots. Radicals recognized this and quickly took action against him. "Finding his life in danger from the violence of the republican faction in New York," a justice of the supreme court noted, Cummins "privately left the colony, and removed to a different part of the continent." After officials questioned Parker, they brought his apprentices in for interrogation and questioned the oldest of his apprentices first. The oldest apprentice eventually "confessed that it was printed by Mr. Parker" after "being threatned with a Commitment." The other apprentices, "after his Example, charged the printing of the Paper on their Master."[18] Parker's apprentices did not have much choice in deciding whether to give testimony, but their statements proved critical to the very unpopular cases against Parker and McDougall.

Young servants and apprentices did not always oppose their masters. Their participation in protests was part of their larger struggle for autonomy and search for identity. Occasionally, servants' and apprentices' desires to punish elites aligned with their masters' goals, and they expressed loyalty to their future occupations and masters by partaking in parades and protests. At other times, their protests expressed their identity as youth. Prior to the acts of resistance during the revolutionary era, young men led disorderly activities in the streets of major cities on Pope's Day, and they continued to make these connections and join in activities with other teenagers. They eagerly joined in events that gave them a voice, and riotous protests were part of their revolutionary experience.[19]

As in earlier eras, servants acted in direct opposition to their masters too, by trying to get free of them, lying, stealing, or making time for themselves. As courts moved away from public mediation of abuse and prosecutions, servants' resistance often became more private. Persuading their families to secure different masters was an important means of protecting their interests and safety, and some children and young adults changed masters several times until a good fit was found. The process of switching masters required communication about servants' experiences at the hands of masters, and parents could play an active role in shaping community opinion about abusive individuals. Communication outside of immediate families and households about the violence of masters was another tool servants used to avoid abuse or contest authority. For two months in 1767, two newspapers ran a notice regarding Richard Speaight, a white apprentice, who admitted spreading false rumors regarding Edward Agar and his wife. Agar was a "chemist" and apothecary in the city, and the advertisement suggests he may have been contracted to learn his trade with Agar as he had "lived with" him. Speaight admitted that the "sundry false and scandalous Reports, very much to the prejudice and tending to asperse the Character of Mr. Edward Agar . . . and of Margaret, his Wife . . . was without any the least Foundation whatsoever." Furthermore, he assured readers that when he lived with the couple he "always received the most civil Treatment."[20] A JP had signed the notice, suggesting the confession was a punishment the courts doled out in consultation with the Agars. The Speaight case served as a reminder to the community not only of the ways that apprentices used gossip to undermine the credibility of masters, but also how they occasionally lied to achieve those ends. Stealing was another means of redressing abuse or addressing other concerns. Taking their masters' property as their own expressed their dissatisfaction with their upkeep and showed servants believed they placed a critical role in the household economy. The private ways of contesting abuse were part of the greater history of servant resistance, but this resistance was considerably less public than official court proceedings.

Larger ideological discussions about the cruelty of servitude were not common during the crisis; however, colonists explored and politicized children's roles and experiences through examinations of their relationship with "mother" England. Colonists used metaphors that positioned England as an abusive parental figure, and the logic in their expressions relied on the belief that force should not be used to direct young adults; rather, they should be persuaded toward righteous conduct and have some agency in their daily lives. The relationships between parent and child were often gendered, with the colonies assuming the role of boys nearing the age of independence. Portraying the colonies as boys was important because young women were not on equal footing when it came to achieving independence.[21] The writing presumed colonists' righteousness in the dispute to align with ideas about how appropriate parental authority over children operated. Some writing attributed the misbehavior of colonists to parents who did not fulfill their roles in properly guiding their "children." Despite the limitations of the parent-child metaphors, these discussions could have radical implications. Historian Gordon Wood explains that "for children and subordinates to disobey their fathers and masters in this still traditional world was so terrifying and unnatural that whigs inevitably resorted to the image of a contract in order to . . . justify their sense of equality and their rebelliousness."[22] Indeed, figuring the relationship as contractual allowed the colonies to draw on certain rights and condemn authoritarian masters or fathers to satisfy polemical attacks on England.

The debates justified the actions of abused servants who walked away or arranged for alternative contracts with better masters. Though courts might not side with servants except in cases of extreme abuse, servants and apprentices construed their situations vis-à-vis their masters in ways similar to the "oppressed" colonists. Ebenezer Fox, a twelve-year-old white boy indentured to a farmer in Roxbury, had ill feelings about his servitude. "I imagined . . . that I suffered many privations and endured much hardship," he recalled. "[D]esirous of some change," Fox and other young men made connections between their countrymen's fight for liberty and their own. Fox "thought that I was doing myself great injustice by remaining in bondage, when I ought to go free," and ". . . should liberate myself from the thralldom of others, and set up a government of my own."[23] Fox eventually did just that, which disrupted the ability of abusive masters to sustain a labor pool.

The societal pressures experienced during the imperial crisis illustrate why, after a century of adjudicating white servant abuse cases, New York City started turning away these cases, and servants began using more private means of resistance. The rejected petitions of white servants did not mean that judges and juries sided with the British. In fact, most judges in New York City did ultimately support the American Revolution; it was the process of the Revolution that led to questions.[24] The threat of violence made citizens anxious for order, but the authority figures they ordinarily turned to faced increased pressure to maintain peace in a highly critical and hostile environment. The rise of artisans and mechanics' power in the body politic occurred during a century-long growth in society's understanding of the important role they played in supervising servants and apprentices. Simultaneously, the resistance movement abetted the preexisting view of young servants and apprentices as disorderly, as they became particularly suspect for undermining the economy and peace of neighborhoods. Viewed in this light, the cases of cruelty reveal a desire on the part of the judiciary to assert its authority in the face of protests and to maintain the economic and social might of masters. In an era in which revolutionaries used violence to circumvent the Crown and local governments, court officials protected the property rights of individuals, and only when there was overwhelming evidence of harm would they protect servants and apprentices.

New trends meant white servant abuse received less publicity in the era leading up to independence, but the instability of the times offered servants other means to get out of abusive situations. The declining number of abuse prosecutions and grants of freedom to servants meant the public was less aware of instances of cruelty and of their ramifications. Of course, this trend did not occur everywhere and it was not long lasting. Individuals still believed that children and youth had a right to serve without excessive punishment, but the larger concerns of society meant private negotiations between masters, families, and communities were surer and quicker ways to attaining servants' safety.

Publicizing the Cruelty of Slavery

In the decade before the declaration of independence, society would do little more to protect slaves than it had in previous generations. African Americans continued to be the leaders in their fight for justice and they pushed back against violence and abuse by using white friends, neighbors, and lawyers who could offer them protection or legal assistance. They publicized the cruelty of slave masters both at home and abroad through the press, lawsuits, and interpersonal communication. While some whites spoke against violence they witnessed, local communities did not fully endorse the idea that African Americans had a right to live without molestation, and many professed that physical discipline was the best way to maintain order. In this regard, African American slaves experienced the revolution in ways similar to white servants. Only the most radical among the white colonists took up efforts to better the conditions of African Americans. The half-hearted attempts of the white revolutionary generation to ameliorate abuse exemplifies the same tensions court officials saw between promoting servants' safety and protecting masters' rights. Individual and community-wide actions taken to publicize the cruelty of slaveholders were often politically motivated, and governments did little beyond what they had done in the colonial era outside of condemning and prohibiting the slave trade. The biggest change to come out of the years before independence, however, was the growth of a movement toward acknowledging that cruelty was a by-product of slavery and the radicalization of some white antislavery advocates.

The antislavery movement had much room for growth among whites. In the colonial era, white northerners had focused on the horrors of slavery in the West Indies or the southern colonies, and this pattern would continue with light criticism that accused northern slaveholders of being unchristian. With the imperial crisis came a new frankness among some white antislavery writers, and they more often discussed the injustice of slavery that occurred at home. In 1766, Timothy Pickering, who would later become a town selectmen and member of the Committee of Correspondence, urged Massachusetts to divest itself of slaves because slavery was immoral. Pickering made note of the horrors of the slave trade but also wrote that if slaves "refuse to work . . . they are severely whipt, by their masters or sent to prisons & whipt there."[25] Acknowledging the abuse of slaves, Pickering made an important critique of slaveholding practices and the government's role in perpetuating violence against slaves. Masters doled out whippings as a form of encouraging work and obedience, and the criminal justice system's incitement to violence against slaves offered another way of maintaining the social economy of violence. The majority of white antislavery writers, however, continued to focus on redirecting the horrors of slavery elsewhere. They questioned the effects of slavery in creating depravity among slaveholders, or the possibility that slavery could undermine the American Revolution, rather than investigating its effects on African Americans.[26] Though these writings did not confront the abuse of slaves, they did provide an opening for more discussion about the immorality of slavery and for African Americans to provide their own perspectives.

African Americans played a central role in the radicalization of white antislavery activists. Taking direct action by seeking out allies or running from abusers, African Americans initiated the conversations and alliances in the incipient antislavery movement that connected colonists with a larger movement in the Atlantic World.[27] Anthony Benezet ramped up his earlier efforts to organize against the slave trade and called for a total cessation of it within the British Empire. He centered his writing on the experiences of Africans in the slave trade and the "cruel chastizements" meted out by slave owners in the West Indies.[28] Though he focused on slaves abroad, Benezet educated African Americans in the colonies, eventually setting up a separate school for them in Philadelphia, and his urgency reflected his awareness of African Americans' perspectives. Benezet exhorted Quakers and others to give up slaves, and in 1775, he founded the first American antislavery organization, the Society for the Relief of Free Negroes Unlawfully Held in Bondage. Benezet influenced others to take up the mantle of antislavery, and he and his allies coordinated their efforts to end the slave trade with Granville Sharp, an abolitionist in Britain.[29] Sharp's radicalization stemmed from meeting Jonathan Strong, a slave so severely beaten by his master he spent four months in a hospital. Sharp and Strong would fight for and win Strong's freedom. Granville's politicization around issues of slavery led to his involvement in other cases, including that of James Somerset. Somerset arrived in England a slave and was resold to another master after running away. He pushed Sharp and the antislavery movement to create legal and ethical arguments supporting a case for his freedom and the illegitimacy of slavery more broadly. In 1772, the Somerset decision resulted in his personal freedom, with Lord Mansfield asserting that English common law did not support slavery and that Africans could not be forcibly removed from England. Though the case did not make slavery illegal, it galvanized those fighting to end the slave trade and sparked further transcontinental communication, particularly between Quakers and British antislavery advocates.[30] Relationships with African Americans were central to the radicalization of white antislavery allies, who learned first-hand accounts of the violence and psychological terror of slavery.

In Massachusetts, slaves initiated at least twenty-four freedom suits after 1763, as opposed to the six suits initiated between 1799 and 1763.[31] Citing cruel usage and the assaults experienced by slaves, the new freedom suits contrasted with colonial-era cases in which slaves sued based on wrongful contracts or having been born free.[32] The individualized stories of violence and suffering had a remarkable effect on the jurists of Massachusetts, who allowed these cases to move forward and most often sided with African Americans (with only one freedom suit denied by the Supreme Judicial Court).[33] Sharing their stories of suffering with whites, African Americans bore their scars and made appeals that led whites to think beyond themselves and to consider the perspectives of slaves. Whites also served as witnesses or even lawyers for slaves, while others would write or speak out on the issue. African Americans' effective marshaling of their stories of enslavement in their interactions with whites pushed debates about slavery, but the right to sue was not available to slaves in New York; this denied an important opportunity to publicly explore their experiences in an environment that demanded decisions.

African Americans and their lawyers used slaveholders' acts of violence to test slaveholders' property rights by blending the successful freedom suits from the past with new evidence of particular assaults. In 1768, Amos Newport sued his owner, Joseph Billing, claiming he assaulted him and falsely imprisoned him by holding him as a slave. Newport and his legal team challenged slavery itself more broadly, and they did not have evidence that a contract or promise of freedom existed between him and his master. Billing's lawyers counter-argued that

Newport's suit "ought not to be Answerd because he says that the said Amos is the proper Negro Slave of said Josephs."[34] Laws required slaves to prove their freedom to contest assaults and imprisonment because from the judiciary's perspective the question was whether slaveholders had a right to dispose of their property as they pleased. By investigating Newport's claims of an assault, Massachusetts opened a debate about the lawfulness of slavery and the inherent violence of the institution. One side held that violence against slaves and the institution of slavery itself were ill-founded. The other side went so far as to argue that a master had the right to take a slave's life. Both arguments set the colony on a clear course to expose the legal and ethical conundrums of slavery.

Freedom suits were critical to the conversations that developed about slavery. At the Hampshire Superior Court, Simeon Strong, a lawyer for Billing, claimed that Massachusetts safeguarded slavery in law and custom, as well as with the approval of England. Although the exact details of Strong's arguments do not remain, John Adams took notes on the broad outlines of both lawyers' arguments. According to Adams, Strong intimated a person had a "A Right to destroy them, if necessary to secure themselves" as they had a "Right to enslave them to repay the Expences of defending ones self." Whether Strong referred to the right to enslave Africans captured in "just wars" or to the right of a master to assault a slave is unclear. However, the origins of Newport's enslavement did not play a role in the case, as the lawyers ultimately argued that the "Presumption here is that an African black is a Slave." At the heart of Strong's defense was the presumption that masters had extensive rights, including the right "to destroy them" by virtue of their property ownership. Although his logic contradicted Massachusetts's laws, it was in line with its practices. Each case tried through the courts resulted in discussions about the nature of the slave contract, a binding agreement to which African Americans were made subject without their consent.

Freedom suits publicized African American experiences and forced their slave masters and white spectators to acknowledge how enslavement occurred. James Putnam, arguing on behalf of Newport, tried unsuccessfully to undermine the legal and moral basis for slavery in New England using a biblical line of reasoning about violence. Putnam referenced Leviticus, which stated a "master might kill his slave" lawfully, to show the hypocritical nature of slavery. He argued against this right, stating that masters "May have a Right to service, during life. But not to life." Putnam believed a higher authority existed and that murder was unlawful regardless of the status of the victim. No person had a right to a person's lifetime of labor or life itself. In Newport's case, it was also important to establish slave murder as morally wrong, given Massachusetts's leniency toward masters. John Sewall, another counselor for Newport, argued that "Humanity, common Justice, and eternal Morality" all went against the existence of slavery in Massachusetts. According to Adams's notes, Sewall made statements regarding "Protection. Break his Head. Indictment will lye." Although we cannot parse out the full argument Sewall made, it is perhaps a reference to the assault made on Newport and the threat Billing posed to Newport's life, given the legal basis for the suit. Adams's notes hint that Sewall questioned the right of masters to ill-treat their slaves.[35] The arguments made by Putnam and Sewall ultimately failed, and Newport remained enslaved. Nevertheless, the antislavery claims and Newport's public testimony about the assault brought attention to the violence he experienced, and the violence of slavery itself, and other suits followed.

In sites such as New York, where freedom suits were not possible, African Americans could not force the matter before the public, and this foreclosed an important means of creating empathy. Nathaniel Appleton, a white Congregationalist minister in Cambridge, wrote "Humanity makes us feel for the evils we know any of our species labour under and unless hardened by education or custom, we naturally resent the pain or hardship of others." As Appleton highlighted, whites had indeed become "hardened" to overlook slavery.[36] Freedom suits were opportunities that enabled a transformation among some whites, who came to recognize the inhumanity of slavery. Each case required a decision—whether in agreement or not with slaves—that made whites consider, however briefly, African Americans' point of view.

Communities pondered the nature of slavery outside of courtrooms, and some Quakers engaged in activities designed to end their communities' involvement in slavery and to protect slaves from excessive abuse. By the 1760s, Pennsylvania's Quakers earnestly appealed to their own membership to divest themselves of slaves, and news of their activities and writings influenced others to reconsider slavery. In 1774, Quakers in New York agreed to penalize those who engaged in slave trading, while other Friends moved to restrict the ill-treatment of slaves. In Rhode Island in 1773, Quakers verbally reprimanded one of their members for tying up her slave and beating her "unmercifully," showing the Friends' movement toward establishing the rights of slaves and limiting slave masters' powers.[37] Interventions like this were rare, but the castigation for abuse shows a major change in some individual and religious communities' perceptions.

Communities outside of the Quakers also considered the treatment of slaves and showed some commitment to socially condemning, if not prosecuting, persons who maimed or murdered their slaves. Amidst the highly politicized context of the American Revolution, individuals spread rumors about abused slaves to indict the political principles of their opposition. Complaints of cruelty against slaves were a stalking horse for other issues that colonists considered more important, but the appearance of concerns about abuse in public papers and commentary marked a change. During the 1770s in Deerfield, Massachusetts, some parishioners of the Church of Christ called into question the ministry of Reverend Jonathan Ashley, and one piece of evidence they used to besmirch him was the charge that he had castrated his slave Cato. On behalf of Ashley, the leadership of the Church of Christ denied the charges and purported that the right to castrate slaves was an offense "a man of Honor (to say nothing of the Christian) would have held most dirty & Infamous." The rumors surrounding Ashley's castration of Cato began after church members suspected Ashely of being a Loyalist, and they propagated the rumor to remove him as their pastor. That the fomenters of this rumor sought to use excessive violence against a slave as a means of ousting Ashley shows that some communities imagined limits on masters' violence and were willing to use gossip to damage their character. Although the law prohibited maiming, officials rarely punished masters for such transgressions. The use of rumors, nevertheless, shows communities conceived of the alleged maiming and sexualized violence against Cato as excessive and an inappropriate use of authority over slaves. Understanding the severe nature of such a charge, the church defended Ashley and its own honor by rebuking Samuel Barnard and the others who continued trying to remove Ashley by spreading this rumor through the 1780s.[38] Others would also fall under suspicion. In 1774, Enoch Bartlet faced accusations of smuggling and selling tea against the wishes of the community of Haverhill, Massachusetts, and the town held a meeting to investigate the matter. According to Bartlet, it was "invidiously suggested" in a newspaper after the town meeting "that I beat and abused my negro for telling the truth, and because he would not lie in my favor, and that I have sold him at a great distance to prevent a discovery about some tea." The allegations suggested he wrongfully sold and beat his slave to cover up his British loyalties, and the gossip persisted even after the community relieved Bartlet of the charges of smuggling tea. Bartlet claimed his detractors sought to "destroy my character . . . and represent me . . . as a vile barbarous and inhuman wretch."[39] The reports about Bartlet reveal the same sense as those in the case of Ashley—that unjust beatings were problematic, particularly in cases where accusations of inflicting them proved a politically expedient means to sully someone's character.

The imperial crisis did not bring about meaningful conversations about the sexual abuse of enslaved women, though gossip about sexual assaults could have similarly undermined slaveholders' claims to public morality and political righteousness. The omission is a telling one that gets at the heart of discussions of cruelty, slavery, and gendered power. The purported sexual violence against Cato and the cruelty against the other enslaved man did not require investigation into their situations. The marks and rumors of violence were indicators of their suffering and the cruelty of their slave masters. Investigating sexual assaults against women required greater commitment to understanding the perspectives of African Americans, as such violence was not always externalized and known outside of the household. Investigations into sexual behavior were decreasingly commonplace by the Revolutionary War, even in Massachusetts, unless it involved well-known cases of adultery. Enslaved women made their suffering known in the same ways as others—through their cries and conversations with others—but finding allies who could be trusted to listen to take action on such information was not likely. African American women knew the odds. Questioning the sexual power and prerogatives of white men to copulate with women was not a significant part of New York or Massachusetts sexual cultures. Both colonies had been much more prone to investigating and ruminating on the sexual behavior of white women and African Americans.[40]

The telling silences in discussions of sexual assaults against enslaved women give evidence of where the movement against cruelty was. It had become expedient to question the ethics of physically abusive slave masters, but whites in New York and Massachusetts did not meaningfully connect the sexual abuse of enslaved women with cruelty or consider the full perspectives of enslaved African Americans. This is clear in all of the abuse cases and murders of African Americans that emerged during the build-up to the Revolutionary War.

Discussions of slaves' rights to humane treatment, even if politically motivated and limited, were steps in the direction of undermining the extensive power of slave masters. Communities that condemned cruelty through gossip inculcated nascent standards about abuse because the perpetrators needed to publicly defend themselves against the charges. Under pressure to account for his activities, Bartlet admitted to selling his slave "for his notorious lying and other faults for which I was unwilling to give due correction, which if it had been applied would have reformed him."[41] In denying the assault on his slave, Bartlet crafted his defense to show his righteousness. He claimed his slave's conduct necessitated physical correction and that he rejected imposing corporal punishment even though it would have solved the problem. To Bartlet's mind, selling his slave, rather than beating him, showed he was part of a modern generation of slave owners who saw physical correction as anathema in the age of reason. Bartlet's sincerity is questionable. Even with his disavowal of his own violence, Bartlet held the assumption that physical punishment remained the best measure to maintain discipline.[42]

In contrast with public condemnations of cruelty, records of African American deaths show communities tolerated extreme negligence, and in some cases, investigations into slaves' deaths seem not to have occurred at all. With white servants, such a practice would be unthinkable. In 1772, *Boston Gazette* reported that a "valuable Negro fellow" drowned by "accidentally" falling into a well. The comment on the value of the slave suggested the loss was for his master, not the man who died or his family. Grand jurors and the government needed cause to investigate deaths, and because the slave had pecuniary value, the town did not envision that his master or others would seek to end his life. Such a mindset denied the humanity of slaves and their many relationships. This death was not isolated. The same year another slave "fell into a Kettle of boiling hot Tar which soon put an end to his Life."[43] Further investigations into how or why these deaths occurred required exploration of the lives of the enslaved, who might have suffered abuse or neglect. Other cases reveal the government's problematic practices in handling and causing slave deaths. In 1772, New York City investigated the death of a slave who had been placed in Bridewell, the city's prison, for misbehavior and drunkenness. While under the care of the city, the slave "underwent the usual discipline of the house for such offences," which included "a plentiful dose of warm water and salt to operate as an emetic, and of lamp oil as a purge, in proportion to the constitution of the patient." After receiving three quarts of water and "2 and a half spoonfulls" of oil, he fell ill which "obliged him to lie down—and between 8 & 9 at night he was discovered to be dead." The government investigated the death and called in surgeons to examine the body. Ultimately, they decided that he died "of excessive drinking, co-operated with the effects of the medicines he had taken." The report suggested the government's culpability given that the city prescribed the "medicines"; however, the coroners determined that "Mr. Dobbs (the operator [in distributing the doses]) was innocent of his death."[44] Though Dobbs did not willfully murder the slave, the "usual discipline" was fraught with danger. Indeed, the reporting on the incident, and of those noted above, avoided assigning agency to anyone other than the enslaved. Newspapers did not hold discussions about whether the city would discontinue the practice given its lethal effects or if whites received such "medicine." The courts let perpetrators go, dismissing culpability even though the cases show, at the very least, extreme neglect of slaves' lives.

Some questioning of governmental and community mishandling of slave murders occurred, and it exposed slaveholders' fears and the role of violence in constructing the racial divide. In 1772, Martin Howard, a chief justice in North Carolina, condemned a grand jury for failing to indict a white man for murdering a slave. *Massachusetts Gazette* republished his essay; he had lived in Rhode Island before being pushed out of the colony for his support of the Stamp Act. Howard believed slavery was a "great evil," and his essay exposed the violence that was crucial to maintaining slavery. "Cruelty is ever bad policy," he wrote, declaring that slave masters should limit their powers (if one allowed slavery) to those that promoted their slaves' labor. He asserted that it "cannot be shown, that a right to murder them will add to our security in their diligence and fidelity." If the institution of slavery left whites fearing for their security, Howard implied it was their own fault for treating slaves harshly and not allowing them access to proper justice. African Americans ran away and committed criminal acts often because of "the rigor or covetousness of his master."[45] White northerners may have initially read Howard's essay as a critique of the South or dismissed it as one penned by a Loyalist, yet his writing fit with their own practices of granting leniency to murderous and violent masters. Howard's defense of slaves' right to life rebuffed that immunity by pointing out that more was at stake in dismissing murder charges against slave masters than giving them total control over slaves' labor. Slaveholders lost in this bargain. Writings like Howard's show an emerging disposition to take slaves' rights seriously, and it was impeccably timed, as a revolution about rights and freedoms was in its inception.

Emerging antislavery literature and the political and religious condemnations of masters' abusive behavior reveal feeble efforts to condemn cruelty during the buildup to declaring independence. Evidence suggests several courts in the revolutionary era also began considering issuing indictments for cruelty, though ultimately masters would not suffer any punishment for their excessive cruelty. In 1773, Henry Marchant, the state attorney general for Rhode Island, forwarded an indictment to the grand jury of the Superior Court after Jabez Reynolds struck his slave Cuff with iron tongs. Cuff bled profusely from his wounds and nearly died. In evidence were the depositions of at least two white witnesses testifying to the effect of Reynolds's attack on Cuff. William Chadsey, a yeoman in North Kingston, disclosed that Reynolds admitted to striking Cuff with his hands and the iron tongs after Cuff refused to go cut wood. Although the court wrote up an indictment, the words "Not a True Bill" were written across the outside of it.[46] The community failed to move forward and press for the indictment, but the possibility of a criminal charge showed a new mindset among the white community. The white witnesses willingly testified to JPs against Reynolds's abusive conduct, because they felt his violence went too far in nearly murdering Cuff. On the other hand, the grand jury failed to take up the case (if it was ever put before them) despite the evidence. Masters remained shielded because the law construed slaves as a mix of property and persons, and courts—made up of community members—did not interfere with masters' rights. So long as slavery existed, there would be limits on legal interventions, even as communities considered the implications of violence.

When communities failed to indict masters for assaults and cruelty, it was not for lack of evidence. Runaway ads detailed the scars of slaves, showing that the effects of violence were visible to whites in their daily interactions with slaves. In 1770, Joseph Moody posted an advertisement asking others to keep a watch out for his slave Prince, who "had his Jaw Bone broke, it is an obstruction to him in Eating, has had his right Leg broke, and is a little crooked, has lost two or three Toes of his left Foot."[47] It's difficult to imagine neighbors and community members not noticing the torment Prince experienced daily, and yet it seems he labored under this situation for some time. Community members may have spoken with Moody to curtail his violence, but the law was on slaveholders' sides and gave them wide latitude in how they treated slaves.

Although governments did not actively prosecute individuals for murdering and assaulting slaves, New York did respond in new ways to violence of slave traders. In 1772, Whitehead Hicks, mayor of New York, investigated John Lovel, a chief mate aboard a slave ship named *York*, for "inhuman treatment of sundry negro slaves." The complaint emerged from one of Lovel's shipmates, and Hicks took depositions from eight of the men aboard the vessel, showing that he took care with the case. Charles Surisco, a member of the crew, described "that he frequently saw John Lovel the Chief mate beat the negro—Slaves on board . . . in a Cruel Manner with ropes, Staves, Hedding, & the handle of a broom." The crew expressed concern about the severity of the beating and the harsh tools (not including whips) used. As Surisco's testimony continued, it became clear that Lovel had done more than assault Africans; he had actually caused the death of one. Surisco noted that Lovel had "particularly [beaten] one Walker who afterwards died." The depositions did not suggest that these beatings intended to discipline unruly slaves, and this might have been an additional factor that spurred Surisco and others to notify the government. Surisco claimed he witnessed "a negro woman, named Neura, whom the deponent saw Lovel tie up to the main shrouds and beat her with a Fishes tale full of Notches, in a very Inhuman manner."[48] Though sexual abuse of women was common aboard slave ships, the witnesses did not identify or indict Lovel for that. Hicks's many depositions suggest that the court of admiralty desired a full prosecution of the case, though records do not indicate the court charged Lovel with murder. The government's interest in the case and the mariners' willingness to report the violence aboard the vessel reveal a growing disdain for life-threatening treatment of slaves.

The slave trade, with its many horrors and barbarity, was the main arena in which white northerners questioned the violence of slavery. Rather than looking inward, the trade served as a convenient foil to investigations of white northerners' own practices, and they made strides in bringing the traffic to a halt. In 1773, the town of Salem urged Massachusetts to consider an act to end the "future Importation of Negroes into this Province; their Slavery being repugnant to the natural rights of mankind." Similarly, in 1774, New York distillers "unanimously" resolved not to "sell any Rum, or other Spirits for the Purpose of carrying on the Slave Trade." That same year the Continental Congress urged Americans to avoid trade with Britain, and the distillers were likely primarily motivated to interrupt their trade in response to the economic boycott. In 1774, Rhode Island, Connecticut, and Georgia prohibited the importation of slaves, and Delaware followed in 1776. Wartime measures limited the slave trade temporarily, and after the war, Congress enacted more permanent measures to prevent involvement in the trade.[49] Charging the British with cruelty for their engagement in the slave trade provided an opportunity to reposition British North Americans as morally upright in contrast with the practices of slave traders. The boycotts and protests to end the slave trade were not only politically expedient, they were indictments of the trade itself.

African Americans demanded that northerners also confront the brutality of slavery at home. Massachusetts slaves repeatedly petitioned their towns and state for an end to the institution, and their writings underscored the hardships of slavery from their point of view. In 1774, enslaved African Americans in Massachusetts asked, "how can the master and the Slave be said to fullfil that command Live in love . . . [and] Beare yea onenothers Bordenes[?] How can the master be said to Beare my Borden When he Beares me down with the Have [heavy] chanes of slavery and operson [oppression] against my will[?]"[50] Proposing a society of brotherly love rather than enslavement went against the internal logic of slavery, in which masters enforced their will through violence. Other writings more pointedly criticized the violence and emotional turmoil of slavery. In 1774, Caesar Sarter, a former slave in Newburyport, Massachusetts, asked whites to imagine what it was like to be a slave and "be plied with that conclusive argument, the cat-o'nine tails, to reduce you to what your inhuman masters would call Reason." He asked whites to acknowledge African American suffering and put themselves in a slave's position rather than viewing slavery as something apart from themselves. In doing so, Sarter subverted assumptions about the kindness and humanity of slave masters in the North and highlighted violence. He noted he had "no less than eleven relatives suffering in bondage" and demanded whites concede the immorality and extensive impact of the institution.[51]

African American partnerships with the British were a form of resistance too, and whites perceived their friendly association with occupying forces as a threat. African Americans leveraged the occupation for financial gain and formed relationships with soldiers. The news of the Somerset case made the British an attractive ally for African Americans. In Massachusetts, fears of commingling resulted in reports of planned insurrections in Boston (1774) and Framingham (1775). Whites found African Americans' activities so questionable that in 1775, Artemas Ward, the commander of American forces at Bunker Hill, issued an order that African Americans found "straggling about the Camps . . . be seized and confined."[52] For whites wanting security and stability during the imperial crisis, African Americans' interactions and dealings with soldiers became suspect and contrary to the institution of slavery. Many already considered African Americans' connections with each other to be a threat, and the occupation forced whites to consider their own role in the bonds created among African Americans and external parties such as British soldiers.

The radicalization of some white antislavery advocates who pressed for more thorough change in response to African American freedom suits, petitions, and writing was the major achievement in the decade before the war. After African Americans petitioned the committees of correspondence in Worcester and Bristol, Massachusetts, officials in Worcester condemned slavery, noting they "abhor the enslaving of any of the human race, particularly the NEGROES in this country."[53] Though they would not add legal enforcement to their statement, Worcester asked the government to adopt abolition as they began making connections between the struggles of the colonies and African Americans. The Dutchess County Friends in New York demanded the New York Yearly Meeting begin the process of divesting their membership of slaves. In 1774, they passed a proposal forcing members to release slaves once they reached the age of 18 for women and 21 for men. The proposal had radical implications for the state and looked much like the gradual emancipation legislation that would emanate first from Pennsylvania followed by other northern states beginning in 1780.[54] Antislavery advocates needed more organizational growth and concrete plans, like that of the Dutchess Friends, to truly begin ridding the region of slavery.

The fractious period that led to the American Revolution did not result in a full-scale change for African Americans. Real change necessitated more than conversations and shaming. Early Americans tolerated extreme abuse and murder in most locations, though Quakers and some communities began demanding more of one another. The possibility of indictments against abuse and the gossip about abusive slaveholders were signs that new standards could emerge. Yet many whites were motivated more by political and social expediency than by concern for African Americans' welfare. African Americans continued revealing their experiences, but more whites like those who testified, wrote editorials, or served as lawyers for African Americans needed to stand up to effect meaningful change. Many whites needed greater reasons and cause to open their eyes to the abuse before them, and they continued to ignore the cruelty of slavery. White New Yorkers did not benefit from the fuller range of discussions about slavery that occurred in places such as Massachusetts, where African Americans shared their perspectives through lawsuits and by serving as witnesses. The next ten years would test the limits of slavery and whites' ability to overlook cruelty as war brought about new realities.

The young men who died in the Boston Massacre had a legacy—one of fear and one of revolution. African Americans' and youths' embrace of the American Revolution challenged society to consider how hierarchy and cruelty were intertwined. The power given to masters meant they could create order, but they could also create backlash. Servants and slaves took the opportunities available to them and ran from cruelty and dependence, making slavery and servitude unstable. The war created even bigger challenges, and the loyalty of all of society become more important and politicized. Wives, servants, and slaves bargained for a new future, one in which violence against them could be construed as dangerous.

Chapter 5

Questionable Loyalties

In 1765, Massachusetts executed Joseph Lightly for the murder of his "pretended wife" Elizabeth Post. Lightly became acquainted with Post after deserting the British Army three times. When he met Post, he had been wandering around the northeast looking to rob people or otherwise support himself. Lightly quickly "made a Suit to her, not with any Intention of marrying her." The aim of his seduction was to get her to "sell her cows," as he had no property himself and was in need of financial means. Elizabeth Post introduced Lightly to her family, and Lightly lied to them about owning a farm, going so far as to ask Post to "go with him" to his fictitious residence. In meeting Post's family and requesting she live with him, Lightly's actions suggested to her family that he intended to formalize their arrangement or that he would cohabit with her in ways that were understood to be similar to a marriage. It would have been particularly brash to suggest Post sell her portion of the family estate without declaring his intentions to the family. Nevertheless, Lightly maintained Post was only his "reputed wife."[1] Lightly must have found taking leave of Post harder than he initially imagined, for they traveled throughout the countryside together, eventually making their way to Waltham. Lightly soon became enraged at Post's behavior. She told others she was married to him, though he denied ever having formalized their arrangement. To his greater consternation, he reported she "behaved in a most adulterous Manner," a term normally reserved for a spouse. Lightly did not share details about what exactly she did, but he claimed her behavior "caused me to be more gross with my Tongue, and use her with bad Language." Post complained to the people they met that he "us'd her ill, in spending her Money."[2] Lightly blamed Post for his treatment of her, claiming her behavior provoked him.

Lurking in the background of this murder case are examples of the major issues facing abused wives, servants, and slaves during the Revolution. The local community knew things were not well with the couple, but they did not intervene beyond acknowledging Post's complaints about Lightly, though the transiency of the couple may have reduced the visibility of their issues. Local communities often ignored the cruelty of slave masters too. By the eighteenth century, the government would step in to prosecute abuse only in cases of extreme violence and murders, and would not intervene for slaves. The criminal justice system categorized the overwhelming majority of reported wife, servant, and slave assault cases as non-offenses—actions that needed management rather than punishment. There are no records of Elizabeth Post turning to the government to sue for a bond for peace against her husband. Massachusetts and New York continued to use bonds as the primary means of dealing with abuse and rarely established penalties, which left wives, slaves, and servants vulnerable. In this regard, wives and servants still had more advantages than slaves, who were unable to find any government protections for abuse. In the case of Post, Lightly denied causing her death. He said she died "of Sickness" and that the four witnesses against him "perjur'd themselves." The indictment for her murder gave the lie to this: authorities determined she was beaten with a club, causing a wound that went three inches deep into her chest.[3]

Perhaps Post would have chosen to return to her family had she thought she could have left without harm. Wives, servants, and slaves abandoned their ties to masters and husbands in greater numbers during the war. This was an indictment of abusive masters and husbands as well as of an unjust system. The decisions wives, servants, and slaves made were intimate and personal, but also political and laden with meaning for a society formally separating from Britain. Though different types of loyalty were expected of wives, servants, and slaves, loyalty played a role in the way each of their contestations of abuse took shape. The Revolutionary War provided greater options for dependent peoples to contest cruelty, and slaves, servants, and wives made progress in identifying abuse as a public problem in their resistance. Though the process was slow, slavery was ultimately purged in Massachusetts through African Americans' and white abolitionists' masterful use of freedom suits and petitions. A shift in societal acceptance of women's right to separate from their husbands was also underway, and this directly related to women voicing their concerns about abuse in print literature and through the legal system. Print literature was an effective space to explore the connections between cruelty and the powers afforded to masters and husbands, because the new context of the Revolutionary War meant they could connect their plight with larger political and legal issues. Yet changes were uneven. New York did not adopt the changes in slavery and divorce, and young white servants and apprentices continued focusing on extralegal forms of mediation for abuse.

Americans discovered that women, young adults, and African Americans could undermine or support war efforts. Running away upset labor patterns, but it also presented a threatening specter in wartime as dependent peoples did not always choose to follow the United States. Loyalty grew in importance, and this gave dependent peoples more power to contest abuse and make it visible to those who previously ignored resistance and violence.

White Wives at War

Post challenged Lightly by discussing his treatment of her with others, and Lightly admitted he resented Post's smearing of his name. He felt her words caused him to get a "worse Name than I deserved," though he disclosed that his intentions with Post were never sincere.[4] Society would allow husbands much leeway in running their households, and abuse was often overlooked. Women defended themselves and their families from abuse, but now did so in context of war, a time in which their sexual and familial loyalty was particularly prized. As in the colonial era, courts were unwilling to prosecute white men for anything less than extreme violence, and abused white wives had to find ways of seeking safety from abuse. White wives persisted in pursuing bonds for peace against abusive husbands and sought legal separations in greater numbers than they had previously. Marriage became a political metaphor to argue for independence, and by the end of the eighteenth century, women began to see shifts in societal acceptance of divorce and separations. However, attempts to expand the natural rights of individuals provided little return for women, who were more often figured as dependent members of households in need of oversight. Widespread acceptance of the righteousness of the hierarchy in marriage served to minimize community support for white women's freedom from abuse, but white wives' resistance show they continued to prioritize their rights to safety and freedom.

Massachusetts maintained its stance on prosecuting, punishing, and socially condemning men suspected of murdering their spouses, and this proved to be more intensive than in cases involving slaves' deaths. Communities drew a clear line that murder and intent to murder were not within the rights of married men, even as they often ignored signs of repeatedly abusive men whose violence escalated. Massachusetts prosecuted at least four men between 1763 and 1789, and the court found one not guilty and three guilty.[5] New York prosecuted at least one man during the same period. Writers in newspapers also spoke against wife murder. When the wife of Mr. Murphy, a shoemaker in New York City, was found dead, newspapers reported he was suspected of "savagely abusing his wife." They condemned "the outrage and barbarity of the monster, her husband," who had left the children with no one to care for them.[6] Such language was not forthcoming in the murder of slaves and no lamentations were made for their children upon their deaths. And unlike in slave murder cases, the rights of men to correct their subordinates were not mentioned as justification for wife murders.

The class and race of perpetrators were larger determining factors for courts in cases of wife murder and intent-to-murder than the rights and privileges men accrued through marriage. Among the four men prosecuted in Massachusetts was Levi Whitney, a white gentleman, who was accused of poisoning his wife. The Superior Court found him not guilty, but guilt in cases involving poison was historically difficult to prove when not involving slaves, who faced a presumption of guilt. Whitney had the means to put up a competent defense, unlike the three other cases of wife murder, which involved men of the lower sort, who used weapons that resulted in loss of blood and tied perpetrators to the crimes. In 1784, William Padley, a white laborer in Boston, stabbed his wife and the court found him guilty of intent to murder. He was sentenced to sit in the gallows for one hour, receive a whipping of thirty lashes, and repay the costs of the trial, revealing the importance of public penance in such cases.[7] Men of color did not find the court willing to reduce charges or punishments in cases of murder. Isaac Coombs, an Indian man, murdered his wife after repeatedly beating her as they traveled through Marblehead to the Great Swamp. Witnesses in a local tavern saw that Sage Coombs had suffered some trauma to her head before the final assault that resulted in her death, and they inquired about it. At Isaac's instigation, Sage did not reveal that her husband had struck her with a stick and a sharp stone. The couple continued to the Great Swamp, but Sage Coombs could no longer walk because she was weak from loss of blood. Isaac confessed to kicking and hitting her with his fists and feet, and to causing her death when he "raised her head & let fall on a Rock two or three times." Massachusetts put Coombs to death for the murder, and its willingness to execute Coombs likely related to his poverty and ethnicity.[8] Coombs did not have the wealth of Whitney, and Massachusetts had practiced greater severity in punishments against men and women of color for crimes. The severity of Padley's punishment is in line with other sentences for wife murder or manslaughter, though occasionally men would suffer imprisonment in addition to whippings and public shaming.

For women, the stakes in committing murder were much higher because husband murder was defined as petit treason, and the punishment for women found guilty was to be burned at the stake. The same was true for slaves and servants such as Mark and Phillis, discussed in chapter 3, who murdered their masters and faced more serious charges and punishments. The gendered charges and punishments in spousal murder laid bare community understandings of women's marital vows. After one woman planned and executed a murder, one editorial hoped that women would "take warning" and "be disposed to behave as become their sex in every relation of life." The writer believed women "were formed for pleasure and finished for delight" and that to gain the esteem of their husbands they should "behave in a discreet and winning manner." Women declared their loyalty and became subjects to their husbands in law upon marriage, even as sentimental literature increasingly portrayed marriage as a match born of reason and love. Wives exerted powers and pressure in marriage, but their claims of self-defense were not legally justifiable causes for reduced charges. In at least three cases, Massachusetts charged women with petit treason and murdering their spouses during the Revolution.[9] It is with some irony that women continued to face charges of petit treason for spousal murder, even as colonists brokered and fought a war for their independence from Britain.

Marriage, like childhood and slavery, served as a metaphor by which supporters and detractors of the crown could understand the stakes of independence. Wives' presumed subordination and loyalty to their husbands were means of exploring the relationship between Britain and the colonies. In 1775, John Leonard, a wealthy lawyer in Taunton, Massachusetts, supported reconciliation with Britain and suggested the colony consider how their actions would look if extended to "private life." Should Massachusetts declare its independence, it would mean that "the least failure in the reciprocal duties of worship & obedience in the matrimonial contract would justify a divorce." Given the importance of marriage to maintaining order and readying children for adulthood, the specter of easily broken marriages was an apt means of prompting colonists to consider the ramifications of their actions. John Adams intended to alleviate fears about how political independence related to marriage by responding that "[E]lopement and adultery would by these principles justify a divorce, but not the least failure or many smaller failures in the reciprocal duties."[10] True to Massachusetts law, Adams did not stipulate that spousal abuse was a cause for a full divorce; he figured sexual loyalty as the key to the marital contract. Other dialogues about how far the marital contract extended demonstrated that spousal assault was not an agreed-upon justification for divorce, even as "cruelty" was the byword to describe British political actions. Writers deployed their ideas about marriage and the dangers of divorce as means of persuading the public to the side of Tories or Patriots, but both sides upheld the marital state as of primary significance and did not wish to see it erode.

In the build-up to independence, white women and their allies used print culture to press their case for more equity in marriage. This strategy was timely because print culture in the United States took on new importance, with newspapers and broadsides informing an eager public about events. Some writers did not explicitly name wife abuse as an issue, but they hinted at the mistreatment of women in marriage. "A lady" wrote, "Wife and servant are the same / But only differ in the name, / For when that fatal knot is ty'd / Which nothing, nothing can divide, / When she the word obey has made, / Then all that's kind is laid aside, / And nothing left but state and pride." Comparisons of wives with servants pointed toward the legal impairment of married women under the doctrine of coverture. Indeed, servants' murders of their masters were defined as petit treason just as wives' murders of their husbands were. "A lady" likened the power of husbands to that of an "Eastern Prince," an image that drew on racial tropes to question the legitimacy of wives' legal subordination. Derisive characterizations of marriages in the East served as a bulwark for Anglo-European patriarchy because they contrasted with the presumed sentimental and loving kindness inherent in European marriages. "A lady" described the power husbands accrued in marriage as leading to a change in their temperament. "Fierce as an Eastern Prince he grows, / And all his innate rigour shows." She moved toward the issue of spousal assault and intimated some of the dangers in women's subjection. At the same time, the comparison with an eastern prince displaced husbands' bad behavior geographically and experientially, as in the case of those who wrote against the slave trade instead of focusing on African American welfare at home. A more explicit discussion of the ramifications of hierarchy and wife abuse occurred in her description of women's perceived powerlessness in marriage. She wrote that wives "fear her husband as her God, / Him still must serve, him still obey, / And nothing act, and nothing say / but what her haughty Lord thinks fit."[11] Observing that wives must submit to the temperament of their husbands, "A lady" explored the problematic nature of women's subordination. Discussions of this nature used wives' suffering to show the inequities in society and push for changes.

White women also directly drew connections between wife abuse and their legal and social impediments in a quest to improve their position as states refigured their constitutions. When Abigail Adams wrote the now famous letter to her husband asking that he "Remember the Ladies" in the new laws the Continental Congress constructed, she reminded him of the importance of protecting women. "Do not put such unlimited power into the hands of the Husbands. Remember all Men would be tyrants if they could. . . . Why then, not put it out of the power of the vicious and the Lawfull to use us with cruelty and indignity with impunity."[12] It would be hard to mistake the meaning and logic in her writing. Early Americans hoped couples would solve their own problems. The abuse of women, Abigail Adams argued, was different and required fixing. To safeguard women, she pointed toward their legal status, as had other women writers in the eighteenth century. Adams asked for new protections, but she also wanted the new government to grant women a larger political role to ensure that such treatment would not be allowed.

Opening a space for the discussion of white women's rights did not lead to granting those rights. Women who faced abuse required more immediate interventions than the process of altering public opinion allowed, and once the war commenced, society's willingness to address wife abuse subsided substantially. Women's sexual loyalty took on political significance during occupation and war, with British forces figured as sexual and political competition for men. Print literature featured men's roles in fighting for colonial independence as sacrifices for the nation in the names of their families and future generations. Enlistment campaigns directly appealed to men's patriarchal roles as protectors of women. In 1778, "Inimiga Tirannis" asked men to imagine the death of their beloved mothers, wives, and children should they not stand up and fight for the states. Consider, the author suggested, "Thy loving spouse, at the motion of whose lips melancholy wing'd her way, on whose brow sat the sweets of love, in whose embrace the dart of pleasure struck thy soul, rifled of those charms, lay soaking in her blood." Not in the least bit subtle, enlistment campaigns used urgent pleas that drew on the fears of colonists surrounding the murders and rapes in the campaigns of the British and Hessians in 1777.[13] Concerns regarding marital violence had no place among wartime narratives. Newspapers would continue to note when wife murder occurred and would condemn the accused, but reflections focused on the barbarity of the murder and the despoilment of the family. New developments in supporting and protecting women from abusive husbands were not forthcoming.

White women took day-to-day actions to restrain their abusive husbands despite the new emphasis on wifely loyalty. Abused white wives turned to JPs for bonds of peace against their husbands during the imperial crisis and war, and the bonds were the primary means through which the government played a role in abused wives' safety. Courts opened only periodically during the crisis due to protests and war, but when women sought out legal interventions from JPs, they did not need to appear in court. For white women in urban areas like Boston and New York City, the proximity of local JPs made bonds a particularly effective means of defending themselves. Between 1764 and 1789, at least nine women in Boston secured bonds against their husbands for abuse;

more complaints likely existed but are lost because of the disruptions in record-keeping during the war.[14] Records in less populous portions of the state reveal that JPs there also responded to white women's abuse complaints, with at least five women in Middlesex, three in Plymouth, and two in Worcester Counties seeking assistance.[15] Like servants, white wives sought to expose the levels of violence against them to attain support from court officials, and they brought witnesses when they could. Much violence occurred in the home, however, and private conflict could be difficult to substantiate in more rural areas. Although wives had a well-established right to seek bonds for peace, they also had to show they were not seeking to undermine their husbands' authority. As in some other assault cases, JPs made sure white wives did not ask for bonds for reasons other than abuse, and some JPs authenticated this in their records. Clear marks of violence and witnesses were especially important for suspicious JPs.

White wives returned to JPs when they suffered repeated abuse from husbands who failed to keep their bonds for peace. Asking for bond extensions could be particularly frustrating for wives because the first instance failed to send a long-term message to their husbands that the community would not tolerate spousal assault. In June 1778, Elizabeth Bemis complained to Justice Thaddeus Mason that her husband "hath already assaulted & beat her, and further hath threatned her in Such Sort, that She is afraid that the Said Samuel Bemis, will beat, wound, maim, kill or do her Some other bodily harm."[16] Bemis had clearly been experiencing abuse for some time when she made this complaint, and she had to repeatedly seek out interventions over the course of her marriage. Though she was likely gratified she had a place to turn for help, at the next sitting of the Middlesex County court, she returned to ask that the court continue her husband's bond until the following year. The court agreed, but a little more than a year later, she returned to a JP, again asking for further protection. Although it was the third time Bemis asked JPs for help, they did not prosecute her husband and instead held him to yet another bond. Between the first series of cases in 1778 and that case in 1780, the Bemis family had moved from Cambridge to Lexington, and she had to develop a relationship with a new JP. Justice Thaddeus Bowman investigated Elizabeth's intentions and found that Elizabeth "Requires the Same [recognizance] not for any Private Male [malice], hatred, or evil will but Simply that She is afraid that her Said Husband will do her Some (further) Bodily hurt."[17] Justice Bowman's scrutiny of her testimony was a regular part of his job, yet Bemis's violence had been repeatedly proven by other JPs who had issued bonds. Changes had to occur more broadly in society to alter the attitudes and actions of JPs to give women greater protections and less scrutiny. Bemis' attempts to protect herself reveal how women's movement from urban to more rural locales could also spread news and use of the legal processes open to women.

Communities continued to see assaults against white wives as lesser offenses than those against nonrelatives, and white women's legal actions to ensure their safety occurred in an environment that did not routinely criminalize abuse. Courts sat irregularly and some records are missing, but what remains shows that in Suffolk County, Massachusetts, the court fully prosecuted only one man between 1760 and 1789; and Plymouth and Worcester Counties also prosecuted one each, and Middlesex County prosecuted two outside the war years. Other prosecutions, such as for fornication, occurred routinely. In New York City, no prosecutions of abusive husbands occurred between 1760 and the start of war in 1776, at which point courts were often closed until the end of war. New York courts had a worse record than Massachusetts for prosecuting abusers, and it's unlikely they would have changed course during the war given their record in dealing with servants.[18] Often white men's abuse of white women in these cases was one charge among others they faced in court or in the short term. Indeed, in at least three of the five cases in Massachusetts, the men faced other charges.[19] The case against John Daniels, a yeoman from Grafton, stands out for being prosecuted during the war. Witnesses saw Daniels take a stone in his hand and heard him state "he would split her brain out." In 1780, JP Josiah Green believed Daniels posed a threat to his wife's life and found him guilty. Green had him swear to the peace in the sum of 800 pounds and asked that he appear in court at a later date. The following year, Daniels was found guilty of cohabitation, which began as early as 1779. For that crime, his punishment was to sit at pillory for one hour, suffer three months' imprisonment, and make a fifty-pound bond to keep the peace for three years.[20] The lack of frequency and the existence of concurrent charges in cases against wife abusers suggest abuse was not well established as an actual crime. However, communities clearly considered wife abuse a greater crime than the abuse of slaves.

The courts continued to neglect enforcing appropriate punishment in prosecuted cases, and even released white men from their fines in most cases, which was a unique aspect to wife abuse cases. Out of four counties in Massachusetts, only Plymouth fined a man for abusing his wife during the revolutionary era, despite the fact that more complaints of violence than that one merited punishment. Fines for wife abuse were light in Massachusetts, usually around five shillings. The penalties were comparable to punishments for other less serious assaults committed by nonrelatives. Husbands like Daniels were usually forced to make bonds even though their violence was more threatening and could lead to murder.[21] As in cases from the seventeenth century, courts were not averse to overturning fines, which posed another problem in creating standards against abuse. In 1771, when a Plymouth court found Joshua Turner guilty of assaulting his wife in a "barbarous and inhuman manner," it fined him twenty shillings. The fine was above the norm due to the severity of the assault and because the court concurrently found him guilty of assaulting another man. When Turner appealed to have his fine for assaulting his wife and the man abated, the court agreed.[22] Because punishments were not upheld, the criminality of wife abuse was dubious, though public prosecutions and bonds for peace set some standards.

As had occurred with servants and slaves in the revolutionary era, white women took direct action outside of the judiciary to serve the immediate needs of securing safety. In one extraordinary case, women formed an ad hoc organization to punish an abuser, which fulfilled the needs of the community to rein in egregious abuse. In 1784, a group of women in Fairfield, Connecticut, punished a man who "had frequently practiced matrimonial discipline, and had made his wife a proselyte to the doctrine of non-resistance and passive obedience." Records do not indicate if the abused wife had sought injunctions for her husband's behavior, but the courts in Connecticut had avoided serving as agents of change or justice in most cases. The courts' abdication of this role opened it up to the "COHORT of her sex," which stripped the abusive husband of his shirt and forced him to "RUN the GANTTOPE [sic] between the two lines of female heroes, who were regularly drawn up for that purpose." The newspaper reporting the event wrote with approval about the events and the "female heroes" involved.[23] The martial description of the women as being "regularly drawn up" suggests the community appreciated their activity in setting standards of appropriate behavior. In serving in this capacity, women took a stand against abuse, but the failure of the courts created the space for their action.

Occasionally white men stepped in to protect white women too, though the lessons society took from these moments varied during the imperial crisis. In Newark, New Jersey, a crowd with "black'd faces . . . seized a man of that place, who was known to be jealous of his wife; and upon a supposition that his jealousy was injurious to his wife, they gave him a severe whipping." The community's punishment of the husband indicates he had taken to beating his wife; defamation alone would not warrant their actions. The newspaper coverage of the event characterized the crowd's violence as an "unlawful enterprise," and the writer warned against it. Actions by the "mob" or "rabble" had come under criticism as a result of the tumultuous protests against the Stamp Act, and the writer used this event as a tool to decry public disorders. After whipping the husband, the crowd learned that the wife had in fact committed adultery, and they believed she and her lover were now in need of punishment. They "gave each of them a still more severe whipping, and left them both tied all night."[24] From the writer's perspective, the moral was that extralegal violence was inferior to other methods of addressing societal ills. In this particular case, public interference into marriage had negative consequences because the husband was right in assuming his wife's guilt.

Bystander intervention like the instances in New Jersey and Connecticut does not appear to have increased during the era of the American Revolution, and many women continued to suffer from abuse without assistance from the community. Only when violence resulted in death or maiming would the community step forward, instead choosing to see fights as private. In 1773, James Bell killed his wife, Christian Bell, in the North End of Boston, a densely populated part of the city. Upon discovery of her body, neighbors immediately assumed her husband committed the murder. One newspaper reported that neighbors suspected him because it was "notorious to numbers of people that this woman had for several years past very undeservedly suffered frequent and cruel abuses from her said husband."[25] That neighbors knew about the abuse and characterized it as "undeserved" makes the lack of intervention particularly noteworthy. The sounds of her being beaten should have alarmed the neighbors to her abuse, but no one helped to save her life. Similar events occurred in New York City. A few friends spent time with Mary and Arthur McNally drinking liquor, and they witnessed the couple fight "several times in the beginning of the evening." Later after the party broke up and the guests went to bed, the McNallys "were heard to fight in the night, when it is supposed she received the wound [a broken skull], which occasion'd her death."[26] The bystanders did little as the fight escalated even though they were awakened by the violence. The liquor would play a major role in the narrative of events as authorities called in multiple individuals to investigate the event.

Women who consistently protested abuse were occasionally viewed with disdain rather than empathy. Neighbors and communities eventually perceived some of the women and families as nuisances, and condemned some women as "barrators" for the public airing of disputes. Cases of murder and government prosecutions of abuse suggest that bystanders could come to view domestic violence as an annoyance and not of primary importance for them to intervene in unless it threatened the larger community.

With few community interventions, white women occasionally took violent action. In at least one of the petit treason murder cases, the tempestuous relationship between the partners played a role in the moments that led to the husband's death. In 1784, James Carrol died after suffering wounds on his head, and he had several other cuts and bruises on his body. As Carrol lay dying, he claimed he fell down the stairs while intoxicated, and Rebecca Carrol, his wife, contended she was assisting him in getting him to bed. Neighbors were suspicious of their protestations of her innocence. Several persons saw the couple quarrel while intoxicated, and witnesses claimed to hear them arguing the day he died. The jury found Rebecca not guilty only because James exonerated her on his deathbed.[27] Whether Rebecca was the instigator of violence in the marriage is unknown, but it is clear that she fought back when her husband beat her. Other cases show wives similarly engaged in physical arguments and using violence to end the matter.[28]

For some wives, the war was a reprieve from violence, and not all women pined for their husbands to return home from war. Some took the moment to free themselves from abuse, and this was particularly opportune for African American women, who had few other interventions available. The dislocations of war meant a greater number of places to turn to for help just as the British occupying forces became a haven for African Americans fleeing slavery. For white women, the absence of husbands provided short-term safety and may have helped wives envision a world in which they maintained an independent household or took up alternative living arrangements. For other white women, the economic suffering that came with war had the opposite effect, and they keenly felt their dependence on their partner in making ends meet even as they recognized their respite from abuse. But for women looking for an opportunity to escape their abusive husbands, the war provided cover.[23] White women in New York were particularly in need of this outlet given their restrictive divorce laws that, in parallel with their decisions on servants, did not extend separations or divorce to women who suffered abuse. White women tried to work out private arrangements with abusive spouses to live separately to attain some safety. Although some men were eager to cast off unhappy marriages, others proved more controlling and unwilling to allow their wives to live independently in peace. White women had to negotiate with these partners and the public to accept their independence. Wives who left abusive spouses tried to keep the children with them, as violence often affected the entire family, but they found community standards undermined their legitimacy as heads of their own households, particularly in rural areas. A further difficulty in New York was that abused wives who privately negotiated separations could not count on regular payments of alimony or the chance to remarry because their separations remained unofficial. Such women needed to find ways of supporting themselves and their children on their own.

White women looking for legal renegotiations of their marriage contracts put laws to work for them when possible. In fact, the number of women's petitions for divorce grew during the American Revolution, which correlates with the rise in runaway wives, servants, and slaves during the same time period. Women's actions had a direct effect on the legal system. Historian Nancy Cott found that 63 percent of all women's petitions between 1692 and 1786 occurred after 1764. The disposition of the Massachusetts courts and governor became more favorable over this period. Between 1692 and 1764, a woman had a 40 percent chance of success in a petition to divorce, whereas between 1775 and 1786 the success rate was 79 percent. Cott attributes these changes to the greater perception of men's adultery as a significant breach of the marital contract. However, in all of the cases involving cruelty during the revolutionary era, the court granted wives separate bed and board from their husbands.[30] The judiciary had come to see the value in separating women who petitioned against abusive husbands because issuing bonds did not resolve recurring abusive conflict. Women's repeated use of bonds and cries for intervention publicized the problem of wife abuse and initiated change in the court system.

Print culture played a critical role in the spread of information about and increased acceptance of divorces and extralegal separations. When husbands and wives separated or divorced, they often posted elopement announcements for several weeks in local newspapers to ensure that they were not responsible for the debt of partners with whom they no longer lived. The advertisements informed the public not to accept purchases from their spouses and that the marriages had ended. Courts also demanded advertisements in cases of divorce and separation to notify the litigants that the court would hear their divorce at its next sitting. While legal and financial necessities proved the primary function of these ads, the ads also served as a means of establishing the guilt or innocence of the parties by occasionally identifying the problem in the marriage, usually adultery, desertion, or cruelty. Often, partners identified as guilty responded by publishing different advertisements to defend their actions and reposition the offending party. These advertisements would be critical to the larger discussions of divorce because their routine appearance in newspapers began normalizing divorce.

For white female divorce petitioners, the advertisements proved particularly crucial: independence from their husbands required more financial and social currency because their independence was not an established norm.[31] In New York, where separations were often ad hoc and not legally supported, women's writing was even more critical. In 1786, Elizabeth Jacobs responded to her husband's advertisement, which claimed that she had been running him into debt. She sought to put the record straight by asserting it was not she who was incapable of financial management. Elizabeth Jacobs was "confident that no person that knows him would trust *even himself* with a shilling." She also defended her reasons for living apart from him, which opened up a discussion about the marital contract in a state that did not allow separations or divorces based on cruelty. She wrote that she was "obliged . . . lately to separate from him . . . after threatning me in the most abusive cruel manner for a considerable time past." Positioning herself as the innocent party was important to Elizabeth Jacobs, who felt her husband "attempted to wound my character by making me the subject of a public advertisement."[32] Benjamin Jacobs had perhaps hoped to force her home by his public statements and lack of financial maintenance, but instead she fought back in newspapers. Her advertisement centered the narrative of elopement to one of abuse and women's suffering and not on the importance of retaining men's power to discipline or financially provide for their wives.

Divorce advertisements became so entrenched in the culture of the Northeast that one writer during the American Revolution described the worsening relationship between England and the United States through a mock divorce advertisement. The abuse of wives and the legal impairment of women served as a metaphor for the emerging nation in the ad, which positioned the United States as the innocent party in an abusive relationship. Signed "American Liberty," the ad asserted that "Whereas my husband Loyalty hath, in a late advertisement, forwarned all persons from trusting me on his account: This is to inform the public, that he derived all his fortune from me." The end of the ad noted that "he behaved in an arbitrary and cruel manner, and suffered his domestic servants, grooms, fox hunters, &c., to direct and insult me."[33] Although the advertisement did not directly implicate spousal assault, colonists' grievances in the ad fell in line with women who placed ads notifying the public of their husband's mistreatment of them. Assuming the aggrieved position, colonists created an effective propaganda piece that related their experiences with the Crown to those of mistreated women. The writer asserted independence as the righteous path for the aggrieved nation, which had profound implications if women were allowed the same options.

The use of this ad as political propaganda illustrates that cultural knowledge about marital issues and divorce had deepened. Although colonists would not advocate divorce as a solution to marital woes, white women's increasing use of divorce petitions and the conversation in print culture surrounding them began to normalize divorce more than in the seventeenth century. Elopements and the expanding print culture provided opportunities for women who could not imagine a world without their husbands. However, divorce was an expensive and geographically privileged option for white women. White women in urban areas were far more likely to use it than those living in the interior and more rural regions of Massachusetts. Beginning in 1787, New York allowed individuals to begin suing on the basis of adultery, and some women later used this law as a way out. Although women had limited access to divorce, by the end of the American Revolution, the changes in women's use of divorce and judicial acceptance of women's suits marked shifts in abused women's options.

An additional change occurred immediately following the war in New York City's courts. New York indicted two white men during the 1780s for abusing their wives. The cases brought New York City in line with Massachusetts's policy of punishing extreme abuse and prosecuting cases in which men simultaneously assaulted wives and neighbors. In 1785, Baker Brasher was up on multiple charges of assault, including one against his wife and a neighbor. Neighbors had come to see Brasher as troublesome, and his first indictment charged him with "disturbing his Neighbors & beating his wife." The court held Brasher to bonds rather than penalizing him for the assault against his wife, matching Massachusetts in its semi-criminalization of wife abuse. In 1787, New York City indicted Henry Brasher and forced him to make a bond for abusing his wife. For assaulting a neighbor, the court issued him a fine of three pounds.[34] Stark double standards existed regarding the assaults of wives, with prosecutions rarely moving forward and punishments not meted out. However, one serious case resulted in a severe punishment of an abuser. In 1787, the jury found Richard Woods guilty of an extreme case of abuse. Like white servants, Mrs. Wood corroborated the assault by showing her wounds and having witnesses, who may have even brought the case to the attention of the special justices. Among the witnesses against Woods were Doctor Lier and two other men. The jury was easily convinced of the severity of this assault and "without going from the bar found the defendant guilty." The court ordered Richard Woods to suffer imprisonment for two months and pay a fine of six shillings, eight pence, upon release.[35] The case against Woods is similar to the types of life-threatening abuse that Massachusetts's communities felt it was important to punish.

Bringing white men forward for prosecution, even with minimal fines or bonds, set some community standards against white husbands who inflicted extreme abuse. Still, Massachusetts and New York had far to go in penalizing abuse and making it a fully prosecuted crime. Wife abuse often figured as more of a nuisance than a societal problem, and bystanders would need to take more action to protect women who were known to be routinely abused in the streets and households. Women's independence from abuse necessitated partnerships in the community, and their increased use of divorce, elopements, bonds for peace, and the printing press began the work of educating communities and setting up divorce as an option for abused women.

Slaves and Servants

The war offered more opportunities for slaves and servants to resist abuse too. They fled their masters in greater numbers, and African Americans in Massachusetts expanded their presence in legal suits and opposed bondage through individual testimony. Their actions set the stage for greater discussions of cruelty and for the emancipation of slaves in Massachusetts, but New York would not take the same radical steps. Slaves' narratives of violence in legal and government petitions increased awareness of the barbarity of the institution. The British occupation, however, led white colonists to fear unrest among slaves and potential rebellion, and this reinforced their belief that violence was the most effective means of promoting order. Though New England and New York differed in their response to the Revolution, the day-to-day protections for servants and slaves appeared unaltered in both states as the war progressed. Governments shielded masters from prosecution for physically assaulting slaves and even murdering them, but war and the activism of servants and slaves limited masters' actual powers.

For their security, young white servants had to turn to options outside of legal suits as war commenced. The British occupations of New York and Massachusetts meant courts did not sit frequently, and judges and juries were not motivated to free servants from abuse during the war and resulting labor shortages. On the other hand, running away became easier for young male servants, and opportunities to enlist and find alternative work outweighed the hazards of prosecution for abandoning their abusive masters. One study found at least six advertisements a year for runaway servants prior to the war, with the numbers rising at least to double that during wartime in New York. Masters were eager to have their apprentices and servants returned to them as they needed assistance. In 1778, Ahijah Jones offered a six-pence reward to anyone who returned Daniel Bostwick, his "apprentice boy." Unfortunately for Jones, Bostwick took several pairs of clothing with him, suggesting he had no plans to return.[36]

Young white girls and women did not have as many opportunities to flee as boys and young men had. The Revolution politicized domestic work, and women's and young girls' labor was more important than ever in meeting household and local needs. Many young women engaged in a larger variety of tasks with male labor shortages, and they had to find ways of living with less due to boycotts and product availability. For most young white girls, it was safer to stay near home and in their domestic employments. Dangers existed for women who traveled alone, especially as rumors of sexual assaults in the Northeast spread in the early years of war. Nevertheless, young women took to the roads and camp life in search of new opportunities, though it was most often alongside their families. Young women provided services and goods, as well as emotional and sexual labor, for soldiers.[37]

The disruptions to the labor force caused by white youth turning to other occupations, enlisting, or switching masters meant that masters' powers weakened during the Revolution, even as courts bolstered masters' authority by siding with them in labor disputes. Masters had a harder time keeping youth in place, let alone in line. Local recruiters took advantage of youthful desires for independence from bad masters, and Ebenezer Fox, an apprentice in Massachusetts, remembered a particularly successful one who targeted young men. "When he espied any large boy among the idle crowd around him, he would attract their attention" with a song that repudiated their masters in favor of joining the war effort. He sang "All you that have bad masters, / And cannot get your due, / Come, come, my brave boys, / And join with our ship's crew." At age seventeen, Fox was now able to sign up.[38] White servants and apprentices sent a clear message to their masters when they ran, but the larger societal implications of absconding were more limited than would be the case with slaves. Society continued to view youth as best overseen by adults. While it was understood that some "bad" masters practiced cruelty, many hoped that the larger practices of servitude and apprenticeship remained safe for their children and productive for society.

African American runaways posed larger issues for the United States, and African Americans ran away with great frequency. As with white servants, running away was an indictment of particular masters, but African Americans applied broader pressure on slavery by revealing the violence of slavery and advocating for slaves' rights to freedom. A study of New England's runaway advertisements found a marked increase in notices during the 1770s; in the 1750s and 1760s, "an average of 100 slaves per decade took flight," and in the 1770s, 125 slaves ran away. A much larger number likely ran away, as many slave masters would not publish ads for slaves who ran away for short periods or whom they had given up hope of recovering.[39] Though all runaways increased, African American women and their families ran in larger numbers than in the colonial era. Historian Shane White studied the runaway slave advertisements in New York City and found that 5.7 percent of ads noted that African Americans ran in response to or in avoidance of punishment.[40] Although such work cannot give us a definitive idea of the varying and competing motivations of slaves who absconded, the runaway ads leave palpable evidence of slaves' motivations and indicate that the public was familiar with many slaves' rationales. Runaways sent a message to their masters and to the United States about the inhumanity the system.

During the Revolutionary War, the British became standard-bearers of liberty for slaves, as they promised freedom to African Americans who rebelled and took flight. In 1775, Lord Dunmore offered freedom to slaves who ran to his defenses in Virginia, and in 1779, General Henry Clinton secured this practice with his Philipsburg Proclamation, opening the British to enlistments by runaways. That same year, twenty slaves in Ulster County, New York, tried to run to Canada for their freedom, openly protesting the hypocrisy of the revolutionary generation who dismissed African Americans' right to liberty. Massachusetts slaves made no pretense about it and charged the state with "inconsistancey" by "acting the part which they condem and oppose in others."[41] The British occupation of New York City, which lasted much longer than in Massachusetts, made the city a destination for runaway slaves because the British offered a safe haven and the possibility of freedom. Boston King, one of the slaves who ran to the British lines in New York, noted, "Many of the slaves had very cruel masters, so that the thoughts of returning home with them embittered life to us."[42] At the end of the war, at least 3,000 runaways occupied New York City before the British evacuated them, and General Guy Carleton ignored the petitions of slaveholding Americans to return runaway slaves.[43]

Fears of slave insurrections mounted as the number of runaways grew and African Americans openly communicated their perspectives on the slave system. States wanted to secure their control over African Americans when threatened, but this was not possible during war. In 1776, the Committee of Safety from Albany sent a letter to New York's delegates, informing them it would be unable to send its militia to support General Philip Schuyler. At the forefront of the Committee's mind were the many Loyalists hiding in the woods and the slaves who might join them. "This County, besides, is full of slaves, who probably may already have been tampered with, and (all our friends being ordered off) may join with the disaffected in the abuse or destruction of our wives, our children, and our effects." Living in fear of a slave insurrection, local governments inflicted harsh punishments on slaves for minor offenses and established new security measures to keep a tighter watch on their mobility and enforce curfews. Threats continued as the war progressed. In 1778, the selectmen of Boston complained to JPs that British soldiers were inciting insurrection among slaves and that John Willson, a British captain, "did entice . . . by a promise of the reward of freedom, certain Negro slaves in Boston . . . to cut their masters throats, and to beat, insult, and otherwise ill treat their said *masters*." Willson reportedly promised "now the soldiers were come, the Negroes shall be free." Boston selectmen stated that the community felt "great terror and danger," and one writer pointed to the policies of Dunmore, Clinton, and speeches made in Parliament as instigating Willson's actions.[44] While conspiracies caused fear, the discussions of the events also exposed the weaknesses inherent in owning slaves during wartime.

In New York, African Americans armed by the British constituted a major threat to the Revolution and the safety of citizens, and this affected white New Yorkers' outlook on slavery for generations. The history of slave rebellions made clear, as historian Benjamin Quarles once noted, that "a slave with a gun was an open invitation to trouble," and British occupation provided opportunities for African Americans to rebel.[45] The British occupied New York City, Long Island, and Staten Island for much of the war, and Rhode Island for several years. Not only did New York slaves run away to the British military, they also allied with the British from the southern campaigns training on Staten Island. Armed African Americans walking the streets of New York City were in stark contrast to the colony's laws that denied African Americans weapons and limited their mobility.[46] African American activities were protests against slavery and made the experiences of white New Yorkers different from those of white New Englanders, who experienced runaways and feared rebellion but never faced high numbers of armed African Americans willing to fight and die for the British. Slaveholders perceived the African Americans who lived in British-occupied New York as a threat to themselves and the early republic.

Slaves capitalized on threats of conspiracies and runaways to highlight the need for a peaceful resolution to slavery in New England by using government petitions. Their formal entreaties to state governments revealed their loyalties and their respect for the rule of law. In 1779, African Americans in Connecticut presented a petition stating, "we are impatient under this grevious Yoke, but our Reason teaches us, that it is not best for us to use violent measures, to cast it off." Though the enslaved claimed they were content to petition the government rather than incite rebellion, their acknowledgement of their power to rebel was a frank admission of the state of things. They wrote, "we not only groan under our own burden, but with concern & Horror, look forward & contemplate, the miserable Condition of our Children, who are training up . . . for a like State of Bondage, and Servitude." The petitioners did not threaten violent conflict, but they did provide the government with an earnest declaration that their patience was running out. The matter needed settling. The petitioners put faith in the government to end slavery.[47] Yet, like Massachusetts, Connecticut denied the petitions by slaves even as conversations about slavery as a liability to colonists continued.

Despite the risks, New England and New York would ultimately decide to arm slaves during the American Revolution, and this decision reflected regional experiences and pressures, as well as some slaves' resistance to their masters. The change in sentiment in New England came about because of massive manpower needs. From early in the imperial crisis, African Americans like Attucks had fought in the first skirmishes and battles against the British in Massachusetts, which was the first state to reconsider its policy in 1776. Other African Americans would similarly choose to side with the Patriots and Continentals to attain freedom, and militias began accepting free black combatants. Serving to defend the states that enslaved them, armed African Americans were promised freedom in return for their service. New York, on the other hand, was much slower to capitalize on African American enlistments. In 1781, New York allowed for black enlistments, but by this time New York had become a haven for African American runaways to the British side, and its policy reflected its own desperation.[48] Armed African Americans had become a force they reckoned with and New York's action merely opened another opportunity to African Americans that many had already chosen to take with the British.

Simultaneous with the war, new freedom suits detailed gruesome pictures of violence to highlight the injustice of slavery in Massachusetts. John Ashley's household, in Sheffield, Massachusetts, became a lightning rod for the growing antislavery movement, largely owing to the political activism of the slaves living in violence. In May 1781, Zach Mullen, a slave in the Ashley household, filed for his freedom, claiming that Ashley "did beat, wound and Abuse, take and Imprison there for a long time."[49] Although the suit follows the ordinary language found in trespass suits, there is reason to believe that Mullen was indeed assaulted and beaten, given the treatment of Elizabeth Freeman and her sister, two other slaves in the household. Hannah Ashley, John Ashley's wife, tried to assault Freeman's sister with a heated kitchen shovel, but Freeman protected her and received the terrible blows. According to Catherine Sedgwick, a neighbor and friend to Freeman, the shovel "cut quite across the arm to the bone," and Freeman carried a scar from the incident the rest of her life. While the assault seems extraordinary, it is likely Hannah Ashley routinely lashed out at the slaves in her household. Sedgwick described Hannah Ashley as "the most despotic of mistresses." John Ashley served as the household judge of his wife's abuse, according to Sedgwick, and the slaves "suffering under her despotism, had always a right of appeal to a higher tribunal."[50] In contrast with Sedgwick's description, the slaves in the household believed they could receive justice only outside of the household. The court never settled Mullen's suit, but by May 1781, Freeman's awareness of the changing temperament in Massachusetts led her and a fellow slave named Brom, also in the Ashley household, to sue for freedom.[51] Freeman's scars would have been visible to the courtroom spectators and jurors, in addition to any testimony made by the pair, and the jury awarded Brom and Freeman damages and their freedom. Proving they lived in violence, the slaves within the Ashley household weakened the basis of slavery in Massachusetts under its new constitution and were the first slaves to do so.[52] The willingness of white jurists to deny the property rights of Ashley in the face of their suit is a testament to the power of individual voices seeking justice.

Freeman's suit was not the only way she promoted her antislavery beliefs. Through her interpersonal relationships with slaves and free people, she made the connections between slavery and violence visible and helped others find their way to freedom. Visitors to the Ashley home became aware of the abuse she suffered as a slave. To call attention to it, Freeman reportedly "never covered her wound," forcing people to bear witness. When questioned about the scar, Freeman always "answered, 'ask Mistress'!"[53] She indicted Hannah Ashley for the assault in her answer but did so with the subtlety necessary to avoid further abuse. Freeman took risks in perpetuating the conversation about her scar by leaving visitors' inquiries unanswered rather than proffering an apology or claiming it was an accident. Using her relationships with neighbors and guests helped her win the case against Ashley as well. Ashley was a lawyer and many persons visited his home, including Theodore Sedgwick and Tapping Reeve, who would become Freeman's lawyers. Sedgwick probably saw and heard reports about the scar and Hannah Ashley's temper before they took on the case. Communication about how to resist slavery also occurred among African Americans. Finding the right person to seek assistance from was critical. After Freeman's case, slaves requiring legal help often reached out to Theodore Sedgwick. Jane Darby, an abused slave from Lenox, Massachusetts, contacted Sedgwick a year after he helped Freeman for similar reasons. History shows that Darby was successful.[54]

Quock Walker's suit against his master, Nathaniel Jennison, quickly followed Freeman's, and his suit led to the official abolition of slavery in Massachusetts.[55] As with Freeman's case, violence was one of the precipitating causes of the conflict. James Caldwell, Walker's original master, told him when he reached the age of twenty-five he would be free, but Caldwell's death left Walker in a precarious situation. Caldwell's widow and her new husband, Nathaniel Jennison, ultimately reneged on the promise of freedom, and in 1781, Walker ran to the remaining Caldwell family in search of his freedom. When Jennison found Walker on the Caldwell estate, he assaulted him and "threw him down & struck him several violent blows upon his back & arm with the handle of a Whip & did him then & there imprison." The wrongful nature of this assault provided one of the initial centerpieces of Walker's case, alongside arguments about his original master's promise to give him his freedom.[56] Walker, like Freeman, held whites accountable for ill treatment and legal chicanery, and he won the case. The court granted him his freedom as well as damages for the assault. Jennison countersued the Caldwell family for assisting Walker in his escape, and he won his case, which did not have as its centerpiece Jennison's violence or Walker's suffering. Walker appealed this ruling and the Supreme Judicial Court upheld the first case, agreeing with the lower court's decision regarding Walker's freedom and fining Jennison for his actions. Chief Justice William Cushing invalidated slavery in Massachusetts with this case, as his decision declared that slavery was incompatible with its new constitution.

Witnesses affirmed the violence Walker suffered, and it affected court decisions. James Caldwell's brothers, Seth and John Caldwell, substantiated Walker's claims and gave detailed information on the assault and on the contract between Walker and their older brother. One of the Caldwell brothers testified that he "heard a Screaming" and went in search of Walker. When he arrived at the scene, he witnessed "Jennison & several others, who had got ye. Negro down." Once he got the men off Walker, he found Walker had "bruised fingers." Walker took the stand next and made statements about his contract with James Caldwell for freedom, and likely spoke of the assault Jennison made when recapturing him. Walker's case reminded Justice Cushing and court spectators of the brutality of slave masters and the harsh existence for enslaved African Americans.

Cushing's notes on the case reveal that larger concerns about the treatment of African Americans affected his decision to end slavery, even though he supported the right of masters to punish their slaves. Cushing believed that after Walker fled, Jennison "had a right to bring him home when run away . . . [and] the deft only took proper Measures for yt purpose." Cushing did not decry Jennison's use of force in capturing Walker, and he based this determination on his assessment of Jennison's larger case, in which his lawyer presented the laws "w[hic]h. give countenance to Slavery." The property rights of slaveholders remained central to Cushing's thinking even as he condemned the institution. He understood assaults against slaves as a form of correction and a privilege of slaveholders. Even in ending slavery, he could not disengage corporal punishment from slavery because it was a centerpiece of racial control. According to Cushing's logic, slave laws were in force during the recapture of Walker even if Walker was illegally enslaved, and thus Cushing allowed for the assault. Cushing asserted that "As to ye. doctrine of Slavery & ye. right of Christians to hold Africans in perpetual servititude [sic], & selling & treating them as we do our horses & Cattle, that (it is true) has been heretofore countenanced." Acknowledging the mistreatment of slaves in the past, however, did not mean Cushing would continue to allow for it. Cushing believed Massachusetts professed greater ideals in its new constitution, and that "Every subject is intitled to Liberty, & to have it guarded by ye. Laws, as well as Life & property—& in short is totally repugnant to ye. Idea of being born Slaves."[57] His final decision explicitly made note that that the treatment of slaves was inhumane. Although Cushing supported Jennison's right to assault Walker as legal custom demanded, he disagreed with the inherent violence of the slave system in which human beings lost their rights to liberty and safety. In this assertion, Cushing pushed back against years of violence and enslavement suffered by African Americans and countenanced by communities and the government.

The numerous petitions, lawsuits, and expressions of patriotism on the part of African Americans changed the perspective of many northerners on slavery, but New York and New Jersey would not immediately agree. Open discussions about the cruelty of slavery were difficult to foster because such narratives prioritized African American perspectives on whites' property rights and desire for a racial order. As the war increased the necessity to determine the political loyalties of African Americans, communities had to confront the reality of African American's lives under slavery. Many African Americans had proven themselves loyal to New Englanders in their fight against Britain, and African Americans also co-opted the rhetoric of the Revolution. The overall decline in slavery would require the people's support, and governmental actions making slavery illegal outside of Massachusetts came from state legislatures. In 1777, Vermont was the first state to end slavery with the passage of its constitution, and in 1780, Pennsylvania approved the first gradual emancipation legislation providing that slaves born after its passage would receive their freedom at the age of twenty-eight. Other northern states followed Pennsylvania's lead and adopted gradual emancipation measures, but New York and New Jersey would not pass similar legislation until 1799 and 1804, respectively. The longer fights to pass gradual emancipation legislation in New Jersey and New York had much to do with their revolutionary experiences. Divesting masters of their ownership was a British tool of war, and the movement had to be better associated with the principles of the new republic for an antislavery movement to succeed. African American Loyalists were a scourge to white populations in New York and New Jersey, not only by giving lie to Americans' claims that the American Revolution was about liberty, but also in their attacks on Patriots and their support of the British. As slaveholders flooded New York seeking to reclaim their slaves from the British, it was clear that some whites held tight to their proslavery attitudes and their belief in the property rights of slaveholders as a form of racial control. Moreover, in New York City, artisans were the largest class of slaveholders, and they were quick to use their voices in dissent of unpopular policies.[58] New York still largely accepted slavery as a means of promoting order in their community even as the cruelty of slavery could not be ignored.

The revolution against enslavement was not complete, even in Massachusetts, and as slaves remained in bondage throughout much of the North, the right to discipline them remained. After Walker's case, slavery died a slow death, and African Americans had to proactively demand their freedom. Some remained endangered in the final throes of slavery, and within a year of Cushing declaring slavery unlawful, one master faced a murder charge against a slave in Massachusetts. Even at this date, masters' extensive rights meant much violence could be construed to fit a narrative suggesting slaves' deaths were accidentally caused by corrective punishment. In 1784, a grand jury in Berkshire, Massachusetts, charged Asa Sparks with abusing his slave Prince and leaving him out in the cold to die. According to the indictment, Prince was sixty years old and infirm, and Sparks "assaulted him and left him in Snow frost and Freezing Air" for twelve hours. Prince developed frostbite and lived only six hours longer. The grand jury charged Sparks with "Willfully" murdering his slave with "malice aforethought." Determining that Sparks deliberatively decided to harm Prince made the murder charge and prosecution possible. At the trial, jurors disagreed and found Sparks not guilty, which is in line with prosecutions from the colonial era and occurrences in other regions.[59] The timing of this indictment is important. It took the end of slavery to begin a more formidable process of making masters defend their violent actions against slaves.

The question remained whether free black lives would be equally valued. Many people continued to turn a blind eye to the violence at home, though cruelty was becoming the byword of antislavery agitation. As some white northerners dispossessed themselves of slaves, people were increasingly confronted with criticisms of the brutality of slavery. Proslavery northerners continued to argue their slaveholding did not empower them to murder their slaves, though, historically, judges and juries did not punish masters for the offense. African Americans' voices provided counterpoints, however, and they were increasingly heard. Acknowledging the violence of slavery and beginning the process of eradicating it challenged the social economy of violence against African Americans. The enforcement of existing legal provisions or the construction of new ones to protect slaves from abuse or murder by their masters was not a legacy of the Revolution.

Patriarchal privileges and property rights would remain a preeminent concern among citizens throughout the war. African Americans in Massachusetts saw more progress than servants in their ability to avoid violence because emancipation proved a clear path to safety; this was important given the level of violence that went unpunished. White servants and wives never faced the same judicial blind eye, but the disorderly years of the Revolutionary War had made it harder for white servants to have their complaints mediated successfully. Servitude and apprenticeship, like slavery, became unstable; many servants and apprentices ran away, and abusive masters were less able to keep servants. The economic pressures on states to produce goods during wartime meant governments would protect slavery, but as the war progressed, most northern states had to make concessions such as arming African Americans. The rising power of artisans was an additional deterrent to further considerations of the plight of abused servants and slaves. Wives saw some improvements in the acceptance of rights to separate from abusive spouses but did not see much more extensive criminalization of their abuse.

Actions by servants, wives, and slaves dealt a considerable blow to the presumption that they would be loyal and stay with abusive masters or husbands. The relative loyalties of African Americans, young white servants, and wives would prove to be one of the major issues that affected their fight for safety and justice. Their battles continued in the early republic, when society stabilized but the issues of violence lingered. The violence of the Revolutionary War did not give birth to an entirely new society but it was used by slaves, servants, and wives to find more paths to autonomy.

PART III

The Early Republic

Chapter 6

Opportunities and Setbacks

In 1797, Reuben Moulthrop, a Connecticut artist who created wax figures drawn from American life, announced an exhibition of his latest work in New York City. Among the figures he advertised was "An Old Woman whipping her negro girl, or domestic discipline," and on other tours he displayed "Mungo disciplined by his master." Appearing a decade after the American Revolution, Moulthrop's work was a tribute to the American experience and part of a larger effort of Americans to cement their new identity. Other installations depicted political and military leaders such as George Washington or John Adams, biblical tableaux, a scene of "Maternal Affection," an Indian with a tomahawk, families playing games, and several beautiful women.[1] Moulthrop's casual inclusion of violence against slaves alongside familial scenes demonstrates that violence was part of the fabric of American life, and he included the depiction even though most northern states, including his own, had legislated gradual emancipation by the time of the exhibition. Visitors could go to Moulthrop's exhibition, identify it as a representation of the South, and discount their communities' part in the violence used to maintain slavery and the racial hierarchy. At the same time, individuals in New York and Massachusetts denied that violence was a theme within marriages or in servants' and apprentices' lives to present a picturesque image of family and household life. The larger opportunities and setbacks for abused wives, youthful servants, and enslaved and free African Americans fell in line with communities' acknowledgement and dismissal of their social economies of violence.

Moulthrop's exhibit drew attention to the hardship experienced by slaves, and in the last decade of the eighteenth century, individuals also increasingly had to face the violence against wives and servants as activism grew in ways that were difficult to ignore. The greatest success prior to the turn of the century was New York committing to gradual emancipation. Slaves' legal condition forced them to make use of cooperative resistance and networks of white sympathizers to define their struggle for freedom and against abuse. Free African Americans and white sympathizers made a case against slavery in New York, with events at home and abroad influencing these discussions. The Haitian Revolution, in particular, was a powerful reminder to white northerners that violence upheld slavery. African Americans' resistance through running away and arson kept violence against them in the public eye, and it made violence like that of the Haitian Revolution an American concern. Strides were made elsewhere too. Governments in New England expanded women's options of divorce and separation, and JPs continued granting them favorable outcomes in divorces and separations. In New York, some courts returned to granting freedom to servants who petitioned against abuse, and in rare instances, JPs even forwarded wife and servant abusers for indictments.

Though opportunities emerged, the last decade of the eighteenth century showed local communities committed to restoring order and hierarchies in the wake of emancipations and the end of war. Servitude and apprenticeship were undergoing changes as society began looking to them as an avenue of training only for the poor and people of color. Though youthful white servants could find some redress for their grievances, free African Americans found it particularly difficult to protect themselves and their children bound in servitude as communities restricted their mobility and denied their independence. State and local governments enacted laws that reduced free African American liberties, and some whites circumscribed African Americans' economic and family lives through violence. Enslaved African Americans were not granted new protections against abuse as slavery declined, and they fought to find allies in the struggle for human rights. Wives were limited in different ways than African Americans. They turned to neighbors for assistance and found legal authorities willing to restrain their husbands, but no association emerged to assist them, as marriage was viewed as natural and vital to the social order. Most immediately, legally dependent people turned to each other and their friends and families, and they set examples for each other in their resistance to abuse.

Gradual Emancipation Comes to New York

The northern ideal of humane slavery was a delusion, as the wax figures showed, but it was a powerful one that needed squaring with the reality of slaveholding. African Americans' communications about violence and their perspectives on slavery were fundamental to the efforts to remove slavery and its attendant brutality from New York. In 1785, the development of the New York Society for the Manumission of Slaves (hereafter NYMS) in New York City gave the enslaved another option to seek intervention for assaults and to argue against slavery. African Americans and antislavery societies created a counter-discourse that highlighted the violence inherent to slavery, as incidents of violence, including the Haitian Revolution, inspired discussion about the nature of slavery and its threats. The larger struggles for freedom in the Atlantic World and the daily resistance of African Americans resulted in a gradual emancipation bill in New York.[2] It became difficult for white New Yorkers to contend that slavery was humane or that its benefits outweighed the threats to their own safety and security. However, no protections were enacted for African Americans who remained enslaved, and slave codes meant the fight against violence was ongoing. African Americans pursued their human rights to safety and freedom by continuing to seek allies in their friends, family, and neighbors, as they could not use freedom suits, serve as plaintiffs, or testify against whites in New York.

During the 1790s, New York's population grew to 340,000 individuals, with just under 40,000 fewer people than Massachusetts, and they continued to hold more than 21,000 slaves, who made up more than 6 percent of the population. Slave rebellions and violence appeared less threatening with the state's decreasing numbers of slaves, but the Haitian Revolution reminded white New Yorkers that such threats existed. White northerners' initial reactions to the rebellion fell in line with their desire to maintain the racial hierarchy and their economic links to the West Indies. They read with dismay about the loss of life and livelihood in St. Domingo. By October 1791, rumors circulated that at least 35,000 slaves rebelled and killed approximately 200 whites and destroyed nearly as many plantations.[3] The links between the northern United States and St. Domingo were clear in discussions about the revolution. One writer described Port-au-Prince as "almost as large as Boston; and containing more inhabitants." Imagining themselves in the narrative, white Americans understood that slave rebellions could happen anywhere. The same writer expressed sorrow for the "misfortunes" that would befall New York as result of a fire, such as the one that destroyed Port-au-Prince, and he suggested "we mingle our sighs with those of our unhappy allies, the islanders of St. Domingo for theirs."[4] The first thoughts of most white Americans were with the Haitian slaveholders with whom they had connections and shared economic and social priorities.

The Haitian Revolution eventually motivated whites to reconsider slavery, as it laid bare the costs of slavery with the destruction of property and loss of lives. Slavery without violence was difficult to imagine in the wake of the rebellion. Discussions about the cruelty of slavery in the West Indies were not new to New York or the North, yet the rebellion resulted in politicized narratives about violence in the West Indies. Criticisms focused white readers on the plight of slaves—a perspective they did not eagerly accept. Many in New York believed slaves owed loyalty to white planters, and the depictions of violence challenged whites to consider the motives of slaves. One traveler to the West Indies described witnessing a mistress, unhappy with a pastry, ordering her cook forcibly put into a hot oven. The traveler depicted another master who reportedly asked his slave to steal trees from his neighbor, and when caught, the slave suffered a "hundred lashes" for obeying the orders. Indictments of individual slave masters from other geographic regions provided alternative perspectives on slavery, and they could openly be discussed as morally problematic. The writer hoped that "Divine Justice" would be served against the cruel slaveholders who were disparagingly described as an "infernal fiend," "dastardly perpetrator," and "monster." In the wake of the Haitian Revolution, these portrayals told the stories that inspired African Americans in rebellion. The narratives of violence from the Haitian Revolution affected antislavery thought, but they also focused that gaze elsewhere rather than on injustice at home.[5]

Slave insurrections in New York brought the fears of the Haitian Revolution to New Yorkers' doorsteps, showing the ways local African American resistance connected with broader struggles for freedom. In November 1793 in Albany, New York, a series of fires set by African Americans led to the destruction of approximately 100 buildings and the property within them, totaling losses estimated at 100,000 pounds.

As with other rebellions, the government showed force to stymie further arson attempts. A nearby paper noted the "night watch is doubled, and a militia company of 60 men do duty every night."[6] In 1796, New York City also experienced a series of fires in two months, which whites blamed on African Americans transported to the city from Haiti. Prior to these fires, the communities surrounding New York City and Albany hampered attempts to pass gradual emancipation legislation, as they were among the larger slaveholding regions. The fires made the danger of slavery palpable to those in urban centers and the surrounding districts while white refugees from the Haitian Revolution were arriving in New York City and other regions. By the end of 1796, after fires had occurred in other cities, one writer commented that "the destruction of property by fire in the United States, within a few years past, has been astonishingly great." Pointing to the fires in "Albany, New York, Philadelphia, Boston, Charleston, Savannah . . . Richmond, Lexington . . . and Baltimore," the writer asked, "shall we ascribe them to accident, or to the malicious designs of a secret and combined enemy?"[7] As the writer hinted, it was clear who whites viewed as the enemy after fires; in New York, they blamed slaves in both instances. Arson had long been a means of resistance for the enslaved, and the new and more broad-based fires showed a more coordinated effort.

The reports of violence emanating from the West Indies and New York affected those with half-hearted commitments to ending slavery, such as William Dunlap, a painter, historian, and writer in New York. In the 1790s, he noted that "slavery appears to be essentially wrong because it is obviously unjust, debasing the holder and brutalizing the slave, to deprive man of liberty when such privation is not necessary for the safety of his fellow men, is undoubtedly wrong." Dunlap's writing suggests moral clarity on the need to end slavery, yet Dunlap argued that ending slavery was not as simple as activists claimed. He believed measures needed to be put in place to acclimate African Americans to freedom and to limit retributive violence against whites. Though he claimed his position came from one of "benevolence," his combined arguments for and against slavery do not make sense without reference to slave insurrections and white fears of it. Slaveholders, Dunlap believed, would "be highly irritated" at emancipation measures, seeing those "they had considered a herd of brutes, elevated to the rank of man, & becoming formidable or dangerous from their numbers, their ignorance, habits & necessities."[8] The loss of property was another consideration of many moderate whites like Dunlap. Dunlap thought it unjust to forcibly remove slaveholders' property though he and others believed slavery immoral, and he did not promote an unconditional end to slavery. Moderates hoped to find a policy considerate of property rights and employed racial controls to limit retaliatory violence.

It was in a context of violence that New York committed to ending slavery. A new framework for understanding slavery existed after the rebellions, with whites increasingly hearing African American perspectives, as well as a larger northern obligation to gradual emancipation. Runaways increased during the 1790s, likely owing to emancipation measures throughout the North and to the revolution in Haiti.[9] In addition, historian David Gellman shows how antislavery thought evolved during the 1790s in New York as discussions of the death penalty, debt, and the kidnapping of Americans in the Barbary War ultimately connected to larger issues regarding slavery, including limits on the lawful use of power over others and the human suffering resulting from lack of freedom.[10] Affected by trends at home and abroad, in 1799, New York passed gradual emancipation legislation, which granted freedom to slaves who served their masters for twenty-eight years for men and twenty-five for women and who were born after the act's passage. The myriad experiences of white New Yorkers as they moved through the 1790s led to their reevaluation of slavery, and they engaged in a slow process to end slavery by freeing individuals one by one as they aged out of the system.

Gradual emancipation in New York did not immediately provide any new legal measures ensuring the safety of slaves, aside from those preventing their sale out of state or southward. In other states, however, legislators expanded the freedom and safety of African Americans and lessened the machinery of violence aimed at slaves. In Connecticut, lawmakers repealed a series of criminal acts specific to African Americans that resulted in severe whippings, including laws on defamation, mobility, and stealing. They even went so far as to repeal the act that punished slaves and servants for striking a white person.[11] In contrast, New York became more explicit about the loophole in cases of murder. When New York reexamined its legislation regarding murder in 1787, it passed a law stipulating that murders would be deemed accidental if the death resulted from "chastising or correcting" servants.[12] Though this had been New York's policy in the colonial era, recommitting to its codification showed that New Yorkers stood with slaveholders, racial order, and property rights in the wake of emancipation processes. New York was clearly still sufficiently concerned about law and order among slaves that it allowed excessive punishments to preserve the racial hierarchy.

As late as the 1790s in New York, masters murdered their slaves with impunity and the legal system did little to punish offenders. However, changes were afoot, and courts indicted several individuals for murdering their slaves, though property rights ultimately trumped slaves' right to life. In 1788, Kings and Suffolk Counties, on Long Island, indicted two men for murdering their slaves, yet neither suffered punishment for it. A case occurring seven years later gives some insight into the half-hearted indictments.[13] In 1795, the court of Oyer and Terminer in New York City indicted Ebenezer and Elizabeth Wilson on suspicion of murdering their slave, Betty. During the trial, witnesses for and against the Wilsons testified, revealing a sense in the community that slaves had some right to life. The all-white jury, however, strongly disagreed with the court for bringing the case forward. It found the Wilsons not guilty "of the felony whereof they stand Indicted and that they did not fly for it." The abrupt statement suggests the jury's disapproval for bringing the case forward and its feeling that the case wasted the court's time. Although the jury expressed dissatisfaction, the fact that the case went to trial shows a change in temperament compared to the colonial era. Lower-level justices and attorneys forwarded these cases to grand juries for indictments successfully, even as jury trials continued to find for defendants in cases involving the death of slaves. In contrast, cases against individuals who were not the masters of murdered slaves did find traction in the court system. In 1807, Suffolk County court found Samuel Cooper guilty of murdering a slave owned by another man.[14] Ownership was crucial to decisions about cruelty and murder, with masters given the right to sue for loss of life, but not being held accountable for taking it.

Jurors depended on government investigations that could point to motive because laws exempted slave masters from murder charges when slaves died during corporal punishment. However, the inability of African Americans to testify limited the discoveries that courts could make to generate suspects and ideas about motive. In 1793, an enslaved man named Loo was found dead in Mill Pond in Westchester, New York, and the town ordered an inquest to discover the cause of his death. They examined his body and called several witnesses, and the jury determined "Loo . . . came to his Death by Accident." He "went into the Mill Pond . . . and from his being overheated supposed to have been Crampt in the water and Drowned." Perhaps believing that slaves were too valuable an investment to harm, jurors do not appear to have investigated the possibility that Loo's master or other individuals assaulted him. Laws forbade Loo's enslaved friends and family to offer evidence of how his master treated him or any locals with whom he had contact. Inquisitions into the deaths of whites show a similar inclination to dismissing wounds if no person could be identified as having a reason for murdering the victim. During the same year, Arnold Bloomer, a white man, was found dead in Mamaroneck, and the jurors found that he died from "Misfortune" after he had "fell" during a bad storm. The jurors reported Bloomer had "Several Bruses in his body and head which was Supposed to have been occationed by the fall and Struggling which fall and the Inclemency of the weather Occasioned his Death."[15] To modern ears, the death of Bloomer appears suspicious given his bruises, but without a motive for the murder the process satisfied citizens of Mamaroneck. Unlike cases against slaves, Bloomer's friends and family testified to his intentions and whereabouts as well as any animosity between himself and others. Looking at these cases together shows that the denial of slave witnesses led to weak investigations of murder cases involving slaves as victims. With governmental oversight limited, slave owners did not fear reprisal for slave abuse.

The antislavery societies that emerged in the era of gradual emancipation furthered the interaction between whites and African Americans and ultimately helped alter white consciousness about slavery and violence. However, these interactions were largely limited to urban centers like Philadelphia and New York City, where such societies existed. White antislavery societies had paternalistic agendas, seeking to eliminate slavery while simultaneously demanding racial "uplift" from African Americans. Although the interactions between these societies and their beneficiaries were racially charged, white antislavery societies provided identifiable allies for African Americans and fostered conversations about the lived reality of enslavement. The membership and leadership of the NYMS were among New York's white elite and middle class, and their connections to the government and business sectors meant antislavery ideas circulated in the top echelons of society as well as in local coffee houses, taverns, and churches. The NYMS started out as a small organization with fewer than one hundred members, but it created an ever-expanding network of activity with African Americans, primarily in New York City, through its construction of outreach projects to the black community. As with other white antislavery societies, paternalistic and racist sentiment tinged its activities designed to engage African Americans, as when it established committees to visit African Americans' homes to encourage the improvement of morals among African Americans.[16] Yet these interactions still had a profound impact on the members of the NYMS as they imagined themselves as protectors of the black community. When they visited African American neighborhoods and schools seeking "vice" and moral reformation, they learned about egregious cases of violence, kidnappings, and poor living conditions. Their interactions with African Americans fueled their challenge to cruel behavior and enslavement, even as many members placed limits on what they deemed possible for free blacks.

The standing committee, an arm of the NYMS that investigated cases of slave masters who tried to abrogate the gradual emancipation laws, was perhaps the most profoundly important component of the NYMS in transforming community standards regarding violence and slavery. The NYMS was responsible for a limited number of manumissions; its real strength lay in its connections with government officials[17] and in providing a space for African Americans to seek justice and support. Similar to the way JPs should have operated, members of the standing committee heard complaints by and about slaves who were mistreated, held in slavery illegally, in jail too long or for wrongful causes, and who were captured and smuggled abroad. Because African Americans actively used the standing committee to further their own agenda, the members of the standing committee shed light on the injustices experienced by African Americans and created legal challenges to slavery and cruelty. As early as 1793, the standing committee heard complaints about the abuse of slaves by their masters, and it directed these complaints to its legal advisors for prosecution. Cases of slave cruelty were legally tied to abused slaves' status as property, and often the committee worked to free the slaves first because laws were not written or prosecuted in ways that assisted enslaved African Americans. In November 1793, the committee reported taking "a long deposition relative to the Cruelty suffered by Lucy Garret," a slave in Westchester County. The next year, it forwarded her case to its legal team, which included Peter Jay Munroe, who sought her and her children's freedom. In October 1794, the committee reported that Munroe had successfully prosecuted the case and recovered twenty-five pounds from the Carman family on the basis of a wrongful contract.[18] Even though it was not always this successful, the standing committee—when it worked best—investigated and attempted to ameliorate conditions it considered inhumane or unlawful, and both whites and African Americans came to see the NYMS as a site to advocate for ill-treated slaves.

The NYMS often worked in tandem with other concerned white citizens who could prevent or forestall cruelty toward slaves. In March 1800, a group of African Americans and whites supported Rose Tussell, a slave in Queens, after a constable accosted her in public. Tussell lived in near freedom with her father, Pompey, but she was in fact a slave to Adam Mall. When Mall died, Pompey, her father, submitted his expenses in caring for Tussell to the administrators of Mall's estate, but they refused to pay, and he considered her free from that point forward because it seemed to him they had given up their rights to her. The administrators of the estate, however, felt differently and sold her away from her employer and placed her elsewhere. In response, Tussell ran away. Barnett Newkirk, a constable, was under the impression that her bill of sale was legitimate and his job was to return Tussell to her owner. Newkirk "seized" Tussell upon finding her and reportedly "beat, choaked, and otherwise inhumanely used her." The violence and noise from the assault "attracted the attention and interference of a Crowd of humane Citizens," and after one individual stepped in, others also joined and prevented further abuse. Joseph King, a shoemaker living nearby, assisted Newkirk after the crowd appeared, which turned the event into a match of wills. Tussell refused to be removed from her front porch and drew attention to the conflict by yelling and fighting to remain in place. King and Newkirk were reportedly "violently jerking & unitedly pulling" to remove her grasp, "which she held in apparent Agony!!" The standing committee recounted that "Such was their inhuman conduct, that some of the Bystanders were apprehensive her Joints would have been dislocated!!! They finally were obliged to desist."[19] The bystanders in this case prevented the further wounding of Tussell and made a report to the standing committee of the NYMS. One of the society members turned to Munroe, legal counsel for the NYMS, who sought to get Newkirk and King tried for assault.

The NYMS could not be fully effective in this legal case or many others involving slaves because it had few legal options. Community concern, however, assisted in the protection of individuals in lieu of legal recourse. Four months after the Tussell case began, Munroe reported that the case against Newkirk and King had stalled out. At issue was the fact that Newkirk believed Tussell was a slave, and Munroe needed proof that "she enjoyed her freedom 6 Years." If Munroe proved Tussell's freedom, the court would allow her to testify, and he could show that the city failed to do due diligence in issuing a warrant for Tussell. Four witnesses to the event agreed to testify, but Tussell's testimony would strengthen the case. By December, the NYMS gave up on the case, and it purchased Rose Tussell from her new master. The NYMS then expected Tussell to work off the twenty pounds the society expended in freeing her.[20] In these early years of the society, its radicalism was limited, and African Americans repaid debts the society incurred on their behalf even as the society contended that slaves had the right to liberty.

New York provided the means to end slavery and cruelty, but major changes were still necessary among the populace to safeguard enslaved African Americans. African American insurrections and runaways forced whites to consider the connections between cruelty and slavery. Those who remained in bondage faced deadly violence, and more needed to be done to secure their safety and independence. The emergence of a white antislavery society gave free and enslaved African Americans a space to direct their concerns, and they continued using the tools they had from the colonial era. African Americans were the driving force in challenging whites, including those in the antislavery society, to think beyond racial order and property rights. They demanded their perspectives be heard as New York took its first steps toward ensuring African American freedom and human rights.

Servitude and Free African Americans

Youthful servitude and apprenticeship was changing from a system of training to one in which race and poverty were primary. Although patterns of apprenticeship continued, children and youth bound into servitude increasingly came from impoverished families and free African American parents, who were expected or forced to indenture their children to white families. Neighbors and juries revealed a disposition to deny the rights of masters to repeatedly and aggressively assault white servants, but they also ignored much of the violence that occurred against servants of color. As with slaves, ideas about dependency, disorderly behavior, and race legitimized their abuse, and such thinking extended to free African American adults. Laws consigned African Americans to an inferior position just as they experienced freedom in greater numbers, and local white communities often behaved in ways that presumed the subordinate position of free African Americans by demanding their deference. Legal redress and personal mobility had been keys to resisting abuse, but governmental policies and social attitudes limited African Americans' ability to access these tools. African American adults did not have the same rights to protect themselves and their children from violence because they were considered dependent people, though they were not under direct legal guardianship. They struggled to assert their civil and human rights to protect their liberties.

The line between apprentices and young servants had always been blurry, and the changes occurring in the early republic resulted in conceptions of servitude and apprenticeship as for only the poorest of children. Communities often used the words "apprentice" or "servant" interchangeably for youth, even though apprenticeship was supposed to signify craft training. Both positions had historically provided meaningful training for future professions and roles while also affording adult oversight as they matured. By the late eighteenth century, the numbers of apprenticeships with craft skill training began declining even while craft industries expanded operations as the economy recovered and grew after the war. Master craftsmen increasingly hired children as wage workers, which reduced the number of child and young adult contractual employees with expectations about their training and care. Servitude without craft training was most common for poor children and children of color, and society perceived servitude as a marker of status. In the 1790s, Boston Overseers, who served the city and surrounding countryside, bound 40 percent of poor boys to craftsmen, but by 1805, that number dwindled to 14 percent.[21] Society did not alter its view that young adults remained best cared for under the supervision of masters or their parents; however, changes in apprenticeship and servitude transformed society's perception of it as an indicator of poverty. Families continued to emphasize their roles in rearing children, and educational opportunities expanded in female academies, Sunday schools, and district schools, which competed with servitude in training and preparing children for future roles.[22]

Servants' and apprentices' resistance in the early republic kept their welfare in the public eye, but changing labor and economic practices meant not all servants and apprentices were equally empowered in their resistance. Postwar stability and the reopening of courts led to a resumption of white servants and apprentices using judicial interventions for abuse. Only those servants and apprentices with formal contracts chose legal interventions. The courtroom adjudications set very public standards about the rights of servants and apprentices; however, servants and apprentices most often negotiated outside of courts. In Massachusetts and other places in the North, servants used private negotiations between Overseers, JPs, and their parents as the norm for getting out of abusive situations. Reverend Jeremy Belknap, a white pastor of the Federal Street Church in Boston, corresponded with his son and his son's master about episodes of violence, which included "free use of 'the fist' and the 'knotted cord.'" Both the master and his son ultimately wanted to end the apprenticeship.[23] Unlike Belknap, who could afford to make a more attractive apprenticeship contract for his son, Overseers of the Poor and impoverished parents balanced their need for financial assistance with finding suitable masters. In addition to parental assistance, some servants sought out masters who were more kind and able to provide for them, while others abandoned servitude altogether. Such resistance made the issue of servant abuse public knowledge, as community members discussed the movement of young persons who ran and switched to other masters. Masters with good reputations had a larger labor pool from which to draw, but masters also had additional options with increased immigration and population growth. They could avoid cantankerous servants, apprentices, or even journeymen, which endangered servants' legal and extralegal resistance.

White servants' and apprentices' legal cases show they used a combination of legal and extralegal methods to prevent abuse, and New York returned to its hospitable reception of their protests. Between 1784 and 1789, eleven white servants and apprentices sued their masters for immoderate correction, and the court discharged seven from their masters. An additional ten made complaints about their contracts, absentee masters, or lack of provisions and training. Some apprentices were particularly adamant that their masters had wronged them even in the face of judicial skepticism. Jacob Tyler, Jr., sued his master three times for mistreatment—twice for cruelty and once for overwork and lack of training. At first, Tyler complained of ill usage from his master's wife, but later he called out his master, too. In Tyler's first complaint, he obtained six witnesses to attest to his perspective, while his master gathered five. The marks of violence and witness testimony remained critical means of showing when masters had taken correction too far. By gathering credible and empathetic witnesses, servants and apprentices undermined the reputation of masters in the community. The court agreed with Tyler's master in each complaint, but eventually his master tired of attending court and dealing with him and let him go.[24] Young white women and girls also used the legal system effectively, though less often. Jane French obtained freedom from servitude by proving she was "in great danger of her life."[25] Tyler's and French's legal persistence suggests other extralegal measures of resistance went on concurrently as they built consensus about their masters' misbehaviors. In addition, some young men and women likely wore down their masters through refusals to cooperate and work.

Young white servants and apprentices found their way free of abuse through the legal system once the revolutionary era fears of disorder had dissipated and discussions about the utility of corporal punishment revived. Although masters' rights to assault their servants in the name of correction continued, a larger movement questioning the use of corporal and public punishments abetted white servants' resistance as northern societies proposed changing practices in schoolhouses, prisons, and families. Much of this writing connected with earlier thoughts on corporal punishment that suggested the use of reason and morality was more beneficial than beatings in altering behavior. Benjamin Rush spoke directly about the corporal punishment of servants and compared it to assaults on adults. He asked, "Why should not children be protected from violence and injuries, as well as white and black servants?—Had I influence enough in our legislature to obtain only a single law, it should be to make the punishment of striking a schoolboy, the same as for assaulting and beating an adult member of society." In proposing that schoolmasters and parents steer clear of corporal punishment, Rush took aim at the privileges of guardianship. He believed the best course was toward a future in which "servants and children are rebuked privately, and where confinement and solitude are preferred for correction, to the use of the rod."[26] Rush's writing was part of a larger milieu of writers who questioned corporal punishment from the Enlightenment through the early republic. They saw the detriments of violence as a means of promoting order.[27]

Most communities were not at the point of widely adopting these ideas in their practices with white children and youth. Declaring some correction to be "immoderate" when they freed servants, courts revealed the community's sense that corporal punishment had legitimate purposes in reforming youth.[28] In some cases, white servants and apprentices tried arguing for their freedom for lack of sufficient cause to use corporal punishment, but they were not successful. James Dunlass Bisset, a white apprentice in New York City, complained his master assaulted him "unreasonably[,] being groundless and ill informed." The court disagreed and ordered Bisset to remain with his master.[29] Because young adults' behavior was viewed with suspicion, a case of wrongful punishment was more challenging to prove than a case of extreme violence. Many community members believed that even well-behaved youth could deserve corporal punishment from time to time on the basis of circumstances and momentary lapses of judgement. People were aware that some youth feigned abuse in search of greater freedoms, and this bolstered ideas about the needfulness of corporal punishment among disorderly groups.

Beyond the causal factors for abuse, race was a critical factor in when and why individuals intervened. Courts and communities most often assisted young white servants and apprentices but showed less concern for young African American or Indian children. Only certain children were sentimentalized in ways that were calls to action.[30] By the end of the century, servitude took on greater importance as a tool of race- and class-based control in the wake of immediate and gradual emancipation experiences in New England and New York.[31] Gradual emancipation legislation demanded the children of slaves be held in servitude until the age of 21 in most cases, and they were often treated like slaves as they waited out their freedom. The passage of gradual emancipation legislation depended upon societal understandings that whites would raise African American children as they had other poor white children. Indeed, in New York, masters unwilling to maintain the children of their adult slaves could relinquish the children of slaves to the Overseers of the Poor, who would then see them bound out to others.[32] As slavery declined in the North, state and town governments passed and continued legislation that free children of color and the poor be bound out as apprentices and servants as well. The pauper apprenticeship of children of color increased with emancipation, and by the nineteenth century in several towns in Rhode Island, 50 percent of the children bound out were children of color, a number that rose from 20 percent in the 1730s, according to Ruth Wallis Herndon.[33] Pauper apprenticeship was important in states like Massachusetts and Vermont that immediately ended slavery, because it provided continued oversight over people of color.

Emancipation statutes also brought scrutiny of African American adults' ability to properly raise their children, which often resulted in forcing young African Americans into servitude under the protest of their parents. White neighbors of Jeffrey Brace, a free African American in Vermont, forced two of his children into servitude despite his repeated protests. His first encounter with the practice occurred in the 1790s, when selectmen of Manchester compelled the children from his wife's first marriage into servitude after neighbors brought complaints to the selectmen. Brace claimed, "The complaint amounted to this, that I was a black man." He claimed slavery, "corruption and superstition . . . made certain people think a Negro had no right to raise their own children." Like white parents, Brace wanted to raise his children and reap the rewards of their labor himself, but he was unsuccessful in his appeals. While all servants had discernible end dates for their servitude, servants of color occupied an ambiguous area in the minds of many whites, who denied their independence by not clearly establishing dates of birth, trying to sell them southward, and claiming they owed more years of service than the law required. African Americans would need to ensure the community recognized their children's age so they could defend and demarcate the boundaries of their freedom.[34] After Brace's disappointments, he moved to Poultney, Vermont, where another neighbor twice sought to force his children into servitude. Brace believed his neighbor's motivation to be more personal this time, as the neighbor made unsuccessful legal cases against Brace and his family in the local courts. When the selectmen first contacted Brace about binding out his children, Brace told them frankly that "as I had suffered so much by bondage myself, my children should never be under the direction of any other person whilst I lived." Brace protested their servitude on each occasion "by telling them that while I lived no authority should bind out my children."[35] However, he and others faced governments that denied African American independence.

For African Americans, being able to claim an independent adulthood meant they should be able to protect their children's childhood. Unfortunately, new and older legislation enforced an understanding of adult African Americans as disorderly and dependent. Like young white servants, they were not trusted, and laws consigned them to an inferior status. In 1788, Massachusetts's legislators passed an "An Act for suppressing and punishing of Rogues, Vagabonds, common Beggars and other idle, disorderly and lewd Persons," which outlined penalties of fines and imprisonment for a range of behavior, including begging, juggling, palmistry, "stubborn servants or children, common drunkards," and those who "neglect their callings or employment, misspend what they earn, and do not provide for themselves or the support of their families." The law targeted African Americans, stipulating that those from out of the state who attempted to settle there for longer than two months would be sent to the House of Correction, where they would work to earn their support. Concerns about the costs and ability of African Americans to support themselves continued into the nineteenth century. Presuming that impoverished African Americans would end up costing New York City money, in September 1807, the government reallocated the work of four constables to the Commissioners of the Almshouse as part of an effort to be more proactive in enforcing African American labor. The constables were to bring "for examination all vagrants, negros, common prostitutes and other persons likely to be chargeable, whom they may suspect have not gained a legal settlement." The council stated they hoped to have people "removed before winter sets in" to reduce the costs of maintaining the almshouse. The new policy asked African Americans to prove their financial stability, regardless of behavior, making their very right to live in New York questionable.[36] New York state laws regarding disorderly persons and the relief of the poor applied to newly freed African Americans who entered the state. Their laws required that persons found begging without proper certification could be removed to workhouses or sent away without jury trials. Neither state was interested in being a haven for African Americans, whose race made them suspects according to these laws.[37]

Mobility was key to establishing that adult and young white servants and wage workers did not have to withstand abuse. Laws limiting the independence and mobility of African Americans and their children hampered effective resistance strategies. As free African Americans relocated, they had to establish connections to certify their freedom and ability to financially support themselves. Even in older habitations, African Americans needed their neighbors or former owners to verify their freedom and industriousness because some officials used the laws to subvert African Americans' new freedoms. In 1792, George Thompson, a free man in Massachusetts, wrote to the editor of the *Massachusetts Spy* about the vagabond law and asserted his right to live unmolested in Massachusetts. According to Thompson, the selectmen of Leicester, Massachusetts, threatened him and ordered him to "depart out of this town." They claimed the law imbued them with the power to "whip tham [African Americans] and put tham in gole . . . tell they will go off." Asserting that he met the residency requirements, Thompson stated "I have lived in it [the county] almost ever since I was twelve years old" to counter the government's claims that he was from out of state or harboring other African Americans. Thompson contested the maneuvers of the selectmen to oust him and asked that "somebody that knows the law may tell me whether he has a right to whip me and put me in jail." The editors of the *Massachusetts Spy* placed Thompson's letter on the front page, giving it a great deal of publicity, but Thompson remained in peril, fearing for his safety and livelihood. The status of African Americans as free people did not change whites' perception that they were inferior and could be abused and assaulted, even as slave codes in Massachusetts and Vermont were no longer in effect. The selectmen's note to Thompson told him to "go off now . . . if you know what is good for your self," threatening they would use the lash as promised.[38] The bullying of Thompson shows that African Americans had to preserve relationships with former masters and other white allies to safeguard their residences and employment.

Many whites failed to accept black freedom and equality, and they engaged in abusive conduct toward African Americans, disrupting their financial positions, families, and right to occupy public spaces. In 1796, the constitution of the NYMS corroborated African Americans' sense that racialized violence was all too commonplace. "The violence still exercised in this state, towards Free Negroes . . . must excite the indignation, and ought to awaken the attention, of every good citizen."[39] A trend in the violence against African American adults and youth was that whites punished them for occupying public spaces. In 1792, Prince Hall, a leader among African Americans in Boston, publicized the problem in his speech to fellow Masons. He expressed his anger that African Americans were subject to degradation and injuries in the streets and parks of Boston. Hall commended African Americans for withstanding "the daily insults you meet with in the streets of Boston; much more on public days of recreation, how are you shamefully abus'd, and that at such a degree that you may truly be said to carry your lives in your hands, and the arrows of death are flying about your heads."[40] The violence Hall referred to was enacted against individual and group gatherings, particularly those times when African Americans claimed space alongside whites, as in parades. The violent acts by whites in these moments had political motivations. In contesting African Americans' right to public space, violence worked to enforce segregation in the emerging economies, transportation industry, residences, and educational institutions.

Personal and political motivations often coexisted in assaults on African Americans; perpetrators intended to use violence to maintain the new racial order and inhibit resistance to it. In more rural Walden, Massachusetts, Brister Freeman, a free African American, found he had to consistently defend himself and his family from neighboring whites. In the 1790s, the town selectmen took Freeman's land in payment for back taxes to remove him from the list of property holders in the region and eliminate his participation in polls and civic life. Freeman tried to lay claim to the property and was known as a person in the community who would fight for his and his family's rights. Freeman failed to pay rent to Peter Wheeler, a neighboring white farmer and miller, who felt cheated and wanted him imprisoned for debt. Historian Elise Lemire believes these factors led to Wheeler's dangerous behavior toward Freeman. When Wheeler desired a bull slaughtered, he gave the unwelcome task over to Freeman, to whom he promised a short-term job if he grabbed an axe from the barn. Without warning Freeman about the danger of the ferocious bull, Wheeler and his companions tricked Freeman and locked him in the barn as the bull lashed at him. Their actions showed disregard for Freeman's life. While Freeman was inside, the white on-lookers took amusement in watching him defend himself rather than assisting him against the bull. Freeman emerged successful, but "white with terror" at the hazard in which his life was placed. Though Freeman did not report the violent incident to a JP, he turned his back on his neighbors who held so little regard for his life and walked away as soon as he was safe. The Freeman family would not find themselves free from molestation even though Freeman chose not to seek legal intervention for this attack. In 1813, Freeman's sister's house caught fire under suspicious circumstances while she was away. The series of events suggested collusion on the part of whites in the community to sustain the racial hierarchy through interpersonal violence.[41] As Freeman's history shows, assaults were rooted in racial and economic tensions that denied African Americans' safety and independence.

Free African Americans had to fight for safety as the social economy of violence against slaves extended to free blacks in the early emancipation period. Prince Hall's writing and speeches broadcast the larger problems of African Americans' right to personal safety, and he claimed their citizenship and worth through their nonviolent resistance to white pugnacity. Like Brister Freeman, he did not use violence to fight back. In 1797, he published his speech to the African Lodge as a means of solidifying the organization and spreading the perspective of African Americans by highlighting their contributions to American society. In regard to violence, he took advantage of patriarchal expectations that men protect and defend women to discredit the violent actions of whites, claiming that in public festivities, "helpless old women have their clothes torn off their backs, even to the exposing of their nakedness." Hall asked for more gentlemanly conduct toward African Americans and pointed out that the executors of violence in Boston were "not . . . the men born and bred in Boston, for they are better bred, but by a mob or horde of shameless, low-lived, envious, spiteful persons, some of them not long since, servants in gentlemen's kitchens, scouring knives, tending house, and driving chaise." Drawing upon increasing social divisions based on wealth, Hall highlighted the poor as perpetrators of racial violence to shame all whites into better conduct. He argued that African Americans were not proper subjects for violent episodes because they were good citizens of the republic. The overwhelming majority of African Americans obeyed state laws, he said, and their good behavior served as a testament to their worth as citizens and Christians. Hall asserted that African Americans did not meet riot with riot and assault with assault because of any cowardice. Like later civil rights advocates, he stated they would prefer to "suffer wrong than to do wrong, to the disturbance of the community and the disgrace of our reputation." Though he wished mobs would act with more dignity and fight man to man rather than "twenty or thirty cowards fall[ing] upon one man," he also presented African Americans' nonviolence as a dignified response to public violence. "For every good citizen doth honor to the laws of the State where he resides," he wrote.[42] According to Hall, African Americans who obeyed the laws also protected the state from its own belligerence.

The violence against free African American adults reveals the way society continued to see African Americans as property and dependents even in places such as Massachusetts, which had ended slavery. Traditions of ownership and the prioritization of masters' rights were not easily broken, and this affected children, too. In 1795, Nancy Washington was born of free African American parents in Boston, but kidnappers took her and her brother John to sell them southward. She eventually returned to Massachusetts, where she "was bought" by Andrew Leach, who removed her to Belfast, Maine. Leach's and Washington's understanding that she was purchased reveal the extent to which ownership figured into the conceptions of servitude for young people of color. The focus on binding out the children of the poor and those of color helped solidify the belief that children of color were property. Slavery gave masters extensive rights over the bodies of African Americans, and African American youth held in servitude were not perceived differently. New York records do not include notations about black servants' complaints to special justices or community members reaching out to assist them. Children of color, like adults, were not provided with many resources to contest abuse.

In contrast, some white servants gained the support of community members to attain safety. Shortly after the American Revolution, the Overseers of the Poor bound Polly Bragg, a young white girl, to Mr. Neet, a store owner in Mendon, Massachusetts. Neet "struck her with a whip because she would not wear a pair of thick shoes that he had got repaired with heavy soles." Her cries and wounds elicited the concerns of neighbors, who "took offense" at the beating. Ideas about ownership and masters' rights do not appear to have figured into their intervention as they would have with African American youth. Neighbors reported Neet's behavior to a local lawyer and, "by their request," Bragg told her story to the lawyer. The community secured her safety by responding empathetically to her cries, learning about her perspective, and contacting lawyers. The courts helped, too. Bragg's brother, who recalled the story in his memoirs, relayed that Neet was tried and the jury "fined debt and cost to the extent of the law."[43] Overseers made a new arrangement for Bragg where she would find security.

For African American children, access to the legal system was more difficult, as was relocating and finding a new master. Their parents could be shackled to a particular location by newly created laws that questioned their rights to establish new residences or even maintain current ones. Continuing relationships with whites in older locales often meant denying African Americans' own perspectives in favor of conversations and actions that would not offend whites. Even in urban New York City, one-third of free African Americans lived in white households, though a larger variety of occupations existed there than in more rural locations.[44]

White and African American servants' use of violence in the home to protest abuse gives evidence of their rejection of corporal punishment and determination to gain more freedom. Gradual emancipation and the American Revolution may not have set them free, but ideologies of individualism and freedom meant the landscape for enslavement and servitude changed. In 1803, Daniel Davis returned his white pauper servant, Sarah Lewis, to the Boston almshouse after tiring of her insubordination. He wanted a compliant and helpful girl, but seven years of misconduct proved she would not change. Lewis reportedly engaged in "stealing, lying, constant and incorrigible disobedience, and other faults not necessary to mention." Of particular concern was the fear she incurred among his family members. Lewis's "disposition," according to Davis, "endanger[ed] the safety of my children, some of whom will carry to their graves the marks of her violence."[45] Lewis's status as a pauper servant meant she did not have a lot of options, as her parents (if they were known to her) might not have the relationships or ability to remove her from the Davis household. As in the other cases of slaves and servants reacting violently toward their masters, Lewis denied her subordination and instead used violence to shape the behavior of her superiors. She made them anxious about interacting with her and lessened their ability to direct her work.

The twin pillars that supported acceptance of corporal punishment for youthful white servants were the understanding of their dependency and of their need for correction, and free African American adults and children of color were also viewed this way in the immediate postwar era. Fearing them as a disorderly group, communities and governmental institutions enforced the dependency of African Americans even after passage of gradual emancipation legislation. Laws and social practices reduced African Americans' ability to access proven methods of resistance, but writings such as Prince Hall's and the editorials by free African Americans began the process of publicly protesting how laws limited African American civil rights and how white violence inhibited their independence. Like enslaved African Americans who used Christianization to claim a space in the community, free African Americans asserted their value and rights to be part of the United States. The meanings of and access to resistance would change as newer models of youthful servitude evolved and whites engaged with what African American freedom and independence meant. For youthful white servants, the conditions that prioritized masters' rights had not dramatically altered, but they found communities more willing to intervene for their rights than for those of children of color. Private negotiations out of abusive situations were favored: parents tried to secure better conditions for their children, and concerned citizens returned abused children to Overseers of the Poor. Though legal mediation was declining, some courts returned to offering freedom to white servants who petitioned against abuse.

White Wives

Moulthrop's wax figures included a scene of a white woman surrounded by her children, emphasizing the centrality of family life to the identity of the United States. In the modern age, the dual factors of companionate marriages and increasingly sentimentalized white women's roles in the family resulted in views of violence as a retrograde response to conflict. Not all wives experienced the idealized view of family life presented by Moulthrop and valorized in novels, magazines, and sermons, however. Abused wives struggled to find pathways to safety for themselves and often for their families. As with servants, the status and location of white wives affected how they resisted, with white women having more options in Massachusetts than in New York. Some white women detailed the violence they experienced in suits against their husbands for breaches of the peace and in divorce petitions, while others left their husbands for short or long periods before reporting abuse to forestall further violence. Taking up with friends or family for a time helped them develop the courage and support systems to report their husbands or sue for divorce. Like free African Americans, white women took advantage of printing presses and the reading public to expand the venues in which their perspectives were heard.

In the early republic, the emphasis on marital and family life as central to the maintenance of a virtuous citizenry reinforced the idea that stable families were important for communities, and this altered the context of white women's resistance.[46] Yet writers of the American Enlightenment rarely focused on women's right to live free from violence (even though reformers reconsidered cruelty through their advocacy of limiting the physical punishment of children and slaves and terminating the public punishment of prisoners). The majority of society believed that women should remain subordinate within marriage and that some conflict was inevitable. A 1795 sermon encapsulated society's interpretation of the power of men within marriage, the expected subordination of women, and the desire of some parts of society to stop the physical abuse of wives. According to a "southern minister's" interpretation of Genesis, Rachel angered Jacob when she demanded children in an unseemly manner. The minister maintained that "Jacob was a brave man, and never disgraced his character as a soldier by striking a woman." He "rebuked his wife by reasoning with her." The minister advocated that modern men do the same and "treat your wives as reasonable creatures. In this way you will not only reform them, but secure their perpetual esteem and affection for you."[47] Appealing to women's intelligence, the minister advised, was more likely to produce harmony and preserve distinctions within marriage. While women were not deserving of violence, according to the minister, they clearly had a subordinate role and were expected to act with decorum and respect for their husbands' leadership. The sermon and its printing attest to an emerging cultural ideal that corporal punishment undermined secure family lives. However, open statements like this in print were rare, and domestic violence was far more often viewed through the lens of humorous anecdotes or discussions about murderous spousal violence.[48] American Enlightenment thinkers similarly proposed that physical punishment was barbaric and unmodern. Benjamin Rush, whose writing focused more on children and slaves, asserted that "husbands—fathers—and masters now blush at the history of the times, when wives, children, and servants were governed only by force."[49] Rush's outlook contrasted with many families' and schools' practices, but his point of view was gaining ground. Physical correction was becoming associated with cruelty and lack of reason in advice literature.

In the 1780s and 1790s, changes occurred in New England that allowed women more room to negotiate out of abusive marriages, and women made increasing use of this option, thereby creating new trends in communities. Vermont (1787), New Hampshire (1791), and Rhode Island (1798) allowed full divorces for cruelty, giving women access to a total break from their previous marriages and future options for remarriage. Connecticut, Massachusetts, and Pennsylvania offered separations, rather than full divorces, to women who experienced excessive violence. Southern states and New York demanded legislative rather than judicial petitions for divorce, and cruelty was not among their actionable causes.[50] Though divorce was still rare, white women turned to it far more often than men and African Americans. Between 1787 and

1799, sixty-nine white women in Massachusetts sued for divorce or separation, while twenty-seven white men did. Comparing women's activism from the previous two decades is even more instructive. Between 1765 and 1774, twenty-nine women sued for divorce or separations, and from 1776 through 1786, fifty-three women petitioned.[51] White women's activism increased, with their petitions more than doubling while population growth was a little more than 60 percent. The fact that African American women were not making use of divorces and separation at this time likely related to the fees involved and to their turning to other means of dealing with abusive spouses. Many women chose to self-divorce, particularly in areas like New York that did not offer divorce or separations for cruelty. Women left their husbands and established new households, but because of the informal nature of self-divorce, data on their actions are unavailable.

After the 1790s, white women's efforts to end unhappy marriages and stop spousal abuse through divorce and separation created a precedent for other women to follow. In each of the ways women used the legal options available to them, they acted as examples to other women and publicized the effects of spousal abuse. Between 1787 and 1799 in Massachusetts, twenty-one white women declared cruelty in their divorce petitions, and in fifteen of these suits, white women also cited adultery, which was a surer means of attaining full freedom from the marriage.[52] Like servants, white wives suing for a separation on grounds of cruelty noted they lived in fear of their lives, and some petitions declared that they were beaten for no fault of their own. Describing the beatings as "inhuman" or leading to "great personal danger," the white wives sought to satisfy court requirements that it was not corporal punishment. Dates, times, places, and witnesses were all important for women to establish their veracity and the severity of abuse.[53] All divorce petitions began formulaically noting that the petitioners were good wives, chaste, and dedicated to their husbands. Some petitioners also took time to characterize the abuse as unwarranted, not only in the extremity of the abuse as most petitions did, but also in that they were not in need of correction. Mary Hurley, of Pownalborough in present-day Maine, wanted the court to know that she was "frequently cruelly and unjustifiably beaten & otherwise abused." Like other women, Hurley left her husband long before she divorced him, but it was through no fault of her own. She was "obliged to depart from . . . the house and habitation of the said John and applied to her friends for relief."[54] Presenting herself as an innocent victim was important in obtaining a favorable verdict from the court.

The petitions reveal that white women took a variety of steps to attain a measure of independence before filing for divorce, including fleeing, even though separations were legally possible in Massachusetts. Women who fled and later filed give a sense of how women in New York fared without access to separations. Self-divorce required establishing an understanding between the partners, and when one of the partners was abusive, this could be especially problematic, as cruelty continued with extralegal separations in some instances. By 1788, Experience Clap had suffered violence from her husband for several years and in response to his "aggravated and outrageous abuse . . . she was driven by him from his dwelling, and compelled to take refuge with her relations and friends." Clap did not flee after the first instance of abuse, nor did she immediately seek a legal separation; it was only in May 1791 that she petitioned the court. Samuel Clap, her husband, contested the petition, but the court dissolved the marriage and forced him to pay her three shillings per week. The months and years she struggled with the abuse created information about her husband that gave her the ability to tell her perspective with witnesses, but she was also in economic distress. Relying upon friends and family was difficult.[55] Physical and financial welfare were sometimes out of reach for women who fled because their assets could be seized by their husbands so long as they were still married. The doctrine of feme covert meant that establishing legal separations was an important right for those with access to it.

Women used any means they could to get free of abuse, and this included alleging adultery in states like New York that did not allow a full divorce for cruelty. In states offering full divorces for cruelty, the number of cruelty cases was higher because women sued for divorce based on the options available to them. Some charges of adultery appear unsubstantiated in women's petitions. In 1792, Lucy Hawkins claimed her husband "beat her so as to endanger her life" and that he "has been guilty of the crime of adultery . . . with divers[e] persons—all of which said Lucy is here ready to prove in court." Elizabeth Davis similarly declared her husband beat her and "committed adultery with divers women of infamous lives" yet she did not name any. The judges felt Hawkins and Davis substantiated their claims and granted the divorces, but most adultery petitions included the name of their husbands' sexual partners, the span of time they coupled, and where. Hawkins noted her husband's adultery occurred in 1791 in Boston, but compared to women like Phebe McBride, who sued for divorce the same year, the charges in her petition were less detailed. McBride noted her husband had deserted her with Abigail Faulkner, and that they went to Uxbridge and stayed there for a week until they moved to Genesee. A total of six of the fifteen adultery and cruelty petitions used language like Hawkins's citing "divers[e] women," "lewd women," or women unknown to them. Community members often knew who sold sex in their neighborhoods, and neighbors who discovered and reported adultery to wives certainly would have named the women they saw. Being as specific as possible about adultery benefitted petitioners who claimed it, and the lack of details in these petitions show women navigating the court in ways that most benefitted their desire for freedom. Judges gave a great deal of latitude to women and granted divorces in cases citing adultery and cruelty in all but two cases. In fact, the two cases with weakest evidence of adultery are the only two cases in which divorces were rejected.[56]

Divorce cases were heard on court days with spectators, but readers of newspapers also learned about the causes of divorce in the advertisement section. White petitioners elaborated on the abusive behavior of their husbands in a way that revealed the horror of living with abuse, and this fit into a narrative arc that northeastern readers of sentimental fiction, crime narratives, and morality tales would have recognized.[57] Because the marital relationship was the centerpiece of the petitions, it drew in readers with the links between violence and sex, and some divorces were commented on in newspapers. Like others, Priscilla Cheney's divorce petition first fashioned her as "a good and faithful wife" before detailing the heart-wrenching abuse she suffered. Situating oneself as an innocent victim, albeit briefly, was a familiar theme in early nineteenth-century fiction and appeals for safety. Cheney noted that her husband treated her with "such extreme cruelty, by beating, bruising, choking and strangling her," and she experienced "continual fear, not only of bodily injury, but of the loss of life." In March, he "seize[d] her by throat, thrust her out of his house, beat and bruise[d] her with extreme cruelty, and ordered her never to return to his house." Cheney's petition chastised her husband for acting in contrast with "his marriage covenant" and "the common principles of humanity.[58] Fragments from divorce petitions printed in newspapers and heard in courtrooms used the same narrative structure: establishing the innocence of the protagonist, creating a vicious antagonist, and revealing the virtuous character's victimization. In Cheney's case, she aired the harm caused by wife abuse and the tyranny that abused women faced.

Suits for divorce and separations were not the only ways in which women told their perspectives and resisted abuse. The first surges in the number of women reporting assaults to JPs began in the 1790s, but the growth of this tool depended on the geography and status of white women. Although new laws did not prohibit spousal assault, the increased availability of divorce empowered women to set standards through the legal system. In Boston between 1790 and 1795, women reported 1.5 cases per year to JPs, with 0.5 cases reported per 1000 people.[59] The urban environment and history of reporting abuse made JPs readily available advocates for abused wives, black and white, but women in more rural areas also took advantage of JPs.[60] Abused wives recognized JPs as having a significant role in protecting them, and the interventions provided by JPs would alert neighbors to abuse in their community, as constables located abusive husbands and forced them to attend to the offices of JPs to make bonds for peace toward their wives.

In addition to the numbers of persons pressing complaints for wife abuse, abuse cases that received public press forced society to confront the problem of spousal abuse in ways similar to the freedom suits of African Americans. This was particularly true in cases where white elite women were plaintiffs, as their cases aroused a great deal of interest and provided a moment for society to consider the ramifications of spousal violence, free women's legal position, and how abuse was adjudicated. One particularly noteworthy case of an elite white family caused considerable alarm in Connecticut. In 1790, Susannah Wyllys Strong made a complaint to Justice Tapping Reeve regarding her husband, Jedediah Strong, a Connecticut judge, state representative, and member of the Governor's council. Her husband's prominence may have initially made her cautious of speaking with a JP, as she recounted a history of abuse when she finally sought out Reeve. However, Strong's social situation also made her familiar with the law and JPs. Reeve would later contest the doctrine of coverture and the right to spousal assault, indicating that Susannah Wyllys Strong might have been aware of his stance on the issue. Reeve also helped slaves such as Elizabeth Freeman attain freedom. On the day of Jedediah's arrest and "trial," newspapers reported a "concourse of people made it necessary to remove to the courthouse, where a full enquiry" ensued. Newspapers across Connecticut, Massachusetts, and New York reported on the incident and detailed that Jedediah had "imposed unreasonable restraints upon his wife, and withheld from her the comforts and conveniences of life; that he had *beat her, pulled her hair, kicked her out of bed and spit in her face*, times without number." The court forced Strong to a bond for his good behavior in the large sum of 1,000 pounds, which he would be forced to pay if he defaulted.[61]

By pursuing their cases, elite women were taking considerable risk to themselves and their families' reputations, as their dissent sparked public interest. The public wrestled with the rights of abused women in these cases. It was not clear to some that Susannah Wyllys Strong had the right as a feme covert to contest mistreatment in the way she did. In a letter to the *Litchfield Monitor*, "Respondent" questioned Justice Reeve's decision to bind over Strong solely on the basis of her evidence. He questioned her testimony by describing the witnesses Jedediah brought forward in his defense. Witnesses "who had lived in the family . . . agreed fully, that his conduct towards her . . . had been uniformly tender and affectionate."[62] For "Respondent," the credibility of Strong's witnesses far outweighed Susannah's testimony. Other questions about the case considered the extent of abuse that was allowable in marriage. "Respondent" highlighted that Susannah was not in fear of her life, which touched on the legal question of when exactly women and servants were empowered to seek mediation of JPs. Many believed wives could bind over their husbands only when they experienced a threat or assault that endangered their life or could cause a lifelong injury. "Respondent" believed the severity of the case against Strong was grossly exaggerated. He wrote that "on particular interrogation" Susannah "finally acknowledged she was not *afraid of her life* from any acts of violence in personal abuse, but rather by wearing her out with secret insults, and *calling her virtues in question*!!!" "Respondent" suggested that the publicity of this trial was caused by political intrigue and an overly emotional woman rather than spousal abuse. He believed Susannah Strong's "peculiar haughtiness, and unmanageable passions" caused her complaints, "rather than any abuse or unkindness in her husband." In fact, he claimed that Susannah was well provided for and comforted according to Jedediah's witnesses.[63] Jedediah appeared in this editorial as the perfect companionable spouse and Susannah as a woman without respect for her station in marriage. In September 1790, Jedediah renewed his bond to keep the peace after a brief defense of himself, with the court accepting Susannah's right to bring Jedediah to the bar.

Newspapers reported that both Jedediah and Susannah planned to file petitions for divorce, and the escalation of the case, as well as Susannah's suit for peace, prompted discussions about the indecency of spousal abuse. Major General George Wyllys, Susannah's father and the leader of the Connecticut State Militia, told the press about Susannah's plans to file for a divorce, which suggested his approval of her decision. The Governor's Council granted the divorce, and the general public appears to have sided with Susannah, despite "Respondent's" defense of Jedediah and his description of the trial. Indeed, the original article informing the public about Jedediah's assault noted that several persons had "long known the infamy of his private character," showing community knowledge and disapprobation of his physical assaults on his wife.[64] When Jedediah swore to his second bond to keep the peace, "A Spectator" claimed he was "accused of the most abominable, cruel, and indecent treatment of his wife," unlike "Respondent's" characterization of events. "A Spectator" asserted that if Jedediah had truth on his side, he should have made more effort to "exculpate himself."[65] Rather than defending the right of men to abuse their wives, the writer gave readers an indictment of spousal assault and ill treatment of wives. By driving the case from a bond to a divorce, Susannah created an opportunity for public discussions about spousal assault.

Many community members were already aware of abusive situations, such as in the case of Susannah Strong, and some bystanders turned to religious communities to reduce violence, but churches were slower to react and less effective in defending women. In 1796, Thomas Knowles reported to the Old South Church in Worcester that he witnessed and heard abusive behavior in the Cook family while he was working on a nearby barn. At one point, Mr. Cook's daughter implored Knowles to come to the house because she feared her father would murder her mother. Once the daughter finally obtained Knowles's attention, he arrived and, through the window, saw Mr. Cook beating his wife, but the door was locked. He saw Mr. Cook hold his wife in one hand and "a whip suitable for driving horse, in the other." In addition to Knowles's report, one other person notified the church that while living in the neighborhood "a considerable number of times, [he or she] heard considerable noise and outcry, in the family of Mr. Cook." Mrs. Cook was witnessed regularly "when her arms and face appeared badly bruised." And in particularly grave instances, Mrs. Cook's neighbor saw "she kept her wounds bound up for several days" as well as the "occasional blackness and blueness about her eyes." For two years after Thomas and another witness reported the abuse, George "refused to be examined by the ch[urc]h," which left them at a standstill to resolve the matter. In 1798, the Old South Church ruled that George would be forbidden from communion, but the church could not compel him to discuss the matter, force him to be peaceful toward his family, or jail him until his temper calmed.[66] Without George's agreement, the church did little besides take depositions and offer emotional support to Cook's wife and daughter. Neighborly inquiries did inform women that their suffering was known and offer them some space for consolation.

Bonds for peace and religious interventions were not ideal solutions to spousal assault, but they provided some oversight of abusive conduct. Mr. Cook's behavior would be monitored by neighbors, though little could be done unless Mrs. Cook took more action to safeguard herself. Legal interventions had stronger force. States penalized men who failed to make bonds for peace after women successfully petitioned for one. In 1796, Henry Smith, a laborer from Natick, did not obtain two individuals to act as sureties for his bond to keep the peace with his wife. Abigail Smith, his wife, did not back down. The court asked her if she continued to desire the bond, and she said yes, knowing that her husband would be imprisoned and under financial loss if he abused her again. The court ordered a 100-dollar bond for peace and that he be committed to jail if he continued to fail in making a bond, and it confined him in jail until March 1797.[67] Henry Smith came to understand the power of the bonds for peace and his wife's ability to effectively marshal the judicial system. Mr. Cook needed the same lesson.

Though separations and divorces gave white women options, they did not set a standard of criminalizing abuse. New York City increased its penalization of spousal assault while Massachusetts, which supported separations and divorce, did not make advances in criminalizing abuse. The rising tide of women reporting abuse to JPs in the postwar era likely forced the hand of New York's special justices, who did not have other options for women. In the 1780s, New York punished two men for spousal abuse, but their abuse of others was critical to the cases seeing the light of day. By the 1790s, the work of punishing abusers gained greater traction, and the city prosecuted at least ten men for spousal assault. The preprinted forms used by special justices in New York City do not offer much detail about what led JPs to push for indictments other than women's growing use of the legal system to restrain their abusers. Ordinarily, in extreme cases of abuse, JPs would take time to denote the exact way men abused their wives and the extent of physical injury, but only one of these cases included extra notes. Juries agreed with the indictments and found at least four of the men guilty, showing a movement toward limiting abuse in the city. Judges generally punished men with fines of at most a few shillings in addition to having to post a bond. Massachusetts and rural New York retained their policies of only punishing the most extreme abuse and remediating the resulting sentences. In 1789, for example, Uriah Hayden, a husbandman from Sudbury, Massachusetts, faced the court on charges that he did "beat, bruise, pinch wound and evil intreat" his wife. The court demanded he make a bond for thirty pounds and pay a one-shilling fine, but it reconsidered his fine in March 1790, and it's likely the court remitted it, as it had so often done.[68] Massachusetts did not break with previous trends, but New York was turning over a new leaf in its more frequent prosecution of men. Its actions moved the state toward criminalizing abuse, which could have a meaningful impact on wives' safety and husbands' thoughts about the legality of spousal assault.

Some judges and JPs became the partners of white women because their work took them beyond the world of idealistic writing about the wrongful nature of cruelty, like members of the NYMS whose work with African Americans pushed them to act. JPs had contact with abused women who revealed the dangers of living with abuse. While they would not declare wives equal to their husbands, officials supported women's rights to live in safety so long as they proved loyal and innocent. With a few exceptions, judges assented to divorce petitions, and JPs forced men to make bonds for the peace. However, as in earlier eras, JPs did not push these bonds into criminal cases as frequently as the cases merited, and they continued differentiating ordinary assaults from those on wives. In 1798, special justice Jacob DeLaMontagnie, of New York City, made a note in the indictment he transcribed against Richard Spencer for abusing his wife to demarcate it as wrongful. New York City used preprinted forms in assault and battery cases and the form used the language that offenders "did then and there beat, wound and ill-treat." In the case against Spencer, DeLaMontagnie used a caret to insert the words "violently & Immoderately" to characterize the spousal assault as illegal. Knowing that an ordinary assault would be viewed as correction in the case of wives, he had to describe the abuse as both extreme and unwarranted. These standards had been the key to any actions taken by the legal and extralegal community to defend or intervene in cases of spousal assault. DeLaMontagnie's actions show how JPs could work to criminalize violent behavior, though indictments were much rarer than women's reporting of assaults. JPs fell short in not seeing all assaults as wrongful and in allowing for the abuse of women whom they perceived as disorderly.

Through more extensive use of divorce and their daily struggles with abuse, white women began making inroads into societal perceptions about the propriety of abuse. After extreme assaults, they fled their homes and asked for help from neighbors and family members. Communities played a role in remediating abuse and allowing women a measure of freedom from abusive husbands, though much of this went on individually and privately. They supported abused wives in their homes and in their independence from abusive husbands. Some women who fled would be viewed by others as disorderly, but they publicized the problem by refusing to live with the threat of violence. Increased access to divorce and separations validated some of the white women who fled as legal processes legitimized their cases and perspectives. The indictments against men for abusing their wives proved additional means of criminalizing abuse. Women's actions forced society to reckon with effects of abuse and to recognize that cruelty required intervention. Ideas about the doctrine of coverture and wives' dependence continued to delay more preventative and punitive measures against abusers, but women fought for the right to safety regardless of societal dispositions.

Individualized protests, such as those by wives, servants, and slaves, continued to be the primary way people challenged abuse and legal dependence in the early national era, but each class of dependents was handled differently. All three groups needed partners in their quest for freedom and safety, and some recognizable organizations and individuals emerged to assist them. Free African Americans joined wives, servants, and slaves as a highly regulated class of persons who became defined as socially dependent and subject to abuse. Though free African Americans retained rights to use the legal system, governments created and upheld statutes that defined them as lesser than free whites, masters, or husbands. White wives had the best chances of redressing abuse in the legal system because of the way their dependence was structured, but extralegal negotiations were important for all dependent classes. White apprentices and servants required parents and Overseers to negotiate freedom from abusive masters, and abused wives relied on neighbors and community members to support their independence. For servants of color and slaves, relationships with neighbors and community organizations were important, as the judiciary underserved them. Publicizing the effects of cruelty and making use of the judicial system would continue to be major strategies in the first decade of the new century, as wives, servants, slaves, and free African Americans contested their dependence and fought for safety.

In 1797, when people toured Moulthrop's exhibit of a woman whipping her slaves alongside the scenes of "Maternal Affection," communities bore witness to a sentimentalized view of a family and a commonplace trend among slaveholders. Violence against enslaved African Americans was culturally and legally approved during the colonial era, but the Haitian Revolution and individual acts of protest in the United States forced whites to confront the problem of slavery and its inhumanity. Stories of cruelty played a critical role in the emancipations and the acceptance of divorces and separations, but much violence persisted. Local communities and governments would have to ultimately rethink the rights of the legally dependent to fully provide for their safety.

Chapter 7

Relationship Building

Peter Wheeler, a slave in upstate in New York, suffered tremendous abuse at the hands of his master, Gideon Morehouse. On a particularly violent day, Morehouse felt that Wheeler betrayed him when he ate and hid the remains of mutton cast aside by Morehouse's family. After finding the bones, Morehouse cried, "You black devil, what did you hide that mutton for?" He whipped Wheeler on the hand, and Wheeler asserted, "Master, I won't stand this," proclaiming his right to food and humane treatment. Wheeler ran to the house, but Morehouse followed, grabbed a gun, and shot at him. After the shots, Morehouse asked, "You dead, nigger?" Wheeler replied, "Yis, Sir," to implore for a reprieve; this only angered Morehouse further, and he took to beating Wheeler with a club. Wheeler explained that after this beating, he "was dead for arnest, enemost" and laid on the ground, exposing his battered body to his master. Using his beaten body to counteract the violence was the only method that worked on this occasion. Seeing his distress, Morehouse exclaimed, "Next time I'll bore a hole through *you*, you black son of a bitch."[1] In the end, it was his body, exhausted from the day's violence, that turned his master from his monstrous temper. Slaves used their pain and suffering to appeal to their masters' humanity, because the violence would destroy them, which was a loss to the masters' investment in them and their own humanity.

Wheeler's suffering shows how important it was that slaves and free African Americans found partners in their struggle for freedom and safety. Although some successes occurred in the early republic, the legal and social prescriptions of slavery and the racial hierarchy undermined the ability of many whites to visualize the hardships of African Americans in a way that moved them to become stakeholders in the fight for justice. In this context, African Americans built relationships to forward their agenda and search for safety. The pathway to change began with the activism of slaves and free African Americans who influenced whites to alter their community norms and better understand African Americans' own conceptions of justice and security. Whites prioritized racial privilege over humanity and justice, and thus the progress of change was slow. In their individual relationships with slaves, however, whites defended African Americans whose plights they were familiar with and whose trust and companionship they held in esteem. They even occasionally fought alongside African Americans in assaults on others or in retributive violence. Interventionist strategies born out of interpersonal relationships resulted in some successful legal suits against abusive whites and protections for African Americans.[2]

The whites serving as helpful bystanders or witnesses in legal suits were not necessarily ideal partners. They did not often prove through actions or words that they believed African Americans had an equal right to independence or the protection of the government. Indeed, some believed corporal punishment had a large role in maintaining discipline. Yet these whites had come to believe some abuse was wrongful, particularly when it targeted enslaved children in cases of torturous and repeated violence. Some of the extreme cruelty used to uphold slavery caused cognitive dissonance when it was used against children, who were increasingly viewed as in need of protection. Antislavery ideology routinely pinpointed the cruelty of slavery, figuring it as bad not only for slaves but for America, as it could result in retributive violence and sully the nation's reputation.

African Americans also used their intragroup relationships to forward their struggle. Geography played a crucial role in the ways African Americans could work together. In 1800, more than 20,000 slaves and 10,000 free African Americans lived in New York out of a total population of approximately 589,000 people. In Massachusetts, nearly 6,500 free African Americans inhabited a state with more than 422,000 people. Just over 2,500 slaves lived in New York City, and they lived alongside more than 3,000 free African Americans. Boston had nearly 1,200 free African Americans, representing almost 5 percent of the total population. Urbanity afforded African Americans greater ease to cooperate in planned resistance, such as creating associations or reporting violence to JPs in groups. The numerous African American religious organizations and mutual benefit societies that emerged in the wake of emancipation reveal that African Americans' first focus was on fueling change for themselves. Only through African Americans' advocacy on behalf of their family members and neighbors would the NYMS, for example, take up cases of abuse.[3] Outside of urban environments, reliance on intragroup strategies of resistance could prove difficult, but African Americans continued to resist by running away and plotting retaliatory violence against masters. Free African Americans' individual and group-based work did not eradicate the culture of violence, but it did secure their legal standing. Their use of the judicial system and resistance to racialized assaults asserted their right to live independently and peaceably in the republic. They fought for their civil and human rights to mobility and economic opportunity, in addition to struggling to secure their families and houses from assaults.

Enslaved Partnerships

Wheeler suffered abuse routinely, and in conversations with his master he used reason, emotional entreaties, and vocal refusals to allay Morehouse's violence. Morehouse appeared unstoppable at times, and Wheeler would flee in the hopes that his master would compose himself during his absence. Outside of running away and trying to defuse dangerous situations, forging relationships with whites was the best means of ensuring personal safety and effecting change in this era. Enslaved African Americans like Wheeler actively sought assistance by creating relationships and crafting pleas for assistance that cut through the prejudicial ideas of whites. New York slaves turned their physical and emotional wounds against their masters, and the NYMS served as an identifiable place for both white allies and African Americans to direct complaints about extremely abusive slave masters. Through this work, a series of small trials against slave masters went through the legal system, which was a major turning point in New York's history. The cases against slave masters forced New Yorkers to confront barbarity at home, as some had well-publicized trials.[4] Changing ideals of childhood meant those most likely to receive help from whites were African American children suffering from unrelenting and extreme violence. African American adults like Wheeler creatively found ways to cut through prejudicial barriers, and they would turn to other African Americans first in resistance.

African Americans' strong relationships with whites altered some whites' perceptions of acceptable levels of violence. Whites stepped in most often in cases in which masters' violence was murderous, revealing their reluctance to interfere with the property rights and power of slave-holders. Sojourner Truth, a slave in southeastern New York, related that her master, John J. Dumont, interceded when the master of her beau, Robert, viciously attacked him. Dumont and Truth had a respectful yet hegemonic relationship while she was his slave. He regularly defended her from his wife's accusations and was "boastful" of her productivity. Truth's narrative exposes that Dumont's economic and personal interest in Truth's welfare and his familiarity with Robert likely influenced his desire to step in when he witnessed Robert's masters assault him. During the assault, Robert's blood "streamed from his wounds, to cover him like a slaughtered beast." According to Truth, Dumont "interposed at this point, telling the ruffians they could no longer thus spill human blood on his premises—he would have 'no niggers killed there.'" Dumont's actions went above and beyond the initial intervention. To prevent further mischief, Dumont "followed them to their homes, as Robert's protector" and did not leave until he was certain their "wrath had greatly cooled." Once at the master's house, he stopped them from tying Robert's hands behind his back as tightly as they wished.[5] Although Dumont wanted to prevent Robert's death, it was his paternalistic regard for Truth and Robert that influenced his condemnation of the slaveholders' violent behavior regardless of their rights—a right he held in common with them. Truth does not give us many details of how she fostered the relationship with her master, but it seems she emphasized her labor productivity and loyalty to Dumont.

Slaves seeking solutions to violence engaged in relationship building, which proved vital in regions that were less densely populated and had limited access to resources such as JPs or antislavery societies. Slaves reached out within and beyond their homes and targeted individuals whose temperaments and belief systems could make them powerful allies. In repeated visits or interactions, African Americans relayed their suffering and cemented white allies' understanding that violent incidents were not onetime events; violence was part of the daily burden of slaves and it exacted a heavy toll. Finding a support system within the home was the best option, and Peter Wheeler reported that Morehouse's violence against his own family made them his natural allies on some occasions, while at other times the family turned against him. Wheeler also reached out to the Abers family, the in-laws of Morehouse, who became his greatest supporters after he saved their daughter from drowning. They regularly offered Wheeler emotional comfort and a place to hide and heal from the wounds Morehouse inflicted. Over time, the Abers shared Wheeler's sense of injustice with his situation, and Mr. Abers intervened on behalf of Wheeler. Abers confronted Morehouse and asked him why he was always "torturin' this boy" and did not just kill Wheeler and "put him out of his misery?" Abers asserted it was his "business, and the business of every human bein' not to see you torture that boy so."[6] Unsatisfied with Morehouse's answer, Abers picked Morehouse up, threw him on the floor, and kicked and beat him. Abers's assault on Morehouse would not have occurred were it not for Wheeler's cultivation of his relationship with the Aberses and his frank relaying of his suffering. The emotional ties forged in the relationships with friends and neighbors shrank the chasm between slaves' sense of righteousness and whites' willingness to intercede.

African Americans also relied on one another to protest cruel treatment and bondage. Friendships forged in homes and communities led to broader actions against violence. In 1801, in New York City, just two years after passage of gradual emancipation, at least twenty "French" African Americans met at Madame Jeanne Mathusine Droibillian Volunbrun's house and threatened to "burn the said Volunbrun's house, Murder all the white people in it," and free the slaves held there. The protest occurred in the wake of the Haitian Revolution, and it ignited discussions about slavery, cruelty, and the propriety of African American resistance. Volunbrun planned to move her household southward, including slaves, and African Americans in New York reported her activities to the standing committee of the NYMS in hopes of intervention. Scholars suggest the protestors were indeed Americans, not Haitian refugees. According to one witness, Volunbrun engaged in "wanton cruelty" toward her slaves, some of whom should have been free, and she "imprisoned [them] in her own House." She "shaved many of their Heads . . . [and] has put them in Irons and beats them inhumanely." The protest against Volunbrun continued to grow, until at least one hundred African Americans were present. Community members called the police to prevent violence and to prevent the liberation of her slaves.[7]

The white public tried to undermine African American rights to protest and emphasized the importance of "disciplining" slaves. The editorials published after the Volunbrun riot denied the legitimacy of African Americans' resistance by blaming the NYMS for instigating it. One writer asked, "When people take their information from negroes, and even from the most abandoned of them, to what errors are they not subject?" Another report suggested that African Americans denied they contacted the NYMS for assistance. The responses cast African American activists as the puppets of the antislavery society, repudiating the issues at stake. African Americans had a clear target and grievance, but many newspapers ignored the humanitarian issues and largely defended Volunbrun as an immigrant in need of government protection from meddling antislavery activists. In the immediate aftermath of the protest, the white public sided with slaveholders by supporting the idea that physically disciplining slaves maintained order. One writer argued the manumission society should encourage slaves to "live quit [sic] and orderly under the discipline of their masters, in common obedience to the laws" rather than wreaking havoc on the formerly peaceful relations between masters and slaves.[8] Indeed, slave masters took the opportunity to complain about the behavior of slaves who had grown "insolent and restless" as a result of the NYMS's efforts to reduce masters' violence and uphold emancipation laws. One writer opined that while slaves formerly received kinder treatment and were docile, the present climate meant "severity is indispensible."[9] This logic was reminiscent of that used against wives and servants. White advocates of slavery used the protest as a rationale for the abuse of slaves, and they swept African Americans' grievances against cruelty and slavery under the rug. Positioning the NYMS as the instigator of the conflict removed African American perspectives from the discussion.

The Volunbrun protests revealed that African Americans' white allies did not always believe African Americans had a role in directly redressing the cruelty of slavery. White defenses of the NYMS after the events characterized African Americans as illegitimate witnesses, too. "A Friend of Justice" applauded the society for ensuring that slaves were "entitled to the protection of the laws," though he would not deem it advisable to extend these laws further. A slave's testimony "might be easily extorted from persons in their circumstances," "A Friend of Justice" suggested.[10] Assuming that slaves could be manipulated, the writer undermined the legitimacy of slaves' perspectives and failed to recognize that white allies still had ill-formed notions about African Americans and therefore were not ideal witnesses either. The logic also precluded enslaved African Americans from the basic right to bear witness against non-slaves, as New York laws upheld. African Americans needed support for their rights to protest and to file legal complaints because the laws made redressing cruelty very difficult and forced their dependence on white interlocutors. Paternalistic whites saw themselves as more appropriate intermediaries for African Americans.[11] Members of the anti-slavery movement would need to resolve their views that slaves should be free and independent but legally impaired while enslaved.

The NYMS required substantial evolution in its membership, but some members understood the urgent need to extend protections and the right to testify to slaves. In 1803, Samuel Brown, the chair of the NYMS, came to believe that cruelty against enslaved African Americans necessitated legislative action in addition to the work the society undertook in trying to foreclose loopholes in emancipation laws. Brown reasoned that slaves needed to have "redress . . . against their Masters who inhumanely beat" them. The committee that was formed to create and examine a bill to allow slaves redress for cruelty recommended forwarding a bill to the New York legislature, but when the committee presented it to the broader society, "after much debate [it] was negatived."[12] In 1803, the NYMS still accepted slaveholders as members of the society and would continue to do so until July 1809.[13] This dampened the more radical efforts of some members, like those on the standing committee, to provide a remedy for slaves and call for a total abolition of slavery.

Amid these discussions, African Americans continued to present cases of cruelty to members of the NYMS standing committee, whose work resulted in New York City drawing up indictments against abusive slave masters; this was uncommon in any other region of the United States before or after the Revolution. Between 1804 and 1810, New York City grand jurors returned seven indictments against slave masters for assaulting their slaves, a truly remarkable occurrence in such a short time.[14] In addition to these cases, the NYMS standing committee investigated three cases of masters who allegedly "inhumanely" treated enslaved women before 1807, but it failed to persuade the government to make indictments.[15] White New Yorkers were particularly inclined to view extreme violence against individual enslaved children as unlawful, with all but one of the seven indictments brought up against slave masters in New York City describing the victims as boys and girls, mostly under the age of twelve.[16] The violence also needed to be life-threatening and routine, such as cases of murderous violence, confinement, lack of sustenance, and exposure that could lead to loss of extremities.

The severe violence it took to engender indictments against slave masters shows a society that continued to believe corporal punishment had value. Only when abuse became torture would individuals step forward, and this was not the case only with slaves. Between 1800 and 1809, only the most extreme cases of white servant abuse resulted in indictments in New York City. In two cases against John Young for abusing his white servants, for example, neighbors described him as having "so inhuman a Disposition as to be quite unfit to have the Charge of any Servant." Young repeatedly assaulted his servants using whips and rods, and witnesses saw him kick and punch them. He malnourished his servants, exposed them to the cold, confined them, left lasting marks on their bodies, and broke their bones. In another case, witnesses saw George Braymer, a cordwainer, whip his apprentice more than sixty stripes, followed by punches with his fists. In all five cases that emerged, the extent of violence was the major causal factor in moving toward indictments. The court prosecuted at least three of the cases, with juries convicting in one case and the parties settling in two.[17] The indictments, like those against slaves, represented some progress when compared with older practices that resulted in civil suits without establishing criminal penalties.

Criminalizing servant and slave abuse sent a powerful message to masters, but the issues in penalization and the extreme violence necessary to prosecute cases weakened the overall effect of the new standards. Very low fines were the norm, as in cases of wife abuse. In the cases involving white servants, masters usually lost rights to maintaining them, but New York did not transfer the ownership of abused slaves or grant them freedom in abuse cases. The majority of abuse cases continued to be handled privately, and most often those private negotiations were about white servants rather than slaves or servants of color. The public airing of cruelty cases did not occur in mediations, though some community knowledge would spread as apprentices and servants left the homes of their masters. Since only the most extreme cases made their way through courts, only violence at the level of torture appeared criminal. Some masters understood that the violence they inflicted was questionable, but they continued assaulting servants, showing the needfulness of establishing more nuanced criminal and societal standards against abuse. When a neighbor threatened to take one of John Young's white servants to the almshouse, Young said "he was afraid that if he sent her to the alms House that . . . [he] would get in trouble about her and therefore did not wish him to do it."[18] Young feared exposure of his deeds, but more intervention was necessary to stop assaults, particularly outside of urban centers, where concerned citizens could not ignore the cries of the abused. Far more often, slaves and white children and young adults needed advocates in the community.

The existing interventions and criminal cases show that enslaved children and poor whites benefitted from newer conceptions of childhood as a time of innocence.[19] Typically, the children defined as innocent in the nineteenth century would largely be considered so in emerging white middle-class ideals and literature. Those with means changed parenting techniques and allowed children to live at home for longer periods, showing an interest in protecting and extending childhood.[20] The servants and slaves who suffered abuse, often poor whites or people of color, are not typically understood as beneficiaries of this emerging ideology in the early nineteenth century.[21] Community and legal actions taken to limit their abuse in the seven indictments against slaveholders and in the five against masters of white servants do not suggest an overhaul in thoughts regarding children and youth. However, the actions taken by New York City courts to protect children of color were not extended to enslaved adults, indicating an understanding of and sensitivity for the innocence of childhood; this correlates with early American literature figuring enslaved youth as having the same emotional capacity to experience loss and joy as white youth.[22] The indictments show that juries, JPs, and bystanders differentiated between African American children, youth, and adults. Once African Americans aged to young adulthood, they lost the protections of white servants, as only slaves younger than the age of twelve or thirteen received the kinds of protections that white young adults received through civil suits or indictments.

Given the extremity and rarity of these cases, it's important to note that the only African American children who saw cases go through courts were those demarcated as slaves. Courts did not take on cases of African American servants' abuse in New York City until after 1810. The concern for enslaved children may have been part of an overall recognition that their state of dependence left them without the succor of other groups, such as white servants who drew on Overseers or parents and were empowered to testify in courts. The young African Americans in these cases were unlikely to find freedom until at least their twenty-fifth year, and the community determined that torturous violence was unjust for them. The courts' and bystanders' trends in ignoring violence against African American children were fractured by the combination of enslaved children's extreme dependency, the severity and repetitious nature of the abuse they suffered, and their young age.

In October 1804, the first of the successful cases against slave masters was tried, and press coverage of the case extended the reach of news from the courtroom. African Americans initiated the larger contestations of violence because they made their suffering known to others with the power to make official complaints. Three white witnesses reported to the special justices in New York City that Charles Hoffman, a furrier, inflicted horrendous punishments on his slave. George Albreight, who lived in the same house as Hoffman, explained he saw Hoffman whip James Wright, a boy between the ages of eleven and twelve, with a horsewhip, and that Hoffman tied Wright's hands above his head and nailed his feet to the floor. After the beating, Albreight swore he saw Hoffman apply "Salt and Vinegar" to the wounds. The sounds of the whips were probably not the only sounds that alerted Albreight to these severe punishments. Wright likely uttered tremendous cries and sought help for the wounds from household members afterwards. Two seamstresses who worked for Hoffman also witnessed and reported Hoffman's violence. Susan McDonald observed Hoffman feeding Wright two tablespoons of salt before confining him in a closet for more than twenty-four hours without air or water. Ann Chace swore that Wright "ran away in consequence of ill treatment," and after his capture and forced return aboard a ferry to New York City, "the Idea of experiencing such usage induced him to spring overboard to destroy himself." In running away and making clear that he would take his own life, Wright put on view that the abuse was too severe to withstand. Outside of running away, Wright could find safety only through the help of whites because he was unable to report violence on his own, and he was a child. Hoffman pleaded not guilty, but the jury convicted him and imposed a fine. The courts did not stymie Hoffman's violence, however. In February 1805, New York City issued another indictment against Hoffman at the insistence of Anna Maria Hunter, a fourth witness who testified against Hoffman for abuse of Wright. Hoffman pleaded not guilty again, but he settled the case outside of court, perhaps knowing he would not be successful. In 1812, James Wright, now a young adult, sought out the NYMS for assistance against Hoffman's brutality, revealing Hoffman's imperviousness to the courts.[23] Only through the interventions of others would Hoffman ever receive a fine or official admonishment for his torture of Wright. And even these proved ineffectual. Wright needed his freedom to achieve any measure of security.

As the details of the first case against Hoffman emerged, some felt the "Horrid Inhumanity" of the case required legislative action to protect slaves. Those advocating for action blended the facts about the violence against James Wright with the sentimentalist undertones of antislavery advocates in the Atlantic World.[24] One writer of an editorial in the *New York Commercial Advertiser* conveyed the details of Hoffman's abuse to garner sympathy and action, expressing "hope, that the members of the Legislature, feeling just indignation, which, at the recital of such shameful acts, must necessarily arise in every honest mind, will enact a law which shall effectually prevent a recurrence." Grounded in a desire to evoke empathy, the editorial noted that the "feeling of humanity" demanded redress for slaves. Broadcasting the violence of slavery was one of the fundamental means of portraying its injustice and immorality.[25] Drawing from these lines, the editorial about Wright's abuse demanded action and appealed to the sensibility of readers and bystanders who witnessed the physical and moral effects of violence.

The spatial organization of New York provided slaves with ample witnesses if they could be effectively marshaled to intervene. It's easy to ignore the cries of slaves as a form of resistance, but their voices were rallying cries for assistance and safety. As new ideologies of childhood innocence took hold, one of the major ways that African American children would be differentiated from whites in the nineteenth century was in their perceived ability to withstand pain.[26] By screaming, young African Americans alerted the neighborhood to altercations that needed interventions. In 1806, Robert Pickering lived in the upper part of a house occupied by Michael Sandford, and he complained to the special justices that he overheard Sandford take Peter, his slave, to the kitchen cellar. Once in the cellar, Pickering heard Peter "Crying and begging 'O! Master O! Master' and the sound of blows for about thirty five minutes with little intervals." Sandford knew that his abuse of Peter upset his neighbors; so did Peter. Peter likely screamed as loudly as possible. Pickering noted that Sandford "locked or bolted all the Doors so as to prevent any one from coming in." Given the precautions that Sandford took, neighbors probably had interrupted his abuse of Peter in the past. Peter's cries afforded the public with the opportunity to scrutinize the cruelty of slavery, after the witnesses took the case to special justices. Pickering likely understood that if he did not act, Sandford's violence might ultimately result in the death or maiming of Peter. The jury found Sandford guilty of assaulting his slave and fined him six cents.[27] Slaves who established relationships with whites fared better in court because the number of white witnesses willing to testify affected the outcome of these cases. In one successful case, four witnesses gave affidavits, and three others offered to give further testimony.[28] In unsuccessful cases, the number of witnesses was three or fewer.[29] Alerting neighbors about violence and developing personal relationships worked to elicit immediate assistance and produce witnesses to acts of violence.

In response to the entreaties of slaves, after 1807, several well-connected members of the NYMS made strides in changing community standards against excessive violence and they considered the legal implications of slaves not having the ability to testify for themselves. In 1807, Christopher Marshal Slocum, who with his family had been members of the NYMS since 1802, drafted a letter to New York City's grand jury advising it to issue an indictment against Joseph Goir for "inhuman conduct" in the abuse of Frances, a slave brought to New York City from the West Indies. Slocum learned about Frances's case "Thro' the community of Thomas Eddy." Eddy, a philanthropist and board member of the NYMS, persuaded Goir to put Frances in the hospital, where Slocum and seven others learned about her miserable situation. Slocum and several others described that Goir whipped Frances with a cowskin and "by reiteration is lacerated from head to foot." Goir "crippled" her hands with frostbite due to exposure and he malnourished her. When Slocum presented the case to the grand jury, he asked "whether such flagrant violations of the Peace will be permitted with impunity?" Underlying this question was a deeper one about the inherent inhumanity of a system that allowed for the excessive abuse of individuals and gave them no legal avenue to protest. Slocum ultimately sought Frances's freedom and tried to circumvent the laws regarding slave testimony by suggesting that Frances be freed to make her "a competent witness in her own case."[30] Like other witnesses who testified about the abuse of slaves, Slocum helped drive the antislavery movement by shedding light on the daily experiences of African Americans struggling for safety, security, and sustenance without any code of laws to protect them.

Under the leadership of the more radical sect on the standing committee within the NYMS, the organization pushed again for legislative change against cruelty after its successes in the legal system. Its members had learned through their engagement with enslaved New Yorkers that change was vital to their very lives. In 1807, William T. Slocum, brother to Christopher, became chairperson of the standing committee of the NYMS and secretary of the overall organization, and he had previously served as a witness in at least one abuse case. He and others advanced the society by demanding more change from inside and outside the organization. Slocum reported the committee had "been attended with success" in some of the cases of "various and aggravated Wrongs inflicted and imposed upon the African Races," including the cases against Goir and Sandford.[31] On November 17, 1807, the society put together a committee of six, including William T. Slocum and Thomas Eddy, to "procure an Act to prevent the cruel treatment of Slaves by their holders." Influenced by their experiences in prosecuting cases of assault, members of the NYMS more greatly empowered this committee because its duty was to seek change rather than to consider the implications of the legislation. The committee reported in April 1808 that the bill passed through the Senate but failed in the assembly. A less noble side to the society lingered, however, even as it adopted more radical advocacy. It continued to engage in projects to reform African Americans' "morals and their manner of living."[32] Believing in their own sense of racial superiority, members cast themselves as the proper persons to propose political and legal changes on behalf of African Americans and denied the legitimacy of African Americans' public action on their own behalf.

The most stunning victory experienced by African Americans and the NYMS was their prosecution of Amos and Demiss Broad in 1809 for brutally beating their two slaves, Betty and her three-year-old daughter Sarah. This case was a turning point in discussions about the inhumanity of holding slaves and the rights of slaves to live unmolested. As in other cases against slave masters, the community acted on behalf of an enslaved woman and child for life-threatening and routine violence. In addition to whippings and forced feedings of salt, Amos and Demiss Broad repeatedly exposed Betty and Sarah to cold temperatures without food and fire in their rooms and left Betty nearly naked and tied up in the cold outdoors. The couple placed Sarah, a toddler, in the cold storeroom for hours until her "feet were frosted . . . so that she was hardly able to crawl." Both kicked Sarah regularly, too. While jurors indicted Amos Broad for beating both Sarah and Betty, Demiss answered only for beating Sarah. Demiss Broad threw a knife at the child, which resulted in "so large a gash" that the wound required a doctor. Reports showed that Demiss Broad also whipped Betty with a cow skin in the front yard and threw cold water on her while outside in winter, and that she was complicit in the denial of food and warmth in Betty's lodgings. However, only Demiss's extreme violence against Sarah merited an indictment, as the youth of slaves and level of violence affected the judiciary's and white community's disposition toward limiting slave masters' violence. The Broads relinquished ownership over Betty and Sarah in the hope of getting more lenient sentences, and the jurors found Amos Broad guilty. The judge issued a four-month sentence in prison and a fine of 1,250 dollars, a far cry from the six cents paid by previous owners found guilty of cruelty. In addition, Amos Broad was held to a 1,000-dollar bond to keep the peace.[33]

Betty and Sarah were pivotal in moving this case forward because they brought attention to their abuse through their cries and their broken and battered bodies. Neighbors and four seamstresses employed by the Broads routinely heard Betty crying and moaning, and they were integral witnesses in the case. By shouting and crying, Betty attracted witnesses even when Broad beat her in his more covert assaults in the cellar or attic. Before bringing news of the violence to the special justices, the seamstresses tried to prevent the violence by contacting a neighbor, David Fielder. Fielder recalled that he ran to the cellar to stop the beating, and that prior to that day, "he very frequently heard her cries." Upon arriving, he saw Betty "standing bent over naked" but did not see Broad whip her because his presence had inhibited Broad. Indeed, Amos Broad seems to have tried to cover up his beating of Betty, as more recently hired seamstresses only heard rather than witnessed the violence. Broad's employees stated they regularly gave food to Betty and her child, who suffered from malnourishment and confinement.[34] Betty must have shared her trials with the women in their conversations, through her anguished cries, and through her lamentations about her situation. She risked additional torture and abuse by publicizing her suffering so loudly that others heard, and her cries of pain and for relief should be read as protests and resistance.

Slaves' use of friendships and their suffering proved essential in legal suits outside of New York City as well. For adults, the ability to attain interventions proved more difficult, but not impossible, as Sojourner Truth's, Betty's, and Peter Wheeler's experiences show. Gideon Morehouse's brutal beatings of Peter Wheeler in Lancaster, New York, resulted in Wheeler's white ally, Mr. Abers, assaulting Morehouse in reprisal. Abers's relationship with Wheeler had been well established by this point. The Aberses witnessed repeated evidence of Morehouse's unrelenting torture of Wheeler, and the event that changed everything was when Morehouse maimed Wheeler. Morehouse stripped and hung Wheeler by his hands in a barn until the "tears fell and froze on my breast." After leaving him in that position for more than twenty minutes, Morehouse whipped Wheeler until his blood "froze in long icicles on the balls of my heels and . . . under my nails and toes." Morehouse ended his torture by throwing a cup of brine on Wheeler's mutilated body. Abers assaulted Morehouse after learning of the torture and in knowledge that Morehouse had fired a gun at Wheeler several times. Morehouse reported Abers's assault against him to a JP, but Abers successfully countersued Morehouse for the excessive violence he exacted on Wheeler that particularly frigid winter evening, among other occasions. The judge and jury believed Morehouse's violence was excessive, and Wheeler recounted that they fined him 500 dollars for the assault, demonstrating that there were constraints on slaveholders' violence against slaves in upstate New York. Like Amos Broad, Morehouse was forced by the court to make a bond for his good behavior in a large sum: 2,000 dollars.[35] As in New York City, a white ally was central to processing the case against Morehouse.

Most slaves would not share Wheeler's experience in being able to cultivate a deep relationship with a white family. The extraordinary way that Wheeler made himself a part of the Abers family relied on his ability to take leave of his master to visit others. Not all masters extended that type of freedom to their slaves. Proximity was an issue, too. Having repeated access to whites was critical to overcome whites' reluctance to take on individual slave masters or report violence to legal authorities. Other hurdles to building relationships included the psychological impact of racism on whites' ability to empathize with adult slaves. Whites were conditioned to ignore violence against African Americans, and ideas about African Americans' ability to withstand pain were pronounced by the eighteenth century. The proslavery ideologies of the nineteenth century would implicate these ideas further in society.[36] Though the ideas about race in the early nineteenth century were very different from today, psychological and neurological tests show whites react less empathetically to the pain of other races even today.[37] Whites in the early republic had been denying the violence in front of them and often failed to relate African Americans' plight to the broader human experience. Whites often feared slaves and suppressed any feelings of empathy, and part of this fear stemmed from whites' inability to control the slaves in their communities.

African American violence directed at masters and whites undermined attempts to enforce dependent relationships on slaves, and the enslaved continued using violence as a tool to claim safety. African Americans understood that violence had risks, but it was an alternative to fostering relationships to attain safety that required African Americans' acquiescence to whites' sense of superiority. In New York City, slaves occasionally abused their masters, and the city prosecuted at least seven slaves for beating their masters between 1795 and 1813, in addition to cases of arson. Certainly, more cases of slaves assaulting their masters occurred, as most slave masters reprimanded slaves with counterassaults. In 1810, Thomas Mace, a white gentleman, reported that his slave Titus threatened to stab him and ran away. Titus declared that "if he went back to Deponent's [Mace's] house he would be put him down so fast that he would not rise up again—and thus would put him asleep so that he never wake more." Mace was reportedly "a Man of an extremely violent character," and Titus likely threatened Mace to prevent him from harming him further.[38] Like African Americans who reported violence to the NYMS and other white allies, slaves used whatever means were available to them to prevent violence and find freedom. These assaults inverted the hierarchy that slavery upheld, and the cases reveal that African Americans used assaults as a means of retribution and to attain an edge in negotiations for liberties. Some African Americans pushed their owners' patience to the limit by continuously rebelling, running away, and threatening their masters' personal safety. Laws limited masters' ability to sell slaves southward, and by repeatedly protesting slavery through lack of compliance, slaves problematized slavery and the expected master-slave relationships for their owners. Slaves did not limit their violent acts to their masters; they subverted white privilege by lashing out at other community members, too. Slaves were responsible for at least forty-eight reported assaults on whites in New York City between 1790 and 1814, and many more unreported assaults likely occurred.[39] Whites demanded that slaves defer to them in public and allow them broad reach, and some reports to special justices show irritation at what whites saw as African American impudence. Slaves did not direct their violence solely at poor whites, who one might assume bore the brunt of violence because of their lesser social and economic capital.[40] Enslaved persons' violence reveals a marked dissonance between the status of the slaves and the expectations of whites.

Slaves looked to one another first to form pacts and find ways to freedom. Creating relationships among each other often had more appeal than alliances with whites. In 1806, Margaret and Diana, slaves of Thomas Snell, colluded to poison the Snell family and burn their house to the ground. Margaret and Diana were young; Margaret was 19 years old and Diana was only 12 or 13. They had experienced the violence of slavery and took aim at those in the household who wielded it against them. Euphenia, an African American hired servant, reported she overheard the young women planning the poisoning over the course of a week. She said their motivation was the whippings they received. They "would not poison any but her old & young mistress because they whiped her." Their plans were not just about vengeance—they also wanted freedom. Margaret desired to be with her husband. It's not clear whether either of the young women would have put their plans in effect. They procured the laudanum but never delivered the dose, and neither did they set the house on fire. Planning their vengeance certainly empowered the young women, and they delighted in discussing it. Their friendship grew as they strategized and imagined the outcomes of their work. Euphenia admitted she was not sure they "were in earnest" but told her mother about it just in case.[41] Courts took these conspiracies seriously, and Margaret and Diana were imprisoned for their scheming. Whites understood that plans such as this could have real-life consequences.

Slave and servant violent and non-violent resistance required whites to rethink their practices, and some whites may have reported masters' flagrant abuse of slaves and servants to authorities because they believed the violence threatened society rather than because of loyalty to those they knew. Before the passage of gradual emancipation, whites acknowledged their fear of retribution from the enslaved, and this moved them to make legislative changes in the wake of the Haitian Revolution and the arson attempts throughout the United States. The activism of African Americans in response to white violence further threatened whites' sense of safety. The Volunbrun protests and individual acts of violence against masters made it known that African Americans would not withstand indiscriminate violence. Early American racial thought attributed a penchant for violence to African Americans, making these events threatening specters. African American revolutions in the Atlantic World, combined with the experiences of the American Revolution, revealed the dangers of maintaining an "enemy within our walls." In a series of antislavery essays Reverend David Rice of Kentucky published in New York, he warned, "A vicious commonwealth, is a building erected on quicksand, the inhabitants of which can never abide in safety."[42] Part of the logic in providing protections for slaves and stemming the cruelty of slavery was to prevent the hardening of African Americans and whites. By limiting cruelty, whites hoped to preserve their society and prevent African American protests.

As whites became more attuned to the wrongful nature of violence against enslaved children, especially through the case against the Broads, they began denouncing it publicly, which was an incredible leap in community disposition considering whites' reactions to African American protests against Volunbrun only eight years earlier. In 1809, Henry Southwick published a tract detailing the testimony of witnesses for and against the Broads, as well as speeches made by the judge, the NYMS, and lawyers. In his descriptions of the violence, Southwick used the language of horror and sentimentalism to capture the audience shocked by the Broads' behavior. He titled one string of advertisements for the tract "HORRID BARBARITY," while other advertisements promised to give details about the "horrid scenes . . . so shocking to humanity." Condemning the Broads for their excessive violence, he called Amos Broad "unmerciful," an "infernal genius," and a person with a "callous" heart. Newspapers similarly denounced the Broads and characterized the NYMS as a "humane and benevolent institution" rather than an organization prone to instigating African American protests, as some had claimed after the Volunbrun protests.[43]

Disdain for the Broads spread elsewhere too, as others stepped forward to condemn their brutality. In Portsmouth, New Hampshire, one advertisement asked citizens to provide information about a "Sea Monster in human shape . . . who some years since was in the habit of trafficking in human flesh on the coast of Africa." The writer accused the captain of lighting gun powder in the hold with the "kid-napped slaves" to prevent their revolt. Hoping the informant would be "the means of bringing to justice another Amos Broad," the writer connected the brutality of slave traders with masters in the North.[44] Cruelty against slaves was routine in the colonial era, but northern society's perspective was changing as it acknowledged and condemned the violent acts of slaveholders.

The Broad case would be a turning point, but it left unanswered the question of whether a master could engage in such extreme violence in correcting an insolent slave. It was clear this level of abuse against white servants would not be tolerated. Repeatedly in the trial, lawyers asked witnesses about Betty's behavior to determine whether the beatings were warranted. Witnesses claimed Betty never tried to run away, and one person described her as "a very willing servant; and . . . with a good master would have been a very good one; but from the witness's expressions it appeared that she was rather stupefied by terror than guilty of any willful fault." Broad treated all his servants and apprentices poorly, and he previously had a white servant taken away because of his merciless and sadistic behavior. The removed servant benefitted from a process and a society willing to negotiate for white children.[45] Although no frank discussion of slave masters' rights to use violent forms of discipline occurred in this trial, it did give New Yorkers considerable details about the experiences of Betty, Sarah, and others in the household. The questioning during the trial revealed a disposition of the legal community to believe that physical punishment of errant slaves and servants remained lawful, though communities placed limitations on violence.

The prosecutions against slave masters gave voice to enslaved African Americans even though legal codes expressly forbade them from serving as witnesses against whites. In the cases against masters, the bodies of slaves and servants served as testament to the horrific violence. In the case against Morehouse, Peter Wheeler reported that he detailed the narrative of Morehouse's assault against him when he presented his body as physical evidence to a judge. "I was brought forward, and had my shirt took off, to show the scars in my meat." Wheeler required two weeks to recuperate after the beating, and the scars he presented shone through the prejudices of the court. After seeing the physical damage done to Wheeler, the judge asked "Peter, how long did he whip you in the barn?" Wheeler testified and "told him the story as straight as I could."[46] The judge told Wheeler to return to him if he experienced further trouble from Morehouse, likely alluding to laws that allowed servants to seek reprieve from violent masters by reporting abuse to JPs. The judge's familiarity with this case meant Wheeler had an additional ally in his quest for justice, but to gain the JP's support, he first required an introduction by his white ally to certify his integrity. Wheeler's extraordinary case shows how slaves subverted the legal system by bearing their bodies as witness to the cruelty of slavery and demanding a response from whites. This pattern also emerged in the case against Hoffman in New York City. The justice who recorded Wright's complaints against Hoffman noted that "The boy has worn an Iron Collar on his Neck about three years, and his Voice is so broken that it is with difficulty he can be heard." Though it is unlikely Wright's testimony made it into the courtroom, the justice recorded that "a Chain is frequently put on his leg with a weight to it and he is forced to labour in that situation." No other affidavit gave this information, and no other source would have informed the justice about the sound of Wright's voice. Justices questioned slaves and considered their experiences in bringing cases to prosecutors and grand juries.[47] The affidavits against Hoffman show that Wright's words and feelings were expressed, particularly in the causes of his attempted suicide.

In contrast with the colonial era, when abuse went unpunished, community disdain for the Broads and the outcome of the Broad trial and others suggest changes in societal acceptance of cruelty. Routinely torturous abuse of slaves, when combined with malnourishment, exposure, or maiming, became illegal in New York City and other sites in New York. Recurring violence weighed on the consciences of white witnesses who saw patterns in masters' dangerous behavior, with all but one of the affidavits noting repeated instances of abuse by slave masters. Most white witnesses who made official complaints did not see one-time happenstances of brutal violence as meriting their intervention, and even in densely populated New York City, whites' complaints of violence against slaves were frustratingly belated. In the cases against Hoffman and the Broads, the witnesses waited months and years before they reported violence. James Wright's suffering was visible to all because Hoffman forced him to wear an iron collar, but only when he tried to commit suicide rather than return to Hoffman did a witness push the case forward. Similarly, Broad kicked Sarah about for at least a year, but only her frostbite and knife wound elicited action. Witnesses' reliance on employment from slaveholders likely impeded their desire to testify to the violence in several instances.[48] Whites sought to prosecute slaveholders for violence only once they had completely lost trust in owners' ability to serve as "humane" masters and they saw slaves' lives at risk. Though not a compellingly humane standard, this was considerable improvement from the colonial era, when slave deaths were not considered significant enough to investigate or bring forth a case.

The relationships built between African Americans and whites made these moments possible. By making others aware of their pain, slaves worked to make their suffering known in a society that undermined their claims to humanity and suffering. Interpersonal relationships helped whites understand that speaking out against slave violence was their responsibility. African Americans' relationships with one another should not be overlooked. Though the NYMS would work toward ending slavery, its acceptance of slow progress and efforts to reduce cruelty did not offer African Americans the radicalism their situation required. African Americans' planned protests and reporting of abuse helped galvanize whites with access to legislative and judicial tools to limit the slaveholders' rights when disciplining their slaves. Their combined work shaped the way the struggle continued.

Fighting for Freedom

Peter Wheeler was not safe so long as he lived with Morehouse, even with the bond for peace in place. He ran away after recovering from the brutal beating and established a new life as a mariner, spending his first winter of freedom in New York City and traveling extensively thereafter. After living in freedom for many years, he reflected that "slavery keeps the foot on the black man's neck all the time, and don't let 'em rise at all; and prejudice keeps a knockin' on him down as fast as he gits up." Wheeler was not just concerned with the growth of segregation and the lack of opportunity afforded to African Americans versus whites, he was also aware of the very real violence that African Americans confronted in their lives as free people. He believed abolitionists should not focus all their energy on southern slaveholding "till we can git the people of the North to treat our color like men and women."[49]

Violence was integral to the negotiations for power as gradual emancipation and changes in population required adaptation to a new racial environment. As early as the 1790s, it had become clear that part of this transformation included individualized and targeted violence against African Americans.[50] Grappling with this violence was critical to the early push for independence in African American communities. As in earlier eras, African Americans instigated assaults or engaged in counterassaults, revealing they literally had to fight for their freedom and right to live unfettered. What was new in the nineteenth century was that formerly enslaved African Americans in New York now had the civil status to report assaults to authorities, which cemented their roles as litigants in the new republic as their population grew. The official registration of complaints through the court system was part of an overall strategy to combat inequality, like the creation of separate black churches and institutions. African Americans served as witnesses in legal suits and partners for each other too. As they built networks and associations, African American perspectives joined others to secure their place in the political, economic, and social growth of the United States. In this work, they continued to use white partners when available to forward their agenda, but African Americans' resistance began with themselves.

Aggressive whites made their views about African Americans' place clear through intimidation and acts of violence. In 1795, Samuel Dexter, who lived in Weston, Massachusetts, described the relationship between whites and African Americans in country towns in Massachusetts, saying that "'harmony in general prevails between blacks and white citizens" but that whites demanded deference. Though Dexter did not elaborate on what disharmony looked like, his writing suggests violence did erupt from time to time. Whites "consider themselves as 'preeminent,'" he noted. Writing in Boston, Thomas Pemberton similarly described the sentiments of whites, claiming they were "tenacious of their superiority."[51] When African Americans refused to accept that they were less than whites, it caused problems, including violence. Coming of age in an era when slavery and the slave trade were legal, some whites believed violence against African Americans was acceptable and even warranted. In 1809, New York City charged James Downey, a white man, with intent to murder after he stabbed Richard Hutson, an African American. Though Downey would be acquitted, two African American witnesses attested that Downey used a club to hit Hutson and stabbed him with a jackknife. Hutson responded by going after Downey until they both fell to ground. It was unclear to bystanders at first who stabbed Hutson, but Hutson and another African American heard Downey "declare that he had killed many a Negro on the Coast of Guineas and mean to kill more."[52] Downey's boasting reveals that the immunity given to those who murdered and assaulted African American slaves affected their sense of right and wrong. To many whites, black bodies were not inviolable. Downey's impudence exemplified how whites made connections between the historical memory of slavery and violence a decade after the state passed gradual emancipation legislation.

Much of the violence between African Americans and whites in New York City and Boston centered on the sites and experiences of the maritime industry. The laboring patterns of African Americans, as well as the commercial activities of northeastern cities, led to increased interracial contact in dockyards and shipbuilding centers and even aboard ships. Work in maritime communities was significant for the growth of African American economic prospects, but prejudice meant violence could be a routine aspect of African American mariners' lives. Discipline was severe aboard ships for all the crew, and African Americans were subject to more frequent floggings than whites as part of shipboard discipline. Racial stratification aboard ships meant most African Americans served in lower-ranking positions such as stewards and cooks. The work was a source of pride regardless of status because it meant being able to provide an income for the family.[53] Some African Americans achieved considerable success as ship owners and traders competing successfully against whites, and this gave them and their crew less fear of violence.

African Americans banded together to create a bulwark against violence and to assert their place and role in the city and industry. In 1805, a series of riots occurred in Boston between African Americans and white mariners, attesting to the deeply felt racial animosity that occurred in the early republic. In March 1805, Jacob Cromwell, Robert Goodridge, and approximately eighteen other African Americans assaulted two white mariners, John Atwood and James Greenfield, who were disembarking from the *Pomona*. The numbers of African American men and women involved in this attack suggest an organized event with readiness on their part to confront the shipmates. Jacob Cromwell, a laborer in Boston, was a routine figure in the Municipal Court of Boston, and he was among the instigators of the attack. White Bostonians and shipmates rallied behind the white victims of the assaults and promised to serve as witnesses in court against the main perpetrators.[54] The local white community responded in kind to the attack. Two months later, in May 1805, Robert Goodridge and several other African Americans complained about four white men's assaults on them. The African American community offered to serve as witnesses for the African Americans assaulted by whites in the subsequent attack.[55] Missing from the events of May was Jacob Cromwell, but he was not forgotten. In November, Boston prosecuted Mathias Murch for assaulting Cromwell, possibly as retribution for the initial waterfront attacks. Cromwell's troubles were not over, and in December, he reported that three men led "a number of persons Names Unknown, who in a riotous manner assaulted his House knocking violently at his door in search" of him and "threatening his life."[56] The numerous directed attacks against Cromwell suggest he had become a target in Boston for actively staking out a role for African Americans and for causing disputes.

Waterfronts were sites where African Americans could assemble to assert their rights and safety as workers, but self-emancipated slaves in less populous regions had a more difficult time trusting others and finding allies. In 1814, William Grimes ran away from his owners in Virginia, first landing in New York and then moving around New England until he settled in Connecticut. He contended that "it [should] not be imagined that the poor and friendless are entirely free from oppression where slavery does not exist: this would be fully illustrated if I should give all the particulars of my life, since I have been in Connecticut." As evidence of his treatment, he detailed several instances of fraud and chicanery, and an assault he suffered at the hands of one student at Yale in New Haven. Grimes felt his race made him a target for mistreatment, though he had positive experiences with more friendly whites. The lawsuits and his status as a runaway slave undermined his chances of financial success and personal security. Being involved in legal matters as a runaway slave was particularly threatening, though he was able to recover damages in one case.[57] Grimes often used his wits and separated himself quickly from perceived threats to avoid incidents.

Trying to avoid or appear congenial to aggressive whites was a common way African Americans dodged violent conflict. Many African Americans learned this behavior while enslaved, and as they navigated roadways and met with new people, it was useful in pacifying aggressive whites who resented their mobility or assumed their criminality. African Americans had to prove their freedom to pass unmolested in some cases; other times, they faced outright hostility for no other cause than their race. Aggressive whites often used the language of racial derision, calling African Americans "nigger" or "boy" to immediately put them in a lesser position when confrontations began. Austin Steward took to the road to settle elsewhere after taking his freedom. As he passed a white man on the road, the white man called him a "nigger." The slur revealed the sensitivity of whites in regard to any perceived slight. The aggression put Steward on notice, and he tried to maneuver around the conflict by acting peaceably. Like Steward, Grimes encountered a group of white men when he traveled from New London to Stonington, Connecticut, in search of work as a barber. Grimes felt "very much frightened" when he saw them. The men were searching for a criminal who had robbed a shop in Stonington, and upon seeing Grimes they called him "boy" and demanded that Grimes allow them to search his baggage. The men told Grimes not to go to Stonington Point because "the people were not civil, but would raise the devil with any person who should undertake to establish a barber's shop there."[58] The message was clear to Grimes, and he returned to New London. Sometimes the threat of being unwanted changed African Americans' plans as they traveled and tried to locate safe spaces. Knowing that the roads were difficult to navigate, African Americans had to share knowledge about how to travel safely.

Schools, churches, mutual aid societies, and associations provided African Americans with a base from which to protest and publicize racially motivated violence, which took their activism in new directions. Much of the daily support African Americans gained from organizational development is lost, but shared spaces offered a place to explore the African American experience and develop political protests as they asserted their equality through speeches, sermons, and parades.[59] Although African Americans engaged in riotous activity and assaults from time to time, many leaders desired that they act as model citizens to counteract prejudice. They advocated improvement and respectability as keys to enhancing the image of African Americans and removing whites' prejudices.[60] Urging peaceful and nonviolent resistance, African Americans created counternarratives about their freedom and progress while also building an integral support network that could be drawn on to fight individual and collective battles. In the 1790s, Prince Hall used the African Masonic Lodge in Boston as a gathering site to advocate for change. Prince Saunders would later use this organization as leverage in his networking with whites to build educational facilities for African Americans. Benevolent societies, such as the New York City African Society for Mutual Relief, were another means of promoting community, while also safeguarding African Americans from poverty by offering financial support to widowed women whose husbands were members.

African American ministers were among the first leaders in the fight for civil rights, and they coordinated with local whites to create peaceful transitions to all-black churches or by serving as leaders for free African Americans. Separate black churches and associations developed a community voice and proved essential to securing dignity and spiritual equality. Meeting regularly was important to developing a shared sense of what issues existed and should be combatted. African Americans used printing presses to promote their associations, gave speeches commemorating emancipations, and advocated against the perpetuation of slavery and the slave trade. They met in buildings and in streets to plan their work; by doing so, they proclaimed their right to peaceably assemble. African Americans sent a clear message about African American resilience and resistance to those who saw or listened.

Some older violent tools of resistance continued alongside association and community building. In street brawls and planned attacks, African Americans showed they would not be trod upon in their freedom. Often, they banded together, as they had on Boston's waterfront, but at other times they fought alone, struggling to escape dangerous situations or looking for greater freedoms. Servitude remained a common focus of contestation for the "free" children of slaves, and some turned to violence to express their desire for freedom or in retribution for mistreatment. The violence of young servants of color sent shockwaves through the white community, which relied on poor black and white youth to provide labor. In December 1806, Eleanor Rawkin, a fourteen-year-old African American indentured servant to William H. Smith, used the household poison intended for vermin and mixed it in her mistresses' coffee. The first time Rawkin used the poison, the mistress immediately fell ill, but it did not slake Rawkin's spirit of resistance. In fact, her success resulted in another bold attack on the family. She served it again to the mistress, the master, and their daughter, and they took ill for weeks until the family doctor became suspicious. Rawkin originally denied poisoning the family, but eventually revealed "she did not like her said Mistress but she did not intend to kill her."[61] Rawkin's youth and the knowledge among servants and slaves that they had a uniquely powerful role in handling the household foodstuffs likely resulted in her choice to use poison to seek revenge.[62] She may not have had parents empowered to remove her from the household, and Overseers may have ignored her pleas for support.

Free and adult African Americans had a greater variety of means to protest their assaults and they showed a willingness to make the judiciary work for them. Their use of the court system likely stemmed from their successes and desire to make use of their citizenship. Legal suits had always been a tool for emancipation in Massachusetts, which informed African Americans' later experiences as free people. Between 1800 and 1810, free blacks reported at least sixty-four cases against whites for assaulting them in Boston and New York City, which is 11.9 reported cases per 1000 free African Americans. In contrast, there were only 5.9 reported cases per 1000 whites between 1808 and 1810, and this was regardless of the race of the assailant. The assault trends continued into the next decade.[63] African Americans asked for bonds of peace against the men and women who assaulted them, but their complaints also demanded the government enforce consequences for the offending whites. Between 1800 and 1810, New York City's and Boston's grand juries decided the complaints against whites merited indictments roughly 66 percent of the time. The cases represent grievous instances of violence as well as seemingly routine assaults, some in chance encounters with individuals, others as targeted attacks based on daily contact or racial animosity.[64] African Americans most commonly initiated legal suits against one another in Boston, which is one measure of the trust they had in the system. Urbanity factored into their reliance on JPs—access was easy, and justice was swift.[65] In rural areas, JPs were scattered through the countryside, but they made themselves available to all citizens. Extensive review of records—in Worcester and Middlesex Counties in Massachusetts and Cayuga County in New York—do not provide instances of cross-racial violence like those in urban areas, but that does not mean it did not exist or that African Americans failed to make use of local JPs.[66] JPs in rural areas often made decisions about assaults in their offices, and many records of assaults do not appear in official records until an appeal occurred. It is also possible that African Americans feared reprisal for reporting violence in less populous areas or did not see the value of involving JPs, who they may not have believed would work for them.

Making complaints, testifying, and gathering witnesses against whites were new assertions of their rights as free people. Peter Wheeler's experiences testifying in court as a free man show the importance of the judiciary in the realization of African Americans' sense of full manhood and citizenship. Wheeler witnessed the murder of a young woman, and he testified in court against a white man, which was a reversal of his previous positions in courts. New York City had prosecuted Wheeler for disorderly conduct after he arrived there, and his body had served as a form of evidence in the case against his former master for assaulting him. In freedom, his fully embodied words served as a vehicle for successfully prosecuting a white man in front of an all-white jury. Wheeler's enthusiastic rendering of this moment in his life reveals the profound effect the state's sanction of his testimony had on him. "*I was treated better than I ever was in an American court in my life; for I never got up in a court room in this country to give testimony or see a black man, who warn't rather laughed at by somebody.*" The magnificence of the room, as well as the spectators and judges, made Wheeler proud. He remembered, "And I tell you if I didn't feel fine to git up afore my lords, (as that ere Attorney General called 'em,) . . . and tell about that poor lady there."[67] The moment profoundly affected his sense of manhood and rights in the United States. As Wheeler notes, African American testimony in court had ramifications beyond those of whites entering the courtroom.

Important components of African American men's freedom were their registration of complaints against other men for assaulting their wives and their serving as guarantors for single African American women needing bonds to swear the peace or to appear in court. In filling these roles, African American men claimed the patriarchal privileges normally accorded to white men under the doctrine of coverture. In 1814, John Reed brought along his wife and two neighbors to process a complaint against Bowen Harrington and William Wiat, both whites, "for attacking his dwelling house with Brick Bats." According to Reed, the attack put his family "in great fear & hazard of their lives."[68] While African American men became agents of patriarchy in assuming this role, they also incorporated themselves into the manliness ideals of the era through their actions, which were claims for equity. It should be noted, however, that they also provided much-needed assistance to women. Independent African American women were particularly endangered in the streets and rural landscapes.[69] African American men registered complaints of assaults alongside and for their wives most often when the violence involved an attack by other African American men, but intraracial assaults were far more commonly reported overall. The cases include complaints for threats of bodily harm, intrusions into homes, and even whippings. Serving as sureties for single African American women's bonds provided a service to the community as well. Single women had less means to support themselves and lacked the protection that a spouse afforded. Offering to be held accountable for single women's appearance in court could be the deciding factor for single women deciding whether to file a suit and hold someone accountable for a violent act.

African American women made use of the courts, too, not only in defense of themselves, but also in defense of their husbands. Wives were particularly important in bringing assault cases against persons who so grievously wounded their husbands that their husbands were unable to appear in court. In 1805, Rosanna Dalton made a complaint on behalf of her husband, Scipio Dalton, for the retributive violence by white mariners on Boston's black community. Susan Butler, on the same day, protested on behalf of Benjamin Paul for an assault on him by over twenty men. The attacks were linked, and the two women appeared as witnesses for each other and went to the same JP. Single women also made use of the judiciary. In particular, several single African American women were routinely threatened and assaulted in Boston, and they made regular appearances to JPs and the Boston Municipal Court to assert their rights. The women were often both victims and assailants, which drove them to the JPs. A common course of action by all litigants was to defend oneself through countersuits when others in an affray determined to use the court system.[70]

Because of the racial climate in the early national era, white assistance was critical to remediating violence. White bystanders could assist African Americans in ways that undermined racially motivated attacks, and they were also important in processing complaints and serving as witnesses. When authority figures such as constables were involved in racially motivated assaults, the role of respectable whites in preventing and reporting violence became even more important. In 1801, white watchmen ordered Louis Cooney, an African American storekeeper in New

York City, to return inside even though it was not quite ten o'clock in the evening. Cooney insisted "that he was a free man & would go in when he pleased. That he disturbed no one." Asserting his own defense was a bold move in front of a group of white men, but Cooney used his knowledge of the law to show he was responsible citizen. The constables, however, saw Cooney as impertinent. One witness described that the watchmen "shoved & Knocked him up against the Window and house two or three different times." The violence was so excessive Cooney bled out of his penis through the night and morning. A helpful neighbor called a doctor, who concluded that "a Blood vessel leading to the said man's Kidneys had bursted" during the violent attack.[71] Several whites acted as witnesses alongside Cooney's own testimony. A nearby museum owner, William Waldron, brought the case to the special justices presumably because Cooney was too injured to leave his bed. Cooney's white doctor also testified about the extent of his wounds, and other neighbors offered themselves as witnesses.

The attack on Cooney occurred shortly after gradual emancipation took effect, and his treatment by constables and the legal system reveals some of the barriers even those with white assistance confronted. The indictment papers in the Cooney case do not include a statement made by Cooney, and several cases involving African Americans leave behind similar trails. When Mary Jones and her child were hit by a horse and cart in the street in 1801, only the testimony of a white witness remains in the indictment records, even though Jones was married and her husband served as a co-litigant. Jones was grievously injured, like Cooney, and likely confined to bed.[72] Justices may not have sought out testimony in these cases, as the first witnesses provided enough detail and believability to move the case forward for an indictment. However, the lack of affidavits from African Americans also suggests that legal custom played a role in the early 1800s. JPs might have been slow to recognize that the legal status of free blacks made them valuable witnesses in these cases. The best witnesses in most assault cases were the victims, and it was an oversight not to include their testimony in records. Only Cooney and Jones could relay the true impact of the assaults on them and add valuable information about the perpetrators. Many cases with solely African American witnesses against whites never made it to indictments and were stalled in the legal system.[73] Other cases of a similar nature resulted in "not guilty" verdicts.[74]

African Americans called on neighbors and strangers for support amid crises, and whites occasionally provided help during violent conflict, even when relationships were not well established. They did so at their own risk and lost their racial privilege in counterattacks. In August 1805, "a mob of People" in New York City attacked an African American man who kept an oyster stand. They "had come to his Stand and had abused him and thrown him down and dirtyed him." After beating him, the white mob of about thirty to forty people went to the cellar he resided in to attack his wife. According to Daniel Sweeney, a white neighbor who kept a junk store nearby, the man "begged for God's sake" to get assistance as the mob had "taken his wife away from him." When Sweeney arrived, he "heard Screaches" of the wife emanating from the cellar. Sweeney answered his cry and admonished the crowd that "it was a Shame to meddle with the Black man's wife" and to leave them alone. Though he did not know his name, Sweeney defended the black oysterman, whom he recognized as one of his many neighbors living on Water Street. The seventh ward was a working-class neighborhood that attracted African Americans and working-class immigrants as the city expanded in size. Sweeney would have had contact with the oysterman and his family during his daily activities, though it does not appear they interacted regularly or socially despite their proximity. The mob turned on him for defending the family. They "began to Damn him and told him they would serve him as they had the black man." Sweeney lost his racial privilege in defending the oysterman, and he was forced to flee to his house, and the mob followed him. In response, he grabbed his pistol and "told the Crowd to keep off or he would Shoot some of them, that they should not serve him as they had done the black man." The crowd continued to press in and Sweeney fired at a man. Ultimately, New York City indicted Sweeney for firing at the mob, though he was found not guilty. Other men experienced the same level of retributive violence for being race traitors. In August 1815, David Cannon, a white ferry master, defended an African American man in his home who was struck by two white visitors. For his assistance, the two men beat him and "nearly cutt off" his ear.[75] Whites' defense of African Americans reveals the importance and complexity of momentary interracial alliances and the way that prejudice did not override all whites' sense of justice.

Whites and African Americans cooperated in perpetrating violence against others, and in some cases, African American men gained the racial privileges of whites. Moments of interracial cooperation, even in acts of violence, reveal the shared bonds of individuals that transcended racial prejudices. Simon Burton, an African American cook on board the ship *Pennsylvania*, "aided and assisted" in the beating of John Williamson, a white chief mate on the ship, by two white men. Burton reportedly encouraged the beating, showing he had a level of power in their relationship. Living aboard a ship could create lasting bonds among shipmates as they faced danger and opportunity together. In another case of interracial violence, John Ennis, a white man from New Jersey, testified he had been beaten by Joseph Williams, a white laborer, and Abraham, an African American man, who "threw a large Stone" at him. The stone "Struck him against his head and bruised him very badly."[76] Strong bonds or shared values often existed prior to the acts of violence involving mixed-race perpetrators. The large population of cities and close living quarters in them encouraged meaningful relationships among immigrants, working-class whites, and African Americans. Open windows and doors as well as porches offered many opportunities to interact. Following these assaults, records do not reveal retributive violence against African American men. The reports to the special justices show a desire to hold the men accountable, but these suits name the white perpetrators, too.

In the wake of emancipations, African Americans built and expanded the vibrant communities already established by free African Americans from earlier decades. They made religious and social associations that erected the political arguments for abolition and the full benefits of United States citizenship. Using their relationships with one another and whites to build a more just and peaceful society was critical to their advancement. African Americans began a movement to end excessive cruelty and laid a foundation for their judicial activism. They also violently fought back. African Americans proved they would not be victims of abuse without a fight.

Charles Edward Lester, a white abolitionist, transcribed Peter Wheeler's memoir and saw it published. Lester understood prejudice existed, but he did not understand the daily burden of confronting white hostility to black progress. Lester recommended, "if you are oppressed by the strong arm of power, and kept down by an unholy and cruel prejudice, forget it and forgive it all, and go to that blessed Redeemer who came to save your souls."[77] This advice was like that given to other dependents in the colonial era, when they were told to withstand excessive or unwarranted punishment and use it as a tool of reflection for personal betterment. He was not being flippant in this advice. When Wheeler recounted his struggles, Lester would often recommend he try to forget and focus on the afterlife, even as he empathized with Wheeler's struggles. Lester took weeks to record Wheeler's life story and months fashioning it into a book, but he did not create a narrative that aimed at the structural issues in the North that perpetuated violence and prejudice, even as he hoped it would show whites the problematic nature of slavery. Lester inscribed the book to the "Free People of Color in the Free States" and expressed paternalistic sentiments in the dedication: "I love you, and feel anxious to have you become intelligent and virtuous." As with many other white partners in the quest for racial justice, the culture of the nineteenth century impaired his vision of African Americans. Lester's advice is a reminder that creating partnerships with whites was not easy. They were implicated in a culture whose view of African Americans was deeply prejudicial and aimed to keep them dependent. By the time Lester recorded his narrative, Wheeler expressed joy in his family and in his commitment to leading a Christian life. Wheeler continued to struggle, though, and so did other free and enslaved African Americans who desired to assert their independence.

Chapter 8

Legal Strategies for Civil Rights

In 1818, Elizabeth Pienovi reported her husband to the special justices for biting off the end of her nose, and a published trial report brought the case to the attention of the broader public. Lawrence Pienovi, Elizabeth's husband, claimed to have gone insane because he believed her to be unfaithful to him. When Elizabeth considered how to deal with her husband's assault, she chose a legal strategy because it was the best means of securing her safety. She knew from experience little would be done to protect her in the moment of crisis, and she needed lasting guarantees. On the night of the assault, Elizabeth screamed in fear and pain, as well as to alert neighbors to her struggles, and Lawrence immediately attended to covering up the assault. Asa Holden, a neighbor, heard the noises and looked out in time to see Lawrence "come to the windows and close the shutters." Asa did not immediately get up and intervene. Instead he commented to his family that "they must be chastising their servant pretty severely"; this misdirected concern for the servant did not motivate Asa to give assistance. Minutes later, Elizabeth opened the shutters to reveal "something black on her face, to appearance something like blood." Asa still did not come to her aid. He learned through neighborhood gossip that Lawrence had fled after biting off his wife's nose. In the meantime, Elizabeth turned to a doctor to help her with the wounds, and she revealed the details of the attack. After she reported the assault to the special justices, Asa agreed to share what he knew of the events along with five other witnesses for Elizabeth.[1] With the assistance of their testimony, the court sentenced Lawrence Pienovi to two years in jail. Bystander intervention could not always be relied upon to prevent assaults, but witnesses provided valuable testimony as individuals took cases to court.

By 1800, wives, servants, and African Americans had a long history of engaging in legal strategies to resist cruelty. In fact, their engagement with the government was increasing due to several opportunities in the early republic's cultural and political landscape. Legally dependent groups made certain that the criminal justice system worked for them by bringing suits forward, thereby ensuring their role as active citizens in the early republic. The ways that those classified or thought of as dependents engaged with the government outside of elections, polling, parades, and public speaking are important to understanding the struggle for civil rights. Abused wives, slaves, and free blacks initiated their own movement to increase their rights by defending their individual right to safety, among other initiatives. Analysis of assaults shows the way people interacted with the government, their conceptions of their own citizenship rights, and their perceptions of the legal and social hindrances they faced. As wives, slaves, and free blacks used the legal system to further their cause, a different kind of civil rights movement emerged among African Americans and women, one that focused on securing public and private spaces from violence. Whether it was a wife suing for divorce or a slave running from a master, resistance highlighted the hierarchy that allowed for their abuse and showed that corporal punishment was not acceptable.

When individuals chose to report abuse to the government instead of friends and neighbors, it was because the government's response was swift; however, legal strategies did not exist in isolation and individuals chose what worked best for them. Poor and urban Americans were much more likely to take cases through the legal system than rural or middle-class and elite victims. Reported assaults often occurred in buildings with shared spaces or in the streets, where disputes were already public, which muted issues of privacy. Constables, special justices, and Overseers of the Poor were integrated into urban communities and were trusted members with the authority to correct wrongs. Those with greater financial means had concerns about privacy that limited their use of the judiciary, and they turned to interpersonal networks for security. They also had access to other governmental and private networks that could provide relief. Young servants and apprentices did not increase their legal activism in this period, though they retained a presence in the courts. Instead, they used neighbors and other bystanders to seek assistance, or engaged in extralegal acts like others.

The reactions of women, African Americans, and young adults to abuse show how the daily struggles for safety were actually human and civil rights issues. With impaired legal statuses, individuals struggled to communicate meaningful criticisms of abuse, and for many, that meant turning to those with whom they had relationships in sharing their struggle. When dependent peoples turned to the government, they demanded the exercise of their citizenship rights. The abused highlighted how subjugated legal statuses hindered their quest for safety and demanded redress; this forced a reckoning of their words with the more socially and legally empowered voices of their masters or husbands. They held the government to providing rights to deliver testimony and bear witness, submit pleas, and demand a hearing of their cases. In some struggles against abuse, the desire for freedom is as palpable as the desire for civil rights. When enslaved African Americans and pauper servants turned to violence or ran, they derided the government, showing they lacked faith in it to resolve conflict and act justly. They demanded human rights to freedom from coercive labor.

Wives' Increased Reporting

No organization developed in the early republic to combat spousal assault and assist women like Elizabeth Pienovi. Women's pleas for support in the early republic worked to ensure that women's perspectives and safety were considered. After 1800, abused wives increasingly used governmental intervention and thereby politicized the abuse they experienced, particularly in asking JPs to issue bonds for peace and address marital violence, and African American women litigants were taking part in this process. Socioeconomic status affected the types of interventions women sought, with poorer women more comfortable using public methods such as suing for the peace. Like others, abused wives resisted violently and created networks of support to assist them in times of need. Finding a haven from abuse required reaching out beyond their homes. In the many ways women resisted, they demanded society confront their abuse and they created a precedent for other women to follow. The agency of women as they protested violence within their marriages is an unmistakable feature of the early republic and was the beginning of a civil rights movement that advanced their own conceptions of their rights within marriage.

Women increased pressure on the judicial system to respond to wife abuse, and they often made repeated efforts to resolve violence. Between

1800 and 1820 in Boston and New York City, records of at least 363 and 320 separate cases exist, respectively, in which wives testified of spousal abuse to JPs. They hoped to force their husbands to make bonds ensuring they would not assault them, or they wanted to move the court to issue indictments. Women increased their reliance on the judiciary to attain safety over the twenty-year period even though doing so came with considerable risks. Between 1800 and 1804, the average rate of reports in Boston was 5.2 cases per year, and from 1816 to 1820, the rate was 39 per year, which is a rise in the number of suits beyond population growth.[2] The report rate per 1,000 people in Boston increased from 1.04 between 1800 and 1804 to 4.43 between 1816 and 1820.[3] Abused wives' complaints of assaults to JPs required persistent efforts on their part to force their husbands to remain peaceful, and their efforts often failed. Women notified JPs when their husbands broke the bonds for peace by assaulting them again. In Boston from 1797 through 1820, women reported that 55 of the 363 men held to bond defaulted on their promise to keep the peace. Gaps in the record-holding of defaults suggest that the real number is much higher.[4] In addition to risks of violence, women suffered the financial sting alongside their husbands when their bond was forfeited; this was especially the case for wives living on slim financial margins—the very women most likely to report abuse. Nevertheless, women maintained their presence in the legal system even with the financial losses and further violence they suffered.

Rising numbers of white women also sued for divorce where it was possible in the late eighteenth and early nineteenth centuries, and New York opened up the process to abused wives. In Massachusetts during the 1760s, women sued for divorce at a rate of 0.005 per 1,000 people, and in the 1800s and 1810s in four counties, this figure went up to 0.036. Though divorce was still rare, white women turned to it far more often than men and increasingly viewed it as an option. Cases citing cruelty as a causal factor were a steady component of pleas for divorce and separation, even though Massachusetts did not grant full divorces for cruelty.[5] In 1813, New York began granting separations to women who suffered cruelty or whose husbands abandoned them. It's difficult to imagine the legal separations being provided to women without reflecting on the many individual protests women made by reporting husbands to JPs for abuse. Women were the individuals who brought the plight of spousal abuse to the forefront, demanding that communities provide them with greater options, as they lacked major advocates.

Prior to changes in New York's law, women cleverly combined legal and extralegal means to combat abuse and forced the government to reckon with the problems of wife assault without legal separations. By 1812, Frances Gautier had suffered repeated abuse by her husband in New York City. Her reports of his assaults to the special justices had not reformed his behavior, even though judges placed him in Bridewell several times in consequence of his actions. Gautier used the legal system because she did not have familial support, and the violence was so extreme she needed intervention. She stated, "I am in a great manner deprived of the use of one of my arms [from the assaults], and I have no relation to whom I can apply for any support in this country." Needing a long-term solution to the problem, Frances Gautier tried to arrange a separation from her husband because she believed the abuse put her "in danger of my life." The separation would be legally contracted, but not officially sanctioned since New York did not allow for it at that time. She and William Gautier signed papers that they "mutually agreed to separate" and that she would not "come after him any more for any support for myself and of my child." Without state sanction, the separation was not financially beneficial to Frances or her child, and she did not have leverage to get more favorable terms. She desired safety for her family, first and foremost, and that was her driving force in this arrangement. William Gautier put notices in the newspaper not to accept charges from her even before she moved out. When she departed his household, she took her things, but the very day after she moved William used the powers he derived through the doctrine of coverture to recover her property even though they had agreed to a separation. Frances Gautier reported "the constables came . . . and took away everything I had as also my childs cloths & sold the whole at auction." Left in a "very destitute situation" she turned to the special justices once more for help. The special justices were familiar with her plight, as were her neighbors, who offered to testify on her behalf, but little else could be done by them. William used all his power to try and get her to return to him, but she knew residing with him put her, and perhaps her child's, life at risk. Frances notified the justices that "he offers me to come and live with him again, but I dare not, as he has frequently come to bed with a Razor, hammer, hatchet &c for to kill me, and is scarcely ever one night Sober." Placed in a difficult situation, Frances tried every maneuver she could—even leaving her husband—to find some safety.

Legal interventions remained important to her even though they had proven ineffective. She tried to have a legal document that would bind her husband to their agreement when they separated, and she demanded the courts protect and provide for her. "My wish is to have some allowance from him, so that I & my child may not become a burthen to the City," she explained after the failed separation. Though the JPs could not arrange for that, the court could take actions to penalize him for the assaults. She asked "to have him bound over so that he cannot come where I am to trouble me as he comes almost every where I am & abuses me so that I can do nothing for my support and that of my child." The court reported the case as settled but it was not, and Frances continued to be in danger. William threatened to leave her even though he was simultaneously coercing her to live with him by taking away her property. Frances reported William for assaulting her again in 1813.[6] She had to remain assertive in her quest for safety and financial security, because the law left her with limited options. JPs were familiar with her and other women's struggles as they processed complaints of abuse, and they were useful as stopgap solutions, but long-term arrangements were not possible so long as she remained tethered to William legally. Allowing legal separations in New York expanded the roles of the government beyond just issuing bonds for peace and indictments for violence.

Extralegal responses to abuse were also mainstays in women's arsenals, even though they could be censured for it. Some women, like Frances, left their husbands regardless of legal understandings, and others violently fought their husbands. Women's relationships with other women could be useful in establishing marital boundaries and finding safe havens, but in some instances wives' support networks struck back against abusers. In June 1822, Titus Oliver, who was likely African American, asked his wife to give him a shirt, and when "she refused . . . He then extended his arm towards her; but whether to strike her or to take hold of her, appeared uncertain." Expecting an assault, his wife hit him, and her two friends, Jane Garretson and Susan Brown also "attacked him violently with their clubs." Oliver defended himself with a club "about the same size" and chased after them. When Garretson found him unaware, she "struck him a violent blow on the back of the head," and he died of the wounds two days later in the almshouse.[7] Garretson and Brown admitted they were moved to get involved because Titus Oliver routinely abused his wife. Prior to the events, Brown was overhead stating, "if you strike her you shall never strike another woman." Oliver's violence within the home was commonplace, and roundly criticized by his wife's friends. Brown further asserted that "she would kill any negro who would whip his wife."[8] These women's extralegal acts intervened in the daily insults they perceived occurring in the Oliver home, and Oliver's wife originally struck back in self-defense as well. Print literature commonly disparaged women's physical and verbal bellicosity to contain their behavior, as it was viewed as dangerous to men's authority and communities. At the heart of the critiques of women's violence was an effort to domesticate them and situate them as modest members of the household. The message that abusive speech was immoral and unfeminine became more pronounced as women aged and married, and the public attention women garnered from these aggressively authoritative actions were censured as unseemly. Women nevertheless saw value in fighting violence with violence, though it could turn deadly.

New ideals regarding womanhood took hold by the early republic, and they fostered women's sense of righteousness in countermanding spousal assault, even as they were told that their voices should be subservient to their husbands'. Increased engagement in writing and public works revealed women believed their public citizenship had value.[9] New ideologies about women, often referred to as "republican wives" or "republican mothers," originated with a push by women and their allies to reconsider the intellectual capacity of women and their place in the republic.[10] This work, which began as early as the colonial era, found women's morality to be a source of power for the republic, and some women hoped to see women's roles within the home and community expanded. Although the beneficiaries of more positive attributions of womanhood are typically associated with wealthier white women, the increased activism of African American women to build and support communities shows women from various backgrounds believed they had valid roles to play outside the home.[11]

African American women in Philadelphia created a novel way to claim respectability and reduce domestic violence: they began policing it themselves through religious organizations. African American women reported domestic discord to church elders and demanded they act to solve familial issues. Historian Erica Armstrong Dunbar views these activities as part of a larger effort of African American women to exert control over their marital lives. In pushing cases forward, they demanded the church adhere to ideals of companionate marriage and prevent the suffering of women married to abusive husbands. Their activities may have had a greater impact on husbands than white women's use of church discipline. Though churches were well integrated into most communities, African Americans' churches were often nearly the only public institutions of which they could claim control. Being ostracized meant a loss of fellowship and access to respectability.[12]

Women's assessment of the risks associated with reporting abuse and emerging class-based values of privacy affected their decisions about how to handle abuse. While submission and privacy were ideals in some upper- and middle-rank models of womanhood, these concerns were less important to poor African American and white women. Women of less wealth, even many in the middle ranks, were more comfortable voicing criticisms of their husbands' behaviors and demanding protection from JPs. Their daily lives often required more public interactions with others in the gathering of water, engaging in markets, and shared living spaces. In Massachusetts between 1790 and 1820, white women and the wives of poorer men were more likely than any other groups of women to turn to JPs for help in peace suits. Laborers' wives' accounted for 40 percent of the plaintiffs, and the wives of mariners and traders made up the second most often noted professions of plaintiffs, but these represent a much smaller pool of 10 and 7 percent of complaints, respectively.[13] Historians estimate laborers made up between 10 and 15 percent of the total population.[14] Many cases were submitted by wives of men in skilled trades and professions, including artisans, traders, musicians, and others, but the wealth of these men cannot be ascertained. In more rural parts of Worcester and Middlesex counties, where fewer records and laborers existed, husbandmen and yeomen appeared as often as other occupations.[15] Given the trend in Boston, it is likely these yeomen and husbandmen were not wealthy and had small landholdings. The majority of complainants were white women, but the racial hostility in Boston did not prevent abused African American women from taking the same steps. African American women brought at least 5 percent of the cases, which is roughly equivalent to their percentage of the population.[16]

In contrast, most elite white wives suffering abuse avoided a public airing of their marital disputes and privately used their families and friends to intercede on their behalf. Between 1790 and 1820, elite women made at least four complaints to JPs in Suffolk, Middlesex, and Worcester counties in Massachusetts, and four in New York City. More elite women likely used JPs to intercede on their behalf, but records are scarce because JPs were occasionally loath to create official paperwork on men of this rank.[17] Elite white women were the beneficiaries of new evaluations of womanhood that valorized their morality and domestic life; and their privacy was highly prized. In reporting assaults to JPs, wives gambled on whether acting as plaintiffs against their husbands was a socially, financially, and personally wise choice—and not all women were equally likely to make that decision.

African American and white women recognized that their residency gave them access to the judicial system, and that the state had a role in protecting citizens of every status. They had a history of using JPs for large and small problems, and JPs proximity made them a valuable tool for women to defend themselves and leverage their citizenship, particularly if they were poor or lived in urban areas. African American and white women often sued other women and men for physical assaults, and women served as witnesses and defendants in other common criminal and civil cases, making themselves heard in public arenas regularly. In 1799, the creation of Boston's new municipal court made seeking justice easier for urban women: cases were heard almost daily, unlike the quarterly General Sessions. They also had a greater number of JPs dispersed throughout the city. New York City had a similarly easy system to access with its steady manning of special justices to handle litigation and constables or watchmen in the streets. Women's familiarity with JPs and the legal system enabled their use of their citizenship and the government to confront their abusers. The numbers of white working-class and African Americans abused wives who registered issues with JPs fostered a legal culture in which they saw themselves as rightful litigants and members of a community.

Communication and exchanges between JPs, constables, and the poor were more commonplace than among wealthier white wives. Historians

have shown that the adjudication of poor laws and efforts to ameliorate the conditions of poverty and fight crime meant charitable groups
and the government routinely interacted with the poor. Fear of crime
in the early republic led to more constables being assigned to prevent
and control vice, and these constables patrolled poor neighborhoods. In
addition, charitable groups often investigated the homes of the poor to
confirm their morality before distributing alms.[18] Such intrusions made
poor white women's and African Americans' access to government and
charitable groups' services visible. Abused wives may have seen these
constables and charitable groups as potential allies when they appeared
amid conflict, even though they would have resented the assumptions
made about their homes and integrity on other occasions. African
Americans had a less positive experience with constables and other public officials, but they sought assistance from charities and associations to
increase educational opportunities and turned to the NYMS to protect
them and others from malfeasance. Wealthier wives were the backbone
of much charity work, and they acted as givers of aid rather than seekers
of it. Their interfaces with charities cemented relationships with other
women in powerful ways, but charitable organizations were structured
in ways that were intended to give women volunteers access to influence
and power to be used on behalf of others.

For wealthy white women, reporting their husbands to the government required a greater flouting of societal conventions. Wealthier
families desired privacy. Their homes were isolated from the poor and
showcased new architectural styles that featured dedicated rooms for
privacy separate from those used for public gatherings. At the turn of
the century, elites sought to distinguish themselves from others through
manners and claims to refinement, and decorum and privacy were an
integral component of this. Abigail Abbot Bailey, a white New Hampshire wife who suffered repeated abuse by her husband, was among the
women in the middle-to-upper strata of society who decided against
making a complaint of abuse to JPs or her church. Both she and her
husband, Asa Bailey, were the children of former selectmen, and he was
a respected member of their New Hampshire community for increasing their family's landholding and economic position. Potential embarrassment from the public exposure of her marital troubles factored into
Bailey's silence. She noted in her memoirs that within the first month

of marriage, she learned to "expect hard and cruel treatment in my new habitation, and from my new friend." She never considered turning to JPs to quell the violence or to redress her husband's adultery with a servant—or his attempted rape of another. Bailey decided "not to make my troubles known to the world, and thus to load my husband with public disgrace." She hoped that by modifying her behavior and by being a good wife, she could manage her husband's violence. It was only after her husband sexually assaulted their daughter that Bailey attempted to get out of her marriage. However, even in this, she avoided the courts and made a private arrangement with her husband to avoid the "dreadful scene of prosecuting my husband."[19] Bailey's hesitancy to seek help stemmed from her belief that the public airing of her marital troubles would be disgraceful, which matches the experiences of other women of her status. In fact, wealth-based identities appear as important as actual wealth. Frances Sedgwick Watson, the daughter of a wealthy and educated family in Massachusetts, worried about how she would support herself if she left her husband, even though he was impoverished. Her elite identity also appears to have influenced her and her family's desire to keep her marital conflict quiet until the 1820s.[20]

Divorce was a more viable option for women with means, given the associated costs and the economic hardships facing women living independently. In Massachusetts, the women who sued for divorce citing cruelty as part of their grounds came more often from the middle and upper ranks of white society, showing they would turn to the government for a final dissolution once they had given up hope of managing their husbands' violence.[21] Women considering divorce also faced similar problems to those suing for peace, including fear of further violence, as well as concerns about privacy, children, and breaking social codes. New Englanders' history of allowing divorce for adultery negated some of the social taboos associated with it, but divorce was a very public matter that was reported in newspapers, gossiped about in the streets, and witnessed in courthouses.

Given that most abused wives turned to the state to stop abuse—through divorce or peace suits—wives of many different social and economic ranks perceived themselves as deserving of the protection of the state, and the government agreed. All women were connected to the state given their vital role in producing citizens, and as citizens themselves they were expected to pay taxes and obey laws, and they had access to legal system. On the other hand, wealthy white women were more timid about leveraging their citizenship in this way, suggesting that their sense of empowerment laid elsewhere. Thus, cultural trends regarding privacy had a negative impact on their exercise of governmental processes available to protect them. Using friends, family members, and neighbors to manage their abuse, wealthier women's sense of their own influence revolved around their interpersonal networks. However, it is important to note that these decisions were made by women, not the government, and that the government still envisioned itself as an important stopgap for those suffering abuse. When wealthy wives did use the judicial system, they proved their citizenship was powerful and that it outweighed their husbands' authority. By leveraging their citizenship, women of all classes compelled their husbands to stop abusing them and forced a reckoning with their own influence as citizens.

Women's appeals for peace or divorce were part of a much more broadly conceived civil rights movement than our current historiography appreciates. Clearly, most women seeking divorce and peace were fighting for their own personal safety and to end unhappy marriages, but the mutual refrain of these women resonates with broader cultural changes in society. Abused wives did not deconstruct gender norms, list an inventory of women's legal and social disadvantages, or act as a group as modern definitions of women's rights movements require. Women in the early republic sought to institute changes related to marital inequality and sex a generation after the radical women of the revolutionary era asserted an environmentalist critique of women's inequality and claimed intellectual and spiritual equality with men. Instead of using a "rights" lexicon, women assumed a position of authority in the home and in sexual matters by limiting births, contesting the sexual double standard, and securing the safety of their homes, among other initiatives.[22] Women's responses to spousal abuse should be viewed alongside these other activities and those of other citizens whose activism affected governmental processes.

The efficacy of the women's movement to stop abuse has not been fully understood or venerated because women acted individually rather than as part of a street protest, parade, petition, or larger milieu of writers. It is in their daily activities that we can see the advancement of women's power and rights in the early republic. The movement to reject patriarchal strictures on sex and violence was more essential to women than movements to obtain a vote; however, this does not mean that their activities did not have political ramifications. Abused wives situated themselves as rights-bearing citizens whom the government could not afford to ignore. Women's judicial activism was important given the reactive nature of local and state judicial practices and the many limitations placed on them in bringing suits forward. The government could not initiate changes in the handling of assault cases if women did not bring forth assault cases. Thus, women's conceptions of themselves, their citizenship rights, and spousal assault were incredibly significant in providing the government with the opportunity to address these issues.

Enslaved Activists

So long as African Americans brought cases of violence to the public eye, white New Yorkers had to face the reality of their slaveholding practices and race relations. Gradual emancipation proved a painfully slow process, and highlighting enslaved persons' experiences was important to eradicating slavery. By 1810, slaves made up less than 2 percent of New York State's total population; out of the nearly 1 million New York residents, 15,000 African Americans remained enslaved, 5,000 less than reported in the 1800 census. Slavery nevertheless remained influential in the marking of African Americans as inferior and in supporting the economic and social privileges of whites. African Americans continued highlighting the cruelty and violence of enslavement and pressed for an end to the institution, and they maintained partnerships in the community. Increased reporting of violence to the NYMS and special justices was a legacy of the early nineteenth century and part of the overall human and civil rights movement to end slavery and gain access to the criminal justice system. Like abused wives, enslaved Americans had their most pronounced legal activism in urban centers where allies were easily found, but tactics to resist violence and slavery were used throughout the state. Enslaved activists also set standards about violence in their daily lives by defending themselves against violence or using assaults to assert their right to safety. They proved unwilling to labor under violence as gradual emancipation continued, and they took opportunities to leave their masters whenever possible.

After the *Broad* cases, more individuals took up the challenge of bringing cases of excessive violence to those who would mediate disputes. African Americans remained the starting point of activism by making their suffering known through verbal cries for help and through seeking out assistance. Prior to 1809, the overwhelming majority of cases heard by the NYMS came from slaves who were seeking their freedom based on false promises, wrongful contracts, or registration issues. After *Broad*, numerous African Americans approached the society in hope of finding some relief from cruel masters, and other community members supported slaves by contacting the NYMS. In the same month as the trial against the Broads, the standing committee heard the details regarding three cases of cruelty; it heard four more cases before year's end. The rising number of cases was a direct response to discussions about the *Broad* cases. One such case was "suppos'd to surpass in cruelty that of Broad's." NYMS notes show growth in what it considered legal practices regarding the disciplining of slaves because it used language such as "unlawful and cruel abuses" when referring to violent incidents.[23] New York passed no new laws regarding the treatment of slaves, but bystanders believed in limits to violence and reported cases for intervention. Between 1810 and 1812, reports of thirteen more cases of abuse emerged, with at least six reported by slaves and the rest by concerned neighbors. One person even turned against his brother in reporting abuse and offered to serve as a witness against him. When reporting abuse, neighbors often noted being "frequently disturbed by the cries," revealing the ways that slaves made their suffering known.[24] Reporting cruelty to the NYMS was a strategy of African Americans and white community members who wanted to persuade the government to intervene.

Although slaves were not allowed to formally testify in court, after 1810, they established their right to sue for peace against their owners through their more frequent and formal protests against abuse. Rather than taking their cases to the NYMS, slaves began directly reporting their mistreatment to the police in New York City, and in 1817, the state formalized the process, which further chipped away at the slave code. Complaints by slaves who served masters as servants until the age of their release would be "heard, tried and determined in the manner, and with like effect, as complaints by and against masters and apprentices, under the laws of this state."[25] The new law effectively admitted that white New Yorkers had falsely claimed they protected slaves by giving them access to JPs to redress their grievances. It was not until after the 1800s that evidence shows the courts respected and pursued cases initiated by slaves. The new law did not assist those who would never see freedom through the gradual emancipation law.

The enslaved were clearly the impetus for the legislative changes because they demanded the government correct their masters' wrongdoing. In 1818, the NYMS learned that Betsey Paulding reported Robert Warnock, her master, to the police for beating her three times, and she continued to suffer from abuse. Justices, however, did not record her complaints, and it was only through the NYMS that her side in the dispute is revealed. Paulding's use of the police to stymie her master's abuse prior to the passage of the legislation shows how New York City adapted to the post-*Broad* condemnations of excessive violence and heard complaints by slaves. After the third beating by Warnock, "Betsey told him [her master] she would make complaint," revealing her sense of power as a litigant.[26] Suits for peace gave her and other slaves some leverage in forestalling and preventing abuse, though it was fraught with risk. Masters' chagrin at their slaves' "insolence" could result in even more damaging assaults, just as it did with wives. Though suing for peace did not require courtroom appearances, slaves' use of this practice goaded justices to expand their view of slaves' legal status, and it broadened the ad hoc practices of justices, some of whom accepted complaints from slaves and took action on their behalf while others did not.

The new law did not mean that the justice slaves received was equal to that of white servants or that they would live secure from violence. Indeed, slave masters developed tools to combat slaves' use of the legal system that relied on the judiciary's view of violence against slaves as a reasonable form of discipline. In the case of Betsey Paulding, Warnock countersued her on each occasion for an assault on his family, which resulted in the police putting her in jail for a trial. In the first report, Warnock claimed Paulding "was very insulting & refused to obey the reasonable orders of deponent & lay violent hands on deponent because he endeavored to prevent her from going out." Characterizing Paulding as a violent and poorly behaved servant swayed special justices to Warnock's perspective. That was not the only way slave masters could refute slaves' accusations. Slaves such as Paulding could be jailed while waiting for trial, and Warnock removed Paulding from jail just prior to her trial to silence her. He gambled that Paulding's experiences in Bridewell would make her desperate to leave jail and give up on her case against him. After Paulding's last beating, Warnock started the cycle over again by making counter accusations and having Paulding jailed. He told the special justices that "he feared she would kill some of the family," and the potential threat the justices saw in the accusations against Paulding caused them to move the trial forward. In the process, they denied Paulding's voice and right to safety and prioritized her master's rights. In 1818, courts twice sentenced her to a week in prison. Paulding's experiences were not singular, and a similar case occurred in 1815. In this case, a neighbor of a slave named Maria reported that Paul Plume routinely and cruelly abused her. Three days before his trial, a countersuit emerged claiming Maria assaulted Plume's wife, and the jury convicted Maria of the crime and acquitted Plume of his charges.[27] Slave masters avoided convictions because assaulting an insubordinate slave was still accepted as a corrective measure.

For slaves living outside of New York City, their civil status proved particularly problematic as they faced more limited prospects for finding allies and bystander intervention. Austin Steward, a slave in upstate New York, noted "nothing could be done to give the slave even the few privileges which the laws of the State allowed them." After witnessing the beating of his sister, Steward considered taking the case to one of the nearby lawyers, but his master had hired out his slaves to all the lawyers in town. Steward perceived that the lawyers' economic and personal connections with slavery negated his pleas for justice, and slaves throughout the state similarly struggled with the practicality of finding advocates. Steward saw and heard about the way other slaveholders treated their slaves, including lawyers and JPs in his community, and he professed these men "treated [their slaves] with more or less rigor" and were thus implicated in the culture of violence existing in the North. Steward believed that "of course they would do nothing toward censuring one of their own number," and he did not seek redress for his sister's beating.[28] Steward's experiences suggest how the social economy of violence affected the mentality of African Americans and their masters.

Like Wheeler, who described his body as "meat" when he was speaking with a judge, many slaves knew society did not grant them basic civil rights and that whites were not prone to assisting them.

Slaves used violence in self-defense and as retribution to demand better treatment. Their sense of their right to live without abuse was fundamental to this resistance, as was the growing antislavery sentiment and existing gradual emancipation legislation. Austin Steward recorded an immediate change in his fellow slaves' conceptions of their rights after they moved from Virginia to the Helm homestead in upstate New York. The overseer demanded that William, a fellow slave, appear for punishment, but after the relocation, William refused to allow the overseer to threaten or beat him with impunity. He "thought as he was no longer in Virginia, he would not submit to such chastisement and the overseer was obliged to content himself with threatening what he would do if he caught him on the west side of the bay." The overseer eventually crossed Sodus Bay to whip William, and William grabbed the cowhide from him and beat the overseer. Nearby slaves exhibited a new sense of their own rights and refused to intervene on the overseer's behalf despite his pleading, and they even threw his "ferocious bulldog" into the fire to prevent it from coming to the aid of the overseer.[29] The dramatic power shift in that moment depended on William's and his fellow slaves' conceptions of their right to resist violence, and their new location in a gradual emancipation state was important. William and Steward might also have been aware of the changing temperament in the legal system in processing cases against abusive slave masters.

The response of whites to slave violence was different in the early republic than it had been in earlier generations, when violence by slaves marshaled white support for the continuance of slavery and the use of force. Slaves destabilized the practices of violence in their individual rebellions against their masters and overseers, and they did so in a climate in which decreasing numbers of slaves existed. Momentarily stripped of their privilege to exact violence, masters and overseers stood before the power and humanity of slaves who were not willing to submit. When William whipped his overseer in upstate New York, he dictated new rules to the overseer and master that would govern discipline on the Helm homestead. William neutralized the racial privileges accorded to the overseer and defied the central tenet of slavery by using the whip on him. Whites did not react by rounding up African Americans for questioning or publicly executing or torturing them as had happened in previous instances when slaves resisted authority. Steward recorded that slavery in New York was less harsh than in the South, and his perception stemmed from slaves' and whites' negotiations in their new location. Slaves used whatever tools they had to create liberties. "Our condition, as I have said before, was greatly improved," declared Steward, "and yet the more we knew of freedom the more we desired it, and the less willing were we to remain in bondage." African Americans demanded more liberties, and the new circumstances resulted in untenable situations for some masters. Steward's thwarted overseer later returned to Virginia, where Steward surmised "he could beat slaves without himself receiving a cowhiding."[30] As gradual emancipation held out the promise of a new society, slaves' conceptions of their right to personal security and liberty altered the practices of slavery—and whites' conceptions of their own place in those practices.

African Americans used their own organizations and the press to broadcast the dangers of slaveholding and white violence, which ensured that the messages about violence in the early republic did not center on transgressions committed by enslaved and free African Americans. A year after the success of the *Broad* cases, Henry Johnson gave a speech to the African Methodist Episcopal Zion Church in New York City, where he defended the character of African Americans by outlining their struggles. Derogatory pronouncements about vice in African American communities and their unsuitability for citizenship routinely circulated in the early republic as a means of supporting the racial hierarchy. Johnson was part of a group of African Americans who were building their own institutions to improve life for African Americans. Cognizant of the growing disdain for free African Americans, Johnson challenged those who would "declare us in a happier state as slaves than as free men" to consider the abuses slaves suffered. At an oration commemorating the end to the slave trade, he noted that the slave master "commands their bodies and minds according to his own will," and slaves are "growning under their savage outrages." Johnson relayed slaves' perspectives, remarking the enslaved had no redress for these injustices. "The country and the country's laws avail me nothing, and here I stand a menial, beaten slave, careless of my fate, regardless of an eternity."[31] Giving voice to African American slaves, Johnson hinted that the ramifications of violence against slaves could be dire. Slaves who were hardened to violence committed physical acts of resistance against individual masters, he implied, and they could even threaten an entire community as seen in Haiti, Albany, and New York City. The threat of rebellion may have been less fearful given the reduction in slave holding after passage of gradual emancipation, but reminding whites that violence against slaves had consequences helped rebuke ideas of northern slavery as a humane institution.

The War of 1812 gave African Americans' resistance added political significance and provided new opportunities for African Americans to assert their belongingness or disdain for slavery. In 1812, the British blockaded New York City, and the city wanted to determine the loyalties of its nearly 2,000 slaves. New York's history of British occupation during the Revolutionary War strengthened this imperative. In 1813, the British threatened Sandy Hook, New Jersey, and rumors of an impending attack near and in New York City continued through 1814. African American associations and churches encouraged their participation in the war to confirm their place in society. Historians estimate that African Americans composed 10 to 20 percent of the men aboard privateers and other seagoing vessels during the war, and their service was essential to trade and war. A fifth of the population at the British prisoner-of-war camp at Dartmoor was African Americans from New England. In addition, African American efforts to secure Harlem and Brooklyn Heights during the threats of 1814 were lauded as they volunteered to reinforce and build fortifications in the wake of threats from the British Navy.[32]

Slaves historically took opportunities to advance their own freedom during times of war and divisiveness. Conversations about increased numbers of runaways and fear of their potential to undermine war efforts heightened the effects of running away. The enslaved did not just turn to the enemies of Americans, however. Running away from masters to serve in the U.S. Navy or aboard privateering vessels proved enticing, even as no official policy welcomed slaves initially.[33] Running away had an immediate impact on the safety of slaves, and they used it consistently to attain freedom. African Americans knew British policies toward slavery to be more favorable, with the British welcoming fugitives in Canada. In 1814, the British made their policy of liberating and transporting slaves to free British provinces official, though they had already offered slaves refuge once they entered British lines. As approximately 4,000 (mostly Southern) slaves made their way to the British, white northerners were aware of the attractiveness of liberty and the danger of holding slaves in wartime.

In their struggle to free themselves from violence, the enslaved affirmed their right to humane treatment and shed light on the legal and moral problems of slavery. This work was part of the overall civil rights movement to end slavery. Though not all slaves could attain bystander interventions or make use of the judicial system, they did protect themselves through violent acts and running away. The enslaved activists who made their master's cruelty known demanded the attention of the government and community members, some of whom would partner with them to help them find safety. By engaging in resistance, they were setting new standards about violence in houses, farms, and workshops, making abuse and slavery less tenable.

African Americans in New York clearly perceived attaining the civil rights to sue and testify in court as important to overturning slavery and stopping abuse. They expressed this through their reports to the police and in garnering white support in their pleas to the NYMS. Enslaved activists knew that using the court system for their benefit would prove essential in securing safety and punishing those who defied community standards. The judicial system did not prove itself to be a full partner for African Americans who reported cruelty, but it did serve as an important community point of arbitration and forced society to confront abuse. The increased reporting of cruelty revealed that for the enslaved to find sanctuary from abuse, they needed power as witnesses and plaintiffs. Chipping away at the slave code weakened the power of masters and slavery, and with greater access to the judicial process came greater numbers of cases for the public to negotiate.

Young Servants, Apprentices, and Slaves

The cases against slave masters and wife abusers did not occur in isolation; they were indicators that society was willing to deal with the abuse of dependents on a broader scale. At the same time, the *Pienovi* case shows that some bystanders did not feel impelled to assist servants or wives suffering abuse. White and African American servants were the only group who did not increase their legal strategies of resistance in the early republic, even as they expanded their conception of what kinds of discipline were intolerable. Some young white servants objected to any corporal punishment by masters, which was a great leap from the colonial era, when servants and apprentices were more apt to push back only in cases of excessive or unjust punishments. Gradual emancipation and new labor protests empowered resistance to corporal punishment and coercive labor arrangements. Pauper apprentices and youth aging out of the slave system saw freedom being redrafted to include a larger class of individuals. Servants and enslaved youth turned to family members, Overseers of the Poor, and bystanders as more immediate options than the legal system for protesting abuse, but they also turned to violence more often to advocate for themselves and attain freedom because legal options appeared less valuable. Early Americans remained committed to the oversight of youth, but it proved challenging for those living in abuse, and they would take steps to resist if they saw the opportunity.

Apprentices and servants retained their rights to sue their masters for cruelty, especially if they were legally contracted to serve, but they had come to rely on a variety of methods to protest their abuse. Turning to neighbors for support proved a favorable method of resistance if they were mandated to serve through pauper apprenticeship or other forms of coercive labor. In 1818, Eliza Sears, a twelve-year-old white servant girl, targeted her neighbors to get help with her abusive masters, William and Sara Gray. She "complained in the presence of those deponents of cruel beatings she has received from her said Master and Mistress." Sears's mother had died, and her father was in the poor house, so she likely came to the service of the Gray family as part of the pauper apprenticeship program. She did not turn to the almshouse or an Overseer of the Poor to find relief. Instead, she turned to those who were more familiar with her situation and were in closest proximity. Urged on by her pleas, seven of her neighbors asked for "process against the aforesaid William and Sarah Gray" and the grand jury issued an indictment, to which they pleaded guilty.[34] Though the legal system proved valuable, poorer children's labor was contracted in ways that did not make it obvious to children that they could reach out to the special justices. By 1820, the roles of apprentices and servants in shops fully transformed as industries and pauper apprenticeship grew and formal legal contracts declined. Many of the girls and boys hired out had families in need of wages rather than contracts for training and provisions.[35] The declining use of children and young adults as witnesses in legal cases also meant they were less familiar with legal processes and the men in the roles of JPs. The almshouse was not a welcoming space either, and though their contracts may have been signed there, children did not want to return there unless their parents remained clients.

Though Sears had many witnesses, bystander intervention did not often take the form of legal intervention. It's clear that the highly publicized cases of cruelty made adults more attuned to the violence of those around them as cases against abusers mounted. Nonetheless, only seven cases of servant and apprentice abuse went through the courts in New York City, which was not a notable rise in legal activism. Neighbors were more routine figures in the life of children like Sears, and she successfully drew on those relationships to receive the help she needed. The neighbors who stepped up for her suggested they had been keeping an eye on her situation.

Though legal challenges were not on the rise, some servants and apprentices developed more radical understandings about masters' rights to corporal punishment. Protests now challenged any sort of physical assault, whereas in the colonial era, servants' protests focused on the use of rods or whips and on punishments that did not have a disciplinary intent. In 1819, two servants in New York City assaulted their masters when they tried to discipline them. In January, Joseph Fox, a white cabinetmaker's apprentice, "seized the deponent [Abijah Matthews, his master] by the collar when he attempted to chastise him for ill behavior." In February, Samuel Dixon, an African American indentured servant to John Skidmore, an innkeeper, similarly resisted abuse. Skidmore complained to the special justices that Dixon "lay violent hands on him when about to correct him & refuses to obey his lawful commands."[36] The servants' intentions in both cases were to prevent punishment before it started, and the fact that the cases were so close together suggests some servants and apprentices had new standards regarding the types of treatment they would withstand. Cases of white and African American servants engaging in violent retribution against masters were not unheard of prior to this time, and arson was among the more prominent forms of protest. However, the combined vocal and violent resistance against correction before being assaulted make Dixon's and Fox's actions noteworthy.

Animating some white and African American servants' new sense that they should not be subject to corporal punishment was their relationship with other laborers. Apprentices and servants in trade industries worked alongside journeymen and other day laborers who hired themselves out to master craftsmen and the entrepreneurs who were expanding the production of goods. The consolidation of craft industries limited career growth opportunities, and some servants and apprentices realized that their anticipated futures as master craftsmen might be impractical.[37] Many jobs were seasonal, and journeymen could not achieve their hoped-for wage level or respectability. Discussions about the changing labor conditions of the industry occurred all around servants and apprentices. The era of the early republic was one of growing agitation, as laborers sought access to better wages and job security. Apprentices and servants witnessed the politicization of the labor force, and it affected their own conceptions of themselves and their masters' rights. From the 1790s, cordwainers in Philadelphia created a society to undercut competition from workers willing to work for lower wages, and in 1805, they initiated a strike for better wages that resulted in a trial against them. In 1805 and 1806, printed remarks about their strike circulated in Boston, New York, and other parts of the North. Shoemakers in New York protested similar conditions in 1808 by initiating a strike and uniting to achieve a standard and better wage. Smaller labor actions also occurred in New York City between 1785 and 1835 among shoemakers, printers, cabinetmakers, carpenters, masons, bakers, stonecutters, painters, and tailors.[38] In some ways, the activities of journeymen were a reaction to their loss of upward mobility, but they were also a response to the growing power of masters and others who were transforming industries. For servants and apprentices who had begun chafing at their dependence, the labor protests proved valuable sources of information about the relative power of individuals to combat unsatisfactory conditions.

The disjunction between new experiences of servitude and the historic relationships between masters and servants set in motion some resistance to physical correction as servants and apprentices aged. In such roles, masters became less the guardians of children and more like employers. The hierarchical relationship between masters and servants remained intact despite changes in the contractual nature of the labor, with masters legally and socially viewed as the guardians of their charges and empowered to corporally punish servants and apprentices. As they aged through the servitude, young men and women resisted being held subject to punishment and were unwilling to withstand assaults. Journeymen, slaves, and wives proved labor and living conditions were negotiable; children and young adults growing up in the early republic desired greater freedoms from masters.

African American servants and apprentices, in particular, wanted to break free of the dependency of servitude, enslavement, and corporal punishment. Perhaps the second most famous crime involving a slave after the *Broad* cases was that of Rose Butler, who risked her own life to find her way to freedom. She lived her life as a slave because she was born in Westchester the same year as New York passed gradual emancipation legislation. The law determined she would be free at the age of twenty-five, and as such, she is more accurately understood as a servant, though society deemed African Americans in her position to be more like slaves. At age eighteen, Butler lived on the harsh dividing line of freedom as part slave and part servant. Had she been born white but impoverished, she might have had the opportunity to release herself from servitude that very year and marry or switch employers. Instead, on March 4, 1818, she set fire to the house of William Morris while the family slept. After two years in the Morris household, Butler no longer wanted to live with a man who assaulted her in the name of discipline. In May 1819, Judge Woodworth sentenced her to death for the arson attempt, though the damage to the house was minimal. He believed she set the fire because she was "offended with one of them for having reprimanded you, and for this cause determined on revenge." At her sentencing, he lectured that she owed the family her "fidelity and obedience—their lives and property were in some measure within your power." In a sense, Butler agreed—their lives were in her hands while they slept. She set the fire on the stairs, and had the fire been stronger, it would have prevented the family from escaping. Prior to this crime, Butler stole from her previous masters, suggesting that her forced servitude and treatment within it had been gnawing at her for some time.[39] Butler's case is one of many coming out of the post-*Broad* and emancipation era in which corporal punishment of those in servitude often led to various forms of resistance, including violence.

Servants who responded violently to abusive conditions felt a sense of urgency in attaining safety. These events show young adults unwilling to wait to age out of their servitude and disposed to defying community standards of ethical conduct to find freedom. As in the case of abused wives and slaves, legal strategies and interpersonal relationships were not always effective during violent conflict, and some servants could not envision a way out of their contracts without turning to violence. The growth of pauper apprenticeship and the irregularity of court adjudications of servant abuse likely informed apprentices that violence was a more viable path out of unfavorable situations. Some servants' arson and assaults against masters show that the courts and neighbors were not viewed as a remedy by ill-treated servants. Of course, not all violence issued by servants was retributive. It's difficult to discern motive in some cases. In New York City in 1812 and 1814, two white servants assaulted their masters; neither case details the reasons behind the assaults, but, given the expected subservience of servants, such behavior was notable.[40] The propensity of individuals to resist corporal punishment and servitude was becoming more widespread.

African Americans used a variety of means to protest servitude and cruelty, but many African American children and young adults also believed no assistance from neighbors or the government would be forthcoming. While in Maine, Nancy Washington, an African American servant, suffered whippings by her master, but she never reported it to authorities. Washington recalled a time when he beat her under false pretenses, for "telling the truth" when she received shoes from a bystander who expressed concern for her uncovered feet during the War of 1812.[41] Though the stranger worried over her exposure, Washington did not believe more would be done for her. Other servants also suffered abuse and similarly viewed much of society as unwilling to assist them. Nancy Prince and her siblings, African Americans living in Massachusetts, were "scattered all about" and were not well cared for by their employers. Prince relates that her brother "was maintained by the government" and her older sister Sylvia lived "with the family that brought her up" in the country. The two siblings were likely part of the Massachusetts pauper apprenticeship system, though Prince avoided it by finding her own employers. She recalled that she earned wages from age eight onwards, but the families in which she resided treated her poorly. In one household, they used "unkind words" and worked her to exhaustion, so much so that, after three months, she reported "her health and strength were gone." Her younger siblings reported cruel treatment, too—she noted that those "who were in families were dissatisfied." Prince does not detail the exact difficulties she and her siblings experienced but her desire to release them from their families suggest they were treated at least as badly as her.[42] Given the reluctance of governments to prosecute even egregious cases of slave abuse prior to the *Broad* case, it seems likely many children did not see the government or other whites as sources of assistance. Both Washington and Prince, young girls at the time, might not have known that Overseers or JPs were persons to whom they could turn. Prince and Washington likely also assumed that the Overseers and JPs cared little about the daily experiences of servants unless masters threatened their lives by the abuse. The court's rare adjudication of such cases certainly supported this belief.

Neighborly interventions were critical to ensuring the safety of white and African American servants, but children reached out only if they thought neighbors would help them. Records of most individual interventions are lost to history, but the persons who came forward in New York on behalf of slaves and at least two servants of color suggest some whites had concerns about the abuse of African American children before and after the *Broad* cases. In addition, several cases exist of white bystanders who alerted authorities to the abuse of African American children and adults in the streets.[43] The density of New York City, however, made it unique, and opportunities for whites to see and hear repeated and non-corrective physical assaults was limited in other areas. Nancy Washington lived in a rural area, while Prince traveled in the more populous areas in and around Salem and Boston. Prince was the more likely candidate for intervention, but the narrative of her experiences suggests she did not believe so. Recently emancipated slaves and those waiting to age out of the system might have been slower to reach out to whites. They experienced discriminatory behavior that trained them not to trust whites or believe that white neighbors cared about their welfare. Experiences of intolerance added up and African Americans learned to distrust whites. Nancy Prince expressed surprise at the kindness of several persons in Boston who went out of their way to assist her in locating her sister Sylvia. However, she also had a lifetime of memories in which she was degraded. In addition to her experiences in white households, she recalled that a white man she knew from her own town tried to force her to ride on top of a carriage rather than permitting her to ride alongside white passengers.[44] It's not surprising some poorly treated servants would not reach out for help.

African American parents tried to limit the servitude and apprenticeship of their children to whites when possible. Creating contracts for their children with African Americans or seeing them placed in black boardinghouses was a way to protect them from excessive violence and see them better cared for. White parents were similarly inclined to place children with caring masters or foster parents, but the poor found almshouses and charities eager to send their children to other persons' homes. Race added an even greater layer of complication. Many African Americans in the early republic were impoverished, which made finding satisfactory occupations and lodging for children important to families' financial welfare. Tracking down safe and rewarding positions in an economically segregated environment was arduous. Boston's Orphan Asylum, for example, did not offer spots to African American children, which added urgency for African Americans to set up positions for poor children who lost their parents.[45]

The pauper apprenticeship system and forced indenturing of African American children meant that legal solutions should have had more value, but resolutions to violence far more often occurred privately—when it did occur. Eliminating employer relationships was more frequently a matter of taking leave than one that required legal interventions. Finding help among bystanders and families was important for all servants and apprentices, though they were differentially willing and able to reach out. Evidence suggests young servants and apprentices were more combative in their roles than they had been previously, and they were beginning to denounce all forms of corporal punishment and occasionally their servitude and enslavement. Their activism related to their desire for independence and the declining economic opportunities of the early republic, with labor protests and demands for equity more commonly heard. The power of masters was changing, but the legal dependency of young adults was not, and their resistance showed a clear desire for more freedom.

Free African Americans

By the 1810s, a decade had elapsed in New York since gradual emancipation legislation passed, and in Massachusetts, it had been thirty years since emancipation. Interracial violence continued to erupt, and governmental arbitrations of violence worked in tandem with African American institutions to promote the civil rights of African Americans. Opposing violent conflict through the courts, African Americans claimed citizenship and secured police and judicial interventions. As with other groups, urbanity played a role in accessing and understanding the courts as effective sites of arbitration. Extralegal solutions to violence existed as well. African Americans used organizations of their own to assert their independence and right to bodily integrity, occasionally using these organizations to make pleas for more constables or government support. African American activists spoke out against violence, too—not only in court arbitration, but also by publishing speeches or writing about their experiences of violence. Publicizing the dangers they faced was important to creating change and supporting an end to their legal impairments, but not all publicity was good. Occasionally, contests for independence were fought out—with African American and white assailants using force to settle conflicts. Though African Americans asserted their independence through violence, these acts could be used by whites to support ideologies of race and undermine the movement for African Americans' full and safe participation in the republic.

African Americans continued using the judicial system to find solutions to violence. At least eighty-seven incidents of white-on-black violence were reported to the special justices in New York City between 1811 and 1819, with the majority against poorer African Americans. By the 1810s, New York and Massachusetts used preprinted forms, so less detailed information about violent incidents are contained in records, but conflicts on the streets, in housing, and in workplaces continued. Often special justices did not denote the occupations of victims in New York City, but laborers were the highest reported occupation among victims and they eagerly used the courts to settle conflicts. Whites and African Americans instigated the reports about violent incidents with African American victims, and married and single African American women stepped forward as part of this movement. African American women represented nearly 37 percent of victims, and they understood they had a rightful place in the process, serving as plaintiffs and witnesses.[46]

Rural African Americans were much less likely to report conflict to authorities, though systemic harassment existed for African Americans. The lesser reporting suggests the residential and social patterns of African Americans affected the way they mediated violence. In rural areas, small populations limited the ability of African Americans to form their own cultural and economic institutions, though they often lived in "clusters" of homes near one another. African Americans also continued to live within the homes of whites in rural areas. In 1820 in Columbia County, New York, for example, only a third of African Americans lived within black households, and similar data exists for rural and small towns in Massachusetts.[47] Daily insults and aggressions could lead to more virulent forms of abuse and assaults, but African Americans likely avoided legal intervention in many cases to retain employment and housing. The economic ties that bound African Americans to whites were a disincentive to using the criminal justice system.

Though rural African Americans were less empowered to report violence, legal interventions remained critical to asserting freedom and citizenship rights throughout the North. Massachusetts had a history of allowing slave and free African American testimony. New York's judiciary did not, and its members questioned the legal status and participation of some free people in courts. New York denied slaves the right to testify even in cases where masters and African Americans had verbal agreements that they were free. In 1816, New York City tried Diana Sellick, an African American woman, for poisoning Hetty Johnson, the child of her babysitter. In the trial, the judge dismissed the testimony of Benjamin Johnson, the stepfather to Hetty, claiming he was a slave. Johnson was born a slave, but his last owner was Mrs. Alexander Jacques, who promised Johnson his freedom at her death. When she died, her husband consented to Johnson's freedom, though Johnson never received his freedom papers. Jacques and Johnson had a cordial relationship, and he lived free for many years. According to the judge, however, the laws of coverture necessitated that Alexander Jacques initiate the formal emancipation of Johnson after the death of his wife. The judge reasoned that the lack of freedom papers meant Johnson's status was indeterminate and open to the interpretation of Jacques, who could claim him at any time. The court also denied Johnson's right to bear witness against Sellick because of the severity of the charges against Sellick, who was prosecuted "in a case of life and death."[48] Many African Americans had a status like Johnson's, in which their previous owners recognized their freedom by verbal agreement. Undercutting the rights of African Americans to serve as plaintiffs and witnesses could be dangerous to a community seeking its rights as free citizens. African Americans needed access to courts to hold individuals accountable for violence, among other issues.

The connections between structural racism and safety were clear to African Americans, and they opposed racism through public speeches and in publications. James Forten, an African American advocate for racial equality in Philadelphia, noted that even "though they know that the law protects all," some whites "will dare, in defiance of the law, to execute their hatred upon the defenceless black." In 1813, Pennsylvania proposed the registration of free blacks, like New York and Massachusetts previously, and this policing of free blacks limited their autonomy and equality in ways that were unthinkable for whites. Forten feared that newly proposed measures would lead constables and other whites to molest African Americans with impunity. Promoters of the legislation claimed African American lawlessness was the reason for its surfacing, but the free black populations' growing wealth and cultural institutions were clearly a target of whites. Forten argued that African Americans were already "subject to the fury and caprice of a certain set of men . . . [and] considered as a different species, and little above brute creation." He wondered why the government would "increase their degradation" when they were already "thought to be objects fit for nothing else than lordly men to vent the effervescence of their spleen upon, and to tyrannize over."[49] Forten showed the relationship between oppressive legislation and violence and demanded that the law always regard men as equals.

Writing such as Forten's used the African American experience to advocate against racialized violence. Like Prince Hall, Forten shamed would-be offenders into better behavior by focusing on the way republican principles were shattered by unequal laws and violence. In 1813, Forten published his "Letters from a Man of Colour" anonymously, and each part opened with a reference to Declaration of Independence and its promise of equality and unalienable rights. The treatment of African Americans contrasted with these principles, particularly in the physical dangers that existed in Philadelphia's streets. He highlighted, "It is a well known fact, that black people upon certain days of public jubilee, dare not be seen after twelve o'clock in the day." Noting the problem of mobility, Forten shared how violence operated in society, but he also sought to show the ignominy of the perpetrators. He contrasted it with the ideals of liberty and justice by pointing out that violence against African Americans often occurred on "the FOURTH OF JULY, . . . the day set apart for the festival of Liberty." He felt violence put a pall on the day, and was "abused by the advocates of Freedom, in endeavoring to sully what they profess to adore."[50] Forten connected the future of the republic with its ability to equally include African Americans, who could not thrive in a culture of violence.

Forten and other writers were associated with African American institutions and societies, which were lodestones for violent offenders. African Americans responded powerfully to attacks on their institutions, using the courts and governmental connections to oppose violence. When white boys began disturbing the worship of members of the African Methodist Church, the members reported it to the Common Council of New York City. Their petition fell in line with actions in New England by African Americans who petitioned to end to slavery during the American Revolution. Acting as citizens, they outed negligent watchmen and demanded that the government do more to protect them. In 1807, George Collins and several other trustees of the African Methodist Church in New York City informed the Common Council about the harassment, and the following year, they reported rioting and a watchman errant in his duty to protect the peace. When the harassment did not abate, the trustees of the African Church did not let the government off the hook. Between September and October 1808, the harassment became so severe the trustees asked that a watch station or watchman be placed in front of the church to protect peaceful congregants. Forcing the government to fulfil its role to protect the peace was important as threats of violence recurred. Despite persistent activism by members, they reported harassment again in 1815 and 1817, and the danger of the situation had increased. In 1815, the church caught fire under unknown causes. Historian Leslie Alexander suspects that the fire at the African Church, in combination with that at St. Phillips Episcopal Church in 1821, shows a virulence on the part of whites to shut down African American organizations.[51] The growth of the African American community as an independent and vibrant presence had made it a target for whites. Fighting violence in their institutions and community was vital for these organizations, which would also join to protest white colonization schemes and other proposed legal inequities.

By the end of the second decade of the nineteenth century, some African Americans lost faith in the government and legal systems of the United States. Prince Saunders, originally from Connecticut, moved to Boston and played an important role in advancing African American educational opportunities. The rancorous racism of whites led him and others to reconsider their future in the North. He partnered with Paul Cuffee to find ways to bring African Americans to Africa and Haiti, where he hoped their economic and social situation would improve. The mission was also one of black uplift. Saunders and Cuffee wanted to bring religious, economic, and political benefits to the peoples of the United States, Sierra Leone, and Haiti. Cuffee had been visiting New Yorkers and exploring the idea with them from at least 1812, and the New-York African Institution was founded shortly thereafter. Peter Williams took the lead in encouraging the plans as far south as Philadelphia, but eventually New Yorkers turned their interest to Haiti and worked with Saunders to build connections there. Like self-emancipation, African Americans' plans for emigration were an indictment of their treatment, and those pursuing these options routinely pointed toward the economic and social degradation experienced by free blacks as among the causes for the movement. Though some whites saw in these plans an opportunity to purge free African Americans from the states, Williams and Saunders lambasted their racism and built international partnerships with Africans aimed at improving the conditions of the African diaspora.[52]

Some African Americans believed that speeches and organizations could not solve the issues they faced, and they turned to violence to assert themselves or respond to violent treatment. Increased social segregation resulted in fractious disputes along racial lines, and African Americans did not shy away from forcefully demanding their inclusion in society. Moses Simons, the first African American lawyer practicing in New York City, assaulted a dance hall owner when he was refused entry based on his race. Simons was born in South Carolina, but his white father sent him North to Yale for brighter prospects. After graduating in 1809, he served as an apprentice in Albany to state attorney general Abraham Van Vechten and eventually made his way to New York City, where he was admitted to the bar in 1816. Simons was no stranger to overt racism, even though he had both African American and white clients in his law practice. In December 1817, he attended a dancehall that operated as a school during the day, and ten to twelve complaints emerged from young white men about the presence of Simons and his brother. When Simons dined at Tammany Hall, proprietor William Cozzens also received complaints about Simons's presence. In response to the dance hall objections, Charles Berault forbade Simons entry because white students threatened to withdraw from lessons if African Americans continued attending. Berault indicated he had written a letter to Simons informing him prior to his arrival, yet Simons felt insulted, "slapped him in the face," and demanded to get the names of those who wanted to prevent his entrance. From Simons's perspective, as soon as he purchased the ticket to the ballroom, he was owed entrance, and his assault on Berault was retribution for not being admitted. The jury disagreed and fined him ten dollars.[53] Simons's behavior may have been regrettable, but he forcefully asserted his right to occupy public space through this incident. African Americans had been barred from many local public parades and segregation was beginning to take hold in neighborhoods in addition to the segmented labor market.

Simons's assault on Berault is a reminder that the civil rights movement of African Americans always included both violent and peaceful means of protest. Disagreements about how to proceed and best fight for equality were legacies of the African American experience. In the second decade of the nineteenth century, African Americans and their allies turned to the special justices in New York more often to report violence, and their work secured some measure of safety for enslaved African Americans. Individual and collective legal strategies fell in line with the tactics African Americans had engaged in as slaves. By petitioning the government and making legal suits, African Americans forced the government to work on solutions that included all citizens. African American networks also played an important role in collecting the voices of African Americans and creating messaging against structural racism and violence. The anonymous and personalized attacks on African Americans remained a problem, even as whites were prosecuted for assaults.

Early civil rights agitation depended on a variety of methods and efforts to achieve security. Violence and association building were critical to putting pressure on unjust systems of dependence, and without this work, legal strategies could not be envisioned. Wives, African Americans, and young adults had power that could be wielded to dangerous ends. Finding allies and building or partnering with organizations to attain safety were important as well. Through private conversations and negotiations with public officials, the emerging middle class found ways to build and draw on networks for personal safety and to get resources they needed to find peace. The ease with which most individuals could seek out legal solutions made them one of the most universally acceptable ways of protesting abuse and having all voices heard. For young servants and apprentices, however, legal strategies appeared less productive. Individuals in rural areas similarly did not have as much access or equal opportunity to make use of these options.

The legal strategies chosen by dependents forced a reckoning with their legal status and the cruelty they endured. The individuals who asserted their right to live free from violence in the early republic did so during a time when more cases of cruelty were litigated by a broader set of the populace. As abused wives, slaves, servants, and free blacks stepped up to challenge violence, they publicized the ways that dependency made them more vulnerable to abuse. The issues brought to courtrooms, lodgings, and the streets demonstrated how those defined as legally subordinate peoples did not perceive themselves as lesser citizens. They revealed a view of themselves as equally endowed with a right to live free from violence and pushed for it more often than they had in the past. In their shared work to protest cruelty, their claims to equality should not be lost on us. They fought for a voice and recognition in governmental processes, and that struggle was part and parcel of a fight for safety and civil rights.

Conclusion

Affecting the Government, Law, and Public Mind

Increased activism in the early republic pressured the government and communities to respond to abuse. The numbers of African Americans and wives who made complaints to JPs about assaults fostered a legal culture in which JPs incorporated protection of legal and social dependents into their daily roles, which secured access to the judiciary and criminalized the behavior of their abusers. The enactment of divorce and separation, as well as movements to end slavery and the slave codes in Massachusetts and New York, related to experiences of and resistance to violence. The War of 1812 and population changes were additional opportunities to reconsider slavery and the civil rights of African Americans. During wartime, slavery was a glaring weakness. African Americans expressed their desire for freedom and patriotism as they had in the Revolutionary War, and their loyalty became more prized. Moreover, in asserting their place in the early republic, African Americans and wives cracked the received wisdom that the racial and sexual hierarchies were righteous. Women's actions undermined the doctrine of coverture and African Americans claimed public spaces and roles regardless of whites' acceptance of them.

Though some action was taken to ameliorate abuse, other signs show violence was increasing rather than abating. The early republic was not the finish line in the quest for human and civil rights. Many Americans were disinclined to add protections for legal and social dependents, and they believed that cruel masters and husbands were rare. The cases that made their way through the criminal justice system gave people faith that justice was being served, even as more femicide and racially motivated violence occurred.[1] New York and Massachusetts passed more legislation to delimit the freedoms of African Americans, and the doctrine of coverture remained in place until the 1850s. Young adults and children did not find their legal rights improved either. Resistance to violence was important for young adults', women's, and African Americans' greater inclusion in society because the law was not the endpoint in establishing their civil rights. Violence was and is a popular method of enforcing racial, generational, and gender based-hierarchies. At the cornerstone of the abuse of dependents was a belief that violence was necessary to discipline them. For many people, the belief that violence could create order did not change though more attention was given to cases of cruelty.

Ending Slavery

The 1810s would be a decade of growth and great challenge for African Americans who struggled under enslavement and continued to bear the burden of society's inclination to both ignore and bear witness to the violence of slavery. As with earlier shifts in thought, news about violence and cruelty proved staging grounds for further efforts to extend civil rights to the enslaved. Legal cases and the pressure of war put the issue of slavery in the forefront of New Yorkers' minds, and the biggest achievement of the decade was undoubtedly when the state settled upon on a final date to end slavery. Even before this time, the pressure on slavery grew from slaves' reports of violence. New York took steps to remove aspects of the slave code that punished slaves more harshly than free persons, and the legislature formally provided a legal process to abused slaves aging out of their servitude. The cooperation between the NYMS, African Americans, and other white allies led to the adoption of new community standards regarding violence and the civil rights of slaves that limited the ability of some masters to abuse their slaves with impunity. Local courts prosecuted abusive slave masters, yet slave masters developed new strategies to hinder legal challenges to cruelty in the wake of several successful suits. New actions to promote slave welfare did not fully protect African Americans, as emancipation was the only true safeguard from abusive masters, but the resistance of African Americans had a definitive impact.

Enslaved African Americans' ability to make alliances with whites and foment legal and legislative activism was historically among the most important to their successes. In Massachusetts, legal suits ended slavery. Only a small number of the legal cases involving New York's slaves went through the criminal justice system, but the reporting of events to special justices and the NYMS represented an ongoing strategy of seeking legal interventions. Between 1810 and 1820, New York prosecuted four cases against slave masters for cruelty, and in two cases juries found masters guilty. In addition, reports given to the NYMS show communities protesting violence against slaves.[2] In challenging abuse and using governmental interventions, the enslaved and their allies publicized and politicized cases of their abuse. As public abuse cases mounted, white northerners had to ignore or create and uphold standards regarding violence. Legal cases also had a remarkable effect on radicalizing the NYMS, and the growth of the membership was clearly a response to its more aggressive actions in legal suits. Starting out as a small organization with fewer than 100 members, the society grew to 250 by 1797 and 340 by 1813, likely as a result of its success in the *Broad* cases. Although the meetings did not draw many members, and the society constantly struggled to get members to pay their dues, joining an antislavery society was a political act and a statement of principle. The newer members drew from the middle class and elites, which meant that the organization continued to have access to governmental leaders and a voice in the broader community.[3]

New Yorkers engaged in community-wide self-licensing after *Broad*, and they congratulated themselves on the triumph of the judicial system, even though they prosecuted only repeatedly violent and life-threatening behavior. In his pamphlet on the cases, Southwick wrote, "never was a case more deserving of universal notice; never one more characteristic of a nation's justice; none ever offered to humanity a more generous triumph—to unfeeling pride, a more impressive lesson—or whispered in the ear of the oppressed, more balmy consolation."[4] The case perpetuated the sense that benevolent treatment of slaves was the norm in New York because the *Broad* cases and other less notorious interventions led many to believe the state would not allow the egregious misconduct of slaveholders. The *Broad* cases simultaneously challenged this view as they made apparent the extensive mistreatment some northern slaves suffered. In some ways, the success of the trial was a disincentive to make changes to slavery or slaves' legal status because it reinforced white New Yorkers' own sense of righteousness for prosecuting the case. Yet they also lived among a nation of slaveholders, and their desire to set themselves aside as unique for the protections they afforded slaves necessitated continued action.

The NYMS would push to eradicate some of the differential treatment of the enslaved, showing progress in the willingness of some whites to accept African Americans' basic human and civil rights over the property rights of masters. This radicalization was born from the resistance of African Americans to violence. From the colonial era, the differing processes and penalties for crimes committed by slaves supported slavery by denying African Americans equal treatment within the judiciary. Governments simultaneously maintained the social economy of violence through harsher sentencing. Violence was inherent to slave codes because whippings were so often the punishment meted out to slaves who committed even petty crimes, in stark contrast to whites. In addition, the government unevenly enforced the hardship of confinement without due process. Slave codes were intended to protect whites from insurrection and the violence of slaves, but the laws appeared anachronistic when the most public and visible sources of violence came from masters, not slaves. The harrowing stories of violence from cases of slave abuse and the campaigning of the NYMS to pass legislation supporting slaves' rights made strides toward a more equal criminal justice system.

Cases of slave abuse brought to the forefront the problem of having a class of citizens without basic civil rights—including the right to bear witness and bring a suit against a person for civil or criminal acts. African American and white activists pursued expanding opportunities for slaves by reporting acts of violence and trying to pass legislation that would free slaves from abusive masters. The new actions revealed major growth in the thought of white antislavery activists regarding the rights of slaves versus masters, but changes occurred too late to help many slaves. By 1810, the NYMS reported that "the inhuman beating of Slaves is a subject which has often engaged the attention of the Society," and it would seek legislation to "punish in an exemplary manner those who may be convicted of such brutal conduct."[5] Slaves' only redress for their masters' cruelty was to report it to the police and seek the assistance of the NYMS. However, they needed other means to defend themselves in a criminal justice system that favored whites and imprisoned blacks at their owners' whims. Although the NYMS successfully opposed the

Broads and other vicious slave masters, newer cases revealed the problems inherent in New York's laws. "Masters . . . convicted of the barbarous & inhuman treatment of their slaves," the society opined, were given "exemplary punishments but [the courts] have not been authorized to withdraw the injured slave from the power of his irritated master or to provide effectually for his further security." Leaving slaves with abusive owners seemed contradictory to the entire process of punishing slave masters, and it was different from the experiences of white servants. Enslaved persons' activism showed the dire effects of this problem. In 1815, Sibby "fled the house of Cornelius Van Winkle . . . after she had experienced the most inhuman treatment from his hands." The NYMS and its supporters understood they were reliant on white witnesses to present testimony in official spaces. A white ally said the "most respectable testimony can be furnished of the deplorable condition she was in and also of her good behavior" since running away. Even with this testimony, however, Sibby's flight was not legal and her place of "refuge" would only remain so at the pleasure of Van Winkle, who could recall her with a warrant. For slaves like Sibby, the transformations occurring in New York happened all too slowly and provided little solace in the daily experiences of living without freedom and under abuse. "Prohibited to bear testimony against a free man the slave has no protection against a cruel master," the NYMS reported, "who need only inflict punishment in private and may then gratify his vengeance with impunity."[6] The problematic nature of slaves' civil status plagued African Americans and the NYMS as complaints continued to flow to the society.

Reconsiderations of slaves' civil status occurred simultaneously with larger movements across the United States to limit the use of the death penalty and public punishments of criminals. The state's machinery of violence, which was critical to supporting slavery and hardening perceptions of race, was less attractive for solving crime and vice in light of modern thinking on the ill effects of public punishments. New York, Pennsylvania, and Massachusetts revised their legal codes to reduce the use of capital and corporal punishments, fearing it played a role in inciting others to violent acts. By 1800, New York abolished corporal punishment except in cases of treason and in criminal cases against slaves.[7] Reformers argued that the degrading effects of slavery and a judicial system that treated African Americans differently prevented racial "uplift." New penal codes and processes were made more inclusive of slaves in response to these criticisms. The NYMS first sought to mandate jury trials for slaves who committed acts of violence against whites. In this work, laws extended basic civil rights that had not previously existed to slaves. Prior to 1813, if a slave struck a white person, two justices would decide on the slave's guilt. If guilty, the slave would be whipped on order of the court. This was a far cry from the experiences of free African Americans and whites, who received jury trials with fines in cases of guilty verdicts. Recognizing the discrimination within the law, in 1810, the NYMS expressed its desire for the suspension of laws preventing jury trials for slaves. It reasoned that a "Slave for striking a white person is liable to be proceeded against in a secret and summary way, without the benefit of Trial by Jury. We therefore propose that application be made to the Legislature for a repeal of that Law, which deprives them of this invaluable right."[8] In 1813, the legislature granted slaves access to the legal system and began treating these crimes more similarly to other petty crimes rather than as insurrections. The 1813 law also began the process of recognizing the civil rights of slaves, including their right to marriage, forbidding illegal bondage contracts, and allowing slaves the same process as servants to complain of their masters when they were not taught reading or Christianity.[9] The NYMS also began work in 1803 on the passage of a law demanding masters give cause and evidence for the imprisonment of slaves after the enslaved fought to bring attention to their imprisonment. It was only after a decade of events and experiences that white New Yorkers extended this basic right of habeas corpus to slaves, and they limited confinement to sixty days.[10]

The lessening of legal strictures on slaves during the 1810s is unsurprising considering the continuous advocacy on the part of African Americans to improve their position and the context of war, which heightened the importance of revisiting the status of slaves living in the state. Changes in the slave codes took place during the War of 1812. During the American Revolution, Massachusetts chose to embrace emancipation, owing to the activism of slaves and the need to secure their loyalty. New York was in a prime location to experience the ravages of war, and it needed a strategy to limit the effectiveness of British incursions into cities and towns on the eastern seaboard as well as along the Canadian border. Anxiety regarding the position of African Americans was further heightened by larger divisions within New York over the war policy. Like some New England states, New Yorkers voted Federalists into office to voice their dissent, and they repeatedly questioned the war. Given these threats, in October 1814, New York made enlistment available to slaves, and the opening of the militia to slaves fractured another aspect of the slave code. The new policy showed whites recognized slaves' strong desire for freedom. Offering small improvements in slave status was advisable given the possible impacts the war would have on African Americans' allegiances.

The population shift in New York was another impetus for changes in the slave code and in perceptions of slavery. Free African Americans began to outnumber the enslaved, and efforts to maintain the racial hierarchy now focused on free people. One of the reasons New York had maintained slavery and slowly adopted gradual emancipation was the threat they saw in slave insurrections and their fears of racialized violence. Only when slavery became a liability in the wake of the Haitian Revolution did New Yorkers embrace the need to emancipate slaves. Cities were particularly attractive to African Americans, given the variety of jobs and the community that could be found there. Free African Americans outnumbered slaves in New York City and accounted for 35 percent of the state's total African American population.[11] As the free black population grew, concerns about slave resistance diminished. New York experienced another sort of population growth that also subtly affected the politics of the region. Between 1800 and 1810, New York's population nearly doubled. The rising number of New Yorkers was partly attributable to the many migrants from New England, who mostly moved upstate looking for land, but others turned to the city to take up new business opportunities.[12] New Englanders committed to gradual and immediate emancipation earlier than New Yorkers, and they had fewer slaves. In addition, New England's laws supported slaves' rights to bear witness against others in court and make suits prior to emancipation. Indeed, slaves' legal access was fundamental to the eradication of slavery, as slaves like Elizabeth Freeman and Quock Walker sued for freedom partially based on the violence they suffered. Changes in New York's slave code fell in line with New Englanders' experiences and expectations of the freedoms given to slaves. New England migrants stayed connected with family and friends, and they brought with them their attitudes and customs regarding racial management. New England also passed repressive legislation pertinent to free blacks in the wake of their emancipation measures earlier than New York, which adapted and considered many of the same measures.

During the 1810s, antislavery activists shifted their attention to the inhumanity of slavery, which helped set the stage for abolition. In 1817, New York passed a law declaring that all slaves born before July 4, 1799, would be freed in 1827. Discussions about the inhumanity of slavery would not be the public face of the bill, but the cases of cruelty had readied the public for passage of such a law. In 1814, the NYMS discussed abolishing slavery with New York's legislators, which represented a major change in its policy of pushing for piecemeal efforts to prevent the growth of slavery and the slave trade.[13] The membership owed its increasing radicalization to the many public cases of cruelty and kidnapping that the society publicized. The message sent to the public by the NYMS and governor regarding this law, however, did not spotlight the inhumanity or injustice of holding slaves in bondage for an additional ten years, focusing instead on the property rights of slaveholders.[14] Making the bill palatable to whites meant denying the perspective of slaves, and its advocates advertised the final blow to slavery as a measure that would not hurt slaveholders.[15] Passage of the bill represented an acknowledgement of the cruelty of slavery, and this was built on the history of slaves fighting against it. Changing conceptions of childhood and violence opened New York's courts to legal cases of cruelty against masters, cases that emerged with greater frequency and more publicity. As white New Yorkers saw the reality of violence in legal cases, their identity as people who maintained what they deemed as a more just system of slavery demanded they continue to denounce acts of violence against the enslaved.

Although New Yorkers set a date to end slavery, justice was not complete, as slaves held in bondage during the next ten years continued to suffer from brutal beatings and murder. Sojourner Truth described how slaves suffered from lack of options to redress cruelty and murder through the story of a fellow slave named Ned who lived on a nearby plantation. His master, Mr. Brodhead, promised Ned that he could visit his wife at the end of the harvest. Once the time arrived, Brodhead forbade him to visit her. Ned decided to disobey his master, and he polished his shoes to prepare himself for the visit and swore to see his wife. For "intending" to disobey, Brodhead hit Ned with a "sled-stick . . . and gave him such a blow on the head as broke his skull, killing him dead on the spot." Truth described that the African American community all "felt struck down by the blow." Olive Gilbert, who transcribed Truth's narrative, amended the text to note that no one inquired into the murder, and the master killed his slave with impunity. Truth characterized the event as indicative of larger trends: "it was but one of a long series of bloody, and other most effectual blows, struck against their liberty and their lives."[16] Truth's insight reveals that as long as slavery existed, the property rights of whites and a legal system willing to look the other way would supersede slaves' rights to personal safety and justice.

Although slaves' use of the judicial system was fraught with issues, community standards continued to evolve about acceptable levels of violence, and the use of weapons against slaves became increasingly impermissible as slavery declined in the north. It is easy to dismiss the importance of this change because legislators had already established the right of slaves to sue for peace, yet society had to create and sustain standards about what constituted unacceptable levels of violence. Only through slaves' repeated efforts to protest violent acts did the government and communities uphold evolving standards. During the 1820s, several cases show that violent acts such as breaking the bones of slaves and the routine use of sticks and whips against them were found unlawful. In 1821, Harry, a slave, reported his master broke his arm and beat him with an oar. The NYMS described the oar as an "unlawful weapon." The community no longer completely ignored abuse, and cases continued to flow through the courts and the NYMS. In 1822, neighbors reported Mrs. Bird for beating her slave on a daily basis with "a large Cow Skin, but at other times sticks of wood, Broomsticks, etc." She beat her slave "in such a Manner that the Blood has ran down her Arms."[17] In both cases, witnesses and victims identified the weapons used by slave masters to prove the beatings were in excess of owners' right to discipline their servants and slaves.

The evolution of community standards and civil rights ultimately depended on the activism of African Americans, who offered a powerful voice that spoke to the severity of their situation. Through their partnerships with whites and each other, African Americans spread knowledge about their experiences of violence, asserting their human right to safety and freedom from coercive labor. The adoption of changes in the civil rights of slaves, which included the right to testify and be free from unlawful imprisonment, were other major successes. The War of 1812 and the population changes in New York made African Americans' and their allies' push for justice timely. With the adoption of a final emancipation statute, African Americans who remained enslaved in New York now faced the pressure of finding ways to contest violence in a society that decreasingly acknowledged its slaveholding. Free African Americans would mount another challenge.

Prosecuting Wife Abusers

Abused wives' resistance demanded a response by the government, and women's individual activities initiated a civil rights movement that chipped away at their legal subordination to abusive husbands. Governmental intervention in spousal assault cases and changing divorce laws reveal that the early republic marked an important turning point in adjudicating wife abuse, though earlier proscriptions against wife beating existed. Communities increasingly protected women and expanded women's rights after the 1790s with more indictments against men for abusing their wives than in previous generations. Not all of this activity was done in the name of women. As with the case of African Americans, some progress in granting liberties was self-serving and intended to preserve the marital hierarchy. Some community action against abusive husbands was intended to shore up patriarchy by punishing errant men. Additionally, the desire of JPs to solidify their authority as important actors in society, particularly over the impoverished men who were disciplined and deemed disorderly in assault cases, readied JPs to assist women in their pursuit of justice. Regardless of their motivations, the number of women plaintiffs forced society to reckon with abuse. Even as communities more often started the judicial process against violent husbands, women remained endangered and much more work needed to be done to protect abused wives.

Legal activism varied by region, but it grew after the 1800s, with greater numbers of indictments for spousal assault in urban areas. In the first twelve years of the 1800s, Bostonians prosecuted more men for spousal assault and intent to murder than during the previous sixty years, which matched the judicial activism of the seventeenth century. Between 1740 and 1800, the Supreme Judicial Court in Massachusetts indicted two men for intending to murder or maim their wives, and in the Suffolk, Plymouth, Middlesex, and Worcester Counties General Sessions five men were indicted on charges of assaulting their wives. In contrast, between 1800 and 1812, the Municipal Court of the Town of Boston and the Suffolk County Supreme Judicial Court, in a much shorter period of time and smaller geographic region, indicted nine men for assaulting their wives. Two further cases involving intent to murder occurred in Worcester and Middlesex Counties Supreme Judicial Courts between 1800 and 1820.[18] Boston courts were slower to embrace indictments as a remedy than New York courts were. In Massachusetts, most cases would be handled as peace suits and without the stiff penalties associated with other assault crimes in the early republic, while New York routinely indicted men for spousal assault after 1800. Comparison with previous decades is difficult for New York City because records are uneven, but a considerable rise in indictments for cruelty emerged there. New York City indicted at least 101 men for abusing their wives between 1800 and 1809, and an additional 219 between 1810 and 1819. Not all of these cases made it through the courts, however. Many failed to be tried, but the indictments show that the special justices saw these cases as worthy of prosecution. Rural areas of New York show prosecutions more in line with similar counties in Massachusetts. Juries forwarded three indictments in Cayuga and three indictments in Essex County in New York.[19] Like slaves, abused wives relied on their communities, legislators, judges, and JPs to hear and act on their pleas, because women were not empowered to serve in governmental positions. It was, however, undoubtedly their pleas that motivated calls to action.

When JPs handled abusers effectively, they secured the community from further disruptions, asserted their authority as JPs, and safeguarded men's power in households.[20] In Massachusetts, where criminal penalties were less frequently established, one of the most striking actions JPs took was writing arrest warrants for, and jailing, men who refused to make a bond to keep the peace. Overly violent husbands fractured the patriarchal ideal in which men provided and cared for their families, and errant men needed to be handled swiftly and discreetly. Men who refused to make bonds also challenged JPs' authority, and confining men to jail was a means of displaying power. In 1815, Justice Stephen Gorham jailed Matthew Peirce for refusing to make a bond, and Peirce wrote a letter to Gorham asking to be released from prison. "I am Sory that Misconduct Laid me to this Place But Conscious of the Justiceings of Your Sentence; and acknowledge my fault this is the first time I transgressed the Laws."[21] Peirce's admission of defeat and experience in jail would have spread beyond the courthouse, with constables delivering warrants for arrest and absences from work and the neighborhood. By enforcing bonds and jailing men who broke them, JPs pushed communities to reckon with a wife's right to personal safety. In his petition to be released from jail, Mathew Peirce promised it would be the last time he hurt his wife or defied a JP. "[If] . . . you wile forgive me this time you never Shall be troubled with me again in Complying to the Request of you."[22] Like other jailed husbands, he humbled himself and promised to keep the peace, a promise he was unwilling to make prior to his incarceration. Forcing men to recognize their wives' right to peace or be jailed served as a public means of demonstrating the limits of husbands' powers. Regardless of motives, JPs responded to the appeals of women, and in practicing their justice, JPs advanced women's rights.

Women needed JPs who were willing to punish their abusers and hold them to bonds, and the fact that poorer men were most often cited as abusers affected JPs' dispositions toward helping women. Poorer men were considered less able to restrain their passions and were deemed proper subjects of governmental discipline. Categorizing poor men as abusers also negated the abuse that occurred in upper- and middle-class homes, even though divorces show that abusers came from all ranks of society. It is with the poor that we see JPs most often engaged in a daily struggle to protect women. As JPs increasingly confined the poor to jail or made them pay fines, society was moving toward increasingly identifying wife abuse as a problem of poverty. The women who availed themselves of the protection of JPs cemented these tropes and helped establish the abuse of wives as uncivilized because it was associated with the poor.

The cultural trends that influenced women protesting abuse also influenced communities to protect women, often without the actual motive of expanding women's freedoms. Some community members

partook in the policing of wife abuse. Between 1800 and 1820, ten records show Bostonians demanding the government intervene in the
households of abused wives, with most cases occurring in the 1810s.[23]
Narratives of abuse, the noise from husbands' violent outbursts, and
physical scars garnered empathy from the community. In 1816, four men
near the home of Elizabeth Katon wrote the police and served as witnesses against Mr. Katon for "cruelly beating his wife." She was "so beat
as not to be able to attend as a witness," so the men stepped forward
in her place.[24] These neighboring men played the roles of responsible
patriarchs, like many JPs, and in protecting Elizabeth Katon from her
husband, they viewed themselves as preservers of the order and peace
rather than as actors who expanded women's ability to contest men's patriarchal privileges or marital rights. Regardless of intent, their actions
restricted men from abusing their wives. The neighbors also created a
support network for Katon, who needed daily protection.

Problems with punishment had historically plagued wife abuse cases,
with many juries willing to find husbands guilty but not to punish them.
The legal system increasingly penalized men who abused their wives,
with the assistance of all-male juries and neighbors of both sexes who
served as witnesses in abuse cases. New York City practiced a policy
of punishing men according to "extent of injury" and the continuing
threat they posed to their wives. In 1805, a judge asked Mary Campbell
about her injuries after her husband pleaded guilty to assaulting her,
and he fined John Campbell five dollars based on her response. Other
men suffered jail time or smaller fines of six cents, similar to some of
the slave masters found guilty of cruelty.[25] These trends existed in Essex
and Clinton Counties of New York, too. Some courts continued to find
men guilty without punishment. In Cayuga County, one judge "arrested
judgement" of one husband found guilty.[26] Bonds for peace remained
part of sentences for men, with men promising bonds for anywhere between 100 and 1,000 dollars. Cases with high bonds often meant wives
suffered repeated abuse and husbands required greater restraints. In
New York, a judge fined William Vallean fifteen dollars for threatening "to HorseWhip" his wife and returning to the family with "a Case
Knife in his Hand." Elizabeth Vallean, his wife, "considered her Life to be
hourly endangered by the ill conduct of her said Husband." She asked for
a "Surety of peace" to maintain her safety and the judges decided on a

bond for 1,000 dollars.[27] William Vallean's repeated assaults and deadly threat likely influenced the judge's light fine with a heavy bond. Indeed, because he walked away and came back with a knife, some premeditation could even be established in his intent to commit harm. In Boston, sentencing could also include jail time, but indictments and prosecutions were much rarer there. In 1819, two cases of wife abuse were fully prosecuted through Boston's municipal court, and both cases resulted in guilty verdicts with men serving jail time. In both of these cases, indictments noted the wife's life was "endangered," which echoed the earlier standard of only life-threatening assaults being prosecuted fully through the judicial system. In other cases, repeated assaults or threats, rather than the use of weapons or maiming, became a new marker warranting a full prosecution.[28] The largest problems in the sentencing of men continued to be the "settling" of cases in between the reporting and trials. As had occurred from the colonial era, women routinely backed away from their charges of abuse fearing financial, personal, or physical suffering.

Judges' decisions in divorce and separation cases, as well as changing divorce laws, also demonstrate movement toward recognizing spousal abuse as illegal. Judges regularly granted separations and divorces on the grounds of abuse, despite the legal logic that suggested abuse did not merit a divorce. Judges averred that consistent abuse warranted separations. Cases in which men offered counterevidence did not affect judges' dispositions toward granting divorces either.[29] The ties that continued to bind women separated *a mensa et thoro* (from bed and board) on the grounds of cruelty attested to the power of men's legal position vis-à-vis their wives, but these separations also gave women much-needed choices in determining how to deal with an abusive spouse. Legislators expanded women's options in the nineteenth century as women's complaints of abuse rose. In 1813, New York granted women the right to separations, likely owing to the problems in restraining repeatedly abusive men, but women desired full divorces so they could remarry. New York would be among the slowest to adopt meaningful reforms to divorce, and it would not be until the 1960s that full divorces were made accessible. Pennsylvania granted full divorces for cruelty after 1817, Connecticut in 1843, and Massachusetts in 1857.[30] Allowing abused wives throughout New England full divorces on grounds of cruelty supported their individual right to testify against their husbands and revealed the fissures in the doctrine of coverture. Women's narratives of violence played an important role in these legislative changes by creating the empathy necessary to effect change. Divorce was not initially viewed as a proper solution to abusive husbands because it interfered with family life and presented the specter of independent women. Allowing women to gain separations and eventually full divorces on the basis of cruelty was a significant change in government administration and a step forward for women living within seventy-five years of the American Revolution.

Jurists were not only issuing indictments and granting divorces; other evidence indicates that, at the insistence of the stream of women who appeared in their offices, they were beginning to dispute the power of husbands to physically correct their wives. JPs who forced husbands to make bonds in urban areas ultimately created a new legal "text" that made spousal assault an offense. By 1816 in Connecticut, the very influential lawyer and judge Tapping Reeve published a condemnation of men's right to abuse their wives, twenty-five years after he assisted Susannah Wyllys Strong in her complaint of wife abuse and worked on Elizabeth Freeman's suit for freedom against her abusive master. Reeve founded the United States' first law school, the Litchfield Law School in Connecticut, and made significant contributions as a teacher, lawyer, judge, and writer. In *The Law of Baron and Feme*, he questioned the English common law traditions that allowed husbands to physically correct their wives. He wrote that "it is not to be denied, that there are to be found brutal husbands who abuse their wives; but the right of chastising a wife is not claimed by any man; neither is any such right recognized by our law." In contrast to earlier jurists, he claimed that the absence of a law forbidding assault did not mean it was a right men held. Showing the effect of women litigants on his thinking, Reeve pointed out that in cases of assault, husbands and wives "may institute a process against each other, the object of which is to compel them to find securities for their good behavior."[31] Of course, it was women who most often made use of this tool. Reeve believed that the binding out of men and women who abused their spouses indicated the illegality of spousal assault. He did not distinguish between women's right to sue for the peace and their husbands' right to physically "correct" their wives, as did other legal minds who disaggregated the two phenomena. Reeve held that husbands and wives could assault each other only in self-defense or if the wife needed confinement for insanity. He argued further that women who fled from their husbands' "brutality" would not be returned by courts to the marriage. A year later, Connecticut's passage of more liberal divorce laws for cruelty supported Reeve's logic.

Reeve's writing suggests he was among those who believed that with modernity and civilization, men should be more highly attuned to women's rights and that physical punishment was the mark of less civilized eras.[32] Similar to those who argued against cruelty to children and against public executions, Reeve believed violence in the home was an archaic form of discipline. His experience with women complainants in abuse cases also likely affected his understanding of the harmful disempowerment of women in marriage. Reeve's use of terms such as "brutal" to describe husbands who assaulted their wives indicated a new social understanding of the limits of husbands' powers and the types of men who beat their wives, and it fell in line with other reformers' talk of corporal punishment.[33] He proposed that from the 1600s, "wives began to receive a more liberal treatment[.] . . . They assumed more the character of companions than of servants to their husbands." In contrast with older ways, he argued the "increased refinements of modern times" lessened the power of husbands.[34] In this way, Reeve intimated that the republic was more modern than old England and demanded better behavior from men. Even if laws did not explicitly prohibit wife abuse, he believed new American common law traditions and modern behavioral standards did. Reeve, however, was merely one of many lawyers, judges, and state representatives, and these new ideas were only beginning to permeate society. As late as 1823, other legal minds still held that a husband had the legal right to "correct his wife."[35]

In addition to expanded access to divorce, indictments against wife abusers and women's petitions for safety revealed the problematic nature of the doctrine of coverture. Married women had already seen the law break down for economic reasons, as in cases when women made agreements with husbands to write wills or wives acted independently (as "femes sole") in business transactions. Assault cases and divorces further ruptured the doctrine by suggesting the difficulty of truly merging two persons' legal identities. Tapping Reeve argued against the doctrine of coverture and tried to show that the "law does not view the husband and wife as one person."[36] Indeed, JPs empowered women's testimonies by placing them above those of their husbands even in cases when their lives were not threatened in peace and divorce suits. Although husbands had legal and economic authority over their households, abused wives forced husbands to submit to their wishes by appealing to the state's duty of protecting women. It would not be until much later in the nineteenth century that the doctrine of coverture broke down further, but women's protests and the diminished divorce laws revealed the law's inherent weaknesses.

Though women saw progress in the judiciary and in some community support, wife murder was becoming more frequent. During the 1820s, fivefold increases in wife murder occurred in New Hampshire and Vermont, with similar increases documented in upstate New York by the 1840s. Historians link the increasing violence to the greater emphasis placed on romantic love and women's options to pursue wages, thus giving them more independence from men. Overall, wife murder remained a rare crime, but the legal inequities of women's position made prosecuting such cases important. Wife murderers would suffer severe penalties, most often the death penalty, revealing constancy in the handling of this crime from the colonial era.[37] Women did not quietly tolerate rising abuse or murder, and the advent of the temperance movement provided a space for women to pose a challenge to wife abuse and spousal murder. They positioned temperance as a cause for women because drunkenness upset stability in the home and could be a major factor in abuse.[38]

The legacy of women's fight against wife abuse was the weakening and questioning of the doctrine of coverture. Though New York was slow to develop divorce laws that allowed women easy access to freedom and safety, it punished wife abuse steadily. Governments changed their disposition toward spousal assault by the 1830s, with more rural counties such as Clinton in upstate New York beginning to prosecute a few offenders engaged in violence. Some of this progress was national in scope. Governments in Baltimore and several counties in North Carolina and South Carolina conceived of themselves as important stopgaps to spousal violence and treated married women's independent personal security as a part of their mandate by issuing bonds for peace.[39] Such work was important in reducing the number of spousal murders, as signs of domestic discord were often ignored or underreported prior to escalation. This problem continues today even with greater protections in place for abused women. One recent study notes that at least "one in ten victims" of intimate partner homicide "experienced some form of violence in the month preceding their death."[40] The growing number of indictments against wife abusers in the early republic shows some advancement toward fully criminalizing abuse and empowering wives' safety and security over the patriarchal rights of the doctrine of coverture. Conversations about spousal abuse in the public sphere outside of these cases did not increase, however, and abused wives faced a considerable fight moving forward to maintain governmental activism in punishing offenders.[41] They needed recognition for full divorces in New York, and abused wives required more partners to secure their safety from violent husbands. It was not until the 1970s that most states adopted specific laws against spousal abuse, but cases made their way through court systems before then.

Needing Interventions

The early republic was not an era of grand reform in the rights of servants, though a greater sensitivity to the abuse of children emerged. Children and young adults remained socially acceptable subjects of corporal punishment meted out by parents, guardians, masters, and even school teachers. On the other hand, neighbors and juries revealed a disposition to deny the rights of masters to make the most egregious assaults, and they were active in ensuring some redress occurred. The government returned to prosecuting abusive masters, even those accused of beating servants of color, but servants' and apprentices' safety remained compromised, and their legal footing was insecure. They needed allies to advocate for freedom from abuse because they lost their ability to stand for themselves in legal spaces. Young adults' servitude and apprenticeship had dramatically altered from the colonial era, with apprenticeship declining and servitude mostly limited to the very poor and African American populations. Resistance to coercive servitude grew. Pauper servants and the enslaved waiting to age out of the system believed their service was unjust and corporal punishment was unwarranted.

Prior to the end of the eighteenth century, governments handled most assaults on servants or apprentices as civil suits, but they began issuing more indictments for mistreatment in the nineteenth century.

Neighbors and servants reported severe or unwarranted assaults, even ones that were not maiming or life threatening, and courts required less extreme levels of violence to issue indictments, much as in the case of wives. After 1810, the court tried seven cases of abuse in New York City.[42] In addition to these cases, at least one additional case appears to reflect concerns about the abuse of a young girl who may have been a pauper servant.[43] Unlike the civil suits from previous generations, cases of servant and apprentice abuse often came from neighbors who overheard the cries of abuse victims. New Yorkers had become more attuned to intervening and reporting cruelty after the *Broad* cases, and their activism goaded courts to action. In April 1812, Peter Lent, who worked across the street from Richard Lowerre, saw Lowerre criminally abuse his white indentured servant. Lent reported to New York City's special justices that he saw Lowerre grab a stick, "and without saying any thing that the Deponent distinctly heard or understand fell to beating the said Jesse Fash who was standing in the Shop until the said Fash cryed Murder." Lent heard Fash "ask for Mercy from the said Lowerre" and Lent believed the "beating an unreasonable one." Lowerre was acquitted for the abuse, but the fact that the case was tried as an assault case, rather than a civil suit, suggests a change in New York City's criminal justice system.[44] The newly politicized context of viewing abuse after *Broad* resulted in greater engagement on the part of neighbors to protect abused servants, but servants were less often bringing cases to courts.

Courts did not take on cases of African American servants' abuse in New York City records until after 1810. After that time, New York City courts established a baseline of treatment that applied to both races. Three of the seven cases after 1810 involved African American servants, and in two of the cases, the grand jury went so far as to express great concern about the safety of the African American apprentices. In 1815, the grand jury in New York City recommended an indictment against Noel Corbet for assaulting Laurent and Alexander Dominick. In pressing for an indictment, the grand jury urged a quick trial and noted their "fear that the lads will be obliged again to return to their master, as also the marks of his cruelty are not fresh and the more obvious." Understanding that the marks of violence were critical to prosecutions as juries became less trusting of young plaintiffs, the grand jury described the "Cruel and Inhuman manner" of the assault, but no other details exist about the case. A month later, Corbet confessed guilt in one suit, and the jury found him guilty in another. The indictment did not identify the race of the Dominick brothers, but the court was aware of it from the first instance of the complaint and throughout the trial. In pressing for a quick trial, the jury described the boys as "a couple of Mullato lads, who lived with him in the character of apprentices."[45] The actions taken to protect the Dominick brothers are hard to imagine occurring without the change in temperament caused by the cases against slave masters in the first decade of the nineteenth century.

Jurors and judges did not change their disposition to viewing corporal punishment as a legitimate means of disciplining unruly servants or apprentices, even though apprentices and servants challenged this standard routinely. In 1813, New York City brought John Towt before special justices for abusing Mary Graham, his African American indentured servant, but the jury found him not guilty after learning of Graham's routine disobedience. Graham was part of the pauper apprenticeship system, and Towt received Graham from the commissioners of the almshouse in 1804. During the last five years of her servitude, Towt found Graham's behavior uncontrollable. She began "absconding and absenting herself for Days and nights," and Graham admitted to running away seven times. Towt tried to control her through "advice, reproof, and correction as he thought most likely to produce that effect, and she still growing more ungovernable proved herself unwilling to conform." The court did not perceive Towt's actions or use of correction as wrongful. From their perspective, he had used discipline in the way it was intended. From Graham's perspective, however, the bondage and her treatment were wrong. She confessed to running away, and the special justice reported "she does not want to go home & serve as she is bound to do." Towt agreed to a formal separation a few days previous to his indictment and turned Graham over to the Commissioners of the Almshouse "to cancel her indentures."[46] It is likely Towt only released Graham because the authorities became involved in the case, and in that sense, she was successful despite the fact that the court found Towt not guilty. Courts upheld the rights of masters to corporally punish their servants, but servants staked out certain standards for correction. They were unwilling to remain with abusive masters and some found ways to freedom regardless of court decisions.

During the second decade of the nineteenth century, urban courts increased litigation to bring guardians in line with standards of what they considered humane treatment. Reformers writing about the misuse of corporal punishment and the sensationalist coverage of cruelty cases in urban courts affected communities' conceptions of the right to commit assaults on children more broadly. Newer understandings of children and young adults that conceived of them as more in need of direction than disciplined into orderly behavior also played a role. Between 1810 and 1820, Boston and New York City indicted ten parents and legal guardians for assaults on children and young adults in their care. This is considerable progress when compared with the four cases in which local governments stepped in to prevent further abuse by punishing parents or removing children from abusive parents in the seventeenth century.[47] The nineteenth-century cases range from abuse of very young infants to an eighteen-year-old girl who suffered a mental disability. Activism on the part of neighbors to see children and young adults treated with care made this possible.[48] Urbanity was an essential driver in attaining indictments, as the close quarters of the cities' residents meant witnesses could identify abuse as repetitive and noncorrective. In contrast, in Cayuga County, New York, and Middlesex and Worcester Counties, Massachusetts, no indictments were made against parents for abusing their children. Some areas in Middlesex and Worcester were more populous, yet courts took no action. While urbanity clearly played a role in the courts desire to intervene, the new sensitivity to children's abuse was important, too. Other caretakers were indicted as well, suggesting a trend in prosecuting guardians for abuse in urban centers of the northeast. In New York City, juries issued indictments against two school teachers and the caretakers of the orphan asylum for abuse of children.[49] The children in the orphan asylum were similar in some ways to pauper servants and African American children, whose guardianship was transferred to other individuals. Criticisms of school teachers using corporal punishment would gain steam in the antebellum era, as reformers like Horace Mann sought to make education more inclusive and humane.[50]

Communities heeded and gave more credence to the advice not to engage in corporal punishment, and this changed the context of viewing assaults on children. Parents discussed and read about how to best develop their children, urging less physical discipline and more attention to their moral and intellectual development. In 1811, James Hardie's son came home without the wages from his apprenticeship, and he refused to beat him. Hardie said he never "chastised any of his children, for what he deemed an accident," and instead he gave his son "friendly and wholesome advice."[51] Some parents practiced moderation at home and focused on reasoning with children to assist their development. These parenting techniques gained even greater esteem as the antebellum era progressed. The romanticizing of children and domestic spaces resulted in less severe use of corporal punishment in some northeastern homes.[52]

Over the centuries, servants and apprentices established that they would not suffer abuse. They engaged in violent acts of retribution and ran away when justice was not possible. It was in urban communities that they found the most success, as the forces against corporal punishment came together with a watchful and diverse population. Although urban courts began classifying abuse of some servants as assaults, the community did not work to end corporal punishment on a large scale in the early republic, and neither did they intervene for all children and servants. By the nineteenth century, servants needed to show scars of abuse and have multiple witnesses willing to testify to their cries and abuse to gain traction. Bystanders would intervene only when abuse was severe and used for reasons other than discipline, and it could be difficult in rural locales to locate support. Servants of color did not feel empowered to reach for help as readily as white servants, and a great deal of evidence suggests that whites did not see African Americans as having the same rights to safety as whites.

Servants and apprentices did not see much advancement of their civil rights in the early republic. Legal guardianship over youth remained secure, and new ideals about their need for development meant middle- and upper-class youth found more direct oversight by their parents, rather than other guardians. As access to education increased, young adults and children found schoolrooms as sites of their development, and new ideas challenged corporal punishment in school settings. Over the antebellum era, campaigns against cruelty would grow, with arguments made that corporal punishment hindered the moral and intellectual development of children. However, some groups would continue to maintain that corporal punishment was critical to children's and young adults' development.[53]

Rising Violence

The first generation of African American northerners freed from slavery focused on establishing their right to safety through legal activism in urban areas and through securing allies in less populous regions. Perhaps the greatest tool African Americans harnessed against violence was their writing and building of institutions to support their success. Increasingly African Americans wrote their own narratives about mistreatment, ensuring whites did not mediate their voices, and they called on Americans to live up to their professed ideals. None of these tactics successfully ended the violence directed against African Americans, and neither did these tools provide additional civil rights. Though African Americans had secured their access to the judiciary, evidence indicates racially targeted violence grew from the 1820s.[54] Newer attacks on African Americans were marked by whites making threats prior to escalating into violence and articulating their racial and ethnic motivations. In addition, African Americans faced new legislation and segregation that limited their rights and mobility. African Americans challenged the new racial ordering of society, but the fight for inclusion and safety was not won in the early republic.

The legacy of slavery had not disappeared, and violence was a greater threat to African Americans than to others. In New York City between 1811 and 1819, the violence experienced by African Americans at the hands of whites was roughly equivalent to that in the first decade of 1800, with 9.04 reports of violence per 1,000 people, but African Americans' likelihood of experiencing violence was greater than whites'.[55] Labor relations and living situations prevented notification of authorities in rural areas, which makes reports of assaults there incongruent with the realities they experienced. Historian Randolph Roth, however, found that violent experiences were part of a deadly trend throughout the North by the 1840s and 1850s. "[W]hites murdered blacks at roughly twice the rate at which blacks murdered one another in rural areas and at five times that rate in cities."[56] Urban areas had become a focus of some of the larger attacks on African Americans. Population growth meant the building of free African American enterprises and community organizations with churches, educational institutions, and community groups focusing on African American welfare.[57] The success of urban black communities and their organizations made them a target, but group-based assaults on African Americans also occurred in more rural areas.

Whites contested the inclusion of African Americans in public spaces by threatening and taking action against them, and the government seemingly abandoned its role in protecting African Americans by disallowing their inclusion in public celebrations. In 1810, the New York African Society for Mutual Relief planned to have a parade to celebrate the state's incorporation of the society, but in an increasingly common aspect of urban life, whites threatened violence. The menace became disappointingly predictable for the free black community. In response to the risk of disorder, white allies to the New York African Society defended the group, noting they had a "perfect right" to form a society and that "the city is bound by its obligations to preserve the peace." Yet they also doubted the ability of authorities to stem violence during the procession. A "friend" advised "such is the malignity of public prejudice that the authorities would be entirely powerless to protect you on the street, and you would be torn in pieces by howling mobs."[58] By the 1810s, gangs of young men who attacked people in urban environs for sport regardless of race were a feature of urbanity, but the writer was clear that racial bias empowered a virulent and dangerous hatred. The fear that the local government could not protect the procession was an alarming development, suggesting racial relations were worsening. Although encouraged to drop the event, the society refused to do so. Public celebrations were under threat from white lawlessness, and cities increasingly asked that African Americans forgo their public celebrations. African Americans were no longer welcome participants in the public parades and militia days in the North, including Independence Day celebrations in Philadelphia, New England, and New York. In 1811, the Common Council of Albany shut down the yearly Pinkster celebrations, claiming the need for law and order. The prohibitions spoke more to growing concerns about the behavior of free blacks and their claims of public space for leisure and work activities.[59]

Threats to public processions were only one facet of the newly intensified racialized violence. In smaller group attacks, whites engaged in racial targeting by publicly declaring their intention to harm individual African Americans. In 1812, William Wilson, an African American chimney sweep master, saw a man mishandle one of his apprentices and he told him "not to strike the boy." Phillip Feris, a white yeoman, was unwilling to let what he perceived as an insult go. Feris and a few others picked up stones, threw them at several African Americans, and cried out "let's kill the Damned Negroes." Nathaniel Bryant, one of the victims who reported the event to the police, noted that Charles Cox suffered a "violent blow against his head by a Stone." The effects of the assault committed by virtual strangers could have been deadly. Bryant was unable to identify most of the attackers by name in his report to the special justices, and the jury declared Feris not guilty. The white attackers made it clear that race was a factor by naming it as such. In addition, chimney sweeping was a segregated occupation in New York City, with primarily African American masters and apprentices. Whites routinely complained about sweepers' presence and considered them dirty and loud, even as many citizens expressed the importance of the work for limiting fires in the city. The attack on Bryant, Cox, and others was not isolated, with whites assaulting at least four African American sweep drivers and masters in 1815 and 1816.[60] Events in rural areas suggest racially targeted assaults, too. In 1811, a mob stoned Ezra Rifle, an African American man, in Hillsdale New York. He died of his injuries, and the grand jury indicted seven men for the crime, but they were acquitted.[61]

Efforts to establish racial boundaries were ongoing in northern cities, and violence was an increasingly common way of surveilling and maintaining segregation. Some whites believed certain areas were forbidden to African Americans or hoped to make them so. African Americans who entered these neighborhoods or blocks were subject to attack. In 1818, Francis More, an African American, reported three white men attacked him for no cause other than his race while traveling through the first ward in New York City, an area with lesser free black settlement. Prior to the passage of gradual emancipation, the first ward represented an area with a high number of slaves, yet by end of the second decade, many African Americans no longer lived there and arrived only as employees. More told the special justices that James McGrath and two other men "came up to him in the street & said there is a negro & struck him & knocked him down."[62] Racial targeting was not new, but the overt announcement of it on an anonymous stranger walking peacefully in the streets suggests whites tolerated and practiced racial policing of the area.

The perpetrators likely saw themselves engaging in protective behavior rather than criminal conduct, though they made dangerous assaults to establish racial boundaries.[63] Whites built their own sense of identity and comradery through these assaults, while also stigmatizing others. Segregation played out beyond urban residences as education, transportation, and labor markets became segregated, and this extended to rural areas of the North where sociability was stratified, too.[64]

The violence in the early republic shows strengthening ideas about race and ethnicity. Assailants announced their racial motivations and ethnic identities and were moved to commit acts based on racial policing of spaces. In June 1816, John Dickerson, John Vann, and William Vincent gathered in the seventh ward and began verbally and physically assaulting African American passersby in front of neighborhood spectators. Patrick Cahil reported the men to the special justices and noted each took "a stick or club in his hand shaking them over the Heads" at "blacks that came their way." The men intimidated African Americans by simultaneously yelling "Huza for the Shamrock." Their actions caused "many persons to collect" and spectate. The motivations of the crowd are unclear—some likely watched in amusement, while others monitored the men's activities to make sure their threats did not go too far. Dickerson, Vann, and Vincent eventually started "an affray with some black man," and a mob gathered "about them." Although they began their activities by singling out African Americans, Dickerson commenced "beating a white man" and asked for assistance from his friends. The white man may have been trying to help the African American targeted by the group, and the entire crowd intervened, and they took the men to the special justices to end the skirmish.[65] It appears that little was done to prevent the three men's actions until a white man was injured. In some ways, the violence was similar to that of the first decade of 1800, when the cities' dockyards became battle zones, but the racial pride expressed by the men also shows an increased awareness of their own ethnicity and assertion of their Irish identity.[66]

Such ethnic identification, in combination with assaults on African Americans, reveals the ways whites' racial differentiation expressed itself through violence in urban centers.[67] The anonymity and group-based offenders are important clues that connect the racial violence in the early republic with modern hate crimes, which are most often perpetrated by strangers and multiple offenders who share common ideas about another group's worth and character.[68] Psychologists, sociologists, and criminologists have several theories about how prejudice turns into violence, and when combined, such explanations provide clues to the violence in the early republic. Conflict group theory explains that the creation of "insider" and "outsider" groups, like the construction of ideas about race, can lead to increased hostility as individuals use baseless judgements about others to boost their own self-esteem, create a sense of belongingness, or reduce their own anxiety about conflict. In the early republic, conflict group theory is pertinent to the social learning of some whites, as they came of age witnessing increased segregation and attempts to limit African Americans to servile occupations. Other forms of systematic subordination added to the hardening of racial categories and assertions of ethnic and racial identification, such as the laws providing for the enforced servitude of many free African Americans.[69] Anxiety and insecurity over racial identities was another factor in growing violence. Major structural changes affected all individuals in the early republic. The movement away from slavery in the North put considerable stress on the formation of whiteness given the growing population of African Americans, particularly in urban areas. African American community organizations and economic enterprises challenged whites' conceptions of themselves as the inheritors of progress. As class and race became the major factors in socially categorizing individuals, violence was often used to help allay fear and insecurities about the changing economic conditions and the marginalization of the white working class.[70] The experiences of journeymen and artisans who challenged their declining roles help inform our understanding of how economic changes undermined some white men's sense of place in a changing society.

African American strategies of resistance to violence did not noticeably alter as violence against them increased, and neither did their activism dissolve these forces. As African Americans asserted their citizenship through military service or legal activism, new props emerged between 1810 and 1830, alongside violence, to support white supremacy. Disfranchisement measures and the growth of the American Colonization Society are among the clearest indicators of societal views showing whites' sense that they were empowered to act out against African

Americans. New Jersey (1807), Connecticut (1818), and Rhode Island (1822) passed legislation eliminating African American men's votes. In 1811, New York required that African Americans prove their freedom at polls when asked, and in 1821 the legislature passed a law demanding property qualifications for African American men while abolishing these restrictions for adult white male voters. The establishment of the American Colonization Society as a solution to slavery and racial inequality in the United States is the clearest indication of many whites' inability to envision African American equality socially and under the law. In considering whether to develop a colonization plan to remove free blacks from the United States to Africa, many whites frankly professed that their own prejudice made equality an impossibility for African Americans. Elias B. Caldwell, clerk of the United States Supreme court, admitted the "declaration of independence" promised that "'all men were created equal' and have certain 'inalienable rights.' Yet," he continued, "it is considered impossible, consistently with the safety of the state, and it certainly is impossible, with the present feelings towards these people, that they can ever be placed, upon this equality, or admitted to the enjoyment of these 'inalienable rights,' whilst they remain mixed with us [in the United States.]"[71] White northerners who supported colonization professed that relocating African Americans elsewhere would allow them to prosper unimpeded by whites. Admitting their own culpability for mistreating African Americans, supporters of colonization essentially disavowed their role in maintaining safe environments or economic equality for African Americans.

African Americans did not cede northern society to whites. Racial violence created and maintained structures of inequality in the early United States, and structural inequality simultaneously set the stage for violence. Violence enforced emerging segregation, limited mobility, and foreclosed some social and economic networks for African Americans. Though the trends toward increased racial violence were clear, African Americans built community organizations and resisted a culture that demanded they be subordinated and separated. African American organizations increasingly looked inward to focus on their own business growth and leadership, rather than partnering with whites whose paternalistic policies often presumed African American subordination.[72] They asserted their role in the republic.

Violence was part of the American fabric, and more frequent murderous violence against African Americans and wives was part of this trend in the nineteenth-century North.[73] The legacy of this violence remains with us today, as people of color are more likely than whites to experience violence, and wives still struggle to find security from abusive spouses.[74] Children remain largely reliant on adults to substantiate and report abuse. Nevertheless, the early republic saw noticeable changes in the way society viewed violence and its utility in disciplining individuals and society. Reduced visibility of public punishments altered the landscape of early America, and public violence was increasingly anathema.[75] Advocates against cruelty began a movement to use tactics of moral suasion and reason to build an orderly society, alongside the legal struggles and relationship building of victims of abuse. Legally subordinate people—wives, young servants, and African Americans—did not find safety and security, however. Slavery ended, but new legislative mandates and violence created a new racial order. Access to divorce opened new freedoms for women, but society clung to the doctrine of coverture until the 1850s.

Women, young adults, and African Americans secured a tradition of civil rights agitation by the advent of the antebellum era, which they would expand upon in later generations. Fleeing from violence and structures of subordination were key to slaves and servants resisting their masters, and free African Americans turned to international partnerships with the African diaspora. Women left abusive spouses and turned to families and neighbors who assisted them in finding security. Relationship building was essential to achieving safety and civil rights. In fact, it would become central to new movements combatting slavery and promoting temperance and women's rights. Forming associations and looking to those within and without the positions of legal inequality were critical to altering beliefs of the larger community. Increasingly, intragroup associations would challenge the social construction of race and sex, among other identities. Progress in access to civil rights, economic viability, and personal security remains critical to lessening violent resistance and violent aggression.

The role of violence in civil rights agitation has perhaps led to the greatest questions about how to foment change. Legally subordinate persons' acts of violence have historically bolstered discourses about their presumed inferiority. Shrill and murderous wives and mothers, combative blacks, and hostile youths have special places in the American lexicon, signifying both a refusal to submit and embodiments of societal fears about their potential to create disorder. Nonviolent protests are favored because of this, but withstanding acts of aggression with peaceful submission has not historically proven itself to be singularly valuable. Surprisingly, it is the combination of the threat of disorder through aggression and the more peaceful protests that has shown the best results.

ACKNOWLEDGMENTS

Everyday Crimes came together with the help of so many generous individuals and institutions. This project would not have been possible or as timely without their many kindnesses.

My most heartfelt thanks, as always, go to Adam Parez and my parents. Working on such a dark topic was troubling—deeply so. Having Adam to return to at the end of the day was particularly galvanizing as I processed the intense cruelty and violence of our nation's history. He refocused me on the stories of courage and resilience and kept me spirited so I could get the work done. My parents raised me to be an independent woman: the best gift parents can give a daughter. They never questioned "why history" or wondered about its relevance. They are proud of me, and I'm terribly proud of them. What a gift!

My academic family began at University of Maryland, under the tutelage of Clare Lyons. She continues to mentor me in so many meaningful ways, perhaps most importantly through her example of never shying away from digging deeply into archives to find voices from the past. Many emails, letters of reference, and a few phone calls got me through this new project. Ira Berlin, who was a generous scholar with meaningful research, was kind in offering encouragement for this project too. He will be missed by many.

Everyday Crimes came together through presentations at conferences and seminars, and the chapters that make up this book had meaningful feedback from scholars who challenged me to do more and offered so many suggestions that improved the final product. Sheila Skemp, C. Dallett Hemphill, James Brewer Stewart, and Nikki Taylor were among the first to read portions of this work and they encouraged its growth and development, taking special time to offer keen insights based on their considerable experience and knowledge. They wrote letters of support that ultimately helped me get the time and space needed to complete the project. They serve as exemplars of senior scholars giving of their time for others. Trevor Burnard and Randy Browne commented on portions of this manuscript, helping me ground this work more deeply in scholarship of resistance. Thank you as well to those who made suggestions and asked questions at various conferences, and the anonymous reviews from New York University Press who also helped define and refine this work.

Members of my local history community in the Kentucky Early American Seminar, reviewed several chapters of this work and offered fellowship along the way. Special thanks to Bradford Wood, Daniel Krebs, Glenn Crothers, and Jane Calvert for seeing me through this project.

I had assistance from several institutions and staff at historical societies who made this work possible. Indiana University generously contributed funding to complete the work with a New Frontiers in the Arts and Humanities grant that made travel to Massachusetts and New York archives possible. In addition, IU Southeast supported this work through grants from the Academy for Diversity and Inclusive Education, a Summer Research Fellowship, and sabbatical. Elizabeth Bouvier at the Judicial Archives of Massachusetts has been so helpful in both of my books, helping me find the materials I need and always ready to answer questions. Other research guidance came from Andrew Smith from the State of Rhode Island Providence Plantations Judicial Records Center, Bill Hulik from Cayuga County Records Management, and Louise Bement of the Lansing Historical Society.

I often had the occasion to seek out advice from my scientist friends. Aaron Setterdahl and Deanne Pierce aided me on statistical and database work, and Pamela and Brandon Connerly helped me understand and interpret causes of death in several mysterious records.

Staff and faculty at IU Southeast's School of Social Sciences have been wonderful supporters of the project. Abbi Kelly, Brigette Adams, Yolanda Zavala Howe, and Mark Falkenstein made it so I had the space to complete the manuscript. Rachel Getz, of IU Southeast's library, has been an enormous help in getting all those books I needed to research, and she deftly negotiated my due dates, often extending me more time.

My friends and family were especially supportive of this work. Angela Tudico offered me her couch, encouragement, and conviviality on my many trips to New York City to research, saving me much money and sanity. I have loads of notes on my phone inspired by our end-of-the-day conversations. My sisters, Tricia and Julie, always asked with interest about the work and supported me through the process. The Parez family remains as wonderful as they were when I was nineteen—always encouraging, never doubting the work would get done, and forgiving my many foibles. Friends celebrated each milestone with me, and to each of them, I am so very grateful to have you in my life.

Clara Platter, editor at NYU Press, took an early interest in this project. Her enthusiasm and efficiency have meant a great deal to me. Amy Klopfenstein's organizational work on this project has been extraordinary, and copyediting support from Beatrice Burton and James Harbeck was invaluable. Martin Coleman's management of production and editing was seamless.

Thank you to everyone in the past and present who fights to protect others and end violence. Everyone deserves a right to safety, and no one's cries for help should go unheard.

ABBREVIATIONS

BPL   Special Collections, Boston Public Library

DAIP   District Attorney Indictment Papers

JAH   *Journal of American History*

MA   Judicial Archives, Massachusetts Archives

MCB   Municipal Court of Boston

NEQ   *New England Quarterly*

NYGS   New York General Sessions

NYHS   New York Historical Society

NYMA   New York Municipal Archives

NYMS   New York Manumission Society

WMQ   *William and Mary Quarterly*, 3rd series

NOTES

INTRODUCTION

1 *Boston Post Boy*, July 20, 1741.

2 For a sample of literature on legal and social dependence, see G. Edward White, *American Legal History: A Very Short Introduction* (New York: Oxford University Press, 2013); Carole Shammas, *A History of Household Government in America* (Charlottesville, VA: University of Virginia Press, 2002), 1–107; Jared Ross Hardesty, *Unfreedom: Slavery and Dependence in Eighteenth Century Boston* (New York: New York University Press, 2016); and Steven Mintz and Susan Kellogg, *Domestic Revolutions: A Social History of American Family Life* (New York: Free Press, 1988), chap. 1–5.

3 Northern states and towns passed regressive legislation demanding freedom certificates for African Americans desiring the vote and limiting how long they could reside without established residency, among other social and political moves. For a sample of historical literature analyzing the legal and social inequities, see Graham Russell Hodges, *Root & Branch: African Americans in New York and East Jersey, 1613–1863* (Chapel Hill: University of North Carolina Press, 1999), chap. 6 and 8; Leon Litwack, *North of Slavery: The Negro in Free States, 1790–1860* (Chicago: The University of Chicago Press, 1961), chap. 3 and 4; Leslie M. Harris, *In the Shadow of Slavery: African Americans in New York City, 1626–1863* (Chicago: University of Chicago Press, 2003), chap. 3 and 4; and Joanne Pope Melish, *Disowning Slavery: Gradual Emancipation and "Race" in New England* (Ithaca, NY: Cornell University Press, 1998), chap. 3 and 4.

4 Allowable extremes of violence depended upon the type of victim, which is discussed in greater detail in chapters 1 through 3. For a sample of literature discussing violence and corporal punishment, see Marisa J. Fuentes, *Dispossessed Lives: Enslaved Women, Violence, and the Archive* (Philadelphia: University of Pennsylvania Press, 2016), 1–69; Myra Glenn, *Campaigns Against Corporal Punishment: Prisoners, Sailors, Women and Children in Antebellum America* (Albany, NY: State University of New York Press, 1984; Philip Greven, *The Protestant Temperament: Patterns in Childrearing, Religious Experience, and the Self in Early America* (New York: Alfred A. Knopf, 1977); Edmund Morgan, *The Puritan Family: Religion & Domestic Relations in Seventeenth Century New England* (1944 Repr.; New York: Harper & Row, 1996), 97, 102–8, 172; Elizabeth Pleck, *Domestic Tyranny: The Making of Social Policy Against Family Violence from Colonial Times to the Present*

(New York: Oxford University Press, 1987), 3, 6, 17–33; and Lea VanderVelde, "The Last Legally Beaten Servant in America: From Compulsion to Coercion in the American Workplace," *Seattle University Law Review* 39 (2016): 727–87.

5 *Boston Post Boy*, July 20, 1741.

6 On public punishments, see Thomas G. Blomberg and Karol Lucken, *American Penology: A History of Control*, 2nd ed. (New Brunswick, NJ: Transaction Publishers, 2010), 11–24; Douglas Greenberg, *Crime and Law Enforcement in the Colony of New York, 1691–1776* (Ithaca: Cornell University Press, 1976); Lawrence M. Friedman, *Crime and Punishment in American History* (New York: Basic Books, 1994), 19–59; Kathryn Preyer, "Penal Measures in the American Colonies," *American Journal of Legal History* 26 (October 1982): 326–53; and David Rothman, *Discovery of the Asylum: Social Order and Disorder in the New Republic*, rev. ed. (New York: Routledge, 2017), 3–56.

7 By studying varying forms of oppression and identities, we can discern larger systemic beliefs and institutions of power. Moreover, intersectionalism shows the ways hierarchies of race, gender, class, sexuality, and generation are "interlocking" and reinforce each other. For founding literature on intersectionalism, see Kimberlé Crenshaw, "Mapping the Margins: Intersectionality, Identity Politics, and Violence Against Women of Color," in *The Public Nature of Private Violence*, ed. M.A. Fineman and R. Mykitiuk (New York: Routledge, 1994), 93–120; Patricia Hill Collins, *Black Feminist Thought: Knowledge, Consciousness, and the Politics of Empowerment*, 2nd ed. (New York: Routledge, 2000), quote p. 18; and Sherene Razack, *Looking White People in the Eye: Gender, Race, and Culture in Courtrooms and Classrooms* (Toronto: University of Toronto Press, 1998).

8 I borrow from Kimberlé Williams Crenshaw, who argued that black women experience unique forms of discrimination based on their identity as African American women, not just a combination of gender and racial oppression felt by black men or white women. See Kimberlé Williams Crenshaw, "Demarginalizing the Intersection of Race and Sex: A Black Feminist Critique of Antidiscrimination Doctrine, Feminist Theory and Antiracist Politics," *University of Chicago Legal Forum* 140 (1989): 149; and Deborah K. King, "Multiple Jeopardy, Multiple Consciousness: The Context of a Black Feminist Ideology," *Signs* 14 (Autumn 1988): 42–72.

9 Samuel Moyn would argue the use of the term "human rights" is an anachronistic rendering of what wives, slaves, and youthful servants fought for, as the United Nation's "Declaration of Human Rights" did not appear until the 1940s. He argues human rights were conceived of to be separate from governments, and that the rights that were fought for prior to this time were those sought from governments. Arguably, some resistance did demand governmental recognition—such as the use of the legal system to attain freedom or seek justice. However, slave insurrections, running away, and violent resistance were not aimed at governmental membership, but were acts to secure protection for those who undertook them—or even to destroy governments. See Samuel Moyn, *The Last Utopia:*

Human Rights in History (Cambridge, MA: Harvard University Press, 2011), Introduction and chap. 1.

10 Analyses of human and civil rights often theorize on stage theories in the development of human rights. In much analysis, natural and civil rights were the precursor to the elaboration of human rights, and I posit here that there is some overlap. Though legally dependent people did not use a rights discourse, they asserted an understanding that abuse was immoral and inhumane, and many critiques of violence pointedly use such terms. See Karel Vasak, "Human Rights: A Thirty Year Struggle: The Sustained Efforts to Give Force of Law to the University Declaration of Human Rights," *UNESCO Courier* 30 (November 1977): 29. On tracing rights historically, see David Boucher, *The Limits of Ethics in International Relations: Natural Law, Natural Rights, and Human Rights in Transition* (Oxford: Oxford University Press, 2009); Robin Blackburn, "Reclaiming Human Rights," *New Left Review* 69 (May/June 2011): 130–3; and Lynn Hunt, *Inventing Human Rights* (New York: W.W. Norton and Company Press, 2007).

11 Michael Barnet describes humanitarianism as distinct from human rights in that it served "immediate needs," though he sees a transition to "alchemical" humanitarianism in the nineteenth century when reformers challenged the structures, such as slavery, that caused pain and suffering. See Michael Barnett, *Empire of Humanity: A History of Humanitarianism* (Ithaca: Cornell University Press, 2011), chap. 3; Christopher Leslie Brown, *Moral Capital: Foundations of British Abolitionism* (Chapel Hill: University of North Carolina Press, 2006); Adam Hochschild, *Bury the Chains: Prophets and Rebels in the Fight to Free an Empire's Slaves* (Boston: Houghton Mifflin, 2005); and Jenny S. Martinez, *The Slave Trade and the Origins of International Human Rights Law* (New York: Oxford University Press, 2012).

12 Civil rights are those granted to citizens from governments and include protections from discrimination. In early America, freedom suits and government petitions are among the more notable legal trends for enslaved African Americans. For a sample of scholarship, see Emily Blanck, *Tyrannicide: Forging an American Law of Slavery in Revolutionary Massachusetts* (Athens, GA: The University of Georgia Press, 2014), chap. 1 and 2; Edie L. Wong, *Neither Fugitive nor Free: Atlantic Slavery, Freedom Suits and Legal Culture of Travel* (New York: New York University Press, 2009), chap. 1 and 2; A. Leon Higginbotham, Jr., *In the Matter of Color: Race and the American Legal Process: The Colonial Period* (New York: Oxford University Press, 1978); and Catherine Adams and Elizabeth H. Pleck, *Love of Freedom: Black Women in Colonial and Revolutionary New England* (New York: Oxford University Press, 2010), chap. 5 and 6. Wives used peace suits and divorce to stymie abuse, but also made use of government petitions, like slaves. For a sample of this literature, see Ruth Bogin, "Petitioning and the New Moral Economy of Post-Revolutionary America," *William and Mary Quarterly* (hereafter (*WMQ*) 3rd ser. 45 (July 1988): 391–425; Nancy Cott, "Divorce and the Changing Status of Women in Eighteenth-Century Massachusetts," *WMQ* 33 (October

1976): 586–614; and Jennine Hurl-Eamon, *Gender and Petty Violence in London, 1680–1720* (Columbus: The Ohio State University Press, 2005), chap. 4.

13 For a sample of historical literature on the difficulties of interracial cooperation, see Glenda Elizabeth Gilmore, *Gender and Jim Crow: Women and the Politics of White Supremacy in North Carolina, 1896–1920* (Chapel Hill: University of North Carolina Press, 1996), chap. 7; Richard Newman, *The Transformation of American Abolitionism: Fighting Slavery in the Early Republic* (Chapel Hill: University of North Carolina Press, 2002); and Alison Parker, "Frances Watkins Harper and the Search for Women's Interracial Alliances," in *Susan B. Anthony and the Struggle for Equal Rights*, ed. Christine L. Ridardsky and Mary M. Huth (Rochester, NY: University of Rochester Press, 2012), 145–71.

14 For example, see Tehila Kogut, "Someone to Blame: When Identifying a Victim Decreases Helping," *Journal of Experimental Social Psychology* 47 (July 2011): 748–55.

15 See Rachel Hope Cleves, *The Reign of Terror in America: Visions of Violence from Anti-Jacobism to Antislavery* (New York: Cambridge University Press, 2009); Glenn, *Campaigns Against Corporal Punishment*, 50–6; Adam Jay Hirsch, *The Rise of the Penitentiary: Prisons and Punishment in Early America* (New Haven: Yale University Press, 1992), 57–62; W. David Lewis, *From Newgate to Dannemora: The Rise of the Penitentiary in New York, 1796–1848* (Ithaca: Cornell University Press, 1965), 32, 46; Louis P. Masur, *Rites of Execution: Capital Punishment and the Transformation of American Culture, 1776–1865* (New York: Oxford University Press, 1989); and Michael Meranze, *Laboratories of Virtue: Punishment, Revolution, and Authority in Philadelphia, 1760–1835* (Chapel Hill: University of North Carolina Press, 1996), 22–4, 62–86.

16 In addition to the foregoing set of practices, the view society has about violent acts is also often considered important in an economy of violence. However, the emergence of social classes is of primary significance in this trend. Though development of economic relations occurred in early America, the true flowering of class-based identities would not be until the end of the early republic. For a sample of literature most affecting my thinking on economies of violence, see Malcolm Greenshields, *An Economy of Violence in Early Modern France: Crime and Justice in the Haute Auvergne, 1587–1667* (University Park: Pennsylvania State University Press, 1994); and John Smolenski, "Introduction: The Ordering of Authority in the Colonial Americas," in *New World Orders: Violence, Sanction, and Authority in the Colonial America*, ed. John Smolenski and Thomas J. Humphrey (Philadelphia: University of Pennsylvania Press, 2005), 1–16. Separate theoretical frameworks and historiographies exist for violence against women, African Americans, and children. For a collection of essays addressing violence against these groups, see Michael A. Bellesiles, ed., *Lethal Imagination: Violence and Brutality in American History* (New York: New York University Press, 1999); and Christine Daniels and Michael V. Kennedy, ed. *Over the Threshold: Intimate Violence in Early America* (New York: Routledge, 1999).

17 Fuentes, *Dispossessed Lives*, 1–69; Saidiya V. Hartman, *Scenes of Subjection: Terror, Slavery, and Self-Making in Nineteenth Century America* (New York: Oxford University Press, 1997), 3–48.

18 For a sample of this literature, see Kathleen Brown, *Good Wives, Nasty Wenches, and Anxious Patriarchs: Gender, Race, and Power in Colonial Virginia* (Chapel Hill: University of North Carolina Press, 1996); Joyce E. Chaplin, *Subject Matter: Technology, the Body, and Science on the Anglo-American Frontier, 1500–1676* (Cambridge, MA: Harvard University Press, 2001); Andrew Curran, *Anatomy of Blackness: Science and Slavery in an Age of Enlightenment* (Baltimore: Johns Hopkins University Press, 2013); Bruce Dain, *A Hideous Monster of the Mind: American Race Theory in the Early Republic* (Cambridge, MA: Harvard University Press, 2002); Cornelia Hughes Dayton, *Women before the Bar: Gender, Law and Society in Connecticut, 1639–1789* (Chapel Hill: University of North Carolina Press, 1995); Winthrop D. Jordan, *White over Black: American Attitudes toward the Negro, 1550–1812* (Chapel Hill: University of North Carolina Press, 1968); Steven Mintz, *Huck's Raft: A History of American Childhood* (Cambridge, MA: Belknap Press of Harvard University Press, 2004), chap. 1–5; Kelly A. Ryan, *Regulating Passion: Sexuality and Patriarchal Rule in Massachusetts, 1700–1830* (New York: Oxford University Press, 2014); and John Wood Sweet, *Bodies Politic: Negotiating Race in the American North, 1730–1830* (Philadelphia: University of Pennsylvania Press, 2006).

19 For examples, see Paul Slovic, "'If I Look at the Mass I Will Never Act': Psychic Numbing and Genocide," *Judgement and Decision Making* 2 (April 2007): 79–95; C. Daryl Cameron and B. Keith Payne, "Escaping Affect: How Motivated Emotion Regulation Creates Insensitivity to Mass Suffering," *Journal of Personality and Social Psychology* 100 (January 2011): 1–15; and Danielle Västfjäll, Paul Slovic, Marcus Mayorga, and Ellen Peters, "Compassion Fade: Affect and Charity are Greatest for a Single Child in Need," *PLoS ONE* 9 (June 2014).

20 Amanda B. Moniz, *From Empire to Humanity: The American Revolution and the Origins of Humanitarianism* (New York: Oxford University Press, 2016).

21 Holly Brewer, *By Birth or Consent: Children, Law, and the Anglo-American Revolution in Authority* (Chapel Hill: University of North Carolina Press, 2005); Linda Kerber, *No Constitutional Right to Be Ladies: Women and the Obligations of Citizenship* (New York: Hill and Wang, 1998); and Rosemarie Zagarri, *Revolutionary Backlash: Women and Politics in Early American Republic* (Philadelphia: University of Pennsylvania Press, 2007), 37–45.

22 Much of the historical literature derives inspiration from Norbert Elias's theory on the "Civilizing Process" and Thomas Hobbes's *Leviathan* (1651) and *Philosophical Rudiments Concerning Government and Society* (1650). See Norbert Elias, *The Civilizing Process* (1939; repr. Oxford: Blackwell Publishing, 2000). For historical literature on violence and the state, see Douglass C. North, John Joseph Wallis, and Barry R. Weingast, *Violence and Social Orders: A Conceptual Framework for Interpreting Recorded Human History* (2009; repr. New York: Cambridge Univer-

sity Press, 2013); Steven Pinker, *The Better Angels of Our Nature: Why Violence Has Declined* (New York: Penguin Books, 2011), 79–102; Randolph Roth, *American Homicide* (Cambridge, MA: The Belknap Press of Harvard University Press, 2009), 17–21; Pieter Spierenburg, *A History of Murder: Personal Violence in Europe from the Middle Ages to the Present* (Cambridge, UK: Polity, 2008); and J. Carter Wood, *Violence and Crime in Nineteenth Century England: The Shadow of Our Refinement* (New York: Routledge, 2014), chap. 3.

23 See Sasha Turner, *Contested Bodies: Pregnancy, Childrearing, and Slavery in Jamaica* (Philadelphia: University of Pennsylvania Press, 2017), chap. 3.

24 Many examples of the centrality of violence to the trajectory of history exist. For a small sample, see Holger Hoock, *Scars of Independence: America's Violent Birth* (New York: Crown, 2017); Robert Maxwell Brown, *Strain of Violence: Historical Studies of American Violence and Vigilantism* (New York: Oxford University Press, 1975); Paul Gilje, *Rioting in Early America* (Bloomington: Indiana University Press, 1996); Carol Smith-Rosenberg, *This Violent Empire: The Birth of an American Identity* (Chapel Hill: University of North Carolina Press, 2010); and Richard Slotkin, *Regeneration through Violence: The Mythology of the American Frontier, 1600–1860* (Norman, OK.: University of Oklahoma Press, 1973).

CHAPTER 1: YOUNG SERVANTS AND APPRENTICES

1 *The Acts and Resolves, Public and Private, of the Province of Massachusetts Bay: To which are Prefixed the Charters of the Province* (hereafter *Acts and Resolves*), vol. 2 (Boston: Wright & Potter, 1874), 182–3, 1067.

2 Benjamin Franklin, *The Autobiography of Benjamin Franklin*, in *The Autobiography of Benjamin Franklin with Related Documents*, 2nd ed., ed. Louis P. Masur (Boston: Bedford St. Martins, 2003), 37–43. Franklin's memory and presentation of events regarding his servitude have been questioned by several scholars. It's clear his ego affected the retelling, as did his agenda in pushing for self-reliance, but this particular story has value because of the similarities between his experiences and those of other white youth who resisted masters by running away, as is shown later in the chapter. For a sample of readings about his motivations in this part of his narrative, see Ralph Frasca, *Benjamin Franklin's Printing Network: Disseminating Virtue in Early America* (Columbia: University of Missouri Press, 2006), 1–6, 24–8, 80–2; David Waldstreicher, *Runaway America: Benjamin Franklin, Slavery, and the American Revolution* (New York: Hill and Wang, 2004), 43–7; Alan Houston, *Benjamin Franklin and the Politics of Improvement* (New Haven: Yale University Press, 2008), 78–81, 203–13; and Nian-Sheng Huang and Carla Mulford, "Benjamin Franklin and the American Dream," in *The Cambridge Companion to Benjamin Franklin*, ed. Carla Mulford (New York: Cambridge University Press, 2008), 145–58.

3 Communities admonished masters who did not regulate the behavior of their servants. For example, in 1661/2, the Plymouth General Sessions whipped Richard Marshall for disturbing the peace of the neighborhood, and his master "was

warned . . . to take course that . . . his servant, shall carry better amongst his naighbours, or otherwise to rid him out of the towne." *Records of the Colony of New Plymouth in New England*, ed. Nathaniel Shurtleff and David Pulsifer, vol. 4 (New York: AMS Press, 1855), 11. On the policing of youth, see Gerald F. Moran and Varis A. Vinovskis, *Religion, Family, and the Life Course: Explorations in the Social History of Early America* (Ann Arbor: University of Michigan Press, 1992), 152–5.

4   Benjamin Wadsworth, *The Well-Ordered Family; or Relative Duties* (Boston: Bartholomew Green, 1712), 106.

5   Franklin, *The Autobiography of Benjamin Franklin*, 43.

6   Mintz, *Huck's Raft*, 23–31; and Brewer, *By Birth or Consent*, 338–67.

7   See notes 16 through 18.

8   *King v. George Betts*, in *Records of the Court of Assistants of the Colony of the Massachusetts Bay, 1630–1692* (hereafter *Court of Assistants*), ed. John F. Cronin, vol. 3 (Boston: County of Suffolk, 1928), 24–31.

9   For example, in 1666, the local court summoned Nicholas and Judith Weeks for abuse of their white servant Nicholas Woodman, York County initially expressed interest in the case after Judith Weeks confessed to "Cutting off her servant Nic: Woodmans tows." She was held to a fifty-pound bond to resolve the matter, but then Woodman died and the court released Weeks from her bond. The coroner's inquest revealed that Nicholas Weeks was culpable for the death of Nicholas Woodman but the grand jury acquitted him. At this point, the colony's General Court stepped in believing that the town was acting in contrast with laws. It found a "mischarage both in bench & Jury" and cited the town of Kittery for not safeguarding Woodman or reprimanding Weeks after the initial complaint. They also found Weeks "defective in his duty to his servant" and the cause of Woodman's death. Claiming the jury did not appropriately consider the coroner's inquest, the assembly ensured that Woodman's death did not go unnoticed. *Province and Court Records of Maine*, vol. 1 (Portland: Maine Historical Society, 1928), 261–2, 272, 286. Details regarding Weeks's punishment could not be located, but he is found in later records of Maine in making suits. See for example, *Province and Court Records of Maine*, 2:294, 346.

10 In the 1680s, the English reinforced the need to protect servants by asking colonial governments to create laws ensuring that servants who suffered cruelty had redress for their grievances. Rather than creating new laws, the northern colonies largely kept in place the measures they had already adopted because they saw their practices as sufficient. Hugo Grotius, *The Jurisprudence of Holland*, trans. R.W. Lee, vol. 1 (New York: Oxford University Press, 1926), 475; *The Colonial Laws of New York From the Year 1664 to the Revolution*, vol. 1 (Albany, NY: James B. Lyon, 1896), 48, 157–8; *The Colonial Laws of Massachusetts: Reprinted from the Edition of 1672, With Supplements through 1686* (Boston: Rockwell & Churchill, 1890), 51, 53, 129; and *Laws of New Hampshire, Including Public and Private Acts and Resolves and Royal Commissions and Instructions with Historical and*

Descriptive Notes and an Appendix, ed. Albert Stillman Batchellor (Concord, NH: Rumford Printing Company, 1913), 2:27, 235, 292.

11 Several scholars suggest that the Dutch had a greater indisposition toward corporal punishment more broadly, though their levels of interpersonal violence are in a range similar to those of other European nations. Writing against corporal punishment, seventeenth-century Dutch writers such as Jacob Cats believed that violence toward children directly resulted in the production of ill-mannered children. On Dutch parents' ideas about corporal punishment, see Steven Ozment, *When Fathers Ruled: Family Life in Reformation Europe* (Cambridge, MA: Harvard University Press, 1983), 144–53; Benjamin Roberts, *Through the Keyhole: Dutch Child-Rearing Practices in the 17th and 18th Centuries: Three Urban Elite Families* (Hilversum, NL: Verloren 1998), 38, 138–9, 165–86; Simon Schama, *An Embarrassment of Riches: An Interpretation of Dutch Culture in the Golden Age* (New York: Alfred A. Knopf, 1987), 555–9; Sherrin Marshall, *The Dutch Gentry, 1500–1650: Family, Faith, and Fortune* (Westport, CT: Greenwood Press, 1987); A.Th. Van Deursen and Maarten Ultee, *Plain Lives in a Golden Age: Popular Culture, Religion and Society in Seventeenth-Century Holland* (Cambridge, UK: Cambridge University Press, 1991), 130–1; and Pieter Spierenburg, *Violence and Punishment: Civilizing the Body Through Time* (Cambridge, UK: Polity, 2013), 39–56.

12 The official Dutch religion was Dutch Reformed, though Catholic elements remained strong in parts of the Netherlands. Philip Greven, *Spare the Child: The Religious Roots of Punishment and the Psychological Impact of Physical Abuse* (New York: Vintage Books, 1992), 60–1, 64–6; Mintz, *Huck's Raft*, 11–20; Edmund Morgan, *The Puritan Family*, 103–4; Moran and Vinovskis, *Religion, Family, and the Life Course*, 112–8; and John Demos, *A Little Commonwealth* (1970; repr. New York: Oxford University Press, 2000), chap. 6.

13 *Records of the City of New Amsterdam in New Netherland*, ed. Henry B. Dawson, vol. 3 (Morrisania, NY: The Knickerbocker Press, 1897), 88; and Mariah Adin, "'I shall beat you, so that the Devil shall laugh at it': Children, Violence, and the Courts in New Amsterdam," in *Children in Colonial America*, ed. James Marten (New York: New York University Press, 2007), 93–4. For example, *see Ruben Hutchins v. John Marshall*, August 1751; *Abraham Hope v. Theophilis Elsworth*, February 1759; *Jacob King v. Peter Tillon*, May 1769, Minutes, New York General Sessions (hereafter NYGS), New York Municipal Archives (hereafter NYMA).

14 Petition of Charles Dupee, July 1710; and Petition of Thomas Griffin, April 1714, Record Book, Suffolk General Sessions, Judicial Archives, Massachusetts Archives (hereafter MA); and Thomas Lechford, *Notebook Kept by Thomas Lechford, Esq., Lawyer, In Boston, Massachusetts Bay, From June 27, 1638, to July 29, 1641* (Cambridge, MA: John Wilson and Son, 1885), 229–30.

15 Laws in the colonial Chesapeake stipulated that white servants could not be whipped on their naked backs, but evidence does not suggest northerners similarly conceived of abuse. For the information on Virginia, see Allison N. Madar, "'An Innate Love of Cruelty': Master Violence against Female Servants in

Eighteenth-Century Virginia" in *Order and Civility in the Early Modern Chesapeake*, ed. Debra Meyers and Melanie Perreault (New York: Lexington Books,
2014), 95; and Greven, *Spare the Child*, 20–1, 69–70.

16 In two cases from Plymouth, the charges were "mistreating" a servant and specific
details about violence are not listed. Another case notes "wronging" a servant, but
is not tallied in the totals here. In one case, the charge was dropped after the servant had died. *Records of the Colony of New Plymouth*, 1:140, 3:63–4, 82, 151, 160.

17 Three of the cases in Essex had uncertain outcomes. *Province and Court Records
of Maine*, vol. 1–3; and Robert B. Morris, *Government and Labor in Early America*
(1946; repr., Boston: Northeastern University Press, 1981), 473.

18 In six cases the court suggested servants return or buy their way out. In one case
the parents of the child used arbitration and decided against further pursuit of
their case. *Records of New Amsterdam*, vol. 2–6; *Minutes of the Court of Fort Orange and Beverwyck*, trans. and ed. A.J.F. Van Laer, vol. 1–2 (Albany, NY: University of the State of New York, 1923); Adriana E. van Zwieten, "Preparing Children
for Adulthood in New Netherland," in *Children Bound to Labor: The Pauper
Apprentice System In Early America, ed.* Ruth Wallis Herndon and John E. Murray
(Ithaca, NY: Cornell University Press, 2009), 95, 98–100; and Adin, "'I shall beat
you,'" 93–4.

19 Ten guilders was worth approximately one pound. The cases from New Am-
sterdam include two adults. *Minutes of the Court of Fort Orange and Beverwyck*,
2:17, 28, 33; *Records of the Colony of New Plymouth*, 3:51; Towner, *A Good Master
Well Served*, 168–9; *Records of New Amsterdam*, 2:247, 3:93–4, 5:11, 332, 345. In
Plymouth, the one fine was for four shillings. The Plymouth Colony Archive
Project gives an overview of practices. See Jason Jordan, "Domestic Violence in
Plymouth Colony," The Plymouth Colony Archive Project (1998), www.histarch.
illinois.edu.

20 *Records of the Colony of New Plymouth*, 1:141–2, 3:64, 3:83, 88. For a discussion of
this practice, see Jordan, "Domestic Violence in Plymouth Colony."

21 *The Colonial Laws of New York*, 1:26; *The Charter and the Acts and Laws of His
Majesties Colony of Rhode-Island and Providence-Plantations in America* (Providence, RI: Sidney S. Rider and Burnett Rider, 1895), 4; *The Colonial Laws of Massachusetts: Reprinted from the Edition of 1672*, 27; *Laws of New Hampshire*, 2:266;
and *Province and Court Records of Maine*, 1:313 and 2:28.

22 *Province and Court Records of Maine*, 2:84, 86; *The Colonial Laws of New York*,
1:356; and *Laws of New Hampshire*, 2:139.

23 *Records of the Colony of New Plymouth*, 3:51.

24 Evidence that JPs occasionally practiced this behavior in fornication and bastardy
suits exists. See Ryan, *Regulating Passion*, 46–7, 57.

25 *King v. Mary Adams*, August 1731, Record Book, Suffolk General Sessions, Judicial
Archives, MA; *Province and Court Records of Maine*, 2:246, 416; and Morris,
Government and Labor in Early America, 417–25, 439–42.

26 Testimony of Thomas Aboot, October 1652, in *Court of Assistants*, 3:31.

27 *Records of the Colony of New Plymouth*, 3:71–3, 82, 143.

28 "Philadelphia," *Boston Gazette*, February 26, 1751; and *Samuel Magoo v. Thomas Hall*, May 1731, Minutes, NYGS, NYMA.

29 The efforts of the Crocket family are illustrative of how active parents were in ensuring their children's development. See *Province and Court Records of Maine*, 5:183–7.

30 Franklin also noted he "had already made my self a little obnoxious, to the governing Party" and may have feared their reaction to his complaints. Franklin, *The Autobiography of Benjamin Franklin*, 44.

31 It is important to note that Dutch law had previously denoted twenty-five or the date of marriage (whichever came first) as the age of adulthood, but the ideas and laws regarding young adults also occurred in English New York. Holly Brewer, "Age of Reason?" 303–27; Brewer, *By Birth or Consent*, 150–287; Fred Anderson, *A People's Army: Massachusetts Soldiers and Society in the Seven Years War* (Chapel Hill: University of North Carolina Press, 1984), 33–4; and Gillian Brown, *The Consent of the Governed: The Lockean Legacy in Early American Culture* (Cambridge, MA: Harvard University Press, 2000), chap. 1 and 2.

32 Minutes, 1731–70, NYGS, NYMA; and Morris, *Government and Labor in Early America*, 478.

33 In one case, the court fined a master for maiming his black servant, which is discussed in more detail in chapter 3. The court required servants to return to their masters in the other cases. Record Book, Suffolk General Sessions, 1702–38, Judicial Archives, MA; and Morris, *Government and Labor in Early America*, 474–5.

34 *Province and Court Records of Maine*, 5:134.

35 *King v. Rice and Dorothy Williams*, August 1756, Minutes, NYGS, NYMA.

36 *King v. Benjamin Lawrence*, August 1751, Record book, Worcester General Sessions, Judicial Archives, MA; *Acts and Resolves*, 4:179.

37 John Locke, *Some Thoughts Concerning Education*, 13th ed. (London: s.n., 1769), 48; Daniella Gobetti, *Public and Private: Individuals, Households, and Body Politic in Locke and Hutcheson* (New York: Routledge, 1992), 82–91; Jacqueline S. Reiner, *From Virtue to Character: American Childhood, 1775–1850* (New York: Twayne Publishers, 1996), chap. 1; and Jay Fliegelman, *Prodigals and Pilgrims: The American Revolution against Patriarchal Authority, 1750–1800* (New York: Cambridge University Press, 1982), chap. 1 and 2.

38 Barnard's tract was sold in New York as well as Massachusetts. John Barnard, *Present for an Apprentice: Or, a sure guide to gain both esteem and estate with rules for his conduct to his master, and in the world* (Boston: Rogers and Fowle, 1747), 65–8. For an advertisement of this tract in New York, see *New York Gazette*, July 30, 1750.

39 Barnard, *Present for an Apprentice*, 9. Massachusetts often produced sermons for young men in addition to advice literature. For examples of advice literature, see Increase Mather, *Solemn advice to young men, not to walk in the wayes of their heart, and in the sight of their eyes; but to remember the day of Judgement* (Bos-

ton: Samuel Phillips, 1695); "Mr. Zenger," *New-York Weekly Journal*, July 8, 1734; Thomas Gouge, *A young-man's guide, through the wilderness of the world, to the heavenly Canaan* (Boston: J. Draper, 1742); and Jacob Green, *A small help, offered to heads of families: for instructing children and servants* (New York: Printed by H. Gaine, 1771).

40 Brewer, *By Birth or Consent*, 150–80.

41 On views about enduring pain, see Elaine Forman Crane, "'I Have Suffer'd Much Today': The Defining Force of Pain in Early America," in *Through a Glass Darkly: Reflections on Personal Identity in Early America*, ed. Ronald Hoffman, Mechal Sobel, and Fredricka J. Teute (Chapel Hill: University Of North Carolina Press, 1997), 380–92.

42 Wadsworth, *The Well-Ordered Family*, 120; and Josiah Quinby, *A short history of a long journey, it being some account of the life of Josiah Quinby, until he came to enter into the 48th year of his age, with remarks and reflections on his own past actions* (New York: Printed by John Peter Zenger, 1740), 52-53.

43 Elizabeth Ashbridge, "Some Account of the Fore Part of the Life of Elizabeth Ashbridge," in *Journeys in New Worlds. Early American Women's Narratives*, ed. William L. Andrews, Sargent Bush Jr., Annette Kolodny, Amy Schrager Lang, and Daniel B. Shea (Madison, WI: University of Wisconsin Press, 1990), 152-153.

44 See for example, Cornelia Hughes Dayton, "Taking the Trade: Abortion and Gender Relations in an Eighteenth Century New England Village," *WMQ* 48 (January 1991): 19–49; Benjamin B. Roberts, *Sex and Drugs before the Rock 'n' Roll: Youth Culture and Masculinity during Holland's Golden Age* (Amsterdam, NL: Amsterdam University Press, 2012); Illana Krausman Ben-Amos, *Adolescence and Youth in Early Modern England* (New Haven: Yale University Press, 1994), chap. 7; and Benjamin Roberts and Leendert Groenendijk, "'Wearing out a pair of fool's shoes': Sexual Advice for Youth in Holland's Golden Age," *Journal of the History of Sexuality* 13 (April 2004): 139–56.

45 *New York Gazette*, June 13, 1757.

46 *Boston Post Boy*, March 19, 1759.

47 The first English laws in New York defined assaults committed by servants against their masters in a different class from other assaults. In routine assault and battery cases, courts held individuals to a bond promising not to engage in further conflict until the court determined fault, but in cases where servants committed assaults against their masters, servants faced imprisonment until the next sitting of the court. If the court found a servant guilty, he "shall receive what Corporrall punishment the Court shall Adjudge Saving life & Member," though fines, rather than corporal punishment, were customary in assault cases for other individuals. *The Colonial Laws of New York*, 1:15; *The Charter and the Acts and Laws of His Majesties Colony of Rhode-Island and Providence-Plantations in America*, 4. Colonists practiced what they preached, and as early as 1642, Massachusetts reported whipping David Conway for "resisting his master." *Court of Assistants*, 2:127.

48 Roth, *American Homicide*, 58–9.

49 *New York Gazette,* June 27, 1757; *Province and Court Records of Maine,* 2:335 and 3:258; and Towner, *A Good Master Well Served,* 177–81.

50 *Boston Gazette,* March 24, 1760.

51 Towner, *A Good Master Well Served,* 172n71.

52 *Manchester v. Hicks,* February 1733; Susanna Manchester Petition, April 1733; and William Hicks, Summons, May 1733, Record Book, Bristol General Sessions, Judicial Archives, MA.

53 *Records of the Colony of New Plymouth,* 3:180. For examples of Hunt's role in the court, see *Records of the Colony of New Plymouth,* 3:222 and 4:13, 21, 23.

54 Margaret Ellen Newell, *Brethren By Nature: New England Indians, Colonists, and the Origins of American Slavery* (Ithaca, NY: Cornell University Press, 2015).

55 Jean O'Brien, *Dispossession by Degrees: Indian Land and Identity in Natick, Massachusetts, 1650–1790* (New York: Cambridge University Press, 1997), 131–8; and Leon Miles, "The Red Man Dispossessed: Williams Family and Alienation of Indian Land in Stockbridge, Massachusetts, 1736–1818," in *New England Encounters: Indians & Euroamericans, ca. 1600–1850,* ed. Alden T. Vaughan (Boston: Northeastern University Press, 1999), 276–358.

56 *Acts and Resolves,* 2:104 and 362–5; Gideon Hawley, Mashpee, to Rev. Dr. Thacher, January 1, 1794, Gideon Hawley Letters, folder 8, Special Collections, Massachusetts Historical Society.

57 For Massachusetts's laws, see *Acts and Resolves,* 2:363–4. On Indian servitude, see David Silverman, "The Impact of Indentured Servitude on the Society and Culture of Southern New England Indians, 1680–1810," *NEQ* 74 (December 2001): 622–66; and O'Brien, *Dispossession by Degrees,* 131–8. In New York, several importers of Indian and African slaves from wars in the Carolinas asked for permission to be allowed not to pay duties on their slaves. See *Laws of Colonial New York,* 1:874–5. On the problem of enumerating Indians (as servants and otherwise) after 1700, see Donna Keith Baron, J. Edward Hood, and Holly V. Izard, "They Were Here All Along: The Native American Presence in Lower-Central New England in the Eighteenth and Nineteenth Centuries," *WMQ* 53 (July 1996): 562–6.

58 No robust literature exists on the experiences of New York Indians as servants or slaves, and scholars have generally conceded that the power of the Five Nations likely prevented the indenturing and enslavement of Indians in northern New York. See Allan Gallay, "Indian Slavery in Historical Context," in *Indian Slavery in Colonial America,* ed. Allan Gallay (Lincoln, NB: University of Nebraska Press, 2009), 27.

59 In an extreme case, in March 1684/5, the court found Thomas Wappatucke, an Indian, guilty of burglary and sold him "for a ppetuall servant." Whites quickly bought Wappatucke's land after he was "sold out of the country." *Records of the Colony of New Plymouth,* 6:31, 153, 160.

60 *A Report of the Record Commissioners of the City of Boston, Containing the Boston Records from 1700–1728* (Boston: Rockwell and Churchill, 1883), 173–4; Ruth Wallis Herndon and John E. Murray, "'A proper and instructive education': Raising

Children in Pauper Apprenticeship," in Herndon and Murray, ed., *Children Bound to Labor*, 3–17.

61 *New York Mercury*, June 19, 1758. The abuse of African American slaves is explored in later chapters. For an example of an African American servant noted as wearing an iron collar, see *Boston Post Boy*, October 6, 1761; and Newell, *Brethren by Nature*, 82–3. Michael V. Kennedy argues that abuse of servants increased after the 1750s when the number of servants declined and marks this time as one where collars, branding, and whipping scars were noted on white servants. See Kennedy, "The Consequences of Cruelty: The Escalation of Servant and Slave Abuse, 1750–1780," in *Essays in Economic and Business History* 22 (2004): 127–41. For a white servant who wore a collar, see Robert H. Bremer, ed., *Children and Youth in America: A Documentary History*, vol. 1 (Cambridge, MA: Harvard University Press, 1970), 308.

62 Petition of Grace Pearson, September 1731, Record Book, Suffolk General Sessions, Judicial Archives, MA.

63 Forty-three servants made complaints between 1740 and 1770. Minutes, NYGS, 1740–1770, NYMA.

64 Record Book, Suffolk General Sessions, 1762–33, Judicial Archives, MA. An additional two cases of cruelty exist during this period, but the cases did not arrive in court as petitions seeking redress for cruelty but rather as criminal complaints.

65 Herndon and Murray, "'A proper and instructive education,'" 14–15.

66 Sharon Block, *Rape & Sexual Power in Early America* (Chapel Hill: University of North Carolina Press, 2006), 63–74, 96–101; Michael I. Fickes, "'They Could Not Endure That Yoke': The Captivity of Pequot Women and Children after the War of 1637," *New England Quarterly* (hereafter *NEQ*) 73 (March 2000): 67–70; Laura Gowing, *Common Bodies: Women, Touch, and Power in Seventeenth-Century England* (New Haven: Yale University Press, 2003), 53–64, 90–3; and Ryan, *Regulating Passion*, 43, 78–9, 166–7. John Pagan reveals the limited options open to servant women in coercive or voluntary sexual relations in *Anne Orthwood's Bastard: Sex and Law in Early Virginia* (New York: Oxford University Press, 2003).

67 *New-York Weekly Journal*, January 28, 1733.

68 Towner, *A Good Master Well Served*, 55; *Acts and Resolves*, 2:182–3, 1067; and 3:30; *The Colonial Laws of New York*, 1:26, 132; Herndon and Murray, "'A proper and instructive education,'" 7, 14–5, 41–2. Because towns and counties usually handled the poor, counties passed New York's poor laws, and they shared the attributes of Massachusetts' laws in allowing for the binding out of children. For an overview, see John Cummings, *Poor-Laws of Massachusetts and New York* (New York: Macmillan and Company, 1895), 75–82.

69 The difficulties in establishing the number of servants for each colony is limited by record-keeping from the seventeenth and eighteenth centuries. It's estimated 79 percent of immigrants headed toward Chesapeake colonies by the 1760s. The following scholars provide valuable estimates: Kenneth Morgan, *Slavery and Servitude in Colonial North America* (New York: New York University Press, 2000), 44–5; Lawrence William Towner, "'A Good Master Well Served': A Social History

of Servitude in Massachusetts, 1620–1750" (Ph.D. diss., Northwestern University, 1955), 62–70; Edgar J. McManus, *A History of Negro Slavery in New York* (Syracuse, NY: Syracuse University Press, 1966), 41–3, 42n5; David W. Galenson, *White Servitude in Colonial America: An Economic Analysis* (Cambridge, UK: Cambridge University Press, 1981), 86, 222–7; Abbot Emerson Smith, *Colonists in Bondage: White Servitude and Convict Labor in America, 1607–1776* (Chapel Hill: University of North Carolina Press, 1947, repr. 1965), 308–315; and Morris, *Government and Labor in Early America*, 347–8. On policies and experiences see, John Wareing, *Indentured Migration and the Servant Trade from London to America, 1618–1718* (Oxford: Oxford University Press, 2017), chap. 3, 4 and 7.

70 *The Countryman's lamentation, on the neglect of a proper education of children, with an address to the inhabitants of New-Jersey* (Philadelphia: Printed by William Dunlap, 1762), 46.

CHAPTER 2: WHITE WIVES

1 Suffolk Files, Judicial Archives, MA, #1148, 57–67; and Lauren J. Cook, "Katherine Nanny, alias Naylor: A Life in Puritan Boston," *Historical Archeology* 32 (March 1998): 15–19.

2 Historians of early North America have overlooked the "assertive" actions of women defending themselves in uses of bonds. Hurl-Eamon uses the word "assertive" to describe wives' use of bonds in her study of assault in London in *Gender and Petty Violence*, 5; see also Laura F. Edwards, "Law, Domestic Violence, and the Limits of Patriarchal Authority in the Antebellum South," *Journal of Southern History* 65 (November 1999): 750–9.

3 Suffolk Files, Judicial Archives, MA, #1148, 57–67; *Court of Assistants*, 1:32; and Cook, "Katherine Nanny, alias Naylor."

4 The early seventeenth century was important in the first transition to a societal understanding that wife abuse was legally and morally wrong, yet widespread community standards against spousal assault never truly developed. Historians agree that the steps that the courts took were neither radical nor ameliorative for the women suffering abuse. See Dayton, *Women Before the Bar*, 136–8; Lyle Koehler, *A Search for Power: The "Weaker Sex" in Seventeenth Century New England* (Urbana: University of Illinois Press, 1980), 137–142; and Pleck, *Domestic Tyranny*, 3, 6, 17–33.

5 *Records of the Colony of New Plymouth*, 5:61.

6 For wife murder, see *Court of Assistants*, 1:295–6 and 303–4; and Cotton Mather, *A Sermon Preached at Boston, December 29, 1689. In the Hearing, and at the Request of One Hugh Stone, a Miserable Man* (Boston: Samuel Green, 1690), 58.

7 T.E., *The Law's Resolutions of Women's Rights; Or, the Law's Provision for Women* (1638; repr. Clark, New Jersey: The Law Book Exchange, 2005), 128; *Baron and Feme: A Treatise of the Common Law Concerning Husbands and Wives* (London: Printed by Eliz. Nutt and Ro. Colling, for John Walthoe, 1719), 9; and *The Laws Respecting Women, As they regard their natural rights, or their connections and*

conduct; in which their interests and duties as daughters, wards, heiresses, spin-sters, sisters, wives, widows, mothers, legatees, executrixes, &c., are mentioned and enumerated: also, the obligations of parent and child, and the condition of minors (London: Printed for J. Johnson, 1777), 54.

8 Hurl-Eamon, *Gender and Petty Violence*, 49–61; Margaret Hunt, "Wife Beating, Domesticity and Women's Independence in Eighteenth-Century London," *Gender and History* 4 (March 1992): 10–33; Elizabeth A. Foyster, "Male Honour, Social Control and Wife Beating in Late Stuart England," *Transactions of the Royal Historical Society*, 6th ser. 6 (1996): 215–24; and Susan Dwyer Amussen, "'Being Stirred to Much Unquietness': Violence and Domestic Violence in Early Modern England," *Journal of Women's History* 6 (Summer 1994): 70–89.

9 Grotius, *The Jurisprudence of Holland*, 1:29; Martin Dinges, "The Uses of Justice as a Form of Social Control in Early Modern Europe," in *Social Control in Europe, 1500–1800*, ed. Herman Roodenburg and Pieter Spierenburg (Columbus: Ohio State University Press, 2004), 1:161–4; Manon van der Heijden, "Women as Victims of Sexual and Domestic Violence in Seventeenth-Century Holland: Criminal Cases of Rape, Incest, and Maltreatment in Rotterdam and Delft," *Journal of Social History* 33 (Spring 2000): 633–5; and Manon van der Heijden, "Women, Violence and Urban Justice in Holland, c. 1600–1838," *Crime, History & Societies* 17 (2013): 71–82.

10 Amanda C. Pipkin, *Rape in the Dutch Republic, 1609–1725: Formulating Dutch Identity* (Netherlands: Brill, 2013), 9–10. Gisbertus Voetius and Jean Taffin similarly rejected wife abuse.

11 *The Colonial Laws of Massachusetts, reprinted from the edition of 1660, with the supplements to 1672: containing also, The Body of Liberties of 1641* (Boston: Rockwell and Churchill, 1889), 51, 171. Plymouth passed a similar law in 1672. *The General Laws and Liberties of the Massachusetts Colony: Revised & Reprinted* (Cambridge, MA: Samuel Green, 1672), 101; Pleck, *Domestic Tyranny*, 21–2, 26–7; and Dayton, *Women Before the Bar*, 136–8.

12 *Court of Assistants*, 2:74, 93; and *Records and Files of the Quarterly Courts of Essex County, Massachusetts*, 1:49, 57–8.

13 *Records and Files of the Quarterly Courts of Essex County*, 2:122.

14 Ann Marie Plane, *Colonial Intimacies: Indian Marriage in Early New England* (Ithaca: Cornell University Press, 2000); Trevor Burnard, "'Theater of Terror': Domestic Violence in Thomas Thislewood's Jamaica, 1750–1786," in Daniels and Kennedy, ed., *Over the Threshold*, 246–7.

15 Pleck, *Domestic Tyranny*, 17–87.

16 Wadsworth, *The Well-Ordered Family*, 25; and William Seckler, *A Wedding Ring Fit for the Finger: or, the Salve of Divinity on the Sore of Humanity* (Edinburgh: Printed and sold by James Watson, 1715), 15.

17 *Records and Files of the Quarterly Courts of Essex County*, vol. 1–8; and Ann M. Little, "'Shee Would Bump His Mouldy Britch': Authority, Masculinity, and the Harried Husbands of New Haven Colony, 1638–1670," in Bellsiles, ed., *Lethal Imagination*, 46–50.

18 For overviews of Dutch Law in the colonies, see Deborah A. Rosen's "Women and Property Across Colonial America: A Comparison of Legal Systems in New Mexico and New York," *WMQ* 60 (April 2003): 355–81; and Kim Todt, "'Women Are as Knowing Therein as the Men': Dutch Women in Early America," in *Women in Early America*, ed. Thomas A. Foster (New York: New York University Press, 2015), 50–3.

19 Van der Heijden, "Women, Violence and Urban Justice in Holland," 71–82.

20 *Minutes of the Court of Fort Orange and Beverwyck*, 1:248.

21 On women in New Netherland's use of courts for economic and familial matters, see Michael E. Gherke, "Dutch Women in New Netherland and New York in the Seventeenth Century" (Ph.D. diss., West Virginia University, 2001); Todt, "'Women Are as Knowing Therein as the Men'," 43–65; and Kim Todt and Martha Dickinson Shattuck, "Capable Entrepreneurs: The Women Merchants and Traders of New Netherland," in *Women in Port: Gendering Communities, Economies, and Social Networks in Atlantic Port Cities, 1500–1800*, ed. Douglas Catterall and Jodi Campbell (Leiden: Brill, 2012), 183–214.

22 *Records of New Amsterdam*, 5:206, 263–5, 271–2, 275–6, 282.

23 I borrow the term "settled" from Eben Mogan, "Settling the Law" (Ph.D. diss., Yale University, 1993).

24 *Records of New Amsterdam*, 6:62, 65, 77, 193, 340; and 7:27; Goodfriend, *Before the Melting Pot*; and Gherke, "Dutch Women in New Netherland and New York in the Seventeenth Century," 24–63.

25 For example, see Abby Chandler, *Law and Sexual Misconduct in New England, 1650–1750* (New York: Routledge, 2015); Hughes Dayton, *Women before the Bar*, 173–207; Ryan, *Regulating Passion*, chap. 1 and 2; Roger Thompson, *Sex in Middlesex: Popular Mores in a Massachusetts County, 1649–1699* (Boston: University of Massachusetts Press, 1986), 19–33.

26 Richard J. Ross, "Puritan Godly Discipline in Comparative Perspective: Legal Pluralism and the Sources of 'Intensity'," *The American Historical Review* 113 (October 2008): 975–1002; and Terri L. Snyder, *Brabbling Women: Disorderly Speech and the Law in Early Virginia* (Ithaca: Cornell University Press, 2003).

27 *Court of Assistants*, 2:74, 93.

28 In Essex County, the court fined a man for being drunk but only held him to bonds "for abusing his wife." It's probable that more cases than these exist and the cases were not entered into official record books, as JPs may have talked with husbands who abused their wives in the first instances. *Province and Court Records of Maine*, 1:264–265, 288, and 300; and *Records and Files of the Quarterly Courts of Essex County*, 4:441. New Netherland courts did not leave records of women seeking them out for safety.

29 Historians of New England and England point out that the courts did not enforce the laws regarding abuse "aggressively or enthusiastically," with most JPs in England and the colonies allowing for moderate correction through the 1700s. See Koehler, *A Search for Power*, 137–142; Pleck, *Domestic Tyranny*, 21–2, 26–7; Margaret Hunt, "Wife Beating, Domesticity and Women's Independence in Eighteenth-

Century London," 10–33; Foyster, "Male Honour, Social Control and Wife Beating in Late Stuart England," 215–24; and Amussen, "'Being Stirred to Much Unquietness,'" 70–89.

30 *Records of the Colony of New Plymouth*, 2:73; and *Province and Court Records of Maine*, 4:247–8.

31 *Records of the Colony of New Plymouth*, 4:103–4.

32 *Records of New Amsterdam*, 4:34.

33 *Records and Files of the Quarterly Courts of Essex County*, 8:272–4.

34 It is estimated that cases in which women abused husbands represent a quarter to a third of all spousal abuse cases. See C. Dallett Hemphill, "Women in Court: Sex-Role Differentiation in Salem, Massachusetts, 1636–1683," *WMQ* 39 (January 1982): 170–1 and 173. See cases of Jane Hallowey and Sarah Morgan for additional penalties on women. Courts sentenced Sarah Morgan to stand in the stocks with a gag in her mouth for a half hour and pay fifty shillings for striking her husband. Morgan would have borne the brunt of community derision and abuse as individuals tossed items at her during her punishment. *Records of the Colony of New Plymouth*, 3:75, 5:31–2, 41, and *Province and Court Records of Maine*, 2:224.

35 *Records of the Colony of New Plymouth*, 3:75.

36 *Records and Files of the Quarterly Courts of Essex County*, 1:136 and 5:363.

37 Snyder, *Brabbling Women*.

38 *Records and Files of the Quarterly Courts of Essex County*, 1:136, 5:363, 8:273.

39 Grotius, *The Jurisprudence of Holland*, 1:29.

40 Gherke, "Marital Litigations," 187–205; and Gherke, "Dutch Women in New Netherland and New York in the Seventeenth Century," 109. For the cruelty cases, see *Records of New Amsterdam*, 3:73, 6:65, 309.

41 George Elliott Howard, *A History of Matrimonial Institutions: Chiefly in England and the United States* (1904 repr. Littleton: F.B. Rothman, 1994), 2:330–41, 349–51.

42 Dayton, *Women Before the Bar*, 112–5, 112n15, appendix 1, 329–33.

43 *Records of New Amsterdam*, 6:65, 77, 193, 340, and 7:27. In 1665, when John Williams appeared in court on charges of verbally and physically assaulting his wife, the court ordered the couple to be peaceful to each other. When he abused Elizabeth Williams again, the court decided that the couple should separate and created a plan in which Elizabeth was maintained by John. See *Records of the Colony of New Plymouth*, 4:92, 121.

44 Ruth Bloch asserts that JPs' issuing of bonds of peace shows that in the eighteenth century, the "dominant trajectory of legal opinion ran against the right of husbands to punish their wives by beating them." Ruth H. Bloch, "The American Revolution, Wife Beating, and the Emergent Right to Privacy," *Early American Studies* 5 (Fall 2007): 231. Although suing for the peace was an important mechanism for ensuring women's safety, fully prosecuting routine wife abuse cases (not of a life-threatening nature) would have been a clearer assertion of JPs' and the community's perception that wife abuse was commensurate with abuse of other adult citizens.

45 Michael Warner, *Letters of the Republic: Publication and the Public Sphere in Eighteenth-Century America* (Cambridge, MA: Harvard University Press, 1992).

46 Roth, *American Homicide*, 108–9; and Randolf Roth, "American Homicide Supplemental Volume: Gender and Homicide," Historical Violence Database of the Criminal Justice Research Center at The Ohio State University (2009), https://cjrc.osu.edu.

47 *King v. Roger Thompson*, September 1741, Record Book, Supreme Court of Judicature, Judicial Archives, MA. The punishment meted out to Thompson was common in Massachusetts for persons guilty of crimes such as adultery and attempted rape. The punishment simulated a hanging with the guilty party tied to the gallows while onlookers pelted and shamed him.

48 The eighteenth-century cases were similar in that both the husbands were accused of poisoning their wives, a crime requiring forethought, but the poison proved difficult to tie to the spouses. In an additional spousal murder case from the eighteenth century, a wife allegedly murdered her husband with poison and she was acquitted as well. In these cases, the poison was mixed with water, eggs, wine, or brandy, making the poison difficult to distinguish and connect to the accused. *King v. Adam McNeal*, February 1762; *King v. Levi Whitney*, November 1779; *King v. Priscilla Woodworth*, April 1782, Record Book, Superior Court of Judicature, Judicial Archives, MA.

49 *A Century of Population Growth from the first Census of the United States to the Twelfth* (Washington, DC: Government Printing Office, 1909), 9–10. Although New York's population was smaller than Massachusetts's in 1760, the colony grew at a faster rate.

50 *King v. John Courses and Peter*, April 30, 1744, Record Book, Suffolk General Sessions; *King v. Ebenezer Proctor*, December 9, 1760, Record Book, Middlesex General Sessions; Record Books, Plymouth and Worcester General Sessions, 1740–63, Judicial Archives, MA.

51 Dayton, *Women Before the Bar*, 136–7; and Cornelia Hughes Dayton, "Women before the Bar: Gender, Law, and Society in Connecticut, 1710–1790" (Ph.D. diss., Princeton University, 1986), 298–9. In England, scholars suggest that that JPs in rural regions likely negotiated and spoke with violent husbands rather than going through the formal process of swearing them to keep the peace. Lack of documentation, however, means records cannot bear this out. Hurl-Eamon also suggests that the higher number of cases in London, as compared with more rural contexts, stems from the fact that women in urban areas were freer from gendered expectations, and the anonymity of the city provided women with a cover for their action. See Hurl-Eamon, *Gender and Petty Violence*, 7–8.

52 For examples of fees issued, see Susannah Piper, petition, September 1754, and Nathaniel Piper, January 1755, Record Book, Middlesex General Sessions, MA; and Jopthah Smith, August 1732, Record Book, New York General Sessions, NYMA.

53 Frederick William, February 1739/40 and May 1740, Record Book, New York General Sessions, NYMA.

54 Jopthah Smith, August 1732, Record Book, New York General Sessions, NYMA. For an example of another case that failed to be pushed forward, see Bethiah Hasten, petition, December 1753 and March 1754, Record Book, Middlesex General Sessions, Judicial Archives, MA.

55 Cott, "Divorce and the Changing Status of Women in Eighteenth-Century Massachusetts," 603, 608–9, esp. 609n69. Cott notes that one woman petitioned for divorce twice, and thus the number of suits is not equal to the number of women suing.

56 Elizabeth Sydenham quoted in Evelyn Sidman Wachter, *Sidman-Sidnam Families of Upstate New York* (Baltimore: Gateway Press, 1981), 54, 253–7. Petitions of Elizabeth Sydenham, in *Calendar of Historical Manuscripts in the Office of the Secretary of State, Albany, N.Y.*, ed. E.B. O'Callaghan (Albany, NY: Weed, Parsons, and Company, 1866) 2:372 and 426.

57 *King v. John Courset and Peter*, April 1744, Record Book, Suffolk General Sessions, Judicial Archives, MA.

58 "The Continuation of our Number 353," *New-York Weekly Journal*, September 22, 1740.

59 Scholars show that some individuals even felt increased pressure and anxiety that their romantic and sexual choices be fulfilling. Thomas A. Foster, *Sex and the Eighteenth-Century Man: Massachusetts and the History of Sexuality in America* (Boston: Beacon Press, 2006), 5–22; Clare A. Lyons, *Sex among the Rabble: An Intimate History of Gender and Power in the Age of Revolution, Philadelphia, 1730–1830* (Charlotte: University of North Carolina Press, 2006), 37–43, 287–8; Ryan, *Regulating Passion*, chap.1; and Lisa Wilson, *Ye Heart of a Man: The Domestic Life of Men in Colonial New England* (New Haven: Yale University Press, 1999), chap. 2.

60 A Friend to Both Sexes, "Messrs. Fowle & Thomas," *Massachusetts Spy*, October 6–9, 1770; and "The Ill-Judged Union: Or, the History of Harpagon and Essilia," *Boston Post Boy*, January 18, 1762. In these pieces the authors debate when a couple should begin courting given the level of affection involved. Both suggest a high level of emotional attachment prior to courting.

61 "The Continuation of our Number 353," *New-York Weekly Journal*, September 22, 1740; and "Mr. Zenger," *New-York Weekly Journal*, July 27, 1741.

62 "Philadelphia, April 17," *New-York Weekly Journal*, May 5, 1735.

63 E.P. Thompson, *The Making of the English Working Class* (New York: Vintage, 1961); E.P. Thompson, *Customs in Common: Studies in Traditional Popular Culture* (New York: Free Press, 1993), chap. 5; Paul A. Gilje, *Rioting in America* (Bloomington, IN: Indiana University Press, 1996), chap. 1; Steven J. Steward, "Skimmington in the Middle and New England Colonies," in *Riot and Revelry in Early America*, ed. William Penack, Matthew Dennis, and Simon P. Newman (University Park: The Pennsylvania State University Press, 2002), 41–86; and Brendan McConville, "Reflections on an Ancient New Custom in Eighteenth-Century Jersey," in *Riot and Revelry*, 87–106.

64 *Boston Evening Post*, July 30, 1764.

65 Certificate of Caleb Hazzne et al., 1759, in John Tabor Kempe Papers, Court Case Records, Special Collections, New York Historical Society (hereafter NYHS), box 11, folder 7.

66 Linda Briggs Breimer, *Women and Property in Colonial New York: The Transition from Dutch to English Law, 1643–1727* (Ann Arbor, MI: University of Michigan Press, 1983); David E. Narrett, "Dutch Customs of Inheritance, Women and the Law in Colonial New York City," in *Authority and Resistance in Early New York*, ed. William Penack and Conrad Edick Wright (New York: New York Historical Society, 1988), 27–45.

67 In contrast with her husband, Mrs. Dyer was admired for "remarkable Piety." "New Haven, April 28," *New York Gazette*, May 7, 1759.

68 Suffolk Files, Judicial Archives, MA, #1148, 57–67; *Court of Assistants*, 1:32; and Cook, "Katherine Nanny, alias Naylor," 15–19.

69 Ryan, *Regulating Passion*, 38–57.

CHAPTER 3: SLAVES

1 Abner Cheney Goddell, Jr., *The Trial and Execution for Petit Treason of Mark and Phillis, slaves of Capt. John Codman* (Cambridge, MA: John Wilson and Son, 1883), 4, 9, 17. Jared Ross Hardesty further explores the violence within the household, including a possibly coercive sexual relationship between Codman and Phillis, in *Unfreedom*, 68–9.

2 Ira Berlin, *Many Thousands Gone: The First Two Centuries of Slavery in North America* (Cambridge, MA: Belknap Press of Harvard University Press, 1998), 369, tables 1 and 3; Graham Russell Gao Hodges, "Liberty and Constraint: The Limits of Revolution," in *Slavery in New York*, ed. Ira Berlin and Leslie M. Harris (New York: New Press, 2005), 114; and Shane White, *Somewhat More Independent: The End of Slavery in New York City, 1770–1810* (Athens, GA: The University of Georgia Press, 1991), 4. More recent historians estimate the number of slaves in Boston to total near 10 to 15 percent of the population. See Hardesty, *Unfreedom*, 5.

3 Hodges, *Root & Branch*, 107–15, 200–8; Melish, *Disowning Slavery*, 15–24; Shane White, *Somewhat More Independent*, 10–23; Gary B. Nash and Jean R. Soderlund, *Freedom by Degrees: Emancipation in Pennsylvania and Its Aftermath* (New York: Oxford University Press, 1991), 14–40; Hardesty, *Unfreedom*, 103–121; and Jeroen Dewulf, "Emulating a Portuguese Model: The Slave Policy of the West India Company and the Dutch Reformed Church in Dutch Brazil (1630–1654) and New Netherland (1614–1664) in Comparative Perspective," *Journal of Early American History* 4 (2014): 3–36.

4 Roth states slave murder "simply stopped" after 1720 in New England, but other cases occurred and some were likely overlooked by governments (see notes 9 and 12). Roth's findings that slave murder declined throughout British North America by the mid-eighteenth century is more accurate for New England than New York. Roth, *American Homicide*, 94–8. Scholars of slavery in the South show domestic labor was not free from cruelty. See, for example, Deborah Gray White, *Ar'nt I a*

Woman? Female Slaves in the Plantation South (New York: Norton, 1985); Fuentes, *Dispossessed Lives*, 8–9, 111–16; and Eugene Genovese, *Roll, Jordan, Roll: The World the Slaves Made* (New York: Pantheon, 1974).

5 Record keeping for legal dependents in early America is not accurate. According to Randolf Roth, whites killed eighteen of the twenty-one African Americans who died before 1775, but not all of these cases involved masters. (Roth, *American Homicide*, 517n83.) Courts drew up indictments against the following individuals for murdering their slaves: Gysbert Opdyck of New Netherland in 1639; James Smith and Thomas Keyser in Massachusetts Bay in 1645; Unknown man in Court of Admiralty in 1733; Charles Dickinson of Rhode Island in 1733; William Bullock of Pennsylvania in 1750; Nathaniel Cane in the province of Maine in 1695; Samuel Smith of Massachusetts in 1719; and William Petit of New York in 1733. Reports of suspicious slave murders by masters occurred in New York (1720s and 1735) by an unknown man and Gilbert Livingston; by Nicholas Lechmere and Nicholas Chatfield in Connecticut (1711 and 1751); and by an unknown man in Roxbury, Massachusetts (London, 1741). One case against a shipmate for murdering a slave is included in these numbers because crews had direct power over the slaves in their care. See notes 9–12 for further reference to these cases.

6 The extent to which slaves had agency to resist slavery is an oft-studied subject, and the particular context of slave regimes was important to African Americans' ability to find ways to resist. Recent historiographical trends urge differentiating between resistance meant to undermine slavery and acts of survival. Much leeway was given to slave masters to "discipline" slaves, including even murder (as is seen below). For examples of literature on slave resistance and agency, see Vincent Brown, "Social Death and Political Life in the Study of Slavery," *American Historical Review* (December 2009): 1231–49; Randy M. Browne, *Surviving Slavery in the British Caribbean* (Philadelphia: University of Pennsylvania Press, 2017); Trevor G. Burnard, *Mastery, Tyranny, and Desire: Thomas Thistlewood and His Slaves in the Anglo-Jamaican World* (Chapel Hill: University of North Carolina Press, 2004); Fuentes, *Dispossessed Lives*, 8–11, 68–9, 102–3; David Barry Gaspar, "Antigua Slaves and Their Struggle to Survive," in *Seeds of Change: A Quincentennial Commemoration*, ed. Herman J. Viola and Carolyn Margolis (Washington, D.C.: Smithsonian Institution Press, 1991), 130–37; and Walter Johnson, "On Agency," *Journal of Social History* 37 (Autumn 2003): 113–24.

7 Natalie Zemon Davis, "Judges, Masters, Diviners: Slaves' Experience of Criminal Justice in Colonial Suriname," *Law and History Review* 29 (November 2011): 925–84.

8 Dinah Mayo-Bobee, "Servile Discontents: Slavery and Resistance in Colonial New Hampshire, 1645–1785," *Slavery and Abolition* 30 (September 2009): 344–5.

9 The cases noted in endnote 5 were located through archival research in New York and Massachusetts, newspaper searches, and the historical literature on slavery in the North. Other indictments may exist as historians continue to dig

through archives, but it is unlikely the number is much greater. See *American Weekly Mercury*, April 29, 1742; *New York Gazette*, December 17–23, 1733; Edgar J. McManus, *Black Bondage in the North* (Syracuse: Syracuse University Press, 1973), 90–1; Lorenzo Johnston Greene, *The Negro in Colonial New England* (New York: Atheneum, 1969), 232–6; George H. Moore, *Correspondence Concerning Moore's Notes on the History of Slavery in Massachusetts*, 1–3, 7–8; Sweet, *Bodies Politic*, 70; and Arnold J.F. Van Laer, trans., *Council Minutes, 1638–9*, vol. 5 of *New York Historical Manuscripts: Dutch* (Baltimore: Genealogical Publishing Company, Inc., 1974), 4:66.

10 In 1645, Massachusetts Bay investigated two men for kidnapping, murdering, and enslaving men on the coast of Africa, and in 1736, the court of admiralty in Massachusetts, a maritime court, indicted and convicted a man for killing a slave aboard a vessel. These men were slave traders, not necessarily slave masters, but the cases reveal some interest in the welfare of Africans. However, the willingness of the admiralty court, in particular, to indict and find guilty a man for murdering a slave while under his care may have been related to the disjunction between this court and the populace. Instead of using jury trials, it was presided over by the colony's governor. The court granted the man "Reprieve for a Year," which enabled him to petition the king for a pardon from the sentence of death. For records and interpretations, see *New-England Weekly Journal*, October 19, 1736; George H. Moore, *Correspondence Concerning Moore's Notes on the History of Slavery in Massachusetts*, 1–3, 7–8; Richard Saltonsall, "Petition of Robert Saltonsall, 1645," in *Documents Illustrative of the History of the Slave Trade to America*, ed. Elizabeth Donnan, vol. 3 (New York: Octagon Books, 1965), 6–7; John Winthrop, *Winthrop's Journal: History of New England*, vol. 2 (New York: Charles Scribner's Sons, 1908), 252–3; and Wendy Warren, *New England Bound: Slavery and Colonization in Early America* (New York: Liveright, 2016), 36–42.

11 In Pennsylvania, the court decided William Bullock should suffer death; historians presume that Bullock did not receive the death penalty as the jury directed because of judicial traditions that lessened penalties as well as because of a lack of evidence that he was put to death. On penalties for murder in Massachusetts, see Edwin Powers, *Crime and Punishment in Early Massachusetts, 1620–1692: A Documentary History* (Boston: Beacon Press, 1966), 404–8.

12 Peter Kalm, *Travels in North America*, 2nd ed. (London: Printed for T. Lowdnes, 1772), 1:306. McManus believes the case noted here refers to a case of slave murder in addition to Bullock, but no evidence exists regarding it, and the printing of Kalm's volume was only six years after Pennsylvania tried Bullock. McManus, *Black Bondage*, 90.

13 Van Laer, *Council Minutes*, 4:66.

14 *Laws and Ordinances of New Netherland, 1638–1674*, ed. Edmund B. O'Callaghan (Albany, NY: Weed, Parsons and Company, 1868), 12, 33; Christopher Moore, "A

World of Possibilities: Slavery and Freedom in Dutch New Amsterdam," in *Slavery in New York*, 40; Harris, *In the Shadow of Slavery*, 16–19.

15 Susannah Shaw Romney suspects Anthonijsen was a servant, not a slave. *Court Minutes of New Amsterdam*, 3:315; Susannah Shaw Romney, "Intimate Networks and Children's Survival in New Netherland in the Seventeenth Century," *Early American Studies* 7 (Fall 2009): 275–9.

16 *Calendar of Dutch Historical Manuscripts in the Office of the Secretary of State, Albany, New York, 1630–1664*, ed. Edmund B. O'Callaghan (Albany, NY: Weed, Parson and Company, 1865), 2: 258–9; Lysbeth Anthonijsen, quoted in Romney, "Intimate Networks and Children's Survival in New Netherland," 277.

17 New York's slave code claimed it gave servants the right to appeal to authorities about cruelty by their masters, but it's not clear that this actually extended to slaves in practice. *The Colonial Laws of Massachusetts, reprinted from the edition of 1660*, 51–3; *The Colonial Laws of New York*, 1:18, 157–8; and Higginbotham, *In the Matter of Color*, 114–15.

18 The act was revised in 1718 at the instigation of the British, and it included protections against cruelty as well. Where New Hampshire differed from other colonies was in the explicit establishment of the death penalty for willful murder of a slave. Scholars tend to see this law as a protection afforded to slaves, as willful murder was stipulated as illegal. *Laws of New Hampshire*, 2:292; and Greene, *The Negro in Colonial New England*, 233–4. By contrast, in southern colonies, legislation set the penalty for slave murder as a fine. South Carolina stipulated a maximum fine of 200 pounds. *Statutes at Large of South Carolina*, ed. David McCord (Columbia, SC: A.S. Johnston, 1840), 7:397–417.

19 The law was reiterated in 1712. *The Colonial Laws of New York*, 1:520, 762.

20 In 1709, Britain's Board of Trade asked Governor Hunter of New York to pass a law "for the restraining of any inhumane severity . . . towards their Christian servants and their slaves," which included a "provision . . . that the willful killing of Indians and Negros, may be punished with death, and a fit penalty imposed for the maiming of them." *Documents Relative to the Colonial History of the State of New-York: Procured in Holland, England, and France* (Albany, NY: Weed and Parsons, 1853), 5:138.

21 Of the fractures, one female had ten fractures; one male had seventeen, one male had twenty-three; and one female had thirty-two. C. Wilczak, R. Watkins, C.C. Null, and M.L. Blakey, "Skeletal Indicators of Work: Musculoskeletal, Arthritic and Traumatic Effects," in *Skeletal Biology of the New York African Burial Ground*, ed. Michael L. Blakely and Lesley M. Rankin-Hill, part I, vol. 1, of *The New York African Burial Ground: Unearth the African Presence in Colonial New York* (Washington, D.C.: Howard University Press, 2009), 221–3.

22 *New-York Weekly Journal*, January 5, 1735. For another case, see Allegra di Bonaventura, *For Adam's Sake: A Family Saga in Colonial New England* (New York: Liveright, 2014), 127–8.

23 Aida Livingston, quoted in Roberta Singer, "The Livingstons as Slave Owners: The Peculiar Institution of Livingston Manor and Clermont," in *The Livingston Legacy: Three Centuries of American History*, ed. Richard T. Wiles (Annandale-on-Hudson, NY: Bard College, 1987), 83.

24 Cotton Mather, *The Negro Christianized* (Boston: B. Green, 1706), 20; Richard A. Bailey, *Race and Redemption in Puritan New England* (New York: Oxford University Press, 2011).

25 Rev. Henricus Selyns, New Netherland, to the Classis of Amsterdam, June 9, 1664, *Ecclesiastical Records of the State of New York*, ed. Edwin T. Corwin, vol. 1 (Albany, NY: J.B. Lyon, 1901), 248; Harris, *In the Shadow of Slavery*, 17–18; and Christopher Moore, "A World of Possibilities," 45.

26 More often, Christianization was a strategy within the British empire to create a link with the members of the body politic. Moniz, *From Empire to Humanity*, chap. 1; and Christopher Cameron, *To Plead Our Own Cause: African Americans in Massachusetts and the Making of the Antislavery Movement* (Kent, OH: The Kent State University Press, 2014), 8–28.

27 Mather, *The Negro Christianized*, 20. Mather focused on the spiritual growth of his slave Onesimus after he became "useless [and] Froward." When all attempts at reformation failed, Mather freed Onesimus, but only did so when he felt he had run out of options. Cotton Mather, *The Diary of Cotton Mather* (New York: Frederick Ungar Publishing Co., 1911) 2:363; Richard F. Lovelace, *The American Pietism of Cotton Mather: Origins of American Evangelicalism* (Grand Rapids, MI: Christian University Press, 1979), 234–6, 363; and Kenneth Silverman, *The Life and Times of Cotton Mather* (New York: Columbia University Press, 1985), 265–6.

28 Mather, *The Diary of Cotton Mather*, 2:686–9.

29 Samuel Willard, *A Compleat Body of Divinity in Two Hundred and Fifty Expository Lectures on the Assembly's Shorter Catechism wherein the Doctrines of the Christian Religion are Unfolded, their Truth Confirm'd, their Excellence Display'd, their Usefulness Improv'd; Contrary Errors & Vices Refuted & Expos'd, Objections Answer'd, Controversies Settled, Cases of Conscience Resolv'd; and a Great Light thereby Reflected on the Present Age* (Boston: B. Green & S. Kneeland, 1726), 615.

30 For examples of suits, see Van Laer, *Council Minutes*, 4:212–13; Christopher Moore, "A World of Possibilities: Slavery and Freedom in Dutch New Amsterdam," in *Slavery in New York*, 38–40, 42–5. For an example of a slave serving as a witness in Massachusetts, see *Acts and Resolves*, 8:392.

31 *The Colonial Laws of Massachusetts: Reprinted from the edition of 1672*, 281; *The Public Records of the Colony of Connecticut*, ed. J.H. Trumbull and C.J. Hoadly (Hartford, CT: Brown and Parsons, 1868), 4:40; and Warren, *New England Bound*, 212–17.

32 Warren, *New England Bound*, 49–81; George H. Moore, *Notes on the History of Slavery in Massachusetts* (New York: Negro Universities Press, 1968), 50; Robert V. Wells, *The Population of the British Colonies in America*, 79–82; Jay Country, *The Notorious Triangle: Rhode Island and the African Slave Trade, 1700–1807* (Phila-

delphia: Temple University Press, 1981); Hodges, *Root & Branch*, 104–5; Edward J. McManus, *A History of Negro Slavery in New York*, 24–32, 44–6.

33 Greenberg, *Crime and Law Enforcement in the Colony of New York*, 72–6. In cases of rape, African American men were more likely to be executed for the crime than white men. Block, *Rape & Sexual Power in Early America*, 169–76; and Ryan, *Regulating Passion*, 115–16.

34 *The Colonial Laws of New York*, 1:157–8, 617–18, and 2:679–81, 684–7; *New York Mercury*, February 27, 1758; *Boston Evening Post*, January 15, 1753; "To the Publisher of the Boston Evening Post," *Boston Evening Post*, April 10, 1738; and "By Order of the Select-Men of the Town of Boston," *Boston News-Letter*, January 16, 1755. The law regarding weapons punished slaves for having or using "any gun, Pistoll, sword, Club or any other Kind of Weapon" not in the "presence or by the Direction of his her or their Master or Mistress."

35 *Colonial Justice in Western Massachusetts, 1639–1702: The Pynchon Court Record*, ed. Joseph H. Smith (Cambridge, MA: Harvard University Press, 1961) 298; *Court of Assistants*, 1: 197–9; John Noble, "The Case of Maria in the Court of Assistants, 1681," *Publications of the Colonial Society of Massachusetts* (Boston; Colonial Society of Massachusetts, 1904), 6:323–31.

36 Joshua Coffin, *A Sketch of the History of Newbury, Newburyport, and West Newbury, from 1635 to 1845* (Boston: Samuel G. Drake, 1845), 153–4.

37 *New-York Weekly Journal*, March 28, 1737, and April 11, 1737. The "Tyranny" of another master was cited as a cause of a revolt in Surinam. *Boston Evening Post*, August 13, 1750. Cotton Mather, for example, expressed alarm after an insurrection in Jamaica. See Warren, *New England Bound*, 233–4.

38 Goddell, Jr., *The Trial and Execution for Petit Treason of Mark and Phillis*.

39 A host of literature debates whether in putting forward narratives of abuse, African Americans supported existing structures that saw them as proper subjects for physical punishment. The starting point for questioning it is Saidiya V. Hartman's *Scenes of Subjection*, 3–48. While such writing is important in considering the long-term ramifications of sentimentalist strategies, the court cases and writing by African Americans were important correctives in a society that focused on violence only from a white perspective. As murder cases show, without testimony and acts of resistance, narratives of abuse would not emerge and only defenses of violence would exist.

40 Greene, *The Negro in Colonial New England*, 161; and *Boston Gazette*, September 28–October 5, 1741. Jill Lepore questions whether the 1741 slave conspiracy was real or a reflection of white fears in *New York Burning: Liberty, Slavery, and Conspiracy in Eighteenth Century Manhattan* (New York: Vintage Books, 2005).

41 Governor Robert Hunter to the Lords of Trade, June 23, 1712, in *Documents Relative to the Colonial History of the State of New-York*, 5:341.

42 Daniel Horsmanden, *The New-York Conspiracy, or History of the Negro Plot, with the Journal of the Proceedings against the Conspirators at New-York in the Years 1741-2*, 2nd ed. (New York: Southwick & Pelsue, 1810), 90, 120, 344, 339.

43 Although responses were fierce, some were dismayed by retributive violence. See Governor Robert Hunter to the Lords of Trade, June 23, 1712, in *Documents Relative to the Colonial History of the State of New-York*, 5:341–2. On New York's conspiracies, see Thelma Wills Foote, *Black and White Manhattan: The History of Racial Formation in Colonial New York City* (New York: Oxford University Press, 2004), 167–9; and Horsmanden, *The New-York Conspiracy*, 11–12.

44 Joshua Coffin, *An Account of Some of the Principal Slave Insurrections, and Others, Which Have Occurred, or Been Attempted, in the United States and Elsewhere, During the Last Two Centuries* (New York: The American Anti-Slavery Society, 1860), 12; and *Acts and Resolves passed by the General Court of Massachusetts* (Boston: Secretary of the Commonwealth, 1839), 998.

45 Horsmanden, *The New-York Conspiracy*, 12, 339.

46 Jeffrey Brace, *The Blind African Slave; or, Memoirs of Boyrereau Brinch, nicknamed Jeffrey Brace* (St. Albans, VT: Harry Whitney, 1810), 152–3; and Walter Johnson, *River of Dark Dreams: Slavery and Empire in the Cotton Kingdom* (Cambridge, MA: Belknap Press, 2013), 207–8.

47 Brace, *The Blind African Slave, 153.* In New York City cases of murderous violence occurred in 1702, 1743, and 1798, and serious assaults against whites in 1696 and 1774. In New England, serious assaults and murders of masters and their families occurred on at least seven occasions over the sixteenth and seventeenth centuries. Foote, *Black and White Manhattan*, 158, 206; Greene, *The Negro in Colonial New England*, 6; Towner, "'A Good Master Well Served,'" 279–91.

48 Arthur, *The life, and dying speech of Arthur, a Negro man, who was executed at Worcester, October 20th 1768* (Boston: s.n., 1768); T.H. Breen, "Making History: The Force of Public Opinion and the Last Years of Slavery in Revolutionary Massachusetts," in Hoffman, Sobel, and Teute, ed., *Through a Glass Darkly*, 80–5.

49 *The Colonial Laws of New York*, 1:762; Edward Cornbury to Justices of the Peace in Kings County, July 22, 1706, in Gabriel Furman, *Antiquities of Long Island*, ed. Frank Moore (New York: J.W. Bouton, 1875), 221–2; and Craig Steven Wilder, *In the Company of Black Men: The African Influence on African American Culture in New York City* (New York: New York University Press, 2001), 12–17.

50 Cadwallader Colden, Philadelphia, March 26, 1717, to Mr. Jordan, in *The Letters and Papers of Cadwallader Colden*, vol. 1, in *Collections of The New York Historical Society For the Year 1917* (New York: Printed for the Society, 1918), 50:39.

51 Elizabeth Elbourne, "Introduction: Key Themes and Perspectives," in *Sex, Power, and Slavery*, ed. Gwyn Campbell and Elizabeth Elbourne (Athens, OH: Ohio University Press, 2014), 9.

52 See, for example, Brenda Stevenson, "What's Love Got to Do with It? Concubinage and Enslaved Women and Girls in the Antebellum South," in *Sexuality and Slavery: Reclaiming Intimate Histories in the Americas*, ed. Daina Ramey Berry and Leslie M. Harris (Athens, GA: University of Georgia Press, 2018), 159–88; White, *Arn't I a Woman*, 27–61; Thelma Jennings, "'Us Colored Women Had to

Go Through A Plenty': Sexual Exploitation of African American Slave Women," *Journal of Women's History* 1 (Winter 1990): 45–74.

53 Block, *Rape & Sexual Power in Early America*, 64–77; Kathleen Brown, *Good Wives, Nasty Wenches, and Anxious Patriarchs*, 120–35; Jennifer Morgan, *Laboring Women: Reproduction and Gender in New World Slavery* (Philadelphia: University of Pennsylvania Press, 2004), chap. 3 and 4; Ryan, *Regulating Passion*, 74–82, 114–16, 163–4; Wendy Anne Warren, "'The Cause of her Grief': The Rape of a Slave in Early New England," *JAH* 93 (March 2007): 1031–49.

54 Cadwallader Colden, Philadelphia, March 26, 1717, to Mr. Jordan, in *The Letters and Papers of Cadwallader Colden*, 50: 39.

55 Brace, *The Blind African Slave*, 143–9.

56 James MacSparran, *A Letter Book and Abstract of Out Services, Written During the Years 1743–1751*, ed. Reverend Daniel Goodwin (Boston: D.B. Updike, 1899), 52, 54–5; Fitts, *Inventing New England's Slave Paradise: Master/Slave Relations in Eighteenth-century Narragansett, Rhode Island* (New York: Garland Publishing, 1998), 107, 120–1; and *Sweet, Bodies Politic*, 71.

57 The history of racial ideas in colonial North America is an oft studied subject and white racial consciousness grew in the North alongside ideas about African Americans and Native Americans. For an overview, see Richard A. Bailey, *Race and Redemption in Puritan New England*; Sharon Block, *Colonial Complexions: Race and Bodies in Eighteenth Century America* (Philadelphia: University of Pennsylvania Press, 2018); Chaplin, *Subject Matter*, 157–98, 201–42, 280–320; Londa Schiebenger, *Nature's Body: Gender and the Making of Modern Science* (Boston: Beacon Press, 1993), 115–42; and Sweet, *Bodies Politic*.

58 Di Bonaventura, *For Adam's Sake*, 126–7; and Mark Levine, "Researching Violence: Power, Social Relations and the Virtue of the Experimental Method," in *Researching Violence*, ed. by Raymond M. Lee and Elizabeth A. Stanko (New York: Routledge, 2003), 126–36.

59 Emily Blanck, "1783: The Turning Point in the Law of Slavery and Freedom in Massachusetts," *NEH* 75 (March 2002): 26–8.

60 In Rhode Island, George Hazard sued Ben for putting his master's cattle in land he owned. Ben's master defended his slave from a civil suit by emphasizing the slave's status and that slaves could not "make any legal appearance or Answer to any Civil Action in the King's Courts." The same master questioned if another enslaved man's evidence was also ineligible "for that the said Negro is a Heathen and a Slave." The Rhode Island court upheld both slaves' rights to testify. *George Hazard v. Ben*, Kings County, Court of Common Pleas, 1765, Judicial Archives, Supreme Court Judicial Records Center, Pawtucket, RI.

61 *The Colonial Laws of New York*, 1:521.

62 During the 1740s, Spanish African Americans and their allies petitioned various officials after they were made prisoners of war and sold into slavery. The forty-five slaves received their freedom, but the opportunities afforded Spanish prisoners of

war were not available to most slaves in New York until the American Revolution, when the British offered slaves new opportunities for freedom. Hodges, *Root & Branch*, 129–30.

63 Venture Smith, *A Narrative of the Life and Adventures of Venture, a Native of Africa: But Resident Above Sixty Years in the United States of America* (New London, CT: C. Holt, 1798), 19–20.

64 Tapping Reeve, *The Law of Baron and Feme; of Parent and Child; of Guardian and Ward; of Master and Servant; and of the Powers of Courts of Chancery. With an Essay on the Terms, Heir, Heirs, and Heirs of the Body* (New Haven, CT: Printed by Oliver Steele, 1816), 340; Nathan Dane, *A General Abridgement and Digest of American Law: With Occasional Notes and Commentary* (Boston: Cummings, Hilliard, & Co., 1824), 2:40.

65 Brace, *The Blind African Slave*, 146.

66 Smith claimed to be standing up for his wife against Mrs. Stanton. Smith, *A Narrative of the Life and Adventures of Venture*, 19.

67 *King v. John Pettell*, October 1717, Record Book, Suffolk General Sessions, Judicial Archives, MA.

68 Because freedom suits were limited to those persons who could argue wrongful imprisonment, scholars often argue that freedom suits did not fundamentally challenge the system. For excellent coverage of these suits, see Blanck, *Tyrannicide*, 34–45.

69 Suffolk Files, *James v. Richard Lechmere*, September 1769, case 147752, Court of Common Pleas, Middlesex County, Judicial Archives, MA. For another example of these terms, see Suffolk Files, Deposition of Charles Hasselton, April 10, 1745, in *Peter Hasselton v. Richard Waters*, April 1745, case 60349, Judicial Archives, MA.

70 John Saffin, *A Brief and Candid Answer to a Late Printed Sheet Entitled the Selling of Joseph* (1705), in Abner C. Goodell, "John Saffin and his Slave Adam," *Publications of the Colonial Society of Massachusetts* 1 (1895): 105; and Suffolk Files, *Prince v. Bull*, May 1763, case 84076, Hampshire Court of Common Pleas, Judicial Archives, MA.

71 John Saffin, *A Brief and Candid Answer*, 105, 109.

72 John Saffin, *A Brief and Candid Answer*, 112.

73 Warren, *New England Bound*, 225–6.

74 Samuel Sewall, *The Selling of Joseph* (Boston: Bartholomew and Green, 1700), 1.

75 Brycchan Carey, *From Peace to Freedom: Quaker Rhetoric and the Birth of American Antislavery, 1657–1761* (New Haven: Yale University Press, 2012), 70–104; Manisha Sinha, *The Slaves' Cause: A History of Abolition* (New Haven: Yale University Press, 2016), 12–13; and Henry J. Cadbury, "An Early Quaker Anti-Slavery Statement," *Journal of Negro History* 22 (October 1937): 488–93.

76 Benjamin Lay, *All slave-keepers that keep the innocent in bondage* (Philadelphia: Printed by Benjamin Franklin, 1737), 45; Marcus Rediker, *The Fearless Benja-*

min Lay: *The Quaker Dwarf Who Became the First Revolutionary Abolitionist* (Boston: Beacon Press, 2017); Carey, *From Peace to Freedom*, 143–219; and Jean Soderlund, *Quakers and Slavery: A Divided Spirit* (Princeton: Princeton University Press, 1985), 15–17.

77 Christopher Leslie Brown, *Moral Capital*, chap. 1; Philip Gould, *Barbaric Traffic: Commerce and Antislavery in the Eighteenth Century Atlantic World* (Cambridge, MA: Harvard University Press, 2003); David Brion Davis, *The Problem of Slavery in Western Culture* (New York: Oxford, 1988), 291–332, 374–42; and David Brion Davis, *The Problem of Slavery in the Age of the Revolution, 1770–1823* (New York: Oxford University Press, 1999), 404–17.

78 Nash and Soderlund, *Freedom by Degrees*, chap. 2.

79 *Boston Evening Post*, February 26, 1759.

80 The choice to commit suicide was an option within an extremely narrow range of agency, as scholars show. See Richard Bell, "Slave Suicide, Abolition and the Problem of Resistance," *Slavery and Abolition* 33 (2012): 525–549; Terri L. Snyder, *The Power to Die. Slavery and Suicide in British North America* (Chicago: University of Chicago Press, 2015); Terri L. Snyder, "Suicide, Slavery, and Memory in North America," *JAH* 97 (June 2010): 39–62; Ira Berlin, *Many Thousands Gone* 2; and Michael A. Gomez, *Exchanging our Country Marks: The Transformation of African Identities in the Colonial and Antebellum South* (Chapel Hill: University of North Carolina Press, 1998), 119–20.

CHAPTER 4: SUSPICIOUS SERVANTS AND SLAVES

1 John Adams, "Case No. 64 Rex v. Weems," December 4, 1770, in L. Kinvin Wroth and Hiller B. Zobel, ed., *The Legal Papers of John Adams* (Cambridge, MA: Harvard University Press, MA, 1965), 3:266; and Eric Hinderaker, *Boston's Massacre* (Cambridge, MA: Belknap Press of Harvard University, 2017), chap. 8.

2 Alfred Young and Holger Hoock show the way the history of the American Revolution was whitewashed to remove the violent elements and secure the authority of the government. Numerous historical works address the violence of the era and they are cited throughout this chapter. See Alfred Young, *The Shoemaker and the Tea Party* (Boston: Beacon, 1999), 92–193; and Hoock, *Scars of Independence*.

3 Steven J. Novak, *The Rights of Youth: American Colleges and Student Revolt, 1789–1815* (Cambridge, MA: Harvard University Press, 1977), 2–4; and Thomas Hine, *The Rise and Fall of the American Teenager* (New York: Avon Books, 1999), 89.

4 The disposition of the court in one of the cases is not rendered in the minutes. Record Books, NYGS, 1774–1776, NYMA.

5 Records do not indicate the kinds of wounds or abuse Crocheron or Cotterill suffered, but by this time, the court freed individuals only when masters took correction too far and threatened the lives of servants. *Nicholas Crocheron v. Thomas*

Cheeseman, February 1774; and *Sarah Cotterill v. Elizabeth Williams*, November 1775, Record Book, NYGS, NYMA. In some records, Cotterill's name appeared as "Cotteril."

6 *Anthony Smith v. John Gilliland*, February 1774, Minutes, NYGS, NYMA.

7 Christine Daniels, "'Liberty to Complaine': Servant Petitions in Maryland, 1652–1797," in *The Many Legalities of Early America*, ed. Christopher L. Tomlins and Bruce H. Mann (Chapel Hill: University of North Carolina Press, 2001), 231–7.

8 Gilje, *Rioting in America*, chap. 2; Hoock, *Scars of Independence*, 16–55; Alan Taylor, *American Revolutions: A Continental History, 1750–1804* (New York W.W. Norton and Company, 2016); Benjamin L. Carp, *Defiance of the Patriots: The Boston Tea Party & the Making of the American Revolution* (New Haven: Yale University Press, 2011); and Barbara Clark Smith, *Freedoms We Lost: Consent and Resistance in Revolutionary America* (New York: New Press, 2010).

9 An Impartial Citizen, "To the Printer," *New York Gazette, or Weekly Post-Boy*, February 5, 1770. For an overview of New York City during the American Revolution, see Richard M. Ketchum, *Divided Loyalties: How the American Revolution Came to New York* (New York: Henry Hold and Company, 2002).

10 William Smith, *Historical Memoirs of William Smith* (New York: Colburn & Tegg, 1956), 1:156, 157.

11 "Messirs FLEETS," *Boston Evening Post*, August 24, 1772; and Jay Fliegelman, *Prodigals and Pilgrims*, 1–66.

12 Leopold S. Launitz-Schürer Jr., *Loyal Whigs and Revolutionaries: The Making of the Revolution in New York, 1765–1776* (New York: New York University Press, 1980), 97–127; Edward Countryman, *A People in Revolution: The American Revolution and Political Society in New York, 1760–1790* (New York: W.W. Norton, 1981), 36–71; Paul A. Gilje, *The Road to Mobocracy: Popular Disorder in New York City, 1763–1834* (Chapel Hill: University of North Carolina Press, 1987), 39–68; Carp, *Defiance of the Patriots*, chap. 8; Young, *The Shoemaker and the Tea Party*, chap. 5–8; Gary Nash, *The Northern Seaports and the Origins of the American Revolution* (Cambridge, MA: Harvard University Press, 1986), chap. 5–7.

13 Staughton Lynd, "The Mechanics of New York City Politics, 1774–1788," *Labor History* 5 (1964): 225–46; Alfred Young, *Liberty Tree: Ordinary People and the American Revolution* (New York: New York University Press, 2006), 46–55, 61–75; Countryman, *A People in Revolution*, 124–6.

14 John Munro, Albany, to Governor William Tryon, November 24, 1772 and August 22, 1773, in *The Documentary History of the State of New York*, ed. E.B. O'Callaghan (Albany, NY: Charles Van Benthuysen, 1851), 4:800–1, 843.

15 The Petition of William Hough and many others of his Majesty's Subjects inhabiting the County of Charlotte and the North Eastern District of the County of Albany, February 2, 1774, in *The Documentary History of the State of New York*, 4:857, 859–69; and Countryman, *A People in Revolution*, 36–71.

16 On the government trying to maintain a balance between asserting their authority and returning to peace, see Thomas J. Humphrey, *Land and Liberty: Hudson*

Valley Riots in the Age of Revolution (Dekalb, IL: Northern Illinois University Press, 2004), 76–8.

17 Thomas Jones, *History of New York During the Revolutionary War* (New York: New York Historical Society, 1879), 1:28–32; and Roger J. Champagne, *Alexander McDougall and the American Revolution in New York* (Schenectady, NY: New York State Bicentennial Commission and Union College Press, 1975), 27–34.

18 Alexander McDougall, "To the Printer," *New York Journal and Weekly Post-Boy*, February 15, 1770; Champagne, *Alexander McDougall and the American Revolution*, 27, 34; and Jones, *History of New York During the Revolutionary War*, 1:28–32.

19 Gilje, *Rioting in America*, chap. 1 and 2; Gilge, *The Road to Mobocracy*, chap. 2; and J.L. Bell, "From Saucy Boys to Sons of Liberty: Politicizing Youth in Pre-Revolutionary Boston," in Marten, ed., *Children in Colonial America*, 204–16.

20 *New York Journal*, October 22, 1767.

21 Laura Janara, *Democracy Growing Up: Authority, Autonomy, and Passion in Tocqueville's Democracy in America* (Albany, NY: State University of New York Press, 2002), chap. 1.

22 Gordon S. Wood, *The Radicalism of the American Revolution* (New York: Vintage Books, 1991), 158–68, quote page 165.

23 Ebenezer Fox, *The Revolutionary Adventures of Ebenezer Fox, of Roxbury, Massachusetts* (Boston: Charles Fox, 1847), 16–21.

24 Court officials had experience on the bench and understood the long history of dealing with cases of abuse. Whitehead Hicks had been mayor since 1766, although he stepped down after the British occupied New York City. Benjamin Blagge, George Brewerton, William Waddle, and John Dikeman were experienced JPs and aldermen in the city who saw the revolutionary crisis deepen year after year. The newest recorder of proceedings, Robert Livingston, would go on to form part of the committee in the Continental Congress that drafted the Declaration of Independence. Hicks would address the mechanics, among others, in the hostile negotiation between the government and populace about what to do with incoming ships bearing tea after passage of the Tea Act. The political loyalties and experiences of this group suggest the reasons that the policies of the court changed lay not solely with their political beliefs but in the process of the Revolution.

25 Timothy Pickering, "Will the Printers (at such a Time as this) be so good as to publish the following Remarks and Cautions," *Boston Gazette*, May 16, 1766. For overviews of abolitionist tactics and thought, see Davis, *The Problem of Slavery in the Age of Revolution*, chap. 6 and 7; Sinha, *The Slaves' Cause*, 37–8.

26 John Saillant, "Slavery and Divine Providence in New England Calvinism: The New Divinity and a Black Protest, 1775–1805," *NEQ* 68 (December 1995): 591–5.

27 Christopher Leslie Brown, *Moral Capital*, chap. 2 and 3. In contrast with Brown, Seymour Drescher believes the American Revolution hindered the transatlantic movement. See Seymour Drescher, *Abolition: A History of Slavery and Antislavery* (Cambridge, UK: Cambridge University Press, 2009), 107–12.

28 Anthony Benezet, *A caution and a warning to Great Britain and Her Colonies in a short representation of the calamitous state of the enslaved negroes in the British Dominions* (Philadelphia: Printed by Henry Miller, 1766).

29 Among those he influenced was Benjamin Rush, who wrote to dismantle the trade. See Benjamin Rush, *An Address to the Inhabitants of the British Settlements in America, upon Slave-Keeping* (Philadelphia: John Dunlap, 1773); Maurice Jackson, "Anthony Benezet: Working the Antislavery Cause inside and outside of "The Society," in *Quakers and Abolition*, ed. Brycchan Carey and Geoffrey Plank (Urbana: University of Illinois Press, 2014), 106–19; and Christopher Leslie Brown, *Moral Capital*, 165–71, 188–92, 259–60.

30 Roger Antsey, *The Atlantic Slave Trade and British Abolition: 1760–1810* (London: Humanities Press, 1995), 221–35, 239–42, 245; and Simon Schama, *Rough Crossings: Britain, the Slaves, and the American Revolution* (New York: Harper Collins, 2006), 21–57.

31 Emily Blanck, "The Legal Emancipations of Leander and Caesar," 245–6.

32 Blanck, *Tyrannicide*, 34–7.

33 Historians argue that the success of freedom suits lay in the fact that African Americans had to convince fewer people to side with them, since slavery was crucial to the household and economic growth in seaport regions, as well as in establishing the wealth and rank of individuals. See Cameron, *To Plead Our Own Cause*, 74; and Melish, *Disowning Slavery*, 16–49.

34 Suffolk files, *Newport v. Billing*, October 1766 and November 1767, case 157509, Superior Court of Judicature, Judicial Archives, MA.

35 John Adams, *The Legal Papers of John Adams*, ed. L. Kinvin Wroth and Hiller B. Zobel (Cambridge, MA: Belknap Press, 1965), 2:56–8.

36 Nathaniel Appleton, *Considerations on Slavery. In a Letter to a Friend* (Boston: Edes and Gill, 1767), 5.

37 Nash and Soderlund, *Freedom by Degrees*, 48–58; and Greene, *The Negro in Colonial New England*, 233.

38 The church committee accused Barnard, the source of the rumor, of "no small degree of malignity" in spreading the gossip. John Hawks, Samuel Childs, Joseph Stebbins, Samuel Arms, Asakel Wright and Johnathan Ashely, Jr., to Colonel David Field and Others, October 22, 1779; and Selectmen of Deerfield, Deerfield Town Warrant, November 25, 1775, Pocumtuck Valley Memorial Association, Deerfield, MA. The charges against Ashley likely stemmed from his presumed disregard for the Patriot cause.

39 Enoch Bartlet, "Messirs. Lunt and Tinges," *Essex Journal*, October 12, 1774.

40 For example, see Thomas Foster, *Sex and the Eighteenth Century Man: Massachusetts and the History of Sexuality in America* (Boston: Beacon Press, 2006), chap. 3; Richard Godbeer, *Sexual Revolution in Early America* (Baltimore: Johns Hopkins University Press, 2004); Lyons, *Sex Among the Rabble*, chap. 1–5; and Ryan, *Regulating Passion*, chap. 2, 4–6.

41 Bartlet, "Messirs. Lunt and Tinges."

42 Denial was a common trend among slaveholders, as seen with Cadwallader Colden. For another example, see *Boston Gazette*, July 16, 1770.

43 *Boston Gazette*, August 31, 1772; and *Boston Evening Post*, May 18, 1772.

44 "New York, May 11, 1772," *Boston News Letter*, May 21, 1772.

45 Martin Howard, "From Cape Fear Mercury," *Massachusetts Gazette*, April 5, 1772.

46 Indictment of Jabez Reynolds, April 1773; Deposition of William Chadsey, May 1, 1773; and Deposition of Benjamin Clarke, May 1, 1773, King County, Rhode Island Superior Court, in Rhode Island Supreme Court Judicial Records Center.

47 *Boston Gazette*, June 25, 1770.

48 *Calendar of Historical Manuscripts in the Office of the Secretary of State, Albany, N.Y.*, 2:818–19; Whitehead Hicks, Document, 1733, July 7 (Deposition of a sailor concerning the cruel treatment of Negro slaves on board the Snow "York" on her late voyage to the coast of Africa, sworn before Hicks, 1773), NYHS.

49 "Salem, May 15," *Massachusetts Gazette*, May 27, 1773; "New-York, Nov. 14," *New York Mercury*, November 14, 1774. Over the 1780s, New York, Rhode Island, and Connecticut prohibited their citizens from taking part in the Atlantic slave trade, though illegal trade proved as profitable for some individuals. McManus, *A History of Negro Slavery in New York*, 165–6; and Melish, *Disowning Slavery*, 67–8, 74.

50 Petition for Freedom to Massachusetts Governor Thomas Gage, His Majesty's Council, and the House of Representatives, May 25, 1774, Massachusetts Historical Society Collections Online, accessed April 17, 2015.

51 Caesar Sarter, "Messrs PRINTERS," *Essex Journal*, August 17, 1774; Cameron, *To Plead Our Own Cause*, 41–2.

52 "A Letter from the Committee of Albany, dated October 21st" in Peter Force, *American Archives*, Fifth Series, 3:266; McManus, *A History of Negro Slavery in New York*, 155–6; and Artemas Ward, *General Ward's Orderly Book*, October 9, 1775, in *The Papers of Artemas Ward*, vol. 5, reel 4.

53 William Lincoln, *History of Worcester, Massachusetts: From Its Earliest Settlement to September, 1836; with Various Notices Relating to the History of Worcester County* (Worcester, MA: Moses D. Phillips and Company, 1837), 99.

54 Sarah L.H. Gronningsater, "Born Free in the Master's House: Gradual Emancipation in the Early American North," in *Child Slavery Before and After Emancipation: An Argument for Child-Centered Slavery Studies*, ed. Anna Mae Duane (New York: Cambridge University Press, 2017), 127–28.

CHAPTER 5: QUESTIONABLE LOYALTIES

1 Joseph Lightly, *The Last Words and Dying Speech of Joseph Lightly, Who was executed at Cambridge, November 21, 1765. For the Murder of Elizabeth Post, at a Place called Ware* (Boston, 1765). On practices of self-marriage and common law marriages, see Lyons, *Sex Among the Rabble*, 33–6; Ellen K. Rothman, *Hands and Hearts: A History of Courtship in America* (New York: Basic Books, 1984); and Lawrence Stone, *Uncertain Unions and Broken Lives: Marriage and Divorce in England, 1660–1857* (Oxford: Oxford University Press, 1995).

2 Lightly, *The Last Words and Dying Speech of Joseph Lightly*.

3 Lightly, *The Last Words and Dying Speech of Joseph Lightly*; and Suffolk files, Indictment, *King v. Joseph Lightly*, April 1765, case 147371, vol. 1006, Judicial Archives, MA.

4 Lightly, *The Last Words and Dying Speech of Joseph Lightly*.

5 For cases of murder, see *Boston Gazette*, November 25, 1765 (Joseph Lightly case); *Massachusetts Gazette*, March 4, 1773 (James Bell manslaughter case); *King v. Levi Whitney*, November 1779; *King v. William Padley*, February 1784; Record Book, Superior Court of Judicature, Judicial Archives, MA; and Joshua Spaulding, *The prayer of a true penitent for mercy; or, The publican's prayer, illustrated. A sermon, delivered at Salem, Dec. 21, 1786, previous to the execution of Isaac Coombs, an Indian, whose crime was the murder of his wife* (Salem, MA: Printed by Dabne and Cushing, 1787) (Isaac Coombs case).

6 *Boston Gazette*, January 29, 1767; and *Pennsylvania Gazette*, April 16, 1767 (Arthur McNeally aka McNally). It's not clear if Murphy was prosecuted. See "New York, August 12, 1773," *Boston Evening Post*, August 23, 1773.

7 *King v. William Padley*, February 1784, Record Book, Superior Court of Judicature, Judicial Archives, MA.

8 "A Sketch of the Life and Confession of Isaac Coombs," *Continental Journal*, December 28, 1786; and *Massachusetts v. Isaac Coombs*, July 1786, Record Book, Supreme Judicial Court, case 133637, Judicial Archives, MA; and *Massachusetts Gazette*, May 29, 1786, December 23, 1786.

9 "Mr. Edes," *Boston Gazette*, August 3, 1778. See *Massachusetts v. Pricilla Woodworth*, April 1782; and *Massachusetts v. Rebeccah Kerilly*, February 1784, Record Book, Supreme Judicial Court, MA.

10 Novangelus, "To the Inhabitants of the Colony of Massachusetts Bay," *Boston Gazette*, January 23, 1775.

11 A lady, "A Caveat to the Fair Sex," *Essex Journal*, March 23, 1774.

12 Abigail Adams, Braintree, to John Adams, Philadelphia, March 31, 1776, in *My Dearest Friend: Letters of Abigail and John Adams*, ed. Margaret A. Hogan and C. James Taylor (Cambridge, MA: Belknap Press, 2007), 110–11.

13 Inimiga Tirannis, "To the Inhabitants of the United States of America," *Independent Chronicle*, March 26, 1778; and Ryan, *Regulating Passion*, 86–97.

14 Given the large-scale loss of records from the Revolutionary War, we can assume that many more women took cases of assault to justices. For example, only one record exists for each of the following years: 1764, 1773, 1774, 1779, 1780, 1781, 1785. No records exist for the time periods 1765–1772, 1775–1777, and 1782–1784. Record Books and File Papers, Suffolk General Sessions of Peace, Judicial Archives, MA; and Elijah Adlow Papers, Special Collections, Boston Public Library (hereafter BPL). For an example, see petitions cited below and Recognizance of William Green, May 12, 1773, Adlow Papers, Special Collections, BPL, Box 71, folder 1.

15 Elizabeth Bemis of Middlesex complained twice and is only counted once. Record Books and File Papers, Middlesex, Worcester, and Suffolk General Sessions of the

Peace; Middlesex Superior Court Justice of the Peace Papers, Judicial Archives, MA; and Plymouth Colonial Records, 3:301, 308. For examples, see Thomas Winch, recognizance, July 7, 1767, File Papers, Middlesex General Sessions, Judicial Archives, MA; and John Daniels, recognizance, May 6, 1780, File Papers, Worcester General Sessions, Judicial Archives, MA.

16 Samuel Bemis recognizance, June 19, 1778, File Papers, Middlesex General Sessions, MA. For an example of the typical language used, see John Barnard recognizance, August 28, 1800, File Papers, Worcester General Sessions, Judicial Archives, MA.

17 Samuel Bemis recognizance, May 2, 1780, File Papers, Middlesex General Sessions, Judicial Archives, MA.

18 Joshua Turner, April 1771, Record Book, Plymouth General Sessions; Ebenezer Proctor, December 1760, and Uriah Hayden, September 1789, Record Book, Middlesex General Sessions; Dennis Cahail, April 1764, Record Book, Suffolk General Sessions of the Peace; and John Daniels, June 5, 1780, File Papers, Worcester General Sessions, Judicial Archives, MA. The record books of New York City and Suffolk County are missing certain years during the Revolutionary War.

19 The other charges were for being a disorderly person (Cahail); assault (Turner); and cohabitation (Daniels). See Dennis Cahail, April 1764, Record Book, Suffolk General Sessions of the Peace; Joshua Turner, April 1771, Record Book, Plymouth General Sessions; and *Commonwealth v. John Daniels*, April 1781, Record Book, Supreme Judicial Court, Judicial Archives, MA.

20 John Daniels, recognizance, June 5, 1780, File Papers, Worcester General Sessions; and *Commonwealth v. John Daniels*, April 1781, Record Book, Supreme Judicial Court, Judicial Archives, MA.

21 For a five-shilling fine, see *King v. Ebenezer Proctor*, December 1760, Record Book, Middlesex General Sessions, Judicial Archives, MA. Fines issued by Middlesex and Worcester General Sessions for single adult men's assaults on other men resulted in fines ranging from five shillings to five pounds between 1770 and 1785. On fornication prosecutions, see Ryan, *Regulating Passion*, 90–1.

22 *King v. Joshua Turner*, April 1771, Record Book, Plymouth General Sessions, Judicial Archives, MA.

23 "New Haven, Sept. 23," *Essex Journal*, October 13, 1784.

24 *Boston Evening Post*, July 22, 1765.

25 "Boston, Feb. 11," *New-York Journal*, February 25, 1773.

26 "New York, January 19," *Boston Evening Post*, January 26, 1767.

27 In the records, Rebecca's and James' surname is spelt variously as Kerilly, Carilla, and Carrol. *Commonwealth v. Rebecca Kerrily*, February 1784, Record Book, Supreme Judicial Court, MA; and Randolph Roth and Cornelia Hughes Dayton, "Massachusetts Homicides, 1781–1790" in "Homicide among Adults in Colonial and Revolutionary New England, 1630–1797," Historical Violence Database of The Criminal Justice Research Center at The Ohio State University (2009), https://cjrc.osu.edu.

28 *Boston Gazette*, December 3, 1783.

29 For an example of an elopement ad from this period, see *Boston Gazette*, January 29, 1776. On self-divorce, see Lyons, *Sex Among the Rabble*, 14–58; and Mary Sievens, *Stray Wives: Marital Conflict in Early National New England* (New York: New York University Press, 2005).

30 Cott, "Divorce and the Changing Status of Women in Eighteenth-Century Massachusetts," 604–6; and Howard, *A History of Matrimonial Institutions*, 2:342–4.

31 Ryan, *Regulating Passion*, 86–92; and Karin Wulf, *Not All Wives: Women of Colonial Philadelphia* (Ithaca: Cornell University Press, 2000), 90–6, 166–79, 200–5.

32 *New York Packet*, January 16, 1786.

33 American Liberty, "To the Public," *Essex Journal*, January 19, 1774.

34 *People v. Baker Brasher*, August 1785; and *People v. Henry Brasher*, August 1787, Minutes, NYGS, NYMA.

35 *People v. Richard Woods*, November 1787, Minutes, NYGS, NYMA.

36 Morris, *Government and Labor in Early America*, 439, 443–4; and *Connecticut Courant*, March 10, 1778.

37 Holly A. Mayer, *Belonging to the Army: Camp Followers during the American Revolution* (Columbia: University of South Carolina Press, 1996).

38 Fox, *The Revolutionary Adventures of Ebenezer Fox*, 57–8.

39 Antonio T. Bly, "A Prince among Pretending Free Men: Runaway Slaves in Colonial New England Revisited," *Massachusetts Historical Review* 14 (2012): 92.

40 Shane White, *Somewhat More Independent*, 127.

41 McManus, *A History of Negro Slavery in New York*, 139; "To the Honorable Counsel & House of [Representa]tives for the State of Massachusetts Bay in General Court assembled," January 13, 1777, in *A Documentary History of the Negro People in the United States*, ed. Herbert Aptheker (New York: Citadel Press, 1969), 10.

42 Boston King, "Memoirs of the Life of Boston King, a Black Preacher," *Methodist Magazine*, April 1798, 110.

43 Benjamin Quarles, *The Negro in the American Revolution* (Chapel Hill: University of North Carolina Press, 1961), 170–2; and Schama, *Rough Crossings*.

44 "A Letter from the Committee of Albany, dated October 21st" in Peter Force, *American Archives*, Fifth Series, 3:266; Sully Americanus, "From the London General Advertiser," *Independent Ledger*, May 3, 1779; and Greene, *The Negro in Colonial New England*, 163.

45 Quarles, *The Negro in the American Revolution*, 13–18, 52–56.

46 Graham Russell Hodges, "Black Revolt in New York City and the Neutral Zone, 1775–1783," in *New York in the Age of Constitution, 1775–1800*, ed. Paul A. Gilje and William Pencak (Cranbury, NJ: Fairleigh Dickenson University Press, 1992); and Graham Russell Hodges, *Slavery and Freedom in the Rural North: African Americans in Monmouth County, New Jersey, 1665–1865* (Madison, WI: Madison House, 1996), 97–104.

47 "To the Honrable General Assembly of the State of Connecticut to be Held at Hartford on the Second Thursday of Instant May [1779]—The Petition of the

Negros in the Towns of Stratford and Fairfield in the County of Fairfield," in Aptheker, ed., *A Documentary History of the Negro People in the United States*, 11.

48 Rhode Island, Connecticut, and Massachusetts made legal provisions allowing African American enlistments, while states like New Hampshire quietly accepted African Americans without legislative action. Charles Patrick Neimeyer, *America Goes to War: A Social History of the Continental Army* (New York: New York University Press, 1997), 71–8; and Judith L. Van Buskirk, "African-Americans in the Revolutionary War and its Aftermath," in *War and Society in the American Revolution*, ed. John Resh and Walter Sargent (DeKalb, IL: Northern Illinois University Press, 2007), 133–36.

49 *Zach Mullen v. John Ashley*, in Arthur Zilversmit, "Quok Walker, Mumbet, and the Abolition of Slavery in Massachusetts," *WMQ* 25 (October 1968): 617–18.

50 Catherine Sedgwick, "Slavery in New England," *Bentley's Miscellany*, XXXIV (1853): 417–24.

51 The Ashley family refused to release Freeman or Brom during the interval when the court decided the case. *Suffolk Files*, *Brom and Bett v. Ashley*, 1781, number 159966, Berkshire Court of Common Pleas, Writ of Replevin, Judicial Archives, MA. Mum Bett was the slave name for Elizabeth Freeman.

52 Ironically, Catherine Sedgwick claimed that Freeman's suit did not stem from "fear of her despotic mistress" and that she was in "awe of" John Ashley. It was clear to Sedgwick that Freeman "felt her servitude intolerable" and it is likely that Sedgwick's own investment in claiming that New Englanders' form of slavery was humane clouded her judgment on the matter. Catherine Sedgwick, "Slavery in New England," 421. Emily Blanck, "1783: The Turning Point in the Law of Slavery and Freedom in Massachusetts," *NEH* 75 (March 2002): 26–8; Theodore Sedgwick, *The Practicability of the Abolition of Slavery: A Lecture, Delivered at the Lyceum in Stockbridge, Massachusetts, February, 1831* (New York: s.n., 1831), 15; and Zilversmit, "Quok Walker, Mumbet, and the Abolition of Slavery in Massachusetts."

53 Catherine Sedgwick, "Slavery in New England," 417–24. Theodore Sedgwick claimed that Freeman ran away after the episode and that Ashley had to sue for her to return, but no other evidence exists to support that assertion. See Theodore Sedgwick, *The Practicability of the Abolition of Slavery*, 15; and Zilversmit, "Quok Walker, Mumbet, and the Abolition of Slavery in Massachusetts," 619.

54 Electa Fidelia Jones, *Stockbridge, Past and Present; Or, Records of an Old Mission Station* (Springfield, MA: Samuel Bowles & Company, 1854), 241; Gary B. Nash and Graham Russell Gao Hodges, *Friends of Liberty: A Tale of Three Patriots, Two Revolutions, and a Tragic Betrayal of Freedom in the New Nation* (New York: Basic Books, 2008), 90.

55 Blanck, "1783," 28, 45–9. Historians most often point to the economic motives for emancipation in Massachusetts, but T.H. Breen suggests that African Americans' push for liberty and liberal discourses on rights effectively ended the institution. See T.H. Breen, "Making History," 67–95.

56 Suffolk Files, *Walker v. Jennison*, 1783, case 153101, Worcester, Supreme Judicial Court, Judicial Archives, MA.

57 Notes on the testimony are limited to Cushing's notebook. William Cushing, William Cushing Judicial Notebook, 1783, Special Collections, Massachusetts Historical Society , 87–99.

58 Shane White, *Somewhat More Independent*, 10–14.

59 Suffolk files, *Massachusetts v. Asa Sparks,* October 1784, case 160036, Berkshire Supreme Judicial Court, Judicial Archives, MA.

CHAPTER 6: OPPORTUNITIES AND SETBACKS

1 "Wax Work," *Weekly Museum*, December 9, 1797; and James Truslow Adams, *History of the Town of Southampton (East of Canoe Place)* (New York: Hampton Press, 1918), 202–3.

2 On the importance of African American activism in ending slavery, see, for example, Shane White, *Somewhat More Independent*; Sinha, *The Slaves' Cause*; and Newman, *The Transformation of American Abolitionism*. Partnerships with whites and larger political issues played a role in the way slavery declined in New York, as scholars such as David Gellman show, though this chapter and the last argue violence was among the most important themes. David N. Gellman, *Emancipating New York: The Politics of Slavery and Freedom, 1777–1827* (Baton Rouge: LSU Press, 2006).

3 "Further European Advices by the Betsey, Capt. Sinclair, from London," *Daily Advertiser*, February 25, 1790; and "Philadelphia, Oct. 15," *Daily Advertiser*, October 20, 1791.

4 "Destruction of Port-au-Prince by fire," *Daily Advertiser*, December 29, 1791.

5 "Refined Cruelty," *Weekly Museum*, June 9, 1798. For an overview of the arguments on the impact of the Haitian Revolution on antislavery thought, see David Brion Davis, "The Impact of the French and Haitian Revolutions," in *The Impact of the Haitian Revolution in the Atlantic World*, ed. David P. Geggus (Columbia, SC: University of South Carolina Press, 2001), 3–9; Seymour Drescher, "The Limits of Example," in *The Impact of the Haitian Revolution in the Atlantic World*, 10–14; and Robin Blackburn, "The Force of Example," in *The Impact of the Haitian Revolution in the Atlantic World*, 15–20. See also David P. Geggus, "The Caribbean in the Age of Revolution," in *The Age of Revolutions in Global Context, c. 1760–1840*, ed. David Armitage and Sanjay Subrahmanyam (New York: Red Globe Press, 2010), 83–100; and Sara Fanning, "The Roots of Early Black Nationalism: Northern African Americans' Invocations of Haiti in the Early Nineteenth Century," *Slavery and Abolition* 28 (May 2007): 61–85.

6 "Fire at Albany," *Columbian Gazetteer*, November 25, 1793; "New York," *Vermont Journal*, December 9, 1793; "New York. Albany, Nov. 23. Fire!," *New Hampshire Journal*, November 29, 1793; Don R. Gerlach, "Black Arson in Albany, New York: November 1793," *Journal of Black Studies* 7 (March 1977): 301–312.

7 "Baltimore, Dec. 22. Serious Causes of Alarm," *Philadelphia Gazette*, December 26, 1796.

8 William Dunlap to Thomas Holcroft, 1797, in *Diary of William Dunlap, 1766–1839: The Memoirs of a Dramatist, Theatrical Manager, Painter, Critic, Novelist, and Historian* (1930; repr. New York: Benjamin Blom, 1969), 1:119–21.

9 Shane White, *Somewhat More Independent*, 141.

10 Gellman, *Emancipating New York*, 78–91. Scholars of northern slavery have rejected earlier arguments that slavery ended because it was not vital to the economy. In fact, the investment in slaves remained a major reason to hold onto slaves. Richard Shannon Moss, *Slavery on Long Island: A Study in Local Institutional and Early African-American Communal Life* (New York: Garland Publishing, 1993), 151–8.

11 Connecticut repealed its slave code in 1797. See *The Public Records of the State of Connecticut* (Hartford, CT: Published by the State, 1953), 9:91–2; and David Menschel, "Abolition without Deliverance: The Law of Connecticut Slavery, 1784–1848," *The Yale Law Journal* 111 (October 2001), 214–15.

12 *Laws of the State of New-York* (Albany, NY: Charles R. and George Webster, 1802), 1:61. Through 1829, the law continued to support accidental death in cases of "lawful correction" of servants and children. See *Revised Statutes of the State of New-York* (Albany, NY: Packard and Van Benthuysen, 1829), 3:660.

13 Edwin Olson, "Negro Slavery in New York, 1688–1827" (Ph.D. diss., New York University, 1938), 73.

14 *New York v. Ebenezer and Elizabeth Wilson*, January 10, 1795, Record Book, New York Oyer and Terminer, NYMA; and Moss, *Slavery on Long Island*, 100–1. In 1797, General Thomas Machlin was also apprehended after killing a slave, but no trial appears to have occurred. See Edwin Olson, "Social Aspects of Slave Life in New York," *Journal of Negro History* 26 (January 1941): 74.

15 Inquisition of Loo, Westchester, August 10, 1793; and Inquisition of Arnold Bloomer, Mamaroneck, January 17, 1793, Coroners Reports from New York State, NYHS.

16 Minutes of Meetings, Records and Reports of Committees, vol. 9, November 11, 1807, and April 12, 1808, New York Manumission Society, Records of the New York Manumission Society (hereafter NYMS), 9:178, 186, NYHS; Robert J. Swan, "John Teasman: African American Educator and the Emergence of Community in Early Black New York City, 1787–1815," *Journal of the Early Republic* 12 (Fall 1992): 331–56; Shane White, *Somewhat More Independent*, 84; Nash and Soderlund, *Freedom by Degrees*, 128.

17 Thomas Robert Moseley, "A History of the New-York Manumission Society, 1785–1849" (Ph.D. diss., New York University, 1963), 113.

18 NYMS, November 7, 1793, January 21, 1794, April 3, 1794, October 16, 1794, 7:23, 27, 34, NYHS.

19 NYMS, March 27, 1800, 155.

20 Among the witnesses was Tussell's employer, James Loines, who had developed concern for her when she was his servant. NYMS, July 3, 1800, August 22, 1800; December 10, 1800, 7:167, 169, 176.

21 W.J. Rorabaugh, *The Craft Apprentice: From Franklin to the Machine Age in America* (New York: Oxford University Press, 1986), 30.

22 William J. Gilmore, *Reading Becomes a Necessity of Life: Material and Cultural Life in Rural New England, 1780–1835* (Knoxville, TN: The University of Tennessee Press, 1989), chap. 3; Mary Kelly, *Learning to Stand and Speak: Women, Education, and Public Life in America's Republic* (Chapel Hill: University of North Carolina Press, 2006), 21–7; and C. Dallett Hemphill, *Bowing to Necessities: A History of Manners in America, 1620–1860* (New York: Oxford University Press, 1999), chap. 5.

23 The story of Joseph Belknap's abuse and Jeremy Belknap's mediation of the conflict is beautifully researched in Rorabaugh, *The Craft Apprentice*, 43–4.

24 In two additional cases, the causes of servants' protests are unknown. Minutes, 1784–1789, NYGS, NYMA; *Jacob Tyler Jr. v. Charles Horton*, May 1784, November 1785, and May 1786, Minutes, NYGS, NYMA.

25 *Jane French v. Michael Hughes*, August 1784, Minutes, NYGS, NYMA.

26 Benjamin Rush, *Thoughts upon the Amusements and Punishments Which Are Proper for Schools* (Philadelphia: s.n., 1790), 5; Benjamin Rush, *An Enquiry into the Effects of Public Punishments upon Criminals and upon Society. Read in the Society for Promoting Political Enquiries, Convened at the House of His Excellency Benjamin Franklin, Esquire, in Philadelphia, March 9th, 1787* (Philadelphia: Printed by Joseph James, 1787), 24; and Hemphill, *Bowing to Necessities*, 173.

27 Mark E. Kann, *Punishment, Prisons, and Patriarchy* (New York: New York University Press, 2005), 22–7, 37–9, 41–2.

28 Hemphill's review of advice manuals also bears this out. See Hemphill, *Bowing to Necessities*, 173 and 176.

29 *Christopher Johnson v. Joseph Haight*, August 1786; and *James Dunlass Bisset v. Robert Carter*, May 1788, Minutes, NYGS, NYMA.

30 Anna Mae Duane, *Suffering Childhood in Early America: Violence, Race, and the Making of the Child Victim* (Athens, GA: University of Georgia Press, 2010), chap 4.

31 Ryan, *Regulating Passion*, 122–4 and chap. 8.

32 Slave owners paid no cost for the maintenance of children as slavery declined, but such laws denied the legitimacy of former slaves caring for their own children. Gronningsater, "Born Free in the Master's House," 123–49.

33 Ruth Wallis Herndon, "'Proper Magistrates and Masters': Binding Out Poor Children in Southern New England, 1720–1820," in Herndon and Murray, ed., *Children Bound to Labor*, 50; Erica Armstrong Dunbar, *Fragile Freedom: African American Women and Emancipation in the Antebellum City* (New Haven: Yale University Press, 2008), chap. 2; and Melish, *Disowning Slavery*, 77–9, 101, and 113.

34 Brace, *The Blind African Slave*, 169-71, 174–77; Robert T. Teamoh, "Kidnapped in Boston," *Boston Daily Globe*, April 18, 1890; "Is 100 Years Old Today," *Boston Daily Globe*, April 15, 1895; Valerie Beaudrault, "Nancy (Minor) Washington: A Woman

of Three Centuries," *American Ancestors* 16 (Summer 2015): 38–41; and Melish, *Disowning Slavery*, chap. 3 and 4.

35 Brace, *The Blind African Slave*, 183-84.

36 John D. Cushing, ed., *The First Laws of the Commonwealth of Massachusetts* (Wilmington, DE: Michael Glazier, 1981), 347; and *Minutes of the Common Council of the City of New York, 1784–1831* (New York: 1917), 1:68.

37 *Laws of the State of New York* (Albany, NY: Webster and Skinner, 1802), 1:123 and 1:566–74.

38 George Thompson, "Pray Masters," *Massachusetts Spy*, November 15, 1792.

39 New-York Society for Promoting the Manumission of Slaves, and Protecting Such of Them as Have Been, or May Be, Liberated, "The constitution of the New York Society for Promoting the Manumission of Slaves, and Protecting Such of Them as Have Been, or May Be, Liberated," (New York: Printed by Hopkins, Webb & Co., 1796), 3–4.

40 Prince Hall, "A Charge," in *Pamphlets of Protest: An Anthology of Early African American Protest Literature, 1790–1860*, ed. Richard Newman, Patrick Rael, and Phillip Lapsansky (New York, Routledge, 2001), 47; and Joanna Brooks, "The Early American Public Sphere and the Emergence of a Black Print Counterpublic" *WMQ* 62 (January 2005): 76–85.

41 Elise Lemere relays the fascinating life of Brister Freeman in *Black Walden: Slavery and Its Aftermath in Concord, Massachusetts* (Philadelphia: University of Pennsylvania Press, 2009), 12, 151–4, 164–168. See also Cyrus Snow, "Memoir of Peter Wheeler," in *The Centennial of the Social Circle in Concord*, ed. Edward Waldo Emerson (Cambridge, MA: Riverside Press, 1882), 1:138, 140–1.

42 Hall, "A Charge," in *Pamphlets of Protest*, 47.

43 Arial Bragg, *Memoirs of Col. Arial Bragg* (Milford: George W. Stacy, 1846), 18.

44 Shane White, *Somewhat More Independent*, 156–7.

45 Daniel Davis to Boston Overseers of the Poor, August 28, 1803, Letters to the Overseers of the Poor, Judicial Archives, MA.

46 On the rise of companionate marriage, gender relations, and early national ideals, see Andrew Burnstein, *Sentimental Democracy: The Evolution of America's Romantic Self-Vision* (New York: Hill and Wang, 2000); Ruth H. Bloch, *Gender and Morality in Anglo-American Culture, 1650–1800* (Berkeley: University of California Press, 2003), 78–101; Anya Jabour, *Marriage in the Early Republic: Elizabeth and William Wirt and the Companionate Ideal* (Baltimore: Johns Hopkins University Press, 2002); and Lyons, *Sex among the Rabble*, 291, 296–8.

47 *The Medley*, October 30, 1795. The third lesson the minister drew from the story of Rachel and Jacob was that modern wives should be less grasping and demanding to secure the love of their husbands.

48 Joshua Stein found that among the more prominent types of violence discussed in newspapers and print literature from local courts were those about the murder and assaults of women, children, servants, and slaves. See Joshua Stein, "The Right to Violence: Assault Prosecution in New York, 1760–1840" (Ph.D. diss., UCLA, 2009), 140.

49 Rush also believed bodily pain was an effective means of punishing individuals, but emphasized other aspects of correction. Rush, *Thoughts upon the Amusements and Punishments Which Are Proper for Schools*, 3–4; Cleves, *The Reign of Terror in America*, 194–229; and Masur, *Rites of Execution*, 50–70.

50 Sheldon S. Cohen, "What Man Hath Put Asunder: Divorce in New Hampshire, 1681–1784," *Historical New Hampshire* 41 (1986): 118–41; and Randolph A. Roth, "Spousal Murder in Northern New England, 1776–1865," in Daniels and Kennedy, ed., *Over the Threshold*, 75.

51 The population in Massachusetts was 378,797 in 1790. The midpoint population (235,600) between 1760 (202,600) and 1780 (268,600) was used to measure the starting point. Record Book, Supreme Judicial Court, 1787–99, Judicial Archives, MA. For divorce data prior to 1787, see Cott, "Divorce and the Changing Status of Women in Eighteenth-Century Massachusetts," 604–6.

52 Record Book, Supreme Judicial Court, 1787–99, Judicial Archives, MA.

53 *Mary Walcut v. Jabez Walcut*, April 19, 1796; *Eunice Hichborn v. William Hichborn*, February 17, 1795; Record Book, Supreme Judicial Court, Judicial Archives, MA.

54 *Mary Hurley v. John Hurley*, July 24, 1792, Record Book, Supreme Judicial Court, Judicial Archives, MA.

55 *Experience Clap v. Samuel Clap*, May 17, 1791. For an example of another woman receiving a stipend, see *Mary Hurley v. John Hurley*, July 24, 1792, Record Book, Supreme Judicial Court, Judicial Archives, MA.

56 *Lucy Hawkins v. James Hawkins*, February 21, 1792; *Elizabeth Davis v. Elijah Davis*, February 17, 1795; *Phebe McBride v. John McBride*, April 17, 1792, Record Book, Supreme Judicial Court, Judicial Archives, MA. For an example of a petitioner able to list prostitutes' names, see *Levina Bigelow v. Francis Bigelow*, April 23, 1793, Record Book, Supreme Judicial Court, MA. For cases in which the judges only granted separations though women claimed adultery, see *Margarett Flinn v. Daniel Flinn*, May 9, 1791; and *Sarah Goodenow v. Frederick Goodenow*, February 18, 1794, Record Book, Supreme Judicial Court, Judicial Archives, MA.

57 Most commonly, petitions detailed that husbands had run away with other women and deserted the family. All New England states demanded portions of the petition be printed, but in Rhode Island petitioners were not required to detail the cause of the divorce. Instead, advertisements referred readers to the petition itself. See *Providence Gazette*, October 14, 1797, and February 10, 1798.

58 Priscilla Cheney petition, *Massachusetts Spy*, May 31, 1792.

59 The General Sessions of the Peace, the court which existed prior to 1800 to serve people in Suffolk County, did not create as many records as those of the Municipal Court of Boston. Record keeping suffered and many gaps exist in holdings prior to 1800. As the court system evolved and the occupation professionalized, JPs wrote more recognizances (bonds) and mittimuses (arrest warrants).

60 For the 1790s, see recognizances of Jonathan Bent (Sudbury), September 5, 1797, and Ruth Wheeler (Carlisle), September 5, 1797, File Papers, Middlesex General Sessions, Judicial Archives, MA; Hiram Stow (Petersham), June 29, 1791, Henry

Smith (Boylston), June 12, 1792, and Asa Fay, September 20, 1796, File papers, Worcester General Sessions, Judicial Archives, MA.

61 *Daily Advertiser,* July 29, 1790. Other newspapers also reported on the case in the exact same language, including *Connecticut Gazette,* July 30, 1790; *Essex Journal,* August 4, 1790; and *Western Star,* September 14, 1790. *Colonial Collegians: Biographies of Those Who Attended American Colleges before the War for Independence,* CD-ROM (Boston: Massachusetts Historical Society, New England Historic Genealogical Society, 2005), online database on https://AmericanAncestors.org (New England Historic Genealogical Society, 2008).

62 Respondent, "Mr. Collier," *Litchfield Monitor,* August 23, 1790.

63 Respondent, "Mr. Collier."

64 According to Franklin Bowditch Dexter, Jedediah Strong became a drunk and a vagrant after the incident, and he lost the esteem of his neighbors and friends. See Franklin Bowditch Dexter, *Biographical Sketches of the Graduates of Yale College: with Annals of the College History* (New York: H. Holt and Co., 1896), 2./10 20.

65 Jedediah countercharged Susannah in his own divorce petition with being "very violent, abuse, and unbecoming conduct," including "often interrupting and preventing FAMILY PRAYER." A Spectator, "Mr. Collier," *Litchfield Monitor,* September 27, 1790.

66 Thomas Knowles Deposition, Old South Church Records (Worcester), American Antiquarian Society (AAA), Box 2, folder 5; and Anonymous Deposition respecting Mr. Cook, Old South Church Records, AAA, Box 2, folder 5.

67 Whether Smith failed to act or others refused him is unknown. *Commonwealth v. Henry Smith,* November 1796 and March 1797, Record Book, Worcester General Sessions, Judicial Archives, MA.

68 *Commonwealth v. Uriah Hayden,* September 1789 and March 1790, Record Book, Worcester General Sessions, Judicial Archives, MA.

CHAPTER 7: RELATIONSHIP BUILDING

1 Peter Wheeler, *Chains and Freedom: Or, The Life and Adventures of Peter Wheeler, a Colored Man Yet Living. A Slave in Chains, a Sailor on the Deep, and a Sinner at the Cross,* ed. Graham Russell Gao Hodges (Tuscaloosa: The University of Alabama Press, 2009), 63.

2 As with the Pennsylvania Abolition Society (PAS), the legal strategy in New York derived from the lived experiences of African Americans who fought for safety. For more information on the PAS, see Newman, *The Transformation of American Abolitionism,* 60–85.

3 Shane White, *Somewhat More Independent,* 26; James Oliver Horton and Lois E. Horton, *In Hope of Liberty: Culture, Community and Protest Among Northern Free Blacks, 1700–1860* (New York: Oxford University Press, 1997), 83; Dunbar, *Fragile Freedom,* chap. 3; Campbell Gibson and Kay Jung, "Historical Census Statistics on Population Totals by Race, 1790–1900, and by Hispanic Origin, 1790–1990,

for The United States, Regions, Divisions, and States," U.S. Bureau of the Census, Population Division, Working Paper No. 56, September 2002, tables 36 and 47.

4 Similar patterns are visible in Jamaica and Guyana in the early nineteenth century. See Turner, *Contested Bodies*, chap. 3; and Browne, *Surviving Slavery*, chap. 2.

5 Sojourner Truth and Olive Gilbert, *Narrative of Sojourner Truth, a Northern Slave, Emancipated from Bodily Servitude by the State of New York, in 1828*, ed. Olive Gilbert (Boston: s.n., 1850), 31–3, 35.

6 Wheeler, *Chains and Freedom*, 71.

7 Deposition of John Marie Garvaize, August 11, 1801, in *People v. Marcell, et al.*, October 9, 1801, District Attorney Indictment Papers (hereafter DAIP), NYMA; NYMS, October 6, 1801, 7:202; Shane White, *Somewhat More Independent*, 144–5; Martha S. Jones, "Time, Space, and Jurisdiction in Atlantic World Slavery: The Volunbrun Household in Gradual Emancipation New York," *Law and History Review* 29 (November 2011): 1031–60.

8 A Friend to Candor, "To a Friend of Justice," *New York Gazette*, September 4, 1801; A Friend to Order, "For this Gazette," *New York Gazette*, August 24, 1801; and "Citizens of New York," *New York Gazette*, September 1, 1801.

9 A Friend to Order, "For this Gazette. To the Friend of Justice," *New York Gazette*, September 5, 1801.

10 A Friend of Justice, "For the American Citizen," *American Citizen*, August 28, 1801. Other defenders of the NYMS simply defended individuals or its history of work to prevent fraud and kidnapping. See S, *For the Daily Advertiser*, September 14, 1801.

11 Indeed, part of elites' self-fashioning of their identity was to display sympathy and assist those they perceived as lesser in status. See Nicole Eustace, *Passion is the Gale: Emotion, Power, and the Coming of the American Revolution* (Chapel Hill: University of North Carolina Press, 2008), chap. 6.

12 NYMS, January 11, 1803, February 1, 1803, 9:90, 93.

13 NYMS, July 11, 1809, 9:214.

14 New York issued two indictments each against Hoffman and Broad. *People v. Carl A. Hoffman*, October 8, 1804; *People v. Carl Hoffman*, February 11, 1805; *People v. Michael Sandford*, May 30, 1806; *People v. Joseph Goir*, April 11, 1807; *People v. Amos Broad* (2 cases), February 25, 1809; *People v. Demiss Broad*, February 25, 1809, DAIP, NYMA.

15 Between 1804 and 1807, the extent of NYMS involvement in the movement to attain indictments is not clear, though the standing committee was clearly active in hearing complaints of African Americans. Abbreviated reports made by the standing committee to the NYMS must be relied on previous to 1807. The standing committee record books are more complete after that time. NYMS, December 24, 1802, March 9, 1805, 7:237, 277.

16 Wright, slave to Hoffman, was noted to be eleven and a half to twelve years old. Betty, slave to Amos Broad, was described as a woman, while Sarah was three years old. No age was given for Frances, who was described as "a Black Girl," and

a fellow slave in the house, who was also named Frances, estimated to be eleven years old. See note 14.

17 *People v. Charles Smith*, November 16, 1801; *People v. George Braymer*, August 13, 1804; *People v. John Butler*, August 1804; *People v. John Young*, February 5, 1807 (two indictments), DAIP, NYMA.

18 Cayuga County indictments do not note the occupations or ages of the defendants. Jacob Fought, deposition, January 9, 1807, in *People v. John Young*, DAIP, NYMA.

19 John S. Yolton and Jean S. Yolton, "Introduction," in John Locke, *Some Thoughts Concerning Education* (New York: Oxford University Press, 1989), 1–69; Alexander Moseley, *John Locke* (London: Continuum, 2008), 118, 169; Jürgen Oelkers, *Jean-Jacques Rousseau* (London: Continuum, 2008), 93, 114–17, 212–13; and Reiner, *From Virtue to Character*, 1–19.

20 Bernard Wishy, *The Child and the Republic: The Dawn of Modern American Child Nurture* (Philadelphia: University of Pennsylvania Press, 1967), vii–viii; Karin Calvert, *Children in the House: The Material Culture of Early Childhood* (Boston: Northeastern University Press, 1992).

21 Robin Bernstein, *Racial Innocence: Performing American Childhood from Slavery to Civil Rights* (New York: New York University Press, 2011), 18 and chap. 1; Viviana A. Zelizer, *Pricing the Priceless Child: The Changing Social Value of Children* (New York: Basic Books, 1985); and Karen Sánchez-Eppler, *Dependent States: The Child's Part in Nineteenth-Century American Culture* (Chicago: University of Chicago Press, 2005), xxi.

22 Bernstein, *Racial Innocence*, 43; and Duane, *Suffering Childhood*, 152–9.

23 "Statement of the cruel treatment of Carl A. Hoffman to James Wright," in *People v. Carl A. Hoffman*, October 8, 1804; *People v. Carl Hoffman*, February 11, 1805, DAIP, NYMA; and NYMS, March 14, 1812, 10:165.

24 Writings about slavery in the early republic often presumed its immoral nature even if little was done on a national level to eradicate it, but antislavery activists used emotional appeals to draw in readers. Brycchan Carey, *British Abolitionism and the Rhetoric of Sensibility: Writing, Sentiment, and Slavery, 1760–1807* (New York: Palgrave MacMillan, 2005); Markman Ellis, *The Politics of Sensibility: Race, Gender, and Commerce in the Sentimental Novel* (New York: Cambridge University Press, 1996), chap. 2 and 3; Paul Finkelman, *Slavery and the Founders: Race and Liberty in the Age of Jefferson*, 2nd ed. (New York: M.E. Sharpe, 2001), 35–6, 115–17.

25 "Horrid Inhumanity," *New York Commercial Advertiser*, February 19, 1805; William Cowper, *The Task: A Poem, In Six Books. To Which Is Added, Tirocinium: Or, A Review of Schools* (Philadelphia: Printed for Thomas Dobson, 1787); and Benjamin Lamb-Books, *Angry Abolitionists and the Rhetoric of Slavery: Moral Emotions in Social Movements* (New York: Palgrave MacMillan, 2016), 93–119.

26 Bernstein, *Racial Innocence*, 30–68; Eustace, *Passion is the Gale*, 41–3, 70–2, 299; Robin Blackburn, *The American Crucible: Slavery, Emancipation, and Human Rights* (London: Verso, 2011), 157.

27 Robert Pickering, affidavit, February 19, 1806 in *People v. Michael Sandford*, May 30, 1806, DAIP Papers, NYMA.

28 *People v. Amos Broad*, February 25, 1809 (two indictments); *People v. Demiss Broad*, February 25, 1809; *People v. Carl A. Hoffman*, October 8, 1804, DAIP, NYMA.

29 *People v. Michael Sandford*, May 30, 1809 (two witnesses); *People v. Joseph Goir*, April 11, 1807 (three witnesses), DAIP, NYMA.

30 Goir failed to register his slaves when they entered New York as the gradual emancipation law required, and Eddy likely threatened Goir that the NYMS would bring a suit questioning his ownership of Frances unless he allowed her medical treatment. C.M. Slocum, letter to Grand Jury of New York City, April 9, 1807, in *People v. Joseph Goir*, April 11, 1807, DAIP, NYMA.

31 *People v. Michael Sandford*, May 30, 1806, DAIP, NYMA; and NYMS, October 14, 1807, and November 1, 1807, 9:174.

32 NYMS, November 17, 1807, April 12, 1808, May 3, 1808, 9:176, 182, 186.

33 Three separate indictments were drawn up: Amos for beating Betty, Amos for beating Sarah, and Demiss for beating Sarah. Mary Tillick, affidavit, n.d.; Levina Van Wyck, affidavit, n.d.; in *People v. Amos Broad* and *People v. Demiss Broad*, February 25, 1809, DAIP, NYMA; and NYMS, April. 11, 1809, 9:212.

34 David Fielder, affidavit, n.d., in *People v. Amos Broad*, February 25, 1809.

35 Wheeler, *Chains and Freedom*, 68-9, 79-80.

36 Among the more highly circulated ideas regarding pain and race during this time period was that women of color suffered less pain during childbirth. See Margaret Abruzzo, *Polemical Pain: Slavery, Cruelty, and the Rise of Humanitarianism* (Baltimore: Johns Hopkins University Press, 2011), 178–9; Robin Blackburn, *The Making of New World Slavery: From the Baroque to the Modern, 1492–1800* (New York: Verso, 1998), 345, 424–5; Thomas F. Gossett, *Race: The History of an Idea in America* (New York: Oxford University Press, 1997), 49; and Jennifer Morgan, *Laboring Women*, 18, 40, 45, 48, 65.

37 For example, see Vani A. Mathur, Tokiko Harada, Trixie Lipke, and Joan Y. Chiao, "Neural Basis of Extraordinary Empathy and Altruistic Motivation," *NeuroImage* 51 (July 15, 2010): 1468–75; and Matteo Forgiarini, Marcello Gallucci, and Angelo Maravita, "Racism and the Empathy for Pain on Our Skin," *Frontiers in Psychology* 2 (May 2011).

38 Thomas Mace, deposition, August 25, 1810, in *New York v. Titus*, October 5, 1810; Paul Cartagnet, deposition, September 12, 1810, in *New York v. Thomas Mace*, October 5, 1810, DAIP, NYMA.

39 Reported assaults were found in the Recognizance Papers, New York General Sessions, 1800–8, NYMA, and an examination of indictment papers from 1790 through 1811. Gaps in the 1790s suggest that more cases exist. See DAIP, 1790–1811, NYMA.

40 Slaves assaulted accountants, tailors, hucksters, grocers, hairdressers, and others. Three cases exist of more than one white person reporting threats by a single slave. See Lott D. Camp, August 22, 1801; Casiir Perrez, August 22, 1801; James

Nelson and Charlotte Weldon, September 3, 1807; Thomas, October 22, 1807, in Recognizance Papers, New York General Sessions, 1800–1808, NYMA.

41 Euphenia, deposition, November 26, 1806, in *People v. Margaret and Diana*, December 8, 1806, DAIP, NYMA. For a case of a slave put to death, see Daniel Allen Hearn, *Legal Executions in New York State, 1639–1963* (Jefferson, NC: McFarland Publishing, 1997), 29.

42 "Slavery," *Republican Watch Tower*, August 25, 1804. For other examples, see "Negro Slavery Unjustifiable," *Daily Advertiser*, February 23, 1803; and "Slavery," *Republican Watch Tower*, August 29, 1804 (from a Kentucky speech on slavery).

43 Advertisement, *Evening Post*, March 6, 1809, p. 3; Advertisement, *Evening Post*, March 9, 1809; "Amos Broad," *American Citizen*, March 13, 1809; "Amos Broad," *Republican Watch Tower*, March 14, 1809. *Evening Post* mocked Amos Broad for his barbarity in a piece that suggested he was being considered for a "Minister to Algiers and the other *Barbary* powers," who were known for their mistreatment of American prisoners. See *Evening Post*, March 9, 1809. Karen Halttunen, "Humanitarianism and Pornography of Pain in Anglo-American Culture," *The American Historical Review* 100 (April 1995): 303–34.

44 "Advertisement," *Portsmouth Oracle*, April 1, 1809.

45 Whether the courts, Overseers, or parents took the servant away is unclear. No record exists in the minutes of New York City. *The trial of Amos Broad and his wife, on three several indictments for assaulting and beating Betty, a slave, and her little female child Sarah, aged three years to which is added, the motion of counsel in Mr. Broad's behalf* (New York: Henry C. Southwick, 1809), 7, 15.

46 Wheeler, *Chains and Freedom*, 68.

47 "Statement of the cruel treatment of Carl A. Hoffman to James Wright," n.d, in *People v. Carl A. Hoffman*, October 8, 1804, DAIP, NYMA. Judges used slave testimony in Maryland as well. See Loren Schweninger, "Freedom Suits, African American Women, and the Genealogy of Slavery," *WMQ* 61 (January 2014): 35–62.

48 Margaret Faupell appears to have reported the violence against Sarah and Betty almost immediately upon leaving the employment of the Broads, and the lawyers questioned her reasons for doing so at the trial. New York issued the indictment on February 25 and she had left the employ of the Broads on the fifteenth. Margaret Faupell, affidavit, n.d., in *People v. Amos Broad*, February 25, 1809.

49 Wheeler, *Chains and Freedom*, 98.

50 Studies touching on violence and African Americans' response during the early national era include Brooks, "The Early American Public Sphere and the Emergence of a Black Print Counterpublic"; Emma Jones Lapsansky, "'Since they Got Those Separate Churches': Afro-Americans and Racism in Jacksonian Philadelphia," *American Quarterly*, 32 (Spring 1980): 54–78; Melish, *Disowning Slavery*, 75 and 199–204; Gary Nash, *Forging Freedom*, 172–211; and Shane White, *Somewhat More Independent*.

51 Samuel Dexter, Weston, February 23, 1795; Thomas Pemberton, Boston, November 12, 1795; in "Queries relating to slavery in Massachusetts," in *Collection of Massachusetts Historical Society*, 3 (1877): 386, 393.

52 John Dickinson, deposition, February 10, 1809; Richard Hutson, deposition, February 10, 1809; in *People v. James Downey*, March 3, 1809, DAIP, NYMA.

53 Jeffrey Bolster, *Black Jacks: African American Seamen in the Age of Sail* (Cambridge, MA: Harvard University Press, 1997), chap. 3; Hodges, *Root & Branch*, 149, 206–7; Horton and Horton, *In Hope of Liberty*, 112–13; and Paul A. Gilje, *Liberty on the Waterfront: American Maritime Culture in the Age of the Revolution* (Philadelphia: University of Pennsylvania Press, 2004), 77.

54 James Greenfield, complaint, March 31, 1805; Obediah Delan, Daniel Proctor, Thomas Gleaves, Robert Matthews, Thomas Edes, Catherine Crafty, Patty Martin, Sukey Flagnor, and Jonathan Atwood, recognizance, March 31, 1805; Jonathan Atwood, complaint, March 31, 1805; File Papers, Municipal Court of Boston (hereafter MCB), Judicial Archives, MA.

55 Three attackers were identified as mariners and one was identified as a mariner alias shipwright. Rozanna Dalton, complaint, May 17, 1805; Reuban Knights, recognizance, May 14, 1805; Samuel Don, recognizance, May 13, 1817; *Commonwealth v. James Wilkins and Henry Hatsom*, Indictment, June 1805, File Papers, MCB, Judicial Archives, MA.

56 Jacob Cromwell, complaint, September 20, 1805, File Papers, MCB, Judicial Archives, MA; *Commonwealth v. Matthias Murch*, September and November 1805, Record Book, MCB; Joseph Brown, recognizance, December 21, 1805, File Papers, MCB, Judicial Archives, MA. *Commonwealth v. Thomas Darling*, October 1801, Record Book, MCB, Judicial Archives, MA.

57 William Grimes, *Life of William Grimes, The Runaway Slave* (New York: s.n., 1825), 58.

58 Austin Steward, *Twenty-Two Years a Slave, and Forty Years a Free Man; Embracing a Correspondence of Several Years, While President of Wilberforce Colony, London, Canada West* (Rochester, NY: William Ailing, 1857), 125; and Grimes, *Life of William Grimes*, 57-58.

59 Leslie M. Alexander, *African or American? Black Identity and Political Activism in New York City, 1784–1861* (Urbana: University of Illinois Press, 2012), 26–31, 45–52; Harris, *In The Shadow of Slavery*, chap. 3; James Brewer Stewart, "The Emergence of Racial Modernity and the Rise of the White North, 1790–1840," *Journal of the Early Republic* 18 (Summer 1998): 181–217.

60 A great deal of literature exists on this topic and the role of institution building in black communities. Among the more recent are Alexander, *African or American?* 1–23; Horton and Horton, *In Hope of Liberty*, 125–54; Patrick Rael, *Black Identity and Black Protest in the Antebellum North* (Chapel Hill: University of North Carolina Press, 2002); and Sinha, *The Slave's Cause*, 113–22, 130–51.

61 Eleanor Rawkin, deposition, November 4, 1806, in *People v. Eleanor Rawkin*, December 8, 1806, DAIP, NYMA.

62 Diana Paton, "Witchcraft, Poison, Law, and Atlantic Slavery," *WMQ* 69 (April 2012): 235–64.

63 Statistical evidence of assaults is problematic because the total number of assaults is unknown—only reported assaults where the race of perpetrator and victim could be established were counted. Race is not typically entered in official record books, with some JPs practicing more definition than others on forms. Cross-analysis with city directories in New York and Boston was also necessary. The irregularity with which JPs and SPs denoted race on recognizances and indictments makes the figure a rough estimate of total assaults. Record Books and File Papers, MCB, 1800–10, Judicial Archives, MA; and DAIP, 1800–10, NYMA.

64 New York issued thirty-one indictments, and Boston tried at least eleven cases. JPs issued sixty-four recognizances denoting complaints of white-on-black violence. The irregularity with which JPs and SPs denoted race on recognizances and indictments make the figure a rough estimate of total assaults. Record Books, BCB, 1800–10, Judicial Archives, MA; and DAIP, 1800–10, NYMA.

65 Between 1790 and 1813 in Boston, African Americans initiated at least seventy-one cases against other African Americans; and in New York City between 1800 and 1810, twenty-six suits emerged. Writs of Commitment, Elijah Adlow Papers, Special Collections, BPL, Box 145, folder 1 and Box 150, folder 2; File Papers and Record Books, MCB, 1800–1810, MA; DAIP, 1800–1810, NYMA.

66 Only one case of cross-racial violence in which a white person was the perpetrator was found in indictment papers for Cayuga County between 1795 and 1810. See *People v. William Martin*, December 24, 1795, Indictment Papers, Cayuga County General Sessions, Records Retention, Cayuga County Government. No records were found in Worcester or Middlesex. See Record Book, Worcester Court of Common Pleas, 1804–10; Record Book, Worcester General Sessions, 1800–3; Record Book, Middlesex General Sessions, 1800–3; Record Book, Middlesex Court of Common Pleas, 1805–10, Judicial Archives, MA; and Record Book, Cayuga County General Sessions, 1799–1810, Records Retention, Cayuga County Government.

67 Wheeler, *Chains and Freedom*, 109.

68 John Reed, Thomas Cooper, Elizabeth Cooper, and Mary Reed, recognizance, May 19, 1814, File Papers, MCB, Judicial Archives, MA.

69 Dunbar, *Fragile Freedom*, 73–4, 116.

70 Rosanna Dalton, recognizance, May 17, 1805; Susan Butler, recognizance, May 17, 1805; file papers, MCB, Judicial Archives, MA. Anna Willis Brown, Louisa Hampshire, and Isabella Marshall were routine defendants and plaintiffs in Boston. For example, see Anna Willis Brown, complaint, January 25, 1804, and March 1, 1806, file papers, MCB, Judicial Archives, MA.

71 The case was settled outside of court and Cooney planned a civil suit. *People v. Henry Stanton, Thomas McGuire, and Coenradt Rawba*, November 14, 1801; and William J. Waldron, affidavit, September 17, 1801, DAIP, NYMA. Shane White also discusses this case in *Somewhat More Independent*, 207–8.

72 John Harring, affidavit, October 7, 1800, in *People v. Michael Gates*, October 7, 1800, DAIP, NYMA.

73 Lack of prosecution is discernible in two ways. Cases in which recognizances for assaults were completed and no indictments were found serve as one group of records. For example, see Juliana Smith and Maschack Stevenson, January 3, 1805, and Cato Randall, August 12, 1805, recognizance papers, NYMA. In addition, New York City indictment records have a number of cases in which the outcome of the case is not listed on the indictment. Usually indictments record the pleas of the defendants as well as the outcomes of the trials. Several cases with African American witnesses note neither of these, revealing that the case likely never made it to trial. For examples, see *People v. David Howell*, October 7, 1800; *People v. Thomas Smith*, April 10, 1802; *People v. Jasper Crospie*, December 9, 1805; DAIP, NYMA.

74 Cases with white witnesses were also not guaranteed success, as in the case of Jones, in which her attacker was found not guilty. For examples of acquittals, see *People v. Louis Humphrey, Alexander Simpson, and Nathaniel Rider*, June 9, 1803, DAIP, NYMA.

75 Daniel Sweeney, deposition, January 2, 1806, in *People v. Daniel Sweeney*, January 17, 1806; and David Cannon, deposition, August 10, 1815, in *People v. Henry Nichols and William Nichols*, September 15 and 16, 1815, DAIP, NYMA; Shane White, *Somewhat More Independent*, 173–179; and Gilje, *The Road to Mobocracy*, 127–8.

76 John Williamson, affidavit, January 2, 1805, in *People v. James Woods, James Shaw, and Simon Burton*, January 9, 1805; George Ennis, affidavit, July 5, 1803, in *People v. Joseph William and Abraham*, August 6, 1803, DAIP, NYMA.

77 Charles Edwards Lester in Peter Wheeler, *Chains and Freedom*, 129.

CHAPTER 8: LEGAL STRATEGIES FOR CIVIL RIGHTS

1 *Report of the trial of Pienovi for biting off his wife's nose: extracted from the New-York judicial repository for September, 1818* (New York, 1818), 5–6; *People v. Lawrence Pienovi*, July 15, 1818, DAIP, NYMA.

2 All of the existing legal papers for the Municipal Court of the Town of Boston (1800–20) and District Attorney Indictment Papers in New York City were examined to discover cases of spousal violence, as were locations in Cayuga County, New York, and Worcester, Plymouth, and Middlesex Counties, Massachusetts. File Papers and Record Books, MCB, Judicial Archives, MA; Elijah Adlow Papers, Special Collections, BPL; and DAIP, 1800–19, NYMA.

3 File papers, MCB, 1800–4 and 1816–20, Judicial Archives, MA; Mixed Recognizances, Mixed Criminal Complaints, and Writs of Commitment Papers, Adlow Collection, BPL, boxes 71, 149, 150, 170, 262, 270A, 316, and 325. The first surges of growth in the number of women reporting assaults may have begun during the 1790s. Remaining records show that between 1790 and 1795, 1.5 cases were reported per year, with 0.5 cases reported per 1000 people.

4 Of the fifty-five recorded defaults, all but five are recorded between 1817 and 1820, suggesting more intensive record notations toward the latter end of the decade. File papers from Middlesex and Worcester counties do not note that any men defaulted. However, this is likely due to a lack of recordkeeping rather than

men's adherence to government strictures. File papers, MCB, 1800–20, Judicial Archives, MA; Elijah Adlow Papers, Special Collections, BPL.

5 Between 1787 and 1820, forty-one women declared cruelty in their divorce petitions. The number of cruelty cases during the period between 1787 and 1799 covered the entire state. In 1797 and 1798, Massachusetts moved to county courts rather than statewide courts as the population grew. For the period after 1800, I focused on Nantucket, Worcester, Middlesex, and Suffolk. The number of divorces in the years 1800–9 and 1810–19 were compared to the combined total of the population from these four counties in 1800 and 1810. For Suffolk and Nantucket, records from the years 1818 and 1819 are missing. To create the figure prior to 1800, an average number of suits per decade was calculated using Cott's findings for divorce for 1755–64, 1765–74, and 1777–86 in comparison with the population of Massachusetts in 1760, 1770, and 1780. See Record Books, Worcester Supreme Judicial Court, 1800–19; Record Book, Middlesex Supreme Judicial Court, 1800–19; and Suffolk and Nantucket SJC, Record Books, 1805–16, Judicial Archives, MA; Cott, "Divorce and the Changing Status of Women in Eighteenth-Century Massachusetts," 592; Jesse Chickering, *A Statistical View of the Population of Massachusetts, from 1765 to 1840* (Boston: Charles C. Little and James Brown, 1846), 15–22 and 33; and Bureau of the Census, *Historical Statistics of the United States: Colonial Times to 1957* (Washington, DC, 1960), 756.

6 *People v. William Gautier*, October 12, 1812; *People v. William Gautier*, April 12, 1813, DAIP, NYMA.

7 Jacob D. Wheeler, *Reports of Criminal Law Cases: Decided at the City-hall of the City of New York, with Notes and References*, vol. 2 (New York: Banks, Gould, & Co, 1851), 347–8; and *People v. Jan Garretson, Susan Brown, and Hannah Thompson*, June 1823, Record Book, New York General Sessions, NYMA.

8 Wheeler, *Reports of Criminal Law Cases*, 2: 348. The race of the participants is not entirely clear in this case. Susan Brown is listed as a black head of household in the 1820 census, but no listing exists for Titus Oliver.

9 On women's rising activism, see Catherine Allgor, *Parlor Politics: In Which the Ladies of Washington Help Build a City and a Government* (Charlottesville: University of Virginia Press, 2000); Anne M. Boylan, *The Origins of Women's Activism, New York and Boston, 1797–1840* (Chapel Hill: University of North Carolina Press, 2002); Lori D. Ginzberg, *Women and the Work of Benevolence: Morality, Politics, and Class in the Nineteenth-Century United States* (New Haven: Yale University Press, 1990); Lori D. Ginzberg, *Women in Antebellum Reform* (Wheeling: Harlan Davidson, 2000), 15–28; and Jane Pease and William Pease, *Ladies, Women and Wenches: Choice and Constraint in Antebellum Charleston and Boston* (Chapel Hill: University of North Carolina Press, 1990), 123.

10 See Linda Kerber, "The Republican Mother: Women and the Enlightenment; An American Perspective," *American Quarterly* 28 (Summer 1976): 187–205; Kerber, *No Constitutional Right to be Ladies*; Nancy Cott, *Bonds of Womanhood: Women's Sphere in New England, 1780–1835*, 2nd ed. (New Haven: Yale University

Press, 1997); Jan Lewis, "The Republican Wife: Virtue and Seduction in the Early Republic," *WMQ* 44 (October 1987): 689–721; Nancy Isenberg, *Sex and Citizenship in Antebellum America* (Chapel Hill: University of North Carolina Press, 1998); Barbara Welter, "The Cult of True Womanhood: 1820–1860," *American Quarterly* 18 (Summer 1966): 151–74; and Zagarri, *Revolutionary Backlash*, chap. 1–3.

11 Jane E. Dabel, *A Respectable Woman: The Public Roles of African American Women in 19th-Century New York* (New York: New York University Press, 2009); Horton and Horton, *In Hope of Liberty*, chap. 6; Dunbar, *Fragile Freedom*, chap. 3; and Alexander, *African or American?*, 66–8.

12 Dunbar, *Fragile Freedom*, 63–8.

13 One hundred forty-two complaints or recognizances listed husbands' occupations in Boston. By 1815, records noted less often the occupation and race of assailants as JPs moved toward preprinted forms. A search of the Boston City Directories was used for cases that did not include occupations, and an additional twenty-six occupations were found. Many of the occupations not mentioned above would be associated with the lower sort, including cartmen, riggers, painters, and truckmen. Men's occupations included sixty-eight laborers; sixteen mariners; twelve traders; seven housewrights; four each of cordwainers, truckmen, and ropemakers; three each of hairdressers and cartmen; two each of gentlemen, yeomen, riggers, tailors, and painters; and various other professions with only one complaint per profession. Record Books and File Papers, Suffolk General Sessions of Peace; File Papers and Record Books, MCB, Judicial Archives, MA; and Elijah Adlow Papers, BPL; *The Boston City Directory,1813, 1816, 1818* (Boston: E. Cotton, 1813, 1816, 1818); *The Boston Directory, 1820* (Boston: John H.A. Frost and Charles Stimson, 1820).

Although occupation does not perfectly correlate with economic status, there are strong indicators that these would most likely be occupations of the lower sort. On occupational categories, see Gary B. Nash, *The Urban Crucible: Social Change, Political Consciousness, and the Origins of the American Revolution* (Cambridge, MA: Harvard University Press, 1979), appendix, table 1, 387–417; and John L. Brooke, *The Heart of the Commonwealth: Society and Political Culture in Worcester County, Massachusetts, 1713–1861* (New York: Cambridge University Press, 1989), 42–7.

14 Several historians have attempted to discern the number of laborers and seamen in early North American cities, but these numbers, as each of these historians suggests, are underestimated. See Jacqueline Barbara Carr, *After the Siege: A Social History of Boston, 1775–1800* (Boston: Northeastern University Press, 2005), 148, 163, and 273n3; Alan Kulikoff, "The Progress of Inequality in Revolutionary Boston," *WMQ* 28 (July 1971): 411–12; Nash, *The Urban Crucible*, 388–91; Richard Oestreicher, "The Counted and Uncounted: The Occupational Structure of Early American Cities," *Journal of Social History* 28 (Winter 1994): 354–6; and Billy G. Smith, *The "Lower Sort": Philadelphia's Laboring People, 1750–1800* (Ithaca: Cornell University Press, 1990), 214.

15 In Middlesex County, men's occupations included four husbandmen, two each
of laborers and yeomen, and one each of clockmaker, gentleman, and miller. In
Worcester County, men's occupations were four yeomen, as well as one each of
blacksmith, gentlemen, laborer, and husbandman/laborer. Record Books and
File papers, Middlesex County General Sessions, 1753–1801; Justice of the Peace
Papers, Middlesex Superior Court, 1789–1806; File Papers and Record Books,
Worcester General Session of the Peace, 1780–1803; Docket Books and File Pa-
pers, Worcester Court of Common Pleas,1800–6, Judicial Archives, MA.

16 Records of eight complaints made by African American women are preserved,
and African Americans made up almost 5 percent of Boston's population between
1790 and 1820. JPs did not note race with regularity after the 1810s, so more records of African Americans may exist. See George Bowers, March 6, 1804; Nancy
Myers, September 13, 1804; Thomas Jackson, June 5, 1805; Thomas Clark, July 25,
1805; Cuff Buffam, August 20, 1805; Anthony Browning, July 10, 1806; Nathaniel
Henry, July 30, 1813; and Samuel Sampson, May 10, 1820, File Papers, MCB, Judicial Archives, MA. On the African American population, see Horton and Horton,
In Hope of Liberty, 83.

17 Characterizations of women as wealthy stem from the occupations of their
husbands. See Jonathan Bent (gentleman), recognizance, September 5, 1797, File
Papers, Middlesex General Sessions, MA; John Barnard (gentleman), August 11,
1800, Docket Book, Worcester Court of Common Pleas; and File Papers, Worcester General Sessions of the Peace, MA; Louis Dumariel (gentleman), September
17, 1807; and John Hill (gentleman), September 1, 1807, File Papers, MCB, Judicial
Archives, MA. For an example of a JP assisting another elite man, see Ryan, *Regulating Passion*, 46–7. For New York, see *People v. William Roberts* (gentleman),
April 11, 1807; *People v. Charles Tooker* (merchant); December 7, 1808; *People v. Edward E. Davis* (physician), November 26, 1812; *People v. Neal McNeal* (merchant),
July 6 and 7, 1815, DAIP, NYMA.

18 David Ralph Johnson, *Policing the Urban Underworld: The Impact of Crime on the
Development of the American Police, 1800–1887* (Philadelphia: Temple University
Press, 1979); and Ryan, *Regulating Passion*, chap. 8.

19 Abigail Bailey, *Memoirs of Mrs. Abigail Bailey, Who Had Been the Wife of Major
Asa Bailey, Formerly of Landaff, (N.H.) Written by Herself*, ed. Ethan Smith, in *Religion and Domestic Violence in Early New England: The Memoirs of Abigail Bailey*,
ed. Ann Taves (Bloomington: Indiana University Press, 1989), 57–8 and 87–8.

20 Custody of children was another important matter influencing Watson. Timothy
Kenslea, *The Sedgwicks in Love: Courtship, Engagement, and Marriage in the Early
Republic* (Boston: Northeastern University Press, 2006), 77–81. On elite southern
women and the ways the family of origin could be used to shelter women from
marital violence, see Lindsey Keiter, "'I fear some interference may be necessary
to rescue her': Out of Court Responses to Spousal Abuse in the Early Republic,"
paper presented at the annual meeting of the Society of Historians of the Early
American Republic, St. Louis, July 20, 2013.

21 Of the nineteen women who sued for divorce with cruelty as grounds in Middle-sex, Suffolk, Nantucket, and Worcester counties, the women were married to three physicians; two each of gentlemen, tailors, and traders; and one each of merchant, yeoman, caulker, stevedore, beef packer, hairdresser, tin plate worker, husbandman, cordwainer, and mariner. See Record Books, Suffolk and Nantucket SJC, 1802–18; Record Books, Worcester SJC, 1798–1820; and Record Books, Middlesex SJC, 1797–1820, Judicial Archives, MA.

22 Women of the early republic actively integrated and pushed for the continuation of new rights to education, respect, and safety in their daily lives prior to the organiza-tion of associations, which would more commonly define civil rights movements of later eras. See Daniel Scott Smith, "Family Limitation, Sexual Control, and Domes-tic Feminism in Victorian America," *Feminist Studies* 1 (Winter-Spring 1973): 40–57; and Susan Klepp, "Women and the Fertility Transition in the Mid-Atlantic Region," *JAH* 85 (December 1988): 910–40. On women who took action against seduction, the sexual double standard, and education prior to the 1830s, see Steven Mintz, *Moralists and Modernizers: America's Pre–Civil War Reformers* (Baltimore: Johns Hopkins University Press, 1995), 66–9; Mary Kelley, *Learning to Stand and Speak: Women, Education, and Public Life in America's Republic* (Chapel Hill: University of North Carolina Press, 2008), chap. 1–3; and Ryan, *Regulating Passion*, chap. 7.

23 NYMS, March 3, 1809, March 21, 1809, April 19, 1809, May 2, 1809, August 11, 1809, November 23, 1812, 10:61, 63, 69, 70, 77, 189.

24 One case was excluded from this time period because it referred to treatment of slaves in Nassau. NYMS, March 20, 1810 (two cases), May 15, 1810 (two cases), July 3, 1810, July 16, 1811, August 25, 1811, October 15, 1811, February 3, 1812, March 14, 1812, May 11, 1812, October 5, 1812, November 23, 1812, 10:95, 98, 99, 103, 136, 140, 148, 162, 165, 173, 184, 189.

25 *Laws of the State of New York*, 4:143.

26 NYMS, February 6, 1818, 11:12.

27 NYMS, February 6, 1818, 11:12; *People v. Betsey Paulding*, February 4, 1817, October 14, 1817, November 10, 1818; Mary Plume, deposition, November 8, 1815, in *People v. Maria*, November 11, 1815; Phoebe Dodge, deposition, October 24, 1815, in *People v. Paul Plume*, November 11, 1815, DAIP, NYMA.

28 Steward, *Twenty-Two Years a Slave*, 99.

29 Steward, *Twenty-Two Years a Slave*, 57–8.

30 Steward, *Twenty-Two Years a Slave*, 59, 107.

31 Henry Johnson, *An oration on the abolition of the slave trade, by Henry Johnson; with an introductory address by Adam Carman; delivered in the African Church in New-York, Jan. 1, 1810* (New York: Printed by John C. Totten, 1810), 11–12.

32 Martha S. Putney, *Black Sailors: Afro-American Merchant Seamen and Whalemen Prior to the Civil War* (Westport, CT: Greenwood Press, 1987), 37–8, 90; Bolster, *Black Jacks*, 114 and chap. 5; Gene Allen Smith, *The Slaves' Gamble: Choosing Sides in the War of 1812* (New York: Palgrave MacMillan, 2013), 49–55, 133–8; Swan, "John Teasman," 352–3; and Shane White, *Somewhat More Independent*, 150–1.

33 Gene Allen Smith, *The Slaves' Gamble*, 51–57.

34 Mary Walker, William Walkers, Sarah Ann Mills, Ann Lozier, Jane Lozier, Margaret McGoran, and Francis Walker, deposition, July 18, 1818, in *Eliza Sears v. William and Sara Gray*, July 14, 1818, DAIP, NYMA.

35 Sean Wilentz, *Chants Democratic: New York City and the Rise of the American Working Class, 1788–1850* (New York: Oxford University Press, 1984), 31–35.

36 The records do not indicate whether this was Fox's or Dixon's first experience with violence, or if they had repeatedly been abused by their masters. If the abuse was ongoing, Fox and Dixon may have been mindful that the courts would not intervene for young adults who routinely resisted commands. *People v. Joseph Fox*, January 8, 1819; *People v. Samuel Dixon*, February 9, 1819, DAIP, NYMA.

37 Lisa B. Lubow, "Artisans in Transition: Early Capitalist Development and the Carpenters of Boston, 1787–1837" (Ph.D. diss, UCLA, 1987), 190–224; Gary J. Kornblith, "The Artisanal Response to Capitalist Transformation," *Journal of the Early Republic* 10 (Autumn 1990), 317–18; Sharon V. Salinger, *"To Serve Well and Faithfully": Labor and Indentured Servants in Pennsylvania, 1682–1800* (New York: Cambridge University Press, 1987), 137–40; Wilentz, *Chants Democratic*, 1–103; Howard Rock, *Artisans of the New Republic: The Tradesmen of New York City in the Age of Jefferson* (New York: New York University Press, 1984), 236–63.

38 The pace toward consolidation was uneven and varied by region. Christopher L. Tomlins, *Law, Labor, and Ideology in the Early American Republic* (New York: Cambridge University Press, 1993), 101–5, 128–152; Wilentz, *Chants Democratic*, 27–60; and Gilje, *The Road to Mobocracy*, 175–202.

39 *New York Daily Advertiser*, May 17, 1819; and Harris, *In the Shadow of Slavery*, 113–15.

40 The court settled one case and convicted in the other. Samuel Warner, white apprentice to a sailmaker, assaulted his master, in 1812; in 1814, Hiram Barter, a dyer's servant, also assaulted his master. *People v. Samuel B. Warner*, April 10, 1812 (convicted); *People v. Hiram Baxter* February 17, 1814 (settled) DAIP, NYMA.

41 Teamoh, "Kidnapped in Boston"; "Is 100 Years Old Today," *Boston Daily Globe*, April 15, 1895; and Beaudrault, "Nancy (Minor) Washington: A Woman of Three Centuries."

42 Nancy Prince, *A Black Woman's Odyssey Through Russia and Jamaica: The Narrative of Nancy Prince* (New York: Marcus Wiener Publishing, 1990), 3–15.

43 For whites who were witnesses to assaults on African Americans, see, for example, *People v. John Curran*, August 6, 1814; "Letter of Grand Jury in *People v. Noel Corbet*," May 6, 1815, in *People v. Noel Corbet*, June 8, 1815, DAIP, NYMA.

44 Prince, *A Black Woman's Odyssey*, 10–11.

45 Jessica Milward shows how extensive and yet invisible African Americans' work became. See Jessica Milward, *Finding Charity's Folk: Enslaved and Free Black Women in Maryland* (Athens, GA: University of Georgia Press, 2015). See also Adams and Pleck, *Love of Freedom*, chap. 5–7; Harris, *In the Shadow of Slavery*, 82; and Horton and Horton, *Black Bostonians*, 22. John E. Murray's scholarship on

the actions poor white women took in Charleston to advocate for their children is instructive. See John E. Murray, "Poor Mothers, Stepmothers, and Foster Mothers in Early Republic and Antebellum Charleston," *Journal of the Early Republic* 32 (Fall 2012): 463–92.

46 By 1810, race of victims and assailants appeared infrequently on paperwork in Boston, so a comparison was made with city directories to locate race, when possible. Between 1810 and 1820 in New York City, special justices did not record sixteen African American men's occupations and the status of fifteen African American women, out of thirty-two African American women victims. Laborers (twelve), servants (five), and sweep masters appeared most frequently in male indictments. Of the women plaintiffs for whom special justices denoted a status, ten were married and they reported violence without their husbands, as did those described as spinsters and servants. Indictments, 1810–20, DAIP, NYMA.

47 John L. Brooke, *Columbia Rising: Civil Life on the Upper Hudson from the Revolution to the Age of Jackson* (Chapel Hill: University of North Carolina Press, 2010), 382–429; Jane Williamson, "African Americans in Addison County, Charlotte, and Hinesburg, Vermont, 1790–1860," *Vermont History* 78 (Winter/Spring 2010): 33–7; Nash, *Forging Freedom*, 165–71; Emma Jones Lapsansky, "'Since They Got Those Separate Churches,'" 54–78; Melish, *Disowning Slavery*, 134–7; and Anthony Martin, "Homeplace Is Also Workplace: Another Look at Lucy Foster in Andover, Massachusetts," *Historical Archeology* 52 (March 2018): 100–12.

48 John Dawson Lawson, ed., *American State Trials: A Collection of the Important and Interesting Criminal Trials, which have taken place in the United States, from the beginning of our Government to the Present Day* (St. Louis, MO: F.H. Thomas Law Book Co., 1914), 2:844–5. In contrast, Richard Shannon Moss claims that in the case of a murder on Long Island in 1807, a slave was able to testify. See Moss, *Slavery on Long Island*, 100–1.

49 James Forten, *Letters from a man of colour, on a late bill before the Senate of Pennsylvania* (Pennsylvania: s.n., 1813), 7–8; and Julie Winch, "The Making and Meaning of James Forten's Letters from a Man of Colour," *WMQ* 64 (January 2007): 129–38.

50 Forten, *Letters from a man of colour*, 8.

51 African American members of St. Phillips separated from Trinity Episcopal in 1819. New York City Common Council, *Minutes of the Common Council*, 4: 389; 5: 272, 278; 7: 729; 9:40. Alexander, *African or American?*, 31. This is in line with growing racial thought. See James Brewer Stewart, "Modernizing 'Difference': The Political Meaning of Color in the Free States, 1776–1840," *Journal of the Early Republic* 15 (Winter 1999): 691–712.

52 Alexander, *African or American?*, 36–44; and Ousmane K. Power-Greene, *Against the Wind and Tide: The African American Struggle against the Colonization Movement* (New York: New York University Press, 2014), chap. 1.

53 Daniel Rogers, *The New York City-Hall Recorder for the Year 1818*, vol. 3 (New York: Clayton and Kingsland, 1818), 39–42; Laura Copland, "The Rise and Fall of

Moses Simons: A Black Lawyer in New York City Criminal Court, 1816–1820," *Afro-Americans in New York Life and History* 37 (July 2013): 81–114; *People v. Moses Simon*, February 3, 1818, DAIP, NYMA.

CONCLUSION: AFFECTING THE GOVERNMENT, LAW, AND PUBLIC MIND

1 For example, see Gilje, *Rioting in America*, chap. 4; Sean T. Moore, "'Justifiable Provocation': Violence against Women in Essex County, New York, 1799–1860," *Journal of Social History* 35 (July 2002): 890–3; Roth, *American Homicide*, chap. 6 and 7; John Runcie, "'Hunting the Nigs' in Philadelphia: The Race Riot of August 1834," *Pennsylvania History* 39 (April 1972): 187–218; and Dabel, *A Respectable Woman*, chap. 5.

2 *People v. Josiah Muir*, July 9, 1813; *People v. Ann Leif*, November 8, 1813; *People v. Elenora Pienoel, Ange Pienovi, and Elizabeth Pienovi*, May 3, 1815; and *People v. John Plume*, November 11, 1815, DAIP, NYMA.

3 Moseley, "A History of the New-York Manumission Society," 27, 33–44. The core group of the NYMS leaders wanted more from its members, and the standing committee routinely chastised them for not fulfilling their duties in investigating the cases assigned to them after the *Broad* cases.

4 *The trial of Amos Broad and his wife*, 3. On self-licensing, see for example, Anna C. Merritt, Daniel A. Effron, and Benoit Monin, "Moral Self-Licensing: When Being Good Frees Us to Be Bad," *Social and Personality Psychology Compass* 4 (May 2010): 344–57; and S. Sachdeva, R. Iliev, and D.L. Medin, "Sinning Saints and Saintly Sinners: The Paradox of Moral Self-Regulation," *Psychological Science* 20 (April 2009): 523–8.

5 NYMS, January 9, 1810, 9:230.

6 "The Memorial of the Subscribers, Inhabitants of the City of New York," NYMS, 9:269; NYMS, July 20, 1815, 10:267.

7 In 1819, New York would reintroduce flogging in its prisons to maintain order. See Hirsch, *The Rise of the Penitentiary*, 57–62; W. David Lewis, *From Newgate to Dannemora*, 32, 46; and Meranze, *Laboratories of Virtue*, 22–4, 62–86.

8 NYMS, January 9, 1810, 9:230.

9 In the same session, the legislators strengthened provisions against kidnapping. William P. Van Ness and John Woodworth, *Laws of the State of New-York: Revised and Passed at the Thirty-Sixth Session of the Legislature* (Albany, NY: H.C. Southwick & Co., 1813), 2:204–10.

10 NYMS, April 11, 1803, 9:102; NYMS, January 26, 1813, and April 13, 1813, 10:198, 230.

11 Everett S. Lee and Michael Lally, "Population," in *The Growth of Seaport Cities, 1790–1825*, ed. David T. Gilchrist (Charlottesville, VA: University Press of Virginia, 1967), 33–4, 37; Cushing, *The First Laws of the Commonwealth*, 347; *Laws of the State of New-York*, 2:253–4 and 3:146; Ryan, *Regulating Passion*, 136–7.

12 W.S. Rossiter, *A Century of Population Growth: From the First to the Twelfth Census of the United States,1790–1900* (Washington, DC: Government Printing Office, 1919), 133; Ira Rosenwaike, *Population History of New York City* (Syracuse,

NY: Syracuse University Press, 1972), 22–4; and Stewart H. Holbrook, *The Yankee Exodus: An Account of Migration from New England* (Seattle, WA: University of Washington Press, 1968), 28–29, 32–33.

13 NYMS, December 12, 1814, 9:378.

14 For an example of a discussions about property rights, see Humanity, "Abolition of Slavery and Imprisonment for Debt," *Ulster Plebeian*, February 22, 1817.

15 On emancipation, see Patrick Rael, "The Long Death of Slavery," in *Slavery in New York*, 113–46; Patrick Rael, *Eighty-Eight Years: The Long Death of Slavery in the United States, 1777–1865* (Athens, GA: University of Georgia Press, 2015), 106–13, 126–31, 142–51; Gellman, *Emancipating New York*, chap. 9; and Harris, *In the Shadow of Slavery*, chap. 2 and 3.

16 Truth and Gilbert, *Narrative of Sojourner Truth*, 40–41.

17 NYMS, July 3, 1821 and August 7, 1822, 11:102, 114. In another case in 1818, a neighbor reported that a twelve- or thirteen-year-old slave was being beaten with a tea kettle. *People v. John and Maria Carpenter*, May 11, 1818, DAIP, NYMA.

18 *Commonwealth v. William Allen*, November 1803, Record Book, Suffolk and Nantucket Supreme Judicial Court; *Commonwealth v. Aaron Mower*, September 1811, Record Book, Middlesex Supreme Judicial Court; and *Commonwealth v. Samuel Winch*, March 1819, Record Book, Worcester Supreme Judicial Court, Judicial Archives, MA.

19 DAIP, NYMS, 1800–19. Cayuga cases represent cases between 1799 and 1820, while in Essex, the cases are from 1800 to 1860. In Cayuga, one of the cases resulted in indictments of both the husband and the wife, suggesting larger community concern about the nuisance of their fighting. Seth Moor, May 1804, case 18040007; and James Clark, January 1808, case 18080011, Indictment Papers, Cayuga County General Sessions; and *People v. Joseph Van Tine*, January 1819, and *People v. Mary Van Tine*, January 1819, Record Book, Cayuga County General Sessions. Records Retention, Cayuga County Government. For Essex County, see Sean T. Moore, "'Justifiable Provocation,'" 904.

20 On legal constructions of these cases as for protecting the peace, see Bloch, "The American Revolution, Wife Beating, and the Emergent Right to Privacy," 234–7, 242–3; and Edwards, "Law, Domestic Violence, and the Limits of Patriarchal Authority," 750–9.

21 Mathew Peirce, recognizance, June 13, 1815, File Papers, MCB, Judicial Archives, MA. For an example outside of Boston, see John Barnard, warrant, March 11, 1800; Martha Barnard, recognizance, March 24, 1800, and June 9, 1800, File Papers, Worcester General Sessions; Docket Books, Worcester CCL, March, June, and August 1800, Judicial Archives, MA.

22 Michael Grossberg defines the judicial protection provided to the less empowered members of society as "judicial patriarchy." He writes that these actions increased the power of the judiciary while they simultaneously fractured male patriarchy. Michael Grossberg, *Governing the Hearth: Law and Family in Nineteenth Century America* (Chapel Hill: University of North Carolina Press, 1985), 289–307. See Mathew Peirce, recognizance, June 13, 1815, File Papers, MCB, Judicial Archives,

MA. For a sample of other men jailed or having warrants for their arrests for refusing to make a bond, see Charles Hunt, recognizance, August 4, 1815; Bethiah Kemp, recognizance, March 13, 1816; Ebenezer Eaton, warrant, May 16, 1816; File Papers, MCB, Judicial Archives, MA. During the 1820s and 1830s in Baltimore, JPs automatically jailed men before holding them to bonds. See Stephanie Cole, "Keeping the Peace: Domestic Assault and Private Prosecution in Antebellum Baltimore," in Daniels and Kennedy, ed., *Over the Threshold*, 159–60.

23 Over the 1810s, seven groups of community members brought forward complaints to JPs about wife abuse in Boston. Trobridge Taylor, David Fay, Rufus Fay, Comfort Fay, and Lydia Newton, September 19, 1796, File Papers, Worcester General Sessions, Judicial Archives, MA. Patrick Miller, Nancy Miller, Gilbert Munzie, and Percevil Hall, January 17, 1806; Thomas Richardson, Samuel Vincent, and Samuel Summer, August 9, 1806; Thomas Townshend, September 28, 1808; John O'Neil, March 29, 1810; Nabby D. Darby, Eliza Gould, Sylvia Mitchell, Judy Cobourn, and James Barker, August 25, 1812; William Clark, August 8, 1813; Joseph Kingsley, Jonas Ames, Gardner Trafton, Hale Kingsley, and John Bannicot, January 1, 1816; John Cleasby, February 21, 1819; Elijah Carelton, June 30, 1819; Charles Lawson, September 11, 1820, File Papers, MCB, Judicial Archives, MA.

24 Joseph Kingsley, Jonas Ames, Gardner Trafton, Hale Kingsley, and John Bannicot, recognizance, January 1, 1816, File Papers, MCB, Judicial Archives, MA.

25 *People v. John Campbell*, June 6, 1805; and DAIP, NYMS, 1800–1819.

26 Seth Moor, May 1804, case 18040007; and James Clark, January 1808, case 18080011, Indictment Papers, Cayuga County General Sessions; and *People v. Joseph Van Tine*, January 1819; and *People v. Mary Van Tine*, January 1819, Record Book, Cayuga County General Sessions, Records Retention, Cayuga County Government; and Sean T. Moore, "'Justifiable Provocation,'" 906, 917–18n86.

27 Record Book, New York General Sessions, 1796–1826, NYMA; *People v. William Vallean*, December 8, 1802, Record Book, New York General Sessions, NYMA; Ellen Vallean, deposition, October 7, 1802, in *People v. William Vallean*, October 11, 1802, DAIP, NYMA.

28 In one of the cases, although the indictment suggested the wife's life was "endangered," the case files do not bear this out. Rather, it was likely the construction of the defendant as repeatedly disorderly that led to his conviction. In 1817, Louisa Robinson first reported abuse by her husband, Abin Robinson, and neighbors reported abuse a second time in 1819. The community report likely instigated the sentencing of Abin to thirty days in prison. *People v. Abin Robinson*, April 1819; *People v. James Riley*, July 1819, Record Book, MCB, Judicial Archives, MA; Alvan Robinson, mittimus, September 15, 1817; John Cleasby, recognizance, February 21, 1819; and Elijah Carelton, recognizance, June 30, 1819, File Papers, MCB, Judicial Archives, MA. Abin was also known as Alvan.

29 For the period after 1800, all five divorce cases with the grounds of cruelty in Suffolk and Nantucket counties were successful; two out of three cases in Worcester; and both cases in Middlesex. See Record Books, Suffolk and Nantucket Supreme

Judicial Court, 1805–18; Record Books, Middlesex Supreme Judicial Court, 1797–1820; and Record Books, Worcester Supreme Judicial Court, Judicial Archives, MA, 1798–1820. On cases with husbands offering counterevidence, see *Experience Clap v. Samuel Clap*, May 17, 1791; and *Mary Walcut v. Jabez Walcut*, April 19, 1796, Record Book, Supreme Judicial Court, Judicial Archives, MA. See Richard H. Chused, *Private Acts in Public Places: A Social History of Divorce in the Formative Era of American Family Law* (Philadelphia: University of Pennsylvania Press, 1994).

30 Norma Basch, *Framing American Divorce: From the Revolutionary Generation to the Victorians* (Berkeley: University of California Press, 1999), 39–41, 48–9; and Merril D. Smith, *Breaking the Bonds: Marital Discord in Pennsylvania, 1730–1830* (New York: New York University Press), 14, 26.

31 Reeve, *The Law of Baron and Feme*, 65–6; and Angela Fernandez, "Tapping Reeve, Coverture and America's First Legal Treatise," in *Law Books in Action: Essays on the Anglo-American Legal Treatise*, ed. Angela Fernandez and Markus D. Dubber (Portland, OR: Hart Publishing Co., 2012), 63–81. Ruth Bloch believes Reeves's thinking extended to a wider swath of legal minds in the early republic. See Bloch, "The American Revolution, Wife Beating, and the Emergent Right to Privacy," 231–2.

32 Rosemarie Zagarri writes about the effect of stage theories of historical progress in regard to sex in *Revolutionary Backlash*, 47–8; and in "Morals, Manners, and the Republican Mother," *American Quarterly* 44 (June 1992): 192–215.

33 Glenn, *Campaigns against Corporal Punishment*, 39–40.

34 Reeve, *The Law of Baron and Feme*, 65–6.

35 In 1823, one writer stated that "great authorities in the law have held it strictly legal to" correct a wife. However, the writer points to English common law from the 1200s and 1700s. See "Matrimonial Rights," *Essex Register*, July 31, 1823. The extreme case of *Bradley v. State* (1824), in Mississippi, also shows judicial acceptance of spousal violence, yet this doctrine has not been tested for its validity in northern states.

36 Reeve, *The Law of Baron and Feme*, 89.

37 Roth, *American Homicide*, 250–72; and Sean T. Moore, "'Justifiable Provocation,'" 890–1, 909–10.

38 Part of this change results from emerging discourses on women's victimization and seduction. For example, see Scott C. Martin, "Violence, Gender, and Intemperance in Early National Connecticut," in *Journal of Social History* 34 (Winter 2000), 309–25; and Martin J. Wiener, "Alice Arden to Bill Sikes: Changing Nightmares of Intimate Violence in England, 1558–1869," *Journal of British Studies* 40 (April 2001), 195, 204, 209.

39 Stephanie Cole found 215 cases of domestic assault between 1828 and 1832 in which government support was sought, while Laura Edwards found fifteen cases in South Carolina in addition to references to peace warrants in North Carolina between the 1810s and 1850s. See Cole, "Keeping the Peace," 163n1; and Edwards, "Law, Domestic Violence and the Limits of Patriarchal Authority," 750n25.

40 Emiko Petrosky, Janet M. Blair, Carter J. Betz, Katherine A. Fowler, Shane P.D. Jack, Brigette H. Lyons, "Racial and Ethnic Differences in Homicides of Adult Women and the Role of Intimate Partner Violence—United States, 2003–2014," Center for Disease Control and Prevention, Morbidity and Mortality Weekly Report (2017), 66:741–746. http://dx.doi.org/10.15585/mmwr.mm6628a1.

41 Myra Glenn charts the lack of public discussion of wife abuse in the northeast in the antebellum era. See Glenn, *Campaigns against Corporal Punishment*, 80–1, 146. Evidence presented by Joshua Stein and Ruth Bloch suggests communities may have required that violence against wives be more extensive to issue indictments after the 1820s. See Stein, "The Right to Violence," 55–70, 77–84; and Bloch, "The American Revolution, Wife Beating, and the Emergent Right to Privacy," 239–46.

42 The parties settled one, the jury acquitted one man and convicted two men, and two more pleaded guilty. *People v. Richard G. Lowerre*, May 8, 1812; *People v. John Towt*, June 14, 1813; *William Esler v. John Edward*, November 14, 1814; *People v. Noel Corbet* (two cases), June 8, 1815; *People v. Nathaniel L. Rose*, July 11, 1818; *People v. William and Sarah Gray*, July 14, 1818, DAIP, NYMA.

43 One case appears to show a child abused in the house of non-relatives, suggesting some kind of guardianship, but no direct relationship was noted. Catherine Kuyler, deposition, August 9, 1815, in *People v. Maryann and John Simerson*, August 11 and 12, 1815.

44 *Jesse Fash v. Richard G. Lowerre*, May 8, 1812, DAIP, NYMA.

45 "Letter of Grand Jury," in *People v. Noel Corbet*, June 8, 1815, DAIP, NYMA.

46 *People v. John Towt*, June 14, 1813, DAIP, NYMA.

47 *Province and Court Records of Maine*, 2:422; *Records and Files of the Quarterly Courts of Essex County*, 3:117, 4:42, 186, 212; 8:295; and *Records of the Colony of New Plymouth*, 5:16.

48 In addition to the cases noted, an additional case against Diana Silleck for murdering her child occurred in May 1816. *People v. James Glass*, August 16, 1810 (stepson); Margaret Watkins, deposition, November 30, 1810, in *People v. Hannah Scott*, December 14, 1810; *People v. Antonie Martin*, October 18, 1811; *People v. Israel Palmer*, January 10, 1812; *People v. Joseph Concklin and Joseph Concklin, Jr.*, July 9, 1813; *People v. John and Mary Ann Simerson*, August 11 and 12, 1815; *People v. Nathaniel S. Davis*, June 7, 1816; *People v. Philadelphia Ludlow*, March 12, 1818, DAIP, NYMA. In the Concklin case, Nancy Dickinson admitted the abuse may have come from the child's brother, not the father. *Commonwealth v. Isam Bundley*, November 1812; *Commonwealth v. Patrick Clark*, August 3, 1818, Record Book, MCB, Judicial Archives, MA.

49 *People v. Catherine McFarlin*; and *People v. John McFarlin*, February 9, 1819, DAIP, NYMA.

50 Glenn, *Campaigns against Corporal Punishment*, chap. 6.

51 James Hardie, deposition, February 11, 1811, in *People v. John Charlwood*, February 13, 1811, DAIP, NYMA.

52 Pleck, *Domestic Tyranny*, 40–3, 46.

53 Myra Glenn, *Campaigns against Corporal Punishment*, 30–4, 40–4, 50–4, 56; Pleck, *Domestic Tyranny*, 47–8; and Greven, *Spare the Child*.

54 A number of scholars show that increased racial hostility emerged from the 1820s onward as new ethnic and racial identification emerged alongside immigration changes, rising abolitionism, and changes in labor. See Gilje, *Rioting in America*, chap. 3 and 4; Roth, *American Homicide*, 310–11; Noel Ignatiev, *How the Irish Became White* (New York: Routledge, 1995), 155; and John M. Werner, *Reaping the Bloody Harvest: Race Riots in the United States during the Age of Jackson, 1824–1849* (New York: Garland Publishing, 1986).

55 The evidence presented here is intended to assist in understanding reported instances, not those that went unreported. Various problems arise from trying to compare crime statistics between the two decades. Both Boston and New York unevenly denoted race on their forms, and the population growth makes accounting for race more difficult for the second decade. Between 1811 and 1819, eighty-seven reported cases emerged, but the year 1817 in the indictments are missing many indictment papers. Trends from previous years suggest approximately eight or nine assaults would have occurred. In 1810 and 1820, 9,832 and 11,404 African Americans lived in the city, respectively; the average population size between the time periods was 10,618. DAIP, 1811–19, NYMA. Randolf Roth found that the murder rate of African Americans was not higher than that of whites during this period overall, though a very small increase over whites in homicides exists in New York City. See Roth, *American Homicide*, 195–6, 534n26.

56 Roth, *American Homicide*, 309.

57 Patrick Rael, *Black Identity and Black Protest in the Antebellum North* (Chapel Hill: University of North Carolina Press, 2002); Alexander, *African or American?*, chap. 1 and 2; Horton and Horton, *In Hope of Liberty*, chap. 6; and Brooke, *Columbia Rising*, 382–429.

58 John J. Zuille, *Historical Sketch of the New York African Society for Mutual Relief* (New York: s.n., 1892), 7; and Swan, "John Teasman," 351.

59 A.J. Williams-Myers, "Pinkster Carnival: Africanisms in the Hudson River Valley," *Afro-Americans in New York Life and History* 9 (January 1985): 7–17; Mary Ryan, *Civic Wars: Democracy and Public Life in the American City during the Nineteenth Century* (Berkeley: University of California Press, 1997), 21–133; David Waldstreicher, *In the Midst of Perpetual Fetes: The Making of American Nationalism, 1776–1820* (Chapel Hill: University of North Carolina Press, 1997), chap. 6; Shane White, "'It was a Proud Day': African Americans, Festivals, and Parades in the North, 1741–1834," *JAH* 81 (June 1994): 17–42; Shane White, "Pinkster: Afro-Dutch Syncretization in New York City and the Hudson Valley," *Journal of American Folklore*, 102 (January–March 1989), 68–76; and Sterling Stuckey, "The Skies of Consciousness: African Dance at Pinkster in New York, 1750–1840," in *Going through the Storm: The Influence of African American Art in History* (New York: Oxford University Press, 1994), 55–9.

60 Nathaniel Bryant, deposition, April 21, 1812, in *People v. John Feris*, May 8, 1812; and John Patterson, deposition, July 5, 1816, in *People v. John Van Houter*, August

12, 1816. For the other assaults, see *People v. John Simpson*, February 10, 1815; *People v. Cornelius Lewis and James Tripler*, February 14, 1815; and *People v. Barney McCafferty*, August 14 and 15, 1815, DAIP, NYMA. Paul A. Gilje and Howard B. Rock, "'Sweep O! Sweep O!': African-American Chimney Sweeps and Citizenship in the New Nation," *WMQ* 51 (July 1994): 512–28.

61 The case of Brister Freeman from chapter 6 is illustrative here as well. Brooke, *Columbia Rising*, 386–91; Nash and Soderlund, *Freedom by Degrees*, 187–8, 191–2; Lemere, *Black Walden*, 164–8.

62 Francis More, deposition, February 8, 1818, in *People v. James McBride*, March 12, 1818, DAIP, NYMA. On settlement patterns, see Shane White, *Somewhat More Independent*, 171–80; and Harris, *In the Shadow of Slavery*, 80–3.

63 Donald P. Green's study of modern hate crimes shows that the most important determinant in white nationalist hate groups' movement to violence is their sense that they need to protect "their turf," while other scholars show perpetrators believed they were provoked to commit violence. See Donald P. Green, Laurence H. McFalls, and Jennifer K. Smith, "Hate Crime: An Emergent Research Agenda," *Annual Review of Sociology* 27 (2001): 479–504; Ryken Grattet, "The Urban Ecology of Bias Crime: A Study of Disorganized and Defended Neighborhoods," *Social Problems* 56 (February 2009): 132–50; and Neil Chakraborti and Jon Garland, "Reconceptualizing Hate Crime Victimization through the Lens of Vulnerability and Difference," *Theoretical Criminology* 16 (April 2012): 499–514.

64 Horton, *Black Bostonians*, 4–7, 19, 23, 76–78; Melish, *Disowning Slavery*, 183–207; Ryan, *Regulating Passion*, 144–48.

65 Patrick Cahil, deposition, June 8, 1816, in *People v. John Dickerson, John Vann, and William Vincent*, June 11, 1816, DAIP, NYMA.

66 Melish, *Disowning Slavery*, 210–37; David R. Roediger, *The Wages of Whiteness: Race and the Making of the American Working Class* (New York: Verso, 1991), 43–92; Mathew Fry Jacobson, *Whiteness of a Different Color: European Immigrants and the Alchemy of Color* (Cambridge, MA: Harvard University Press, 1998), 15–38; Nell Irvin Painter, *The History of White People* (New York: W.W. Norton, 2010), 104–31; and Ignatiev, *How the Irish Became White*.

67 Curran, *Anatomy of Blackness*, 167–215; Bruce Dain, *A Hideous Monster of the Mind*; Sweet, *Bodies Politic*, 271–397; George M. Fredrickson, *The Black Image in the White Mind: The Debate on Afro-American Character and Destiny, 1817–1917* (1971; reprint, Middletown CT: Wesleyan University Press, 1987), 1–42; and Melish, *Disowning Slavery*, 119–280.

68 "Offenders," 2015 Hate Crime Statistics, Criminal Justice Information Services Division, Federal Bureau of Investigation, United States Department of Justice (November 2016), https://ucr.fbi.gov; Jack McDevitt, Jack Levin, and Susan Bennett, "Hate Crime Offenders: An Expanded Typology," *Journal of Social Issues*, 58 (Summer 2002): 303–17; and Mark Austin Waters, "A General Theories of Hate Crime? Strain, Doing Difference and Self Control," *Critical Criminology* 19 (November 2011): 313–30.

69 For examples of scholarship on racialization and hate crime, see Green, McFalls, and Smith, "Hate Crime: An Emergent Research Agenda," 479–504; Mark S. Hamm, *American Skinheads: The Criminology and Control of Hate Crime* (Westport, CT: Praeger, 1999); Phyllis B. Gerstenfeld, *Hate Crimes: Causes, Controls, and Controversies*, 4th ed. (Los Angeles: Sage, 2018), chap. 3; and Randy Blazak, "White Boys to Terrorist Men: Target Recruitment of Nazi Skinheads," in *Hate and Bias Crime: A Reader*, ed. Barbara Perry (New York: Routledge, 2003), chap. 22.

70 Michael Kaplan, "New York City Tavern Violence and the Creation of a Working-Class Male Identity," *Journal of the Early Republic* 15 (Winter 1995), 591–617.

71 Elias B. Caldwell in *A view of exertions lately made for the purpose of colonizing the free people of colour, in the United States, in Africa, or elsewhere* (Washington, DC: Printed by Jonathan Elliot, 1817), 6; and Nicholas Guyatt, *Bind Us Apart: How Enlightened Americans Invented Racial Segregation* (New York: Basic Books, 2016), 220–24, 267–69.

72 Rael, *Black Identity and Black Protest in the Antebellum North*; Alexander, *African or American?*; Horton and Horton, *In Hope of Liberty*; and Brooke, *Columbia Rising*, 382–429.

73 Roth, *American Homicide*, chap. 7; Eric H. Monkkonen, *Murder in New York City* (Berkeley: University of California Press, 2001). Joshua Stein argues rising rates of assault were an additional factor in escalating violence. See Joshua Stein, "Privatizing Violence: A Transformation in the Jurisprudence of Assault," *Law and History Review* 30 (May 2012), 423–48; Leonard L. Richards, *"Gentleman of Property and Standing": Anti-Abolition Mobs in Jacksonian America* (New York: Oxford University Press, 1970); David Grimsted, *American Mobbing, 1828–1861: Toward Civil War* (New York: Oxford University Press, 1998), 33–66; Linda K. Kerber, "Abolitionists and Amalgamators: The New York City Race Riots of 1834," *New York History* 48 (January 1967): 28–39; and Runcie, "'Hunting the Nigs' in Philadelphia," 187–218.

74 Studies of use of force by police today show African Americans and Hispanics are 50 percent more likely to experience non-fatal force than whites. Though differences in racial structure between today and the early republic are profound, racial bias in interaction is clear in both contexts. Roland G. Fryer, Jr. "An Empirical Analysis of Racial Differences in Police Use of Force (NBER Working paper No. 22399), National Bureau of Economic Research (issued in July 2016, revised in January 2018), www.nber.org. Similarly, drivers today are less likely to yield to pedestrians of color. See Tara Goddard, Kimberly Barsamian Kahn, Arlie Adkins, "Racial Bias in Driver Yielding Behavior at Crosswalks," in *Transportation Research Part F: Traffic Psychology and Behavior* 33 (August 2015): 1–6.

75 Cleves points to the importance of the French Revolution in this turn away from violence, and Glenn argues republicanism and the replacement of prisons for public punishments affected perceptions of violence. See Cleves, *The Reign of Terror in America*, 84–8, 105; and Glenn, *Campaigns Against Corporal Punishment*, 50–56.

print literature (*cont.*)
  religious documents as, 13; white wife
    abuse in colonial era and, 47; white
    wife abuse in early republic and, 192,
    193, 244; white wife abuse in eigh-
    teenth century and, 69–70, 75; white
    wife abuse in Revolutionary War and,
    139–40, 143–45, 152–54
Putnam, James, 126–27

Quakers, 13, 124, 125; antislavery writings
    and, 106; slaves in eighteenth century
    and, 105–6; white antislavery activism
    and, 127–28, 136
Quarles, Benjamin, 159
Quimley, Jeremiah, 72
Quinby, Josiah, 36–37

Rawkin, Eleanor, 230
Reeve, Tapping, 100; on doctrine of cov-
    erture, 288; Freeman, E., and, 198; on
    self-defense, 287–88; Strong, S., and,
    197–98
relationship building. *See* slaves, relation-
    ship building
resistance. *See* nonviolent resistance;
    violent resistance
Revolutionary War, 14, 337n2; Commit-
    tee of Safety in, 158; courts in, 155–56;
    divorce and, 140, 143, 151–52, 155;
    female labor and, 156; judges sup-
    porting, 122; Native American wife
    abuse in, 141–42; patriarchy and, 165;
    self-emancipation and, 4, 151, 155–56,
    157. *See also* slaves, Revolutionary War;
    white wife abuse, Revolutionary War;
    youthful servant, Revolutionary War
Reynolds, Jabez, 132–33
Roth, Randolf, 38, 64, 295
Rush, Benjamin, 183, 193

Saffin, Adam, 103–5
Sandford, Michael, 215

Sarter, Caesar, 135
Saunders, Prince, 229, 269
Sears, Eliza, 258–59
Sedgwick, Catherine, 345n52, 345n53
Sedgwick, Theodore, 161
self-divorce, 11, 70–71, 152–55; of African
    American wives, 194; of Native Ameri-
    can wives, 50; for white wives in early
    republic, 195
self-emancipation, 10–11; of African
    American wives, 71; of Franklin, B.,
    45; gradual emancipation in New York
    and, 174; in Revolutionary War, 4, 151,
    155–56, 157; of slaves in early repub-
    lic, 4, 220, 256–57, 277; of slaves in
    eighteenth century, 88, 94–95, 157; of
    Wheeler, 225; white wife abuse in eigh-
    teenth century and, 70–71; youthful
    servant in colonial era and, 26, 29–30;
    youthful servant in early republic, 292;
    youthful servant in eighteenth century
    and, 38, 156
Selyns, Henricus, 85–86
servant: apprentice compared to, 19, 180.
    See also youthful African American
    servant, early republic; youthful
    servant, colonial era; youthful servant,
    eighteenth century; youthful servant,
    imperial crisis; youthful servant, Revo-
    lutionary War
Sewall, John, 127
Sewell, Samuel, 105
sexual abuse: in antebellum era, 96;
    cultural acceptance of, 43–44; rape
    trials and, 43; of slaves in eighteenth
    century, 96; slaves in imperial crisis
    and, 129–30, 134; youthful servant in
    eighteenth century and, 43–44
Sharp, Granville, 124, 125
Silverman, David, 41
Simons, Moses, 269–70
slaves, colonial era, 14, 179, 222, 224, 237;
    allies of, 91; Anthonijsen and, 82–83;

ABOUT THE AUTHOR

Kelly A. Ryan is Dean of the School of Social Sciences and an Associate Professor of History at Indiana University Southeast. Ryan specializes in race, gender, sexuality, and violence in early United States history. Her previous book, *Regulating Passion: Sexuality and Patriarchal Rule in Massachusetts, 1700–1830* (2014), analyzed sexual trends in Massachusetts to discover changes in early American hierarchies of gender, race, and class.